WINSTON AND JACK
The Churchill Brothers

Also by Celia Lee

Jean, Lady Hamilton 1861 – 1941: A Soldier's Wife

Also by John Lee

A Soldier's Life: General Sir Ian Hamilton 1853 – 1947
The Warlords: Hindenburg and Ludendorff

CELIA AND JOHN LEE

WINSTON AND JACK:
The Churchill Brothers

[signature: Celia Lee]

[signature: John Lee]

CELIA LEE 2007

First published 2007
Celia Lee
"Middlemarch"
12 Longhurst Road
London SE13 5LP
Tel. No. 0208-318-4940

ISBN 978-0-9539292-1-4

A CIP catalogue record for this book is available from the British Library.

Typeset by Phoenix Photosetting, Chatham, Kent.
Printed and bound in Great Britain by
Mackays of Chatham, Chatham, Kent.

Dedicated to
the memory of

Peregrine Churchill
1913–2002

"Peregrine had a burning loyalty to the truth, which he often saw as overwhelmed by innuendo and bad research. …
He was a great man who was devoted to history and saw Sir Winston in a balanced way, virtues and faults both."

Richard M. Langworth, Editor FINEST HOUR
(www.winstonchurchill.org) from a letter of condolence to Peregrine's wife, 22nd March 2002.

Contents

Acknowledgements

The late Mr Peregrine Churchill, and Mrs Churchill: enormous thanks and gratitude are due to the late Peregrine and Mrs Churchill for their support, and for allowing us unrestricted access to all their private papers, letters and photographs.

His Grace The Duke of Marlborough: thanks are due to His Grace for allowing photographs to be taken at Blenheim Palace of the Jerome rocking chair, (bequeathed by Peregrine Churchill), and for granting us permission to reproduce photographs.

The Lady Soames LG DBE: thanks and gratitude are due to Mary for a lengthy afternoon interview, and the lovely tea and delicious chocolate cake, served on her late mother's china. Mary also corrected the typed draft of the interview, and provided some very helpful hints.

The Countess of Avon: thanks and gratitude are due to Lady Avon for her hours of painstaking work and help, both during an interview and in listing the names and events in a series of home movies made by her late father, Major John Churchill.

Mrs Minnie Churchill and Mr Simon Bird: thanks are due to Minnie and Simon; to Minnie for allowing us to reproduce a picture of the oil painting of Lord Randolph's famous racehorse, the *L'Abbesse de Jourarre*.

Sir John Leslie, 4th Baronet, Castle Leslie; thanks are due to Sir John for granting us an interview and for receiving us with great courtesy and kindness, at Castle Leslie.

The Earl of Roden: we are most grateful to His Grace for supplying us with a photograph of his ancestor the 5th Earl of Roden, John Strange Jocelyn.

Mr Ian Hamilton: thanks are due to Ian for his kindness in granting us the copyright of several passages from his great Aunt Jean Hamilton's diaries. Thanks are also due to Mr and Mrs Hamilton's two sons, Felix and Max.

Barbara Kaczmarowska Hamilton (Basia): more thanks than can ever be recorded are due to Basia, who introduced us to Mr and Mrs

Peregrine Churchill in 2001. Basia has been an enthusiastic supporter throughout the writing of WINSTON AND JACK.

Dr John H. Mather MD and his wife Dr Susan Mather; enormous thanks are due to John and Susan for a lengthy interview in London. John most generously allowed us to quote freely from his paper, "Lord Randolph Churchill: Maladies et Mort" (pub. *Finest Hour*; Winter 1996–7 edition; No 93). Dr Mather's expert medical knowledge was paramount in guiding us through the medical aspects of the allegations that Lord Randolph Churchill died of syphilis of the brain.

Mr Richard M. Langworth, CBE; Editor, The Churchill Centre, USA; Richard was a great friend of Peregrine Churchill and fully understands Jack's role in the family. www.winstonchurchill.org.

Mrs Rita Boswell Gibbs, MA, RMSA, Archivist, Harrow Public School; thanks are due to Mrs Boswell Gibbs, for providing copies of examination results and other help and guidance on a number of occasions from the public school where Winston and Jack Churchill were educated.

Miss Pamela Clark, Registrar, The Royal Archives, Windsor; thanks are due to Miss Clark, who has helped us on several occasions with information of an historical nature.

Mr John Forster, Head of Education, Blenheim Palace; thanks are due to Mr Foster for his painstaking help on the letters of Lord Randolph Churchill and Winston, for his knowledge of the family and Blenheim Palace, and for arranging several photographs to publish in the book.

Claire Aston, guide, Kensal Green Cemetery; thanks are due to Claire who told us the story of how Winston, even after he became wartime Prime Minister, used to stop the official car outside the cemetery, and sit on a bench and meditate at the grave of his deceased daughter, Marigold.

Mr Geoffrey Bailey, Pan Bookshop; thanks are due to Geoffrey who is a fount of knowledge, for academic and other advice, acquired through his many years of experience in the publishing industry.

Mr Robin Brodhurst, Head of the History Dept., Pangbourne School, for much advice on relevant books to read in relation to the politics of Ireland and for academic guidance with regard to the terminology used in public schools.

Mr Richard Cragg, photographer, Blenheim Palace; Mr Cragg took the wonderful photographs of the 'historic' Jerome family rocking chair, and provided us with a copy of the wedding portrait of Major John and Lady Gwendeline Churchill with the Oxfordshire Hussars.
Dr Robin Darwall-Smith, Archivist, Magdalen College, Oxford; thanks are due to Mr Darwall-Smith, who painstakingly produced figures of the costs involved for a student taking a degree at Oxford in 1897–8.
Mr Neil Lang: enormous thanks are due to Neil, who produced the brilliant jacket design for the book, having worked on it during his August Bank Holiday weekend to get it out on time.
Mr Julian Mitchell: Julian was co-author with Peregrine Churchill of *Jennie – Lady Randolph Churchill – A Portrait with Letters*. The book was published in association with Thames Television's film JENNIE: LADY RANDOLPH CHURCHILL, for which Julian was the scriptwriter. He was a friend of Peregrine's, and during an interview with him we learnt much of value about the Churchill family history, which he had gained from his unique experience.
Mr Allen Packwood, Director, Miss Katharine Thomson, Mr Andrew Riley, and the staff of the Churchill Archives, Churchill College, Cambridge; more thanks are due to Mr Packwood and his staff than can ever be recorded. On so many occasions when we visited the impeccably arranged Churchill Archives, every effort and help was provided to us.
Mr Andrew Roberts; Andrew is a well-known author and journalist; enormous thanks are due to Andrew for assisting our press publicity.
Mrs Elizabeth Snell, author of *The Churchills*: Elizabeth most generously allowed us access to her writings on the ancient Earls of Abingdon, the ancestry of Lady Gwendeline Bertie.
Mr Paul Strong, a fellow member of the British Commission For Military History, who put us in touch with Sir John Leslie, 4th Baronet.
Mr Hugo Vickers, Gladys Deacon's biographer; we are much obliged to Hugo for his knowledge of Jack Churchill's employment at Vickers da Costa, and family history he obtained from an elderly aunt.
Mrs Tara Wigley, editor; thanks are due to Tara, who spent many painstaking hours reading our manuscript, and making numerous recommendations for improvement.

Quotations from Sir Winston Churchill are reproduced with permission of Curtis Brown Ltd, London on behalf of the Estate of Winston Churchill: Copyright Winston S. Churchill.

Quotations from Clementine Churchill are reproduced with permission of Curtis Brown Ltd, London on behalf of the Estate of Clementine Churchill: Copyright The Lady Soames.

All quotations from Lord Randolph, Lady Randolph, Jack and Peregrine Churchill are by kind permission of Mrs Peregrine Churchill.

Quotations from Jean, Lady Hamilton are by kind permission of Mr Ian Hamilton.

List of Illustrations

1. Lord Randolph Churchill c. 1874
2. Miss Jeanette Jerome c. 1874
3. Lord Randolph Churchill, at the height of his power.
4. Lady Randolph Churchill, at the height of her beauty.
5. Randolph as a child.
6. Winston as a child.
7. Jack as a child.
8. The 'Jerome' rocking chair (p.29), now at Blenheim Palace.
9. Randolph and Jennie, soon after the birth of Winston.
10. Winston, aged 10; Jack, aged 5.
11. Jennie in her riding habit, Ireland 1877.
12. *L'Abbesse de Jouarre,* painted by Emil Adam, Newmarket 1889.
13. Left to right: Jack, Jennie and Winston.
14. Jennie and her boys, Winston (front) and Jack (standing).
15. Jennie walking out with the Prince of Wales, Tower of London c. 1896
16. Jennie making free with the Prince's headed notepaper.
17. Jennie as the Empress Theodora, 1897.
18. George Cornwallis-West, 'the most beautiful man in England'.
19. Winston in the South African Light Horse, 1900.
20. Jack in the South African Light Horse, 1900.
21. Jennie working in her office aboard *The Maine,* 1900.
22. Jennie and Jack, recovering from his wound, *The Maine,* 1900.
23. The officers of the Oxfordshire Hussars.
24. The 'family regiment': Colonel The Duke of Marlborough, KG, PC; Major Viscount Churchill; Major W. Churchill, MP; Major J. Churchill.
25. Jack: one of the best riders in the regiment.
26. The King of Portugal visiting the Oxfordshire Hussars.
27. Arthur Bertie, 7th Earl of Abingdon, Goonie's father.

The illustrations are from the private collection of Mrs Peregrine Churchill, with the following exceptions:
8 and 33 – by kind permission of His Grace the Duke of Marlborough.
12 – by kind permission of Mrs Minnie Churchill.
34 – by kind permission of The Lady Soames.

In the Shadow of a Great Oak

On 16th June 1996, in the American *Parade Magazine,* Michael Ryan wrote a review article entitled 'Who is Great?' In discussing the criteria of 'greatness', he drew upon the work of a California professor of psychology, Keith Simonton, and his 1994 book *Greatness: Who Makes History and Why.* Since one of his categories was a 'never surrender' attitude, it is no surprise that Winston Churchill figured in his study. Simonton 'discovered the striking pattern' that firstborns and only children tend to make good leaders in time of crisis, as they are used to taking charge. Then comes the astonishing assertion, "Churchill, an only child, was typical". A sidebar to an illustration of Winston repeats the question, "Was being an only child a factor in his greatness, as well as his defeats?"

More recently a biography of Jennie Churchill, with a sub-title referring to the mother of Winston Churchill, took a well-known photograph of Jennie and her children, cropped one out of the picture and left in the 'wrong' son![1]

These are somewhat extreme examples of a general phenomenon regarding the life of Winston Churchill and his wider family. Winston, of course, was not an only child. His brother, John (always known as Jack), was born in Dublin, some five years and two months after Winston. The brothers loved each other dearly, and Jack was frequently of service to Winston in unsung ways.

Winston is, by popular ballot, 'the greatest Briton' who ever lived. Many millions of words have been and continue to be written about him, in books, articles, the press and a journal devoted entirely to preserving his memory and the lessons for the world today of his ideas.[2] With a few honourable exceptions, most of this writing mentions Jack either in passing, or not at all. Yet to fully integrate Jack into the family history is to explain many contentious issues that bedevil writings on the Churchills.

If we only view Lord Randolph Churchill through the eyes of his eldest son and some of his in-laws, we end up with statements which relegate him to being, for example, "a busy father who did not like children and who treated him [Winston] with calculated coldness".[3] Winston's cousin, Shane Leslie, would write the outrageous assertion: "Few fathers have done less for the sons."[4] Jack is not mentioned or considered in these findings. A closer reading of the family's letters about and between all four members paints a very different picture. Randolph was certainly a busy man, often leading the fight for and – because of the high moral positions he struck – just as often against his own party. He attracted a great deal of opprobrium from the Tory-dominated press. Through all this he suffered from very poor health, often exhausting himself and requiring frequent rest cures. His letters to and about his sons display great affection, but also an increasing exasperation with the intractability of Winston to apply himself to his studies. This annoyance, which could be impassioned, can only be understood if compared to the model behaviour of young Jack. Jack applied himself diligently at all the schools he attended, and won the affection of as many teachers as Winston managed to antagonise. Through all this Lord Randolph was trying to secure the future of both his boys, and he went to a good deal of trouble on their behalf, for which he gets no consideration whatsoever. For this reason our book spends a good deal of time explaining the life and times of both parents, in order to better understand their relationship with, and the development of, their two sons.

In 1930, Winston published a highly entertaining account of his upbringing, *My Early Life*. It is witty and compelling, and the stories and basic assumptions in it are repeated in numerous subsequent accounts of his life. It really needs to be read with a critical eye. It too easily creates an image of parents who took little interest in their children. This, together with a highly coloured account of his schooling, is probably meant to leave the reader with the impression that Winston achieved so many great things entirely by his own efforts and against a tide of circumstances impeding his general progress. The book appeared after the broadcast of much scandal attached to Lord Randolph's name, courtesy of the disreputable journalist, Frank Harris, and Winston may have had an added reason for 'distancing' himself from his family. The idea, wholly false, that Randolph died a raging syphilitic madman was made public at a time when Winston was under heavy political attack for changing parties – again. His enemies in the Conservative Party he was just then re-joining loathed him with a fervour that a previous generation had directed against his father for his 'disloyalty' to the Party.

Winston and Jack were the sons of a Victorian aristocrat and his wife. Notions of child rearing in the nineteenth century were very different from today, though children could still be spoilt by doting parents and nannies. It was entirely the norm for children to be handed over to nurses and governesses, and to be sent away to boarding school. By the standards of the day this was as much to develop their character as for their education. The surviving letters of both Winston and Jack are a cacophony of requests for more letters, more visits, more parcels and, above all else, more money. Taken alone this correspondence could be seen as 'evidence' of neglect. We have come across many instances where such letters are only quoted partially to reinforce this general impression, in accordance with the story according to Winston, but which is not borne out by the writings of young Jack. The fact is the correspondence is anything but complete. It needs to be read carefully and analytically. Then patterns begin to emerge. Letters are often acknowledging the receipt of other letters, gifts or even visits, for which no other record exists. The letters between both parents and their two sons were always read out aloud and shared between all parties. Thus cross-referencing between letters gives a much fuller picture of a close and loving family. It is worth remembering that when Randolph or Jennie talk of sending the boys postal orders or cash of one or two pounds, we should multiply the value by anything between fifty and seventy times to get an idea of its worth in today's terms. When Lord Randolph shared his racing winnings with his boys, sending them three or five pounds he was making a gift equivalent in value to over two hundred pounds today.

It is also true that Jennie's own account of her life, the *Reminiscences* written at a time when she was desperately short of money, exaggerated many aspects of her early social life to appeal to the buying public, especially in her native America. This added to an image of her as a feckless mother, which reinforced Winston's descriptions of her being worshipped 'from afar' by 'a lonely little boy'.

It might be surprising that such a well-documented family should have so many gaps in surviving correspondence. While writers on the

Churchills are usually hampered by an excess of material on which to work, these lacunae are regrettable but understandable. The storage and preservation of the family papers has been fraught with difficulty. Jack and his wife, Lady Gwendeline ('Goonie'), were storing large quantities of papers at their last London home, Chester Terrace. On the outbreak of war in 1939, three steel trunks full of papers were sent down to Winston's country home, Chartwell, in Kent. Other papers were still at Chester Terrace when it was bombed in 1940, and the damaged property sealed up until after war had ended. Other papers relating to Jennie were driven to a barn belonging to the Duke of Westminster in Berkshire. It was with great difficulty, and no chance of reconciling any losses, that Jack's second son, Peregrine, recovered as much of the family archive as possible. They were to be stored first at his home at Holworth in Dorset, and subsequently in a hidden room at 'Fairdown', Vernham Dean, Hampshire. It is this previously unused material to which we have been given unique access, together with permission to use all the material for which Peregrine and Yvonne hold the copyright.

When Winston's son, Randolph, began to write the official biography of his father, later completed by Sir Martin Gilbert, there was a great upheaval in many archives. Randolph's son, Winston, has left a picturesque, and somewhat alarming, record of 'raiding expeditions' on various locations, including that other great repository of Marlborough family papers, Blenheim Palace. He describes the 'carrying off' of all papers relevant to the biography.[5] We have it from both Peregrine and his sister, Clarissa that items loaned for this purpose seldom returned to their original donors.

To illustrate how precarious is the fate of Churchill manuscript letters, the original of one quite well known Winston letter, printed in the first of the Companion Volumes to the biography started by his son, Randolph, has been re-discovered by us amongst Peregrine's papers. A woman found it amongst a 'job lot' of documents at a local sale. With commendable honesty she passed it to Sothebys, suggesting it belonged in the Churchill papers. They were uncertain of its authenticity and referred the matter to Peregrine. After checking with Churchill College and Blenheim Palace, it was finally declared to be the original, with no explanation as to how it went missing. It was subsequently wrongly filed away, and was found by Celia Lee when she was sorting papers relating to the family graves at Bladon! It has been returned to the Churchill Archives at Cambridge.

Now this particular letter has been used to show Lord Randolph as a neglectful father. It was written by Winston just before his first examinations for entry into Sandhurst, and contains some rather exaggerated estimates of how he would do. It is written on a very expensive 'Joynson Super Fine' paper, headed '2 Connaught Gardens' and begins by saying that he had waited as long as he could to see his father but had to leave to catch the train back to Harrow. A full knowledge of the family letters would show that Winston had suggested this meeting with his father at their London home at very short notice, and without checking to see if his father was in London or not. On more than one occasion he did this, and there are letters extant from Randolph telling everyone not to worry about such accidents and saying that he simply did not receive the initial letter. Winston had, on occasion, been scolded for using his father's expensive headed notepaper for such notes written within the family. A few months later he had done almost exactly the same thing, and had received a kind letter from his father saying how sorry he was not see the boys. He had obviously expressed some concern about using the 'forbidden' paper yet again, and confided as much with Mrs Everest and Jack. Here is an example of how bringing Jack's letters into the picture gives us a much better understanding of the true family dynamic. He wrote to his mother, who had been very ill, "I hear from Everest that you are much better today, she also says Papa on reading the letter which Winney wrote down stairs, was not angry and was so sorry that he did not see us".[6] Randolph had said that he would very much like to have seen the boys and his letter[7] is from "your affectionate father".

It became Peregrine's intention to write a new study of his Uncle Winston, that would show how he had exaggerated many aspects of his early life, and which would endeavour to reinstate Peregrine's father, Jack, in the family history. Having completed biographies of General Sir Ian Hamilton, and his wife, Jean, Lady Hamilton, we were introduced by Mrs Barbara Hamilton to Peregrine and his wife, Yvonne, in the year 2001. After several meetings and discussions it was suggested that we might assist Peregrine, then eighty-eight years old, in organising the papers and research for this work. Before this co-operation could begin Peregrine died suddenly and unexpectedly in 2002. At the request of his widow, we have undertaken to write a new look at the Churchill family in the spirit in which Peregrine intended. To our own surprise we would uncover a great injustice done to Jack after the death of Lord Randolph.

The family papers of Jack, and his father and mother, including large numbers made available to us for the first time, have enabled us to challenge the myth of distant and uncaring parents. Instead, we see a family struggling with many difficulties – political and social ostracism, more than their share of ill health, and impossibly way-ward finances. Randolph and Jennie, two young people very much in love when they first met, are seen to adapt their lifestyles to the demands of the bid for political power and influence, to the demands of 'Society', and to the normal tendency in those days for aristocratic husbands and wives to spend a great deal of time apart from one another. They cared for their children. They were unfortunate indeed to select a first school for their firstborn that belied its high reputation and was later seen to be a monstrous place, ruled by a sadist straight from the pages of Charles Dickens. The upbringing of their two sons was a constant concern for them both. After the death of Lord Randolph, his carefully laid plans for his boys were quickly and irrevocably overturned. One would use the army as a stepping-stone towards a path in politics with many twists and turns, earning admirers and enemies in equal measure, until he was in place to achieve a greatness that will echo down through the ages. The other would be forced into the last possible career he would have chosen for himself and live out his life a devoted and supportive prop to his brother. It is our fond wish and hope that Jack will emerge from the shadow in which he is cast and take his deserved place in the story of this remarkable and important family.

Author's note

To avoid the repetition of the word 'Churchill' hundreds, if not thousands of times, all the principal members of the families of Lord and Lady Randolph Churchill are referred to throughout by their first name, or the name by which they were known in the family.

CHAPTER I

Love at First Sight
1873–1876

Miss Jeanette Jerome kept the card inviting her to a prestigious reception and ball aboard HMS *Ariadne* during Cowes Week 1873. Held in the presence of the Prince and Princess of Wales, it was to introduce members of the visiting Russian Imperial family to English society. Where the printed invitation said, 'To meet', Jennie (as she chose to be known) had written in the name 'Randolph'. This delightfully romantic touch by the nineteen-year-old American was entirely in keeping with this, the very definition of a whirlwind romance.

Having known the splendours of the court of Napoleon III before the defeat of France in 1870, Mrs Jerome had raised her three daughters to have a high regard for European 'society'. She had taken a pretty little cottage with a garden facing the sea, at West Cowes, on the Isle of Wight, to enjoy the last great event of 'the Season' – Cowes Week. The Russian Imperial family was staying with Queen Victoria at Osborne House, and the ball on 12th August was for the younger Russian royals to enjoy. In this age before electric light, dancing was from 3.30 to 7.30 pm on an English warship, bedecked with lanterns and draped with the national colours of Great Britain and Imperial Russia. The guests, in their finest clothes and jewels, were serenaded by a band of the Royal Marines.

Jennie, resplendent in white gown and diamonds, attracted enormous attention. She was, quite simply, stunningly beautiful. Lord Randolph Churchill had seen her whirling about the deck and stood staring, spell-bound by her dark good looks and sparkling violet blue eyes. The Honourable Frank Bertie, a junior Foreign Office clerk, was a neighbour of Randolph's in Oxfordshire, and had met the Jeromes in Paris. It therefore fell to him to introduce the couple. Jennie later recalled the exact words used: "Miss Jerome, may I present an old friend of mine who has just arrived in Cowes, Lord Randolph Churchill".

Jennie was intrigued by this English aristocrat. He was of medium height and slim build, pale of complexion, fair-haired and with a full moustache. His blue eyes were a little protuberant. He was, of course, immaculately dressed and charming to speak to. Though he was no great dancer, he seized the moment and asked Jennie for the next quadrille. At the earliest opportunity he made excuses to leave the floor and they sat together on deck, sipping champagne and talking of the many things they had in common. Both had travelled widely in Europe, and both were fluent in French and German. But what drew them most closely together was their intense love of all things equine. They both rode well, hunted to hounds and were enthusiastic race-goers. They were quite lost in each other's company until Mrs Jerome appeared, anxious that her daughter was too long away from the dance floor, and whisked her away.

Jennie prevailed on her mother to invite Lord Randolph and his friend, Colonel Edgecumbe, to dinner. She enlisted the support of her elder sister, Clara, and they practiced piano duets to entertain and impress their guests. Barely twenty-four hours after she had met him, Jennie confided in Clara that she had "the strangest feeling that he is going to ask me to marry him". Her mind was made up. "I am going to say yes". Randolph confided to Edgecumbe that "he admired the two sisters, and meant, if he could, to make 'the dark one' his wife". Jennie had cleverly mentioned in passing that she strolled along a certain, deserted path at the same time each day. The next day she took particular care of her looks and, sure enough, Randolph was waiting on the path for her. Alone at last, they resumed their animated conversations. He explained that he was expected to leave for his family home, Blenheim Palace, next day. After their tryst, Jennie asked her mother to invite him to dinner again that evening. Mrs Jerome was already alarmed at the speed with which this relationship was moving. She had her sights set a little higher than the 'second son' of a duke for her daughter. She relented and issued a formal invitation that was again, like the invitation to the ball, kept by Jennie all her days. Mrs Jerome excused herself after dinner with a headache, but left Clara as chaperone. Clara, of course, was party to the romance and contrived to leave the couple alone. They strolled in the garden on a beautiful summers evening. The moment was perfect for a proposal of marriage and Jennie accepted without question. They both

agreed not to say anything to her mother, "as she would not understand the suddenness of it". Randolph, hopelessly in love with this
delightful young American, changed his plans and stayed four more
days, during which time they saw as much of each other as they
could.

At the end of Cowes Week Jennie told her mother that she was
betrothed to Lord Randolph and the reaction was everything she
might have feared. "She thought we were both quite mad and naturally would not hear of anything so precipitous". She forbade Jennie
to see or write to Randolph, closed down the holiday home and
returned the family to Paris forthwith. Her response was mild compared to the hostility to come from the great Churchill family.

Lord Randolph Spencer Churchill was the second surviving son of
the 7th Duke of Marlborough, John Winston Spencer Churchill, and
his wife, Frances Anne Emily Vane, daughter of the 3rd Marquis of
Londonderry. This was a union of two of the great Conservative
families in the land. The Churchill's family seat was the huge and
imposing Blenheim Palace, at Woodstock in Oxfordshire, built to
celebrate the victories of one of England's greatest soldiers, John
Churchill, 1st Duke of Marlborough. The dukedom had passed to a
grandson, Charles Spencer; the family name became Spencer
Churchill. The estate was grievously wounded by some particularly
profligate dukes, but, in the 7th Duke, it was once more in sober
hands. His marriage with a daughter of the powerful Londonderrys,
owners of large properties in the counties of Derry, Down and
Durham, brought much-needed money into Oxfordshire. However
his eldest son and heir, George Charles, Marquis of Blandford,
(known always as 'Blandford'), was another dissolute character in
the making. He had made an unhappy marriage in 1869 to Albertha,
daughter of the 1st Duke of Abercorn, and would cause grief to the
family. Randolph was very much the favourite son of the Duke and
Duchess.

The Londonderry connection may also have introduced a genetic
weakness into the male line of the Churchills. They were not long-
lived, and were delicate in their health. In successive years, at the age
of nine and ten, Randolph saw two of his younger brothers die, (one
aged two, the other just ten months); one brother had died before
him, aged four; Blandford would die aged forty-eight; Randolph

himself would be dead before his forty-sixth birthday after a series of illnesses. All six sisters would live into the twentieth century, dying between the ages of forty-six and eighty.[1]

Born on 13th February 1849, Randolph had the usual upbringing of an aristocratic child in Victorian England. He was given into the care of nannies and governesses, seeing his parents perhaps once a day, before going away to boarding school (Eton) at about eight years of age. He did moderately well at school, but the Duke had occasion to write to Eton a number of times, almost apologising for his son's behaviour. "He is a boy who I believe is readily moved, he has a quick sense of right and wrong, I do not think he has vicious tendencies; and there is a good sub-stratum of conscientiousness to work upon: his great faults are want of self control in his language, temper and demeanour and an imperiousness of disposition to those under him"[2]. Winston would display many of these characteristics at school.

Randolph already displayed a propensity to pick up every cough and cold going. His health was always precarious; he had a weak heart. The Duke, his father, was grooming this favourite son to be the Member of Parliament for Woodstock, a borough in the pocket of the Marlboroughs. In 1864, aged fifteen, Randolph had delivered a political speech on behalf of his father, and they discussed political affairs in their letters to one another. He toured Europe, improving his grasp of French and German, and becoming familiar with European culture. After two months in Switzerland and Italy in 1867, Randolph returned to pass his matriculation exams, and went up to Merton College, Oxford to study history and law. He developed an interest in chess, and became a founder member of the university chess club. He once took the world champion, Steinitz, to thirty-three moves before losing, though the Grandmaster was playing blindfolded at the time! Randolph got in with a 'fast set' and generally misbehaved, once avoiding police prosecution only by suing a police witness for perjury and seeing the case dropped. In 1870 he graduated with a Second Class Honours degree, having narrowly missed a First. This was something he would regret in later life, and would hold up as a bad example to his errant son, Winston.

Once graduated, he was, as he put it, kept 'hanging about' by the Duke, waiting for a general election to see him into Parliament. During this enforced idleness he became a well-known figure at the racetracks, and was considered something of a dandy. He certainly expressed no interest in a life in politics. He was naturally quiet and reserved, and seemed more intent on pursuing a life of pleasure than of duty.

Jennie's father was of considerable note in New York society. Leonard Jerome was a successful businessman, not above making a large fortune by the most blatant manipulation of stock prices through the good offices of friends who were leading financial journalists. He was busy in the corrupt world of New York politics and was U.S. Consul in Trieste for a while. He was a great patron of the opera and, in another aspect of his remarkable character, often had singers as mistresses, actually living in his household. His long-suffering wife, Clarissa, bore him three living daughters – Clarita (who called herself Clara), Jeanette (Jennie), and Leonie. All were raised in a style familiar to any European aristocrat. There were nannies and governesses, and as good a private education as money could buy, with the proper emphasis on the genteel arts – music, drawing, languages.

In 1858, when Jennie was four, the family lived in Paris for a year or more, which is where Mrs Jerome acquired her great love of France. When Jerome insisted on returning to the United States he had to provide a palatial home as compensation. It had a ballroom fit for 300 guests, a theatre that could seat 600, a dining room for 70. But his incessant womanising was too much for Mrs Jerome to bear, and in 1867 the couple separated. They never divorced and remained on relatively friendly terms. With a good financial settlement, and with money of her own, Mrs Jerome was able to remove to Paris.

Mrs Jerome and Clara became intimately acquainted with the court of Napoleon III, forming a particular friendship with the Empress Eugénie. Mrs Jerome became ambitious for her daughters, with the prospect of marriage into the European aristocracy very much in view. The Franco-Prussian War in 1870 ended all that. In September the Jerome women fled to England, settling first at Brighton. Leonard Jerome came as quickly as he could and installed them in London's prestigious Brown's Hotel. He took care to see that the girls continued their piano lessons; Jennie had been taught in Paris by Stephen Heller, a noted Hungarian teacher and composer. An Austrian tutor walked the girls every day in Hyde Park as they

perfected their German. Mr and Mrs Jerome went back to Paris to
salvage what they could from their house there after the ravages of
the siege and the communard revolution.

They were able to renew their friendship with the exiled French
Imperial family and enter polite society in England. France soon settled down and Mrs Jerome was able to return to their house in the
Boulevard Haussman, little changed but for the unexploded shell in
the cellar! Thus it was that Jennie was at Cowes Week in 1873, and
lost her heart to Lord Randolph Churchill.

Randolph had returned from Cowes to Blenheim Palace in a state
of high excitement and despair. He expected difficulties from his parents. His father was in Scotland on a shooting and fishing trip; his
mother's reaction, when Randolph first declared his love for Jennie,
was every bit as frosty as he feared. On 20th August he wrote a long,
ebullient and slightly clumsy letter to his father, trying to convey the
happiness he had found:

> I must not keep you in ignorance of a very important step I
> have taken – one which will undoubtedly influence very
> strongly all my future life. I met, soon after my arrival at
> Cowes, a Miss Jeanette Jerome, the daughter of an American
> lady who has lived for some years in Paris and whose husband
> lives in New York... before leaving I asked her if she loved me
> well enough to marry me; and she told me she did. I do not
> think that if I were to write pages I could give you any idea of
> the strength of my feeling and affection and love for her; all I
> can say is that I love her better than life itself, and that my one
> hope and dream now is that matters may be arranged that
> soon I may be united to her by ties that nothing but death itself
> could have the power to sever.
>
> I know, of course, that you will be very much surprised, and
> find it difficult to understand how an attachment so strong
> could have arisen in so short a space of time, and really, I feel
> it quite impossible for me to give any explanation of it that
> could appear reasonable to anyone practical and dispassionate.

Randolph then asked the Duke to increase his allowance to enable
him to marry and reassured him:

I enclose you her photograph, and will only say about her that
she is as nice, and loveable, and amiable and charming in every
way as she is beautiful, and that by her education and
bringing-up she is in every way qualified to fill any position.

We cannot be sure whether Randolph went on to conceal the true
state of the Jerome's marriage or whether, in the short time he had
known Jennie, he did not know of the separation:

Mr Jerome is a gentleman who is obliged to live in New York
and look after his business. I do not know what it is. He is
reputed to be very well off, and his daughters, I believe, have
very good fortunes, but I do not know anything for certain. He
generally comes over for three or four months every year.
   I believe and am convinced that she loves me as fully, and as
strongly as possible, as I do her; and when two people feel
towards each other what we do, it becomes, I know, a great
responsibility to assist in either bringing about or thwarting a
union so closely desired by each.[3]

There was no instant blessing, nor any increase in allowance. Instead
a rather formal letter from the Duke, which concluded: "I only
hope you will be willing to be guided by your mother and me". He
immediately set in train an investigation of Leonard Jerome's circumstances in America. The results were not encouraging. Jerome
was held to be "a well-known man with a fast reputation", whose
large fortune was matched by his extravagant expenditure. It was
known that he had been nearly bankrupted but had hung on to sufficient property to ride out the storm. One report might say he was
thoroughly respectable; the next might imply that he spent as much
money as he made.
   There followed a letter from his father as damning as Randolph's
worst fears might have expected:

It is not likely that at present, you can look at anything but
from your own point of view but persons from the outside
cannot but be struck with the unwisdom of your proceedings,
and the uncontrolled state of your feeling, which completely

paralyses your judgement. Never was there such an illustration
of the adage, *'love is blind'* for you seem blind to all
consequences in order that you may pursue your passion; blind
to the relative consequences as regards your family and blind
to the trouble you are heaping on Mamma and me by the
anxieties this act of yours has produced... .[4]

However attractive the mother and daughters were, 'Mr J.' was a
"vulgar kind of man", and the connection would not be respectable.
It was not long before Randolph's older sister, Cornelia, weighed in
with advice of the 'marry in haste, repent at leisure' variety. The rake,
Blandford, who had made a disastrous marriage, wrote a spiteful,
fifteen stanza 'Elegy to Marriage', mocking Randolph's fate if he
married too quickly. Finally his mother, the Duchess, delivered a
wounding blow:

> You must imagine to yourself what must be our feelings at the
> prospect of this marriage of yours... . Under any
> circumstances, an American connection is not one that we
> would like... you must allow it is a slightly coming down in
> pride for us to contemplate the connection... .

The news of Jerome's philandering added fuel to the opposition.
Lurking in the background was yet another story about Mrs
Jerome's antecedents; one that Winston Churchill used to take great
delight in spreading, as it added a hint of exoticism to his roots.
Attention has already been drawn to Jennie's remarkable dark
beauty. This almost certainly came from her father's Cornish ancestry, but some would have it that these genes came from Mrs
Jerome's grandmother having been ravished by an Iroquois Indian.
The story has been investigated and utterly disproved; the lady in
question could not at any time have been in any danger, either by
place or date, of befalling such a fate.

The Marlboroughs were frankly astonished when they heard that
it was the Jeromes who were so vehemently opposed to their daughter marrying a Churchill. Mrs Jerome had written to her husband
denouncing Jennie as 'hasty', 'rash', 'headstrong', 'unconsidered' and
'impulsive'. She implored Mr Jerome to come at once and try to influ-

ence this, his favourite daughter, who idolised her father so. He was more concerned that Randolph was only toying with her affections and begged her to think again.

Jennie bombarded her mother with tearful entreaties to be allowed to marry, and she was firmly supported by sister Clara. Randolph wrote to Mrs Jerome often and, finally, won her over. She once replied: "I must acknowledge that you have quite won my heart by your frank and honourable manner"[5]. She was the first of the parents to give way, and told her husband, Leonard, that she consented to the marriage. Jerome then telegraphed that he would provide a dowry of £50,000, an allowance of £2,000 a year, and leave one third of his estate to Jennie. This was a powerful incentive to a cash-strapped English aristocratic family.

Randolph cleverly changed tack and wrote to his father that, having drifted aimlessly in life, he now felt that marriage would give him a new sense of purpose and encourage him towards making a name for himself. As the Duke set his legal representatives to negotiating about the financial side of the arrangements, he was now talking about getting the young couple to wait for a year, secretly hoping that it would all die out before then.

Then Jerome found out about the investigations into his affairs in New York and sent an angry telegram: CONSENT WITHDRAWN. Through it all Randolph and Jennie wrote to each other of their undying love and affection. He had worked out a strategy for coping with his recalcitrant parents, by either refusing to stand for the parliamentary seat at Woodstock unless he be allowed to marry, "or else, and this is still more Machiavellian and deep, to stand, but at the last moment threaten to withdraw and leave the Radical [the opposition candidate] to walk over. All tricks are fair in love and war... ."[6].

Jennie had written a charming letter to the Duchess, which is said to have pleased her very much. The Duke commented that her fine handwriting expressed a deal of character.

Randolph confided to Jennie that public life held no great charms for him, as he was naturally very quiet, and shunned publicity. He would do it if it pleased her, hoping she would take an interest and encourage him to keep up to the mark. To become active in politics would require a considerable change in personality for Randolph, and Jennie would be a major influence upon him. She was already excited about becoming the wife of a Member of Parliament, and was reading up on British politics.

At last, in January 1874, Leonard Jerome came to Britain and met Lord Randolph. With their shared passion for horse racing, they became the best of friends. Randolph found that he had to defend himself against some scurrilous stories circulating in America that he was a heavy drinker. A proposed trip by Randolph to Paris to see Jennie was cancelled when the Duchess insisted that he attend an ailing aunt, Lady Portarlington, in Ireland. These thinly veiled attempts to keep the lovers apart were soon ended by the calling of a General Election.

Randolph was up against a formidable Liberal candidate, George Brodrick, who made heavy and sustained attacks on the way the Churchills had run the constituency in the past. Randolph knew he had a fight on his hands and he was terribly nervous at the prospect. Already a heavy smoker, his consumption of cigarettes increased, to the great detriment of his delicate health.

The Conservative Party provided him with a seasoned 'minder', the barrister Edward Clarke. Together they worked on prepared answers to questions planted amongst their supporters in meetings, and Randolph found he was developing a good memory. But Clarke was forced to observe: "Lord Randolph...certainly seemed to have the most elementary ideas about current politics". He put in some rather nervous performances but worked hard, visiting all parts of the constituency. His last letter to Jennie before the vote said it all:

> If only we had been married before this! I think the reception
> you would have got would have astonished you. The number
> of houses I have been into – many of them dirty cottages – the
> number of unwashed hands I have cordially shaken, you would
> not believe. My head is a whirl of voters, committee meetings
> and goodness knows what. I am glad it is drawing to an end,
> as I could not stand it very long; I cannot eat or sleep".

On 4th February 1874 Randolph won a resounding victory by 569 votes to 404, a far better majority than any Churchill had ever achieved. He cabled Jennie immediately to expect him in a day or so. The Duke and Duchess gave their consent to the marriage. Better still, the Duke agreed to travel to Paris to meet the Jeromes. Mrs Jerome found him 'a perfect dear'. Jennie, just turned twenty years of age, conducted a charm offensive, playing Beethoven sonatas for him, and discussing British politics with marked intelligence. The Duke took an immediate liking to her, and would cherish her all his days. As a marriage settlement the Duke agreed to settle any and all of Randolph's existing accounts, grant an allowance of £2,000 a year, and pay all his annual expenses as an MP. Randolph had never been good at handling money, and wrote to his father with an extravagant promise:

> I am quite decided that Jennie will have to manage the money, and I am quite sure she will keep everything straight, for she is clever, and like all Americans, has a sacred, and I should almost say, insane horror of buying anything she cannot pay for.

How little he could know of what the future held out for them. While Jennie was in the care of her mother this may well have been the case. In every other respect this declaration was as wrong as it is humanly possible to be.

There were further wrangles about financial matters as Mrs Jerome held out for clarification of what might happen if the marriage failed. But eventually these things were settled and a dowry of £50,000 (£2.5 million today) and a joint income of £4,000 a year was deemed sufficient for the young couple to start their life together.

The Prince of Wales, a friend of Lord Randolph's and an ardent admirer of Jennie since they had been formally introduced at Cowes, later claimed to have been instrumental in securing the agreement of the Marlboroughs to the wedding. He could not claim to have influenced the Duchess, who never warmed to the woman who had 'stolen away' her darling son.

The date was set for 15th April 1874; the venue was the chapel of the British Embassy in Paris, the only acceptable place available at short notice. If their day was spoiled by the absence of Randolph's mother and father, because the Duchess could not bring herself to associate with the Jeromes, in every other way it passed off well. The Jeromes spent lavishly to see that it did. Blandford stood by his brother; wedding presents poured in from the great and the good in British society. Jennie wore white Parisian satin, under Alencon lace, with a simple string of fine pearls and a corsage of American orange blossom, all designed to enhance her dark beauty. After a sumptuous wedding breakfast, the couple left in a smart coach for their honeymoon tour of Europe.

Their honeymoon was a great success. Given that we know Jennie returned from it pregnant with her first child, and from what we know of her future patterns of behaviour, it is safe to assume that her introduction to the joys of sex was as complete as anyone might wish for a young bride.

They returned to England in late May to live at Blenheim Palace. Jennie was deeply impressed with the grandeur of the place, though it was far from comfortable as a home. It was, of course, the first time she had met Randolph's mother and sisters. Despite the warm greeting by the Duke, the Churchill womenfolk remained stern and unforgiving. Jennie made a real effort to get to know them. She may have tried too hard; she may have simply been showing off. She knew she was beautiful; she dressed in the height of fashion. Neither of these attributes applied to the Duchess and her daughters. Jennie was a vastly better pianist, and a truly accomplished horsewoman. Everything she did seemed to them calculated to offend.

The stultifying, old-fashioned routine of the palace soon wore her down. As the pregnancy developed, she took proper care of herself. Soon she was denied the chance to ride as Randolph went off with the Heythrop Hounds. She was confined to Blenheim, playing the piano, viewing its paintings, and reading in its magnificent library. She accompanied the Duchess on dutiful visits to the local poor and did her best to fit in. But this was not what she had married for. She agitated for a home of their own, and Randolph was soon able to rent a small house for them at 1 Curzon Street, in London's Piccadilly.

In later years, Jennie would write a very colourful account of her life, full of balls and banquets, travels and endless socialising. The book *Reminiscences* is so completely self-centred that it hardly mentions her husband at the time, George Cornwallis-West, and certainly sidelines her children when young. No aristocratic woman in Victorian and Edwardian Britain was expected to tell the world about the upbringing of her children. Written to earn some very much-needed cash, it went a good way towards painting her as a frivolous and somewhat neglectful mother. Reality was a good deal more prosaic.

It was during a visit to Blenheim in November 1874, when Jennie was out walking on a game shoot with Randolph, that she went into premature labour. She was rushed back to the house and, being unfit to climb the stairs, was put to bed in a downstairs cloakroom, that still contained a bed from its time as quarters of the chaplain to the first duke. There was no time to send to London for the distinguished obstetrician they had planned for. After a difficult eight-hour labour, the local doctor, Frederic Taylor, delivered the baby at 1.30am on 30th November. The premature Winston Leonard Spencer Churchill had amber-red hair and blue eyes. There had been no time to assemble his new clothes and so he was dressed in some given by the local solicitor's wife, herself expecting at any time.

A recent biographer[7] has made the extraordinary claim that Jennie deliberately provoked this emergency delivery, including the elaborate deception of not having clothes or a specialist doctor to hand, in order to conceal the 'fact' that she was pregnant before she married. Others suggest that such a healthy baby could not have been premature and that the couple had consummated their relationship ahead of their wedding. Leaving aside the physical separation of Jennie and Randolph before their wedding, in Paris and Woodstock respectively, this is another example of a general ignorance of the true family circumstances. Both Jennie's sons were delivered prematurely, and there was a medical problem at the neck of her womb that caused this to happen twice. It was thought that one of the several falls that this fearless young horsewoman suffered had caused a pelvic injury that made it hard for her to carry her babies to full term.[8] We seem to be the first to have made a very simple calculation that goes a long way towards scotching this story. People routinely state that Winston was born at seven months, when he should have been weak and in some danger in the medical conditions of the day. From the date of the wedding, 15th April, to the date of the birth, 30th November, is 230 days, or one day short of 33 weeks. Being just three weeks early is not nearly so alarming, and could easily have been the result of strenuous exercise. The doctor in attendance stated quite clearly that the child was premature but healthy; the Duchess of Marlborough described him as 'strong and healthy'.

Randolph was a proud and dutiful father. He wrote a detailed letter to Mrs Jerome in Paris:

> ... all has up to now thank God gone off very well with my darling Jennie ... the baby was safely born at 1.30 this morning after about 8 hrs labour. She suffered a good deal poor darling, but was very plucky & had no chloroform. The boy is wonderfully pretty so everybody says ... and very healthy considering its prematureness ... we have got a most excellent nurse & wet nurse coming down this afternoon ... I telegraphed Mr Jerome; I thought he would like to hear. I will write again tonight. Love to Clara... I hope the baby things will come with all speed. We have to borrow some from the Woodstock Solicitor's wife.[9]

Winston was baptised on 27th December by the Duke's Chaplain in the private chapel at Blenheim Palace, and was named after Randolph's father, whose middle name was Winston. Lady Camden was his godmother and at Randolph's request, Leonard Jerome was his godfather, though he is not thought to have made it on time from the US. Jennie was very weak after the birth; a photograph at this time shows her pale and tired, slightly overweight still. Her adoring husband sits at her feet. They rested together at Blenheim Palace until the New Year.

In January 1875, they returned to Curzon Street. Jennie appointed Mrs Elizabeth Everest, an experienced nurse and nanny. This single lady, the 'Mrs' was an honorific title, became an enormous influence on the Churchill boys. When Winston learnt to talk he called her Woom meaning woman. She is the 'Woom' or 'Woomany' to whom they constantly refer in their letters, an adored and adoring companion for twenty years.

Though money troubles were already beginning, the young couple seemed 'in denial' as they vigorously embarked on establishing themselves in society. Leonard Jerome did not pay all of the dowry expected, and the Duke also seems to have failed to pay the full allowance he had promised. He did, however, buy a leasehold (for

£10,000) on a new house for them, 48 Charles Street, Mayfair. This was a four-storey house in a fashionable part of town, where the couple could set up home properly for the first time. They hired an excellent French cook and a number of servants. They were able to entertain very successfully but at some expense. Jennie was thrilled whenever the Prince of Wales came to dinner. Being seated beside the future king of England was exactly what she aspired to when she married Randolph. The Prince always complimented them on the meals served, and clearly enjoyed their company a good deal.

Randolph had his parliamentary duties to attend to; Jennie sometimes visited her family in Paris, taking the baby with her. They kept up a delightful correspondence if they were parted for too long. Jennie wrote to Randolph after he had left her in Paris:

> It seemed so lonely not to find you dearest. I took particular pains to shut the door of your room. I could not bear the desolate look it had ... I hope your cold is no worse and remember only 6 cigarettes ... . Please take care of yourself darling boy and come back soon to your lonely Jennie ... . The baby is such a darling, he is growing so fat and nearly walks alone.

We can see that Jennie was already concerned about Randolph's excessive smoking, and about the continuous minor ailments that seemed to dog him. Another letter shows what a close and loving family they made:

> Tell me really how you are ... please dearest get well and come back ... . The baby is most flourishing, but he never will kiss me unless I say "For Papa".

During a few days spent at the Marlborough Club on business, Randolph wrote to Jennie:

> I have the same rooms we had the last time we were here together. I thought of you so much last night: I wish I was back with you, it seems an age since I saw you.[10]

This is hardly the letter of a man sexually estranged from his wife, as some writers would have us believe. An extraordinary and persistent idea suggests that Randolph was infected with syphilis during the time Jennie was pregnant with Winston. Not only did Randolph acquire political enemies who were ready to spread such tales, but there were even elements within his extended family who would become the primary source of slander against him, as we shall reveal in due course.

Charles Street turned out to be a draughty house and Winston was unwell. In October 1875, after a successful visit to the Newmarket races where he cleared £400 in winnings, Randolph wrote, "I still feel rather anxious about the baby. I hope you will be very careful of him in that draughty house". Early in 1876, he was trying to rent a house in the country, which he felt would be healthier for them all. Letters from this period always send his love to 'Skinny', their comical nickname for this plump baby. The winter was hard on Randolph's health and his doctors suggested a rest in the south of France. Jennie demurred, saying it would be too expensive and an imprudent journey to make with the baby. This was a happy family, but one already beset with money worries. Much more serious trouble was to overtake them soon.

Randolph's brother, Blandford, had been having an affair with Edith, Lady Aylesford, a former mistress of the Prince of Wales. The Prince suddenly struck a high moral tone and wrote to Blandford demanding that he divorce his wife and marry Lady Aylesford. An abusive row developed, in which Randolph and Jennie took Blandford's side against the Prince's ridiculous suggestion. The Prince of Wales let it be known that he would never again enter a house where the Churchills were guests. The family was suddenly dropped from the invitation lists of most of their friends and acquaintances. There were awkward moments when the Prince would arrive at short notice at a house, and Randolph and Jennie had to be bundled out by another door least they should meet. To try and calm matters, Randolph took his brother off to Holland in April 1876. From there he wrote the most loving letters to Jennie, sending kisses to the baby. He found his brother to be a crashing bore and deeply deplored his idiotic behaviour. Thinking he could force the issue, Randolph then somewhat rashly threatened the Prince with the publication of intimate letters he had written to Lady Aylesford, who had unwisely given them to Blandford. Not surprisingly the Prince was enraged and even swore he would fight a duel with one of the Churchill brothers, he didn't much mind which. Peregrine Churchill was quite convinced that Randolph took such a strong stand against his former friend, the Prince, because he was becoming alarmed at the very great interest this most lascivious of royal princes was taking in Randolph's beautiful young wife. Randolph refused to fight the heir to the throne, but offered to fight another man of the Prince's choosing. Lord Hartington intervened and, having asked Randolph to hand over the Prince's letters to Lady Aylesford, he walked over to the fire and threw them onto it. On his return to England, Randolph apologised, but the Prince was still not satisfied.

The row was so embarrassing that Prime Minister Disraeli proposed that the Duke of Marlborough should accept the vacant position of Viceroy of Ireland, and take his family out of England altogether. This he reluctantly agreed to do. Blandford played his part by taking his mistress away to live with him in France.

Jennie went for a long visit to her mother in Paris, leaving Winston with his father and Mrs Everest in London. Randolph wrote to her often expressing how much he missed her and sending regular news of the baby's antics:

> I don't like this house without you it is awfully dull ... . The
> baby is very well. He came in to see me this afternoon &
> carried off the paper basket in triumph.[11]

Money matters also formed a constant topic. Loans were being sought; less expensive houses were being looked at. Randolph's letters to Jennie included the admonition, "Don't you go and spend too much money". He complained that her letters were too short and that she should tell him more of what she was doing. Her reply to her "darling *petit* R" insisted that she was living quietly:

> ... the fact is there is so little to tell you – ... Can't you manage
> to meet me Monday night? – How delicious it will be – to be
> together again – I hope you have missed me & feel that you
> can't do without little J -? ... . I have no news to tell you we

potter about all day playing the piano, reading & driving – &
pass the evenings quite alone so I can't have much to say
except that I love you & am longing to see you. ... Good night
dearest I should like to kiss you ... .[12]

As she was getting ready for this trip, Jennie's maid packed away various medicines, which included that prescribed to Randolph for his current malady. Jennie wrote to him from Paris, full of apologies for the error, and promising to send him the prescription, which was amongst her papers. If Randolph's medicine was kept in a cabinet beside Jennie's, and was easily accessible to the servants, it can hardly have been the telltale compounds of mercury prescribed for syphilis.

At the end of the year the new Viceroy left for Ireland, taking Randolph as his private Secretary. With wife and child at his side, the next few years were to have the most profound effect on Lord Randolph Churchill.

CHAPTER 2

An Irish 'Exile'
1876 –1880

In December 1876 the installation of a new Viceroy in Dublin was a major state occasion. The 7th Duke of Marlborough wore a full dress uniform, and his family and staff entered the city in a cavalcade of coaches to a salute of cannon fire befitting the representative of Queen Victoria. The cheering crowds could see that Lord and Lady Randolph had brought their two-year old son, Winston, in the carriage with them. After the fashion of the day, he wore a white satin frock, with petticoats, and a royal blue coat, with his red hair done up by Mrs Everest in ringlets hanging to his shoulders, and tied with a white ribbon. Less devoted parents might have left him in the care of the nanny, but Jennie thought he should be given the chance to participate in this, his first great state event.

The Duke embarked on this career reluctantly, knowing that his expenses of £20,000 a year in keeping up this high office would far exceed the grants allowed for it. He and the Duchess lived in the Viceregal Lodge in Phoenix Park. Randolph, as his (unpaid) private secretary, lived in the 'Little' White Lodge close by, with Jennie, Winston, Mrs Everest and a small staff. Randolph's duties were not onerous at first, and he and Jennie quickly took to the life of the Anglo-Irish gentry, with its heavy emphasis on riding, hunting, fishing, shooting and sailing.

During one vigorous ride, Jennie was galloping through a farmyard gateway when a gust of wind blew the gate shut and her horse crashed into it, spilling her from the saddle. She later recalled:

> Luckily I fell clear, but it looked as if I might be crushed
> underneath him, and Randolph, coming up at that moment,
> thought I was killed. A few seconds later, however, seeing me
> all right, in the excitement of the moment he seized my [hip]

flask and emptied it. For many days it was a standing joke
against him that *I* had the fall, and *he* had the whiskey.[1]

This incident illustrates both the loving concern Randolph felt for his
wife, and his highly nervous disposition.

There were still the duties of the Member of Parliament for
Woodstock to be attended to, and Randolph was obliged to spend
time away from his family because of it. His letters to Jennie always
said he was "dying" to get back to her, and that he was "bored" in
London. Having won a remarkable success in getting elected,
Randolph had slipped quietly onto the backbenches and did as little
as he could by way of parliamentary duty. His maiden speech of
1874, had been rather an unfortunate beginning. The House was
debating the creation of a new military barracks at Oxford. Randolph
spoke against the proposal, saying there was no place for "roistering
soldiers and licentious camp followers" in a university town.
Oxfordshire MPs had already had to fight against industrial development in the city, saving it from "railway roughs" and "navvies". Was
Oxford to become a garrisoned city like London, Dublin or
Edinburgh, with troops on hand to control an unruly populace?

It would be hard to contrive a speech calculated to offend quite so
many people in one sitting. Sir William Harcourt was shocked that a
descendant of the great Duke of Marlborough could speak in such
vulgar terms about the army. He also reminded this new Member
that he owed his place to the votes of "rough" working men in his
constituency. The Lord Mayor of Dublin also took exception to the
characterisation of his city as lawless and in need of patrolling. The
motion was defeated and Randolph left a first impression of being an
unpleasant little reactionary. Prime Minister Benjamin Disraeli, a
friend of the Duke of Marlborough, is known to have had a quiet
word with Randolph about his performance. Randolph took almost
no part in future debates that session, speaking only occasionally on
matters relating to his Woodstock constituency.

In Ireland, however, he was thrown into the company of some very
impressive intellects. Chief among them was Lord Justice Gerald
FitzGibbon, the Law Adviser at Dublin Castle, the seat of British rule
in Ireland. He dealt with questions of law from every part of the
country and from every department of government. His knowledge

of the country and its problems was unsurpassed. He was also the centre of a circle of fine minds, who met often to discuss politics and high culture. Through his great friendship with FitzGibbon, Randolph was drawn into this circle. It included the Roman Catholic priest, Father James Healy, who became a regular visitor, and who interested Jennie greatly in the issues surrounding Irish Home Rule. As he got to know this group better, Randolph came to rue his earlier description of Dublin as a 'seditious capital'. He expressed his regret, admitting, "I have since come to know Ireland better".

The spring and summer of 1876 had been unusually wet and, that year, the potato harvest was very poor, leaving a serious shortage of seed for the following year. When the bad weather continued in 1877 a most serious failure of all harvests, potato and wheat, and the lack of useable peat for fuel, led to very great hardship for the people of Ireland. Repeated crop failures led to a famine in the years 1878–1880, evoking memories of the more infamous 'Great Hunger' of the eighteen-forties. The British government response, in the form of easier for loans for landlords who might (or might not) then help their suffering tenants, was completely inadequate.

The Duchess of Marlborough set up a Famine Relief Fund, with Randolph as its secretary. Jennie became much involved in its work. Its purpose was to provide food, fuel and clothing, especially for the elderly and the weak, and small sums of money to keep able-bodied men, temporarily in distress, out of the workhouse. Grants were also available to schools, that they might provide meals for the children. It was intensely practical help, and it was offered without any sectarian bias, to Roman Catholic and Protestant alike. With the prestige of the Marlborough/Churchill name behind it, the Fund attracted substantial gifts from Queen Victoria, the Prince of Wales, and all the great families of the mainland. It raised over £135,000 in all; over £8,000,000 in today's valuation. Jennie wrote to Randolph in London where he was attending the Commons, keeping him abreast of family matters in Ireland. In one she mentioned the fuss Winston created when she had to leave with the Duchess to carry out famine relief work:

> Winston has just been with me – such a darling he is – 'I can't have my Mama go – & if she does I will run after the train &

jump in' he said to me. I have told Everest to take him out for
a drive tomorrow if it is fine – as it is better the stables should
have a little work.

In the course of administering these funds, often dispensed through
local committees, Randolph and Jennie visited all thirty-two counties
of Ireland, meeting large numbers of her best citizenry. Together they
became more than familiar with Ireland's problems, and these times
would have a lasting influence on them both. It went a long way
towards radicalising Randolph's politics, and set him on a collision
course with his own party, then in government. In September 1877,
at a speech in Woodstock, he was discussing the rise of an Irish
Nationalist movement and the disruptive role of its Members of
Parliament in the House of Commons:

> I have no hesitation in saying that it is inattention to Irish
> legislation that has produced obstruction. There are great and
> crying Irish questions which the Government have not attended
> to, do not seem inclined to attend to and perhaps do not intend
> to attend to...
> Who is it, but the Irish, whose eloquence so often commands
> our admiration, whose irresistible humour compels our
> laughter, whose fiery outbursts provoke our passions?

Randolph became a formidable expert on Irish matters. He took
upon himself a survey of the need for educational reform in the country. He criticised the diversion of funds to the Church of Ireland at
the expense of other institutions. He persuaded the Government to
set up a small commission, on which he and Lord FitzGibbon sat, to
enquire into the condition, management and revenues of Ireland's
schools. Fact-finding for this work also took him all around Ireland.

This fairly lacklustre backbencher, with a natural aversion to the
clamour of politics, had become a man with a mission. Soon he was
roundly condemning England's record, proclaiming that she had
"years of wrong, years of crime, years of tyranny, years of oppres-
sion, years of general misgovernment to make amends for in
Ireland". It must not be imagined that this radical stance made him
in any way sympathetic to the flourishing nationalist movement,

under the charismatic leadership of Charles Stewart Parnell. Their
call for a degree of Irish Home Rule, what we would call a devolved
parliament, was more moderate than the small band of revolutionaries who sought complete independence from Britain. But this was
anathema to Randolph, who would have liked to make a huge range
of reforms to improve the standard of life for all the Irish people, to
give them equal status with all citizens of the United Kingdom.

With a new confidence, Randolph was now vigorously opposing
the more militant policies of his own party and government. During
the crisis occasioned by the Russo-Turkish war of 1877–78, it was to
the great Liberal politician, Sir Charles Dilke, that he wrote, on 7th
February 1878, suggesting ways that several Balkan provinces might
gain their freedom from Turkey (which country had the backing of
Disraeli's government), and he even promised to enlist the Irish
Nationalist vote for the project. He later told Dilke that he did not
want these new republics to fall under some Russian or German
prince, who would be a mere puppet under the guise of a constitutional monarchy. This son of a duke had no great regard for
aristocratic rule. As a 'war fever' swept the country, Randolph
denounced it, saying: "I think the Conservative Party are gone mad".
How interesting that his correspondents were leading Liberals, and
what a transformation from the young man who had deplored the
vexations of political struggle.

How was Jennie adapting to this new life? It had certainly not
turned out as she might have planned. After a wonderful honeymoon, she had returned to the icy atmosphere of Blenheim Palace
and her unforgiving female relations. Her early pregnancy had placed
further restraints upon her. She and Randolph adored their new baby
and, when they set up home together in London, they were able to
begin entertaining and be entertained in society. Then came the terrible rift with their erstwhile friend, the Prince of Wales, and this 'exile'
in Ireland. There were pleasures enough to be had in the company of
the Irish and Anglo-Irish gentry, but it was not the same as the glo-
ries of 'The Season' that she had so recently been a part of – that
great round of balls, banquets, and festivities that defined the lives of
the British aristocracy.

Jennie was supportive of Randolph's newfound interest in politics.
There was, of course, the possibility of advancement in this field and

Jennie would become fiercely ambitious for her husband. The famine in Ireland gave Jennie some meaningful work to do, something usually and cruelly denied to women of her class and station. It even brought her a little closer to her austere mother-in-law. She greatly enjoyed the opportunity to share in Randolph's work as they travelled about Ireland together.

But he was increasingly absent due to his political work, needing to attend sessions of the House of Commons and staying away in London. Letters between them in 1877 began to speak of Jennie feeling "lonely and wretched"; his replies begged her not to be angry with him. He sent her a fine new saddle, and was "relieved" when she said how much she liked it. Jennie's sisters, Clara and Leonie, visited her in Ireland. At a reception at Dublin Castle, Leonie was to meet her future husband, John Leslie of Castle Leslie, County Monaghan. These Americans could display their natural high spirits when things got a little dull, or when Dublin Castle convention got too stifling. Jennie was known to race one of her sisters on the vice-regal lawn in their nightgowns, whilst the servants were at supper.[2]

Their dear son, Winston, was a constant topic of interest. In Jennie's letters to Randolph a precarious 'W' began to appear at the bottom, as Winston added his first attempts at a signature. He was a greatly indulged and boisterous child.

> Winston is here making such a noise I can hardly think of what
> I'm writing. I hope you are enjoying yourself. The house does
> pretty well with only Kate [a servant], her style of waiting on
> table is peculiar – but as long as one gets something to eat
> what does it matter. Clara & Winston send their love.

The letters are full of the usual stories of child development and baby talk. "I bought Winston an elephant this afternoon which he has been asking me for for some time, & I was on the point of saying to the shop-woman 'An ephelant'. I just stopped myself in time". "Winston is flourishing and has learnt a new song, 'We will all go hunting today, etc.'". News of winter colds brought concern from the absent father: "I shall leave for Ireland Monday night and be with you Xmas day morning … . I am rather uneasy at your account of little Winston and hope you will get the Dr. to see him". Winston had been a robust baby but the atrocious weather in Ireland was giving regular chest trouble to the child. This, and the weakness in the male line of his family, seems to have left him prone to ill health. At one stage Randolph considered bringing him back to England to rest in a sanatorium, but it was not necessary. This is a devoted and concerned father and not the unfeeling, distant figure of legend.

In 1878 Winston had his portrait painted by the Dublin artist, P. Cyron Ward. The most remarkable features were still his mass of red ringlets, tied in ribbons, and his beautiful blue eyes. Mrs Everest took him walking in Phoenix Park most days when the weather permitted. With his head filled with stories told by her and the servants, he expected to encounter 'Fenian ruffians' at any moment. While out riding his donkey one day in 1879, he had a serious fall and was badly concussed. Both parents were greatly alarmed, and he was to suffer serious headaches for years to come – an added trial to a, by now, somewhat delicate child.

On 14th April Randolph sent birthday greetings to his mother, and took the opportunity to let her know just how happy he was at that stage in his life:

> I write to wish you many happy returns for your birthday to-morrow, which is also, as perhaps you may remember, our wedding-day; and having been married five years I begin to feel highly respectable … .

In the summer of 1879, the Empress Elizabeth of Austria was holidaying in Ireland, having taken Lord Longford's house, 'Summerhill', in County Meath, for the summer. She was reputedly the most beautiful woman in Europe, and a superb horsewoman. She and Jennie rode out together often. On 22nd August, the Empress began to reminisce about the birth of her son, the Crown Prince Rudolph:

> One hundred guns pounded. My boy was born. On August 22nd … he is a nice boy … perhaps a little too full-blooded and excitable. You will meet him. I'll bring him next summer … You see he is not quite the product of my education. I was allowed to give him life, but he has never belonged to me. He

grew up under the care of 'Wowo'... his nurse, Baroness
Welden, I mean ... .[3]

Jennie was suddenly seized with the idea that she had not being
seeing enough of Winston lately, and she took her leave of the
Empress, saying, "Excuse me, Madame, I must beg to be permitted to
return home. I should look after my boy". The Empress replied,
"How fortunate you are! I was never permitted to look after my
boy".

Besides the constant attention of Mrs Everest, Jennie also read to
Winston on a regular basis. Then Mrs Everest introduced a book
called "Reading Without Tears" and began his proper education.
This was in preparation for the appointment of a governess, who
would be brought in one day a week to teach lessons. Winston took
an immediate dislike to her and to the whole idea of 'compulsory'
learning. Winston later recalled the "steadily gathering shadow"
over his daily life, and how he would run away and hide in the extensive garden shrubberies. The descent into "a dismal bog called
sums", and the knowledge that his mother "sided with the Governess
almost always" was a blow to the little chap. This display of rebellion, and inability to adjust to any degree of discipline, bore all the
hallmarks of an over-indulged, not to say spoilt, child. Jennie did get
stricter with him, but it was the start of a series of misadventures
relating to Winston's education.

The book My Early Life (1930) has affected most subsequent
books about Winston Churchill but there are problems if it is taken
entirely at face value. Winston was in Ireland between the ages of
two and five. Any 'memories' he had of this period were quite clearly
being reflected back from later impressions. How many of us can
truly recall, in detail, memories of our parents from such a young
age? Winston claims to remember his mother in Ireland wearing a
riding habit, "fitting like a skin and often beautifully spotted with
mud", and that she and his father "hunted continually" on their
large horses. Now there is certainly a very fine photograph of Jennie
looking as beautiful as ever in just such a costume, and in her later
Reminiscences she did paint a picture of an endless round of sporting
and social events, but surely it is the photograph Winston is describing rather than the 'memory'? Attention has already been drawn to

the fact that his mother's book, published 1908, (which she was writing at the same time as Winston was writing his father's biography in 1906, and they were working together), was made as exciting as possible with the sole purpose of maximising its sales. It undoubtedly contributed to Winston's 'memories' and, though he may not have intended it so, it has added to an impression of Jennie as neglectful of her children. Most famously he described how he 'loved her dearly – but at a distance', and implying that Mrs Everest was his one constant companion and confidante. We have seen enough, and will see more, of the close personal attention Jennie gave her children to know that this is a long way short of an accurate 'memory'.

If the dreadful weather in the summer of 1879 deprived the Randolph Churchills of the opportunity of as much riding as they might have liked, it did throw them more into one another's company. Sometime late in June they conceived their second child, the arrival of which Jennie declared to be her most joyful experience in Ireland. Once again Jennie took good care of herself, giving up her riding interest, but finding time to accompany Randolph on his school inspection tours.

For a second time she was not able to carry the baby to full term. On 4th February 1880, after some thirty-two weeks, she delivered John Churchill into the world. Peregrine was able to tell us that his father was described as a 'blue baby', after a difficult birthing, and a baptism had to be arranged very quickly. The baby's full name was John Strange Spencer Churchill. John was for his paternal grandfather; Randolph always called him Jack in honour of the famed 1st Duke of Marlborough. Strange was for the 5th Earl of Roden, John Strange Jocelyn, who stood in at very short notice as godfather.

For this act of kindness to a family he knew well, Strange Jocelyn (as he was usually known), is routinely, and ignorantly, cited as Jack's true father. In 1969, Peregrine, sickened by the repeated allegations of his father's illegitimacy, took an author to court to prevent the slur being repeated. He presented such a weight of evidence that a settlement was made out of court, which included the destruction of the first print run of the offending book and a written promise not to repeat the allegation. It came as a blow to see the story repeated in cavalier fashion, by Roy Jenkins, in a hugely successful biography of Winston, published in 2001. Jenkins freely confessed that he made no original research for the book, basing it entirely on secondary sources and his own considerable experience of British political life. Yet, seven pages into the book he could assert:

> If the legitimacy of Jack Churchill is challenged, a more likely candidate seems to be the Dublin-based Colonel John Strange Jocelyn, who succeeded his nephew as the fifth Earl of Roden later in the year 1880. He was thirty years older than Lady Randolph but that was no necessary bar.[4]

Strange Jocelyn was a happily married man, who had been a professional soldier, leading his battalion, 2nd Scots Fusilier Guards, with distinction in the Crimea. He was a particularly devout Christian. Mabell Airlie wrote of him that, "He became deeply religious, even in youth, and his simple piety grew and persisted in old age". Peregrine entered into a long correspondence with the Jocelyn family and made this precise and forceful statement in a letter published in 1990:

> The Rodens allowed me, some years ago, to copy their family records and the facts are as follows:
>   My father was born in February 1880. The year 1879 was the year of the famine in Ireland and my grandmother [Jennie] and the Duchess [of Marlborough] were occupied with relief work. Lord Randolph was horrified when he first saw the poverty and distress of the people of Ireland ... .
>   John Jocelyn, 5th Earl [of] Roden, lived in England and was there during all 1879. He arrived in Dublin in February after my father's birth, having succeeded to the title on January 9th 1880.[5]

Colonel Jocelyn, born in 1823, was a friend of the Duke of Marlborough in England, and was named as an executor to his will. He was not 'Dublin based' and was not in Ireland when Jack was conceived. His nephew, the 4th Earl of Roden, had died unmarried and Strange Jocelyn suddenly and unexpectedly inherited the title in January 1880. He was in Ireland in February 1880 to visit the estate at Tollymore, in County Down, that was part of his inheritance. He was visiting the Viceregal Lodge to see his friend, the Duke, when he was delighted to be asked to stand as godfather to the new baby that would bear his baptismal name.

This flailing about for an alternative father for Jack, and there were and are other names bandied about, only makes sense to those gossip-mongers who insist that Randolph was seriously afflicted with syphilis almost from the moment he was married and that, as a consequence, sexual intercourse with his wife had ceased. There is nothing in the couple's correspondence, or in the medical records, to suggest any such thing. Indeed, they express a continuing affection for each other's company and the only discordant notes are when they are kept apart for too long.

Jack had fair hair and blue eyes though his hair would darken to jet black like his mother's. Photographs of him as a child and young man would show a striking resemblance to those of Randolph at similar stages in his life, and Jack's sons would be unmistakably Churchillian in aspect. Randolph would never have doubted the paternity of his second son for a moment. This point is laboured because as we shall later see, Winston himself, under the influence of at least one of his aunts, grew to believe the syphilis slur, and it is even possible, tragically possible, that Jack may have thus been made to doubt his own paternity.

The arrival of a new baby was, of course, a source of upheaval in the household. To the five-year-old Winston it was something of a mixed blessing. Jennie had brought a rocking chair from her family home in America, in which she used to rock Winston, but now rocked Jack[6]. It would be a while before Jack would be a playmate. Meanwhile Winston lost the undivided attentions of his mother and Woomany, and had to share them with a brother. This is usually resented by a first child and, as an entirely natural development, need not be exaggerated. If his mother or Mrs Everest were attending to Jack, then the other was free to devote her time to Winston.

The Duke of Marlborough's time as viceroy was coming to an end. A General Election had been called for 2nd April, so Randolph, Jennie and family came back early to England. They lived in a hotel near Blenheim, until their latest new house, 29 St. James's Place, London, could be got ready. Randolph worked very hard to retain his seat at Woodstock. He wrote to his mother on 21st March that he was campaigning from nine o'clock in the morning until eleven at night. Bad weather in England had also seen the rural workers suffer hardship, and the Blenheim Estate Land Agent had not handled the tenants with a great deal of tact. Luckily the splendid work the whole family had put into the Duchess's Relief Fund in Ireland earned them a good deal of political sympathy in Oxfordshire. Thus, while the Conservative Party crashed to a heavy defeat in the election[7], Randolph retained his seat by 512 votes to 452. For a new MP who had to divide his time between his constituency and Dublin Castle, this was a creditable performance. To examine the causes of their defeat, the Conservatives would set up a Central Committee tasked with 'reforming, popularising and improving the party organisation'. Randolph would, somewhat surprisingly, become a major force in party and national politics.

CHAPTER 3

A Political Star is Born
1880–1882

The newly elected House of Commons assembled for its first session in May 1880, and Randolph immediately seized on an awkward matter for the Liberal Party and established himself as the darling of the Conservative opposition, both in the House and in the country. The Liberal MP for Northampton, the atheist Charles Bradlaugh, refused to take the bible oath required of all elected members before they could take their seats. When the Liberal government, anxious to get on with other things, suggested setting up a committee to investigate the issue, Randolph swung into action and delivered one of his most brilliant speeches, insisting that it was for the whole Parliament to decide the matter. For theatrical effect he threw down a pamphlet written by Bradlaugh and trampled it underfoot. Randolph was not a particularly religious person, and Bradlaugh's atheism was of no particular interest to him. But the opportunity to take a stand for the sovereign rights of Parliament, and cause deep embarrassment to the new Liberal administration, was seized and what should have been a minor procedural affair was dragged out for months. He drove such deep wedges into the ranks of the Liberals that the Government was defeated by 275 votes to 230 on the issue. When Bradlaugh eventually agreed to take the oath, Randolph gleefully led a revolt that denied him the chance to swear an oath he so obviously did not believe in. The largely Tory press loved every moment of it, and Randolph's fame was established as the scourge of 'the enemy'. This launch into the front line of political action would have deep, not to say dire, consequences for his family life.

The defeat in the 1880 General Election was a shock for the Tory establishment, and an opportunity for their critics to begin a campaign for change within the party. Randolph joined a group calling itself the 'Fourth Party' (allowing the Liberals, Conservatives and Irish Nationalists as the first three). This group included Sir Henry

Drummond Wolff, MP for Portsmouth, a senior figure in the Conservative Party; John Gorst, MP for Chatham, whose organisational skills led Disraeli to credit him with the electoral victory of 1874; Lord Randolph Churchill, and the new MP Arthur Balfour, nephew of Lord Salisbury, who was somewhat more loosely associated with them. These four sat together on the opposition front bench, and met regularly and in secret. They devised strategies to fight the Liberals and also to galvanise what they saw as a thoroughly inadequate Conservative opposition. Randolph's acerbic wit was given free rein. He could be rude to the point of vulgarity and made as many personal enemies as he made friends in his own party. The leader of the opposition in the Commons, the heavily be-whiskered Sir Stafford Northcote, was promptly nicknamed 'The Goat'.

The first battle in Parliament was over the Employer's Liability Bill, in which the Liberals tried to offer some protective legislation to their working-class supporters, while simultaneously trying not to over burden their powerful manufacturing backers. The bill was riddled with anomalies. Expecting the official opposition to argue in the interest of the capitalist class against new liabilities laid upon them, the Liberals were astonished when the Fourth Party denounced the bill as not strong enough in the interests of injured workers and proceeded to expose its inadequacies. Randolph poured ridicule on the Liberals, and easily emerged as the real champion of the working-class on this issue.

Every piece of legislation brought before the House found the Fourth Party well informed and in combative mood. Their arguments were often more progressive than the 'left' of the Liberal Party, and simply ignored the old Tory leadership entirely. Prime Minister Gladstone certainly took the Fourth Party more seriously than the official opposition.

One important figure deeply impressed by the Fourth Party was Benjamin Disraeli, now Lord Beaconsfield. He personally encouraged Wolff and Gorst in their work, and shortly before his death in April 1881, he predicted to Sir William Harcourt that Lord Randolph Churchill would become a powerful figure in the Conservative Party: "… when they come in they will have to give him anything he chooses to ask for and in a very short time they will have to take anything he chooses to give them".

Jennie's elder sister, Clara, married Moreton Frewen in New York in June 1881. He was English, and a renowned horseman and sportsman from an old but impoverished family of Sussex gentry. He had uncertain business interests in America, and Jennie had considered him an unsuitable match for her sister and let her feelings be known quite freely. Clara was considered a great beauty, and had received attention from notable European aristocrats, and Jennie must have thought that she could do much better. She was not at the wedding, but before long the newly-weds were inviting Randolph and Jennie to visit them at their home in the ranching country of Wyoming. The couple would later settle in England. That he evolved the nickname 'Mortal Ruin' tells us all we need to know about the financial disasters that dogged him for many a long day.

Still vexed at the social ostracism caused by the rift with the Prince of Wales, Jennie took great pride in Randolph's success, and clearly hoped it would bring them some social advancement. Her note of 12th July 1880 to her mother in Paris was only a little short of a begging letter, with its heavy emphasis on their shortage of money, but it evinces a deep understanding of her husband's character and is full of sound advice. Winston was still a handful.

Dearest Mama

Old Everest got a cold and I had to give her a holiday – and she is still away. Luckily I found a very good monthly nurse who looks after the Baby [Jack]. Winston is a very nice boy, and is getting on with his lessons, but he is a most difficult child to manage – so much for the infants.

You will be glad to hear that R.[andolph] has been covering himself with glory, and I am told he has made himself a wonderfully good position in the House. Last Monday he spoke on an Irish Question which interests all the landlords at the moment, and he has made a *really* splendid speech – everyone says so – and Gladstone got up and answered him for an hour … . When this Government goes out (which they say will be soon) I fancy R. and his boon companion Sir Henry Drummond Wolff must be given something. I am only so afraid of R. getting spoilt – he would lose half his talent if he

did. I keep reminding him of it. London is very gay just now. I
haven't been to many balls as I simply can't afford to get
dresses and one can't always wear the same thing. Besides I am
not bidden to the ones I want to go to and I do not care about
the others. This week I am going out every night, tomorrow to
the opera; I was sent a box .... I shall send Winston and John
to Ventnor for a month. Money is such a hateful subject for me
just now don't let us talk about it. [1]

Jennie attended many of the debates at the House of Commons and
her dinner table saw many schemes hatched by the Fourth Party. By
a delicious irony they lived right next door to 'The Goat'. The group
became fast friends, and, as Gorst and Balfour were both music
lovers, Jennie frequently joined them at concerts. She and Balfour
played the piano together very well.

The 1881 sitting of the House of Commons was entirely dominated by Irish affairs. The increasing unrest in Ireland saw the
Liberals introduce a Coercion Bill to maintain law and order.
Randolph spoke passionately against it, defending the "high qualities" and "many virtues" of the Irish people, and deploring this act
that would criminalize many men seeking to protect their homes and
families. He caused great disquiet in the ranks of the Liberals as he
ruthlessly exposed just what an illiberal bill this was.

Randolph was working so hard in the political sphere that he was
nearing exhaustion. Partly to get out of London and into the fresh
air, partly to save money and partly to continue political discussions
with his father, the family moved into Blenheim Palace for some
months. It was good to be able to ride and hunt in Oxfordshire, and
the naturally friendly and exuberant Jennie did all she could to make
the stay pleasant. But the hostility of her mother-in-law was an insu-
perable barrier and on 21st November 1881 Jennie wrote to her
mother expressing her abiding unhappiness at Blenheim:

It is such ages since I've seen you. It is really too long. I quite
forget what it is like to be with people who love me. I do so
long sometimes to have someone to whom I could go and talk.
Of course, Randolph is awfully good to me and always takes
my part in everything, but how can I always be abusing his

mother to him – The fact is I *loathe* living here. It's not on
account of its dullness, *that* I don't mind, but it is gall and
wormwood to me to accept anything or to be living on anyone
I hate. It is no use disguising it, the Duchess hates me simply
for what I am – perhaps a little prettier and more attractive
than her daughters. Everything I do or say or wear is found
fault with. We are always studiously polite to each other, but it
is rather like a volcano, ready to burst out at any moment … .
Meanwhile our money affairs are pretty much like everyone
else's it seems to me, hard up notwithstanding Papa's generous
'tips'… . Randolph is obliged to spend so much in a political
way … . You don't know how economical we try to be.[2]

We have already discussed how Jennie had tried, and failed, to
impress her female in-laws when they first met. The beautiful and
vivacious Jennie would never win the favour of the Duchess of
Marlborough. Clearly Randolph defended his wife from much of the
criticism. Jennie's idea of being 'economical' would almost certainly
be at variance with the normal use of the word. However, much of
the young Churchills' money was being eaten up in paying for political dinners, entertaining, and hiring halls for large public meetings.

For Winston's seventh birthday (November 1881) he was given the
first of what grew into a huge collection of toy soldiers, which interest would eventually lead him into an army career. The collection
was added to that Christmas and at all subsequent festivities. At this
age Winston was noisy, boisterous and disruptive, like most boys his
age. Jennie spent a good deal of her time engaging his interest and
attention, while Mrs Everest saw to the two-year-old Jack. Jack was
already a quiet, placid, well-behaved child, with a slightly serious
aspect. Winston saw this inherent 'goodness' as something of a challenge: something to define himself against. One houseguest asked
Jack if he was a good boy, to which the little chap replied, "Yes, but
brother is teaching me to be naughty".

We are very fortunate that Peregrine preserved his grandmother's
only diary for the year 1882. It gives us a faithful picture of the sort
of life Jennie really led, a corrective to the extravagant picture she
would create in later years. In January they were still resident at
Blenheim Palace and the diary describes a contented family scene.

Jennie was attentive to her husband and her sons. Despite Winston later writing that his mother took no part in his education, crediting all to Mrs Everest, Jennie regularly recorded having given Winston his lessons, taking him for walks and reading to the children.

The other principal activity that she recorded was her painting, which she indulged in almost every day. It had been part of her genteel upbringing, and she had developed the interest in Ireland. Her sister Clara was an early model to practice her skills in portraiture. Back in London, she took lessons from Mrs E. M. Ward, the wife of a prominent painter, who later wrote, "Lady Randolph Churchill showed a decided talent for painting ... and on more than one occasion was accompanied by her son Winston, a delightful little boy in short trousers".[3] Again we have the testimony of Peregrine, with whom his father lived in his later years and from whom he learnt a good deal of the family history, that first Winston, and later Jack, were taught to draw and paint by their mother. This is another important corrective to Winston's myth making about how he took up that great love of his life during the First World War. Both boys regularly illustrated their letters within the family, and Jack would keep up the tradition in writing to his own children when they went to school.

The diary, besides dutifully recording the weather every day, holds many references to domestic contentment, including playing billiards with the Duke and other Churchills, to charitable duties with the Duchess and to attending political meetings with Randolph. Amongst the many friends she recorded visiting or being visited was Blanche Hozier (Lady Blanche Ogilvy), the mother of Winston's future wife, Clementine.

On a foggy 4th February 1882 Randolph, Jennie and their family moved back to their London home in St James' Place. She resumed her painting on a daily basis, which included portraits of some of their close friends,[4] and was getting back into life in the capital city when things took a dramatic turn for the worse.

In mid-February Randolph's health collapsed completely. Officially diagnosed as an acute inflammation of the mucous membrane, it was a result of his working too hard, coupled with his serious chain-smoking of very strong cigarettes and Cuban cigars. It led to a deterioration of his immune system, leaving him vulnerable to other infections. His principal physician was Dr Robson Roose, a specialist in nervous disorders who had written a number of medical studies on the strain on some men of hard, mental work. Randolph's enemies began to circulate the slur that he was ill with syphilis, but nothing in his medical record or in his treatment indicates any such disorder.

Mrs Everest took the boys away to Blenheim Palace for the duration of the illness. It would be five months before their father could return to the House of Commons. Despite his doctors ordering a complete rest, there were streams of visitors coming to see Randolph and to argue questions of policy and strategy. While there was a day nurse in attendance, Jennie personally looked after Randolph every evening, and coped with the crowds who came to see him.

Randolph's condition worsened towards the end of February and he suffered a physical collapse. Still he would not reduce the number of visitors he received, or refrain from the excitement of politics. One entry on 2nd March was significant, recording for the first time a visit by Count Charles Kinsky, a personal friend of Randolph's through their shared passion for horse racing. Jennie had first met him in 1881, and would become very greatly attached to him in the future. For eleven days there are no entries in the diary as Jennie coped with the crisis in her husband's illness. He began to improve. Jennie was able to take one break from her bedside duties and recorded something of a turning point in her place in Society. After a party at the Salisburys on 15th March, she was taken on to a ball given by Randolph's eldest sister, Cornelia, Lady Wimborne. This kindly woman was working to heal the breach with the Prince of Wales, and the Prince and Princess were present at the ball without any major upset in protocol. They did not actually meet Jennie, and she recorded that the ball was "not wildly exciting", but it was the first small step towards a reconciliation.

Jennie took Randolph away to a hotel in the Crystal Palace area of London, then still quite rural in aspect and a much better environment for a convalescent. The children were able to visit there, in the company of their aunt Cornelia. Jennie attended closely to her husband, taking him for improving walks, and keeping near him as she got on with her painting and reading. Randolph improved a good deal by the end of March, which is more than can be said for their finances. Considerable extra expense was being incurred, the doctors who attended Randolph, one of whom was a Harley Street specialist, Oscar Clayton, FRCS, had to be paid. Leonard Jerome was in arrears with Jennie's allowance. They were obliged to send four of their best horses to Tattershalls for sale, but even then only two went, with the other two failing to make the reserve price. The £142 gained would not have made much of a dent in their spiralling debts.

The Marlborough family took good care of Winston and Jack. The gap in ages between the brothers meant it would be some years before Jack could really become a playmate. Winston had his cousins to play with in the wonderful grounds of Blenheim Palace. Jack, though still a toddler, was getting his first access to the toy soldiers. In one of the first letters from the child, Winston, to his 'dear Papa', dated 20th March, he hopes he is getting better, and makes reference to the many primroses he sees at Blenheim. He had evidently picked up on the idea that these were the late-lamented Lord Beaconsfield's favourite flower, and probably heard them described as such by the adults in the garden. After this charmingly precocious observation, he sends "Best love to you and dear Mamma".

Jennie was very tired during this ordeal. She sometimes recorded that she read all through the night as she kept a close eye on Randolph's health. Her painting sustained her all the while though oils and canvasses did not come cheap. Through a harsh winter, she finally curtailed the number of visitors and Randolph improved a good deal. They were able to return home, with the children, to St James' Place on 1st April. On the doctor's advice they immediately arranged for Jennie and Randolph to go for a long trip to America, where the cleaner air was expected to assist his recovery. It would also keep him away from the hurly-burly of politics, for the stream of visitors had resumed the moment he returned to London. They would be able to see Jennie's father, and have a serious talk with him about her allowance, as well as see Clara and Leonie, who were both visiting their father at that time.

Leaving the children at Blenheim, they travelled to Liverpool with one maid and one valet. They sailed for America on 21st April, and had the most awful crossing. The weather was very bad and they were both seasick. Jennie's diary recorded the consolations of paint-ing, playing the piano and reading. At last, on 2nd May, they docked in New York and the Jerome family were all there to greet them. Leonard and Randolph always got on well together, through their shared love of the races. Despite continuing bad weather, they enjoyed a lively time of visits to friends, to the theatre, the racetrack and eating out.

Historic events in Ireland brought the holiday to an abrupt end. In Phoenix Park, Dublin, Irish revolutionaries stabbed to death Lord Frederick Cavendish and Mr Burke, the Chief Secretary and Permanent Under-Secretary to the Lord-Lieutenant of Ireland respectively. Randolph saw that this would create a new crisis in that troubled country and insisted on returning to England immediately. On 17th May Jennie described "an enormous crowd" of family and friends seeing them off from New York. Head winds made it a rough passage but otherwise the weather was warm.

They were back in St James' Place on 27th May, and the dizzying round of visitors and dinner parties resumed at once. Randolph may have been eager to return to the political fray but his doctors certainly did not agree. They advised that his improvement was fragile, that he should avoid crowds and take further rest and fresh air. London in general was smoggy and unhealthy, and their house had a peculiar, ill-smelling miasma about it. Jennie began to look for a home in the country, other than suffer a further spell at the detested Blenheim with her mother-in-law.

She rented a 'cottage', Beech Lodge, in Wimbledon. One recent writer, basing his words on another misleading recollection of Winston's[5], has commiserated with the family and their 'hard times', that they were reduced to living in a cottage. One glimpse at a photograph of it would have shown it to be an airy, elegant mansion of a place, fully staffed with servants. Its spacious lawns and rose garden provided a fine setting for some rest and relaxation. They spent a very happy summer there with the boys. Being able to rent out their London house helped their finances somewhat. It was sufficiently removed from London to reduce the usual stream of visitors to Randolph's immediate family, the pals from the Fourth Party and some of Jennie's American friends. Jerome had provided some much needed funds, as Jennie was able to gleefully record one of her favourite pursuits on 7th June: "Shopped all the morning". This was a very pleasant summer. The fine weather allowed for lots of painting, and there were visits to Blenheim, where Winston was delighted to find the yeomanry cavalry encamped.

On 3rd July, Randolph finally returned to the House of Commons and immediately took up the reins as the scourge of the Liberal government. He led a fight against an attempt by the Liberals to legislate for a two-thirds majority being required to pass new laws. If a simple majority got one elected to Parliament, he argued, why should that not be enough to win a vote in the House? He so discomforted the Liberals that they had the unusual experience of seeing all the Irish Nationalists line up behind this firebrand Tory radical against them. He got even more radical when Britain waged war on Egypt in 1882. Randolph had actually backed the revolt of Egyptian officers against Ottoman rule, and saw the British interference there, to protect British financial interests, as a "wicked war, an unjust war, a bond-holders' war". Again it took a leading Tory to expose this illiberal government move.

The Fourth Party was developing a philosophy known as 'Tory Democracy'. They could see that the 'old gang' of Tory leaders were hopelessly out of touch with the mass of the population. Randolph and his friends wanted to devise a political programme that would directly represent the interests of the working people. They would address the issues that mattered to them – housing, education, health, national insurance, access to common land and open spaces, muse-ums, libraries, galleries. Many of these advanced ideas, well ahead of the Liberals in social awareness, would challenge the interests of powerful backers of the Conservative Party. The Fourth Party rel-ished these fights. Seeing the dead hand of the 'old gang' on the Central Committee, they backed a new organisation called the National Union of Conservative Associations (NUCA). When Randolph was put up for election to the committee it split fifty-fifty, and he was only successful with the casting vote of the Chairman. Randolph wrote to Wolff on 28th September that he intended to "declare war against the Central Committee and advocate the plac-ing of all power and finance in the hands of the Council of the National Union". Success at the national conference of the NUCA gave Randolph a platform from which to launch his bid for the high office that everyone felt was his due.

While her husband resumed his spectacular political career, Jennie set about finding a school for Winston. Like all boys of his age and class, the time for him to go to a preparatory boarding school was fast approaching. It has to be said that both parents agreed that this rather difficult, over-indulged, boy would probably benefit from the disciplined routine of a boarding school. Together they finally decided to send him to St George's, Ascot. Founded in 1877 by Mr Herbert William Sneyd-Kynnersley, this was an impressive, modern school, with small classes (ten boys to a tutor), electric light, a fine swimming pool, gymnasium and playing fields, with an intelligent programme of out-of-school visits. At £55 a term, it was expensive and fashionable.

Jennie accompanied Winston there on his first day, 3rd November 1882. They set off together in a carriage to the railway station. Winston always remembered that his mother gave him as pocket money three half crowns which he awkwardly dropped on the floor. After a private interview with the Headmaster, she left him in the care of the school. His parents could have had no idea what a hellish place they had delivered him to.

CHAPTER 4

A Sea of Troubles
1882–1885

At just a few weeks before his eighth birthday, Winston was nearly a year older than most of the boys starting at St. George's, and hence a year 'behind' in the expectations of his masters. This helps to explain the difficulty he experienced on his very first day, when a tutor took his innocent, indeed intelligent, questions about some wholly unfamiliar Latin grammar as a sign of impertinence. Instead of encouragement he was offered the threat of severe punishment. To a little boy raised by an army of loving women – mother, nurse, grand-mother, and aunts – this was a grim introduction to the world of the British public school.

His first letters home to both mother and father were however, a convincing declaration of his happiness at school. On 3rd December he wrote:

> My dear Papa
> I am very happy at school. You will be very pleased to hear I
> spent a very happy birthday. Mrs Kynersley [*sic*; the
> Headmaster's wife] gave me a little bracket. I am going to send
> a [school] Gazette wich [*sic*] I wish you to read.
> With love and kisses, I remain your loving son
> Winston.

> My dear Mamma
> I hope you are quite well. I am very happy at school.
> You will be very glad to hear I spent a very happy birthday. I
> must now thank you for your lovely present you sent me. Do
> not forget to come down on the 9th December.
> With love and kisses I remain your loving son
> Winston.[1]

Winston's letters to his parents always had dozens of kisses at the bottom, and his parents would naturally have assumed that he had settled in with boys of his own age. Punishment at school had probably not begun at this early stage.

While not all the correspondence has survived, it can be construed that there was a regular exchange of letters between parents and child, and there are references to visits to the school by Jennie but mostly by Mrs Everest. Of course, Winston was begging for a visit almost as soon as he had arrived and Jennie probably thought it best not to give in to these frequent requests or it would unsettle him. The perceived lack of visits became a source of complaint to Winston, and Jennie is often criticised as an uncaring mother. Sending sons to boarding school was the norm for the Victorian aristocracy, and Jennie was both the actively supportive wife of one of the most famous politicians of the day, and had just selflessly nursed her husband through a most serious illness.

We know Winston was very unhappy at this school, and that his parents did not understand this to be the case. What Winston did not know at the time was that, soon after he started school, his mother became so ill that she was close to death.

Randolph had been ordered by his doctors to take another holiday in the fresh air, and he was touring in Algeria. Jennie was enjoying furnishing their new London home, 2 Connaught Place, near Marble Arch. But on 17th December she pencilled a note to Randolph saying she was ill and in the care of Dr Laking[2]:

> Dearest R –
> I am sorry to say I am in bed with a slight feverish attack.
> Laking says I will be all right in a day or 2, if I remain perfectly quiet, so here I am an angel – taking my medicines and not stirring. ... By the time this reaches you I shall probably be as well as ever – Mind you enjoy yourself – Mama & Leonie are here & are nursing me.[3]

Randolph did not get this, or a subsequent letter, for several days or he would have been alarmed at its rather feeble handwriting. Jennie was much sicker than her doctors told her. It was the onset of typhoid fever, perhaps contracted at their thoroughly unhealthy previous house at St. James' Place. When skeletons started to come up through the cellar floor, the Churchills found out that the house had been built on top of the graveyard of Tyburn Prison. Mrs Jerome feared for her daughter and brought in the eminent doctor, Sir William Gull, Physician in Ordinary to Queen Victoria. He ordered complete bed rest and the full time services of a trained nurse, and together they got Jennie through the crisis.

Randolph sent a telegram expressing his great alarm at the news of Jennie's illness, and there followed an exchange of letters and cables between two people clearly still very much in love. Some confusion about exactly where Randolph was, or was going to be, added to the drama. Their handwriting was execrable and frequently the names of places just could not be made out! Jennie wrote on 29th December, "Dearest R. Your telegram distressed me so... . You poor darling I did feel for you so last night ... . I know how you worry – How naughty of you!" Randolph had started for home, and was in the south of France on New Year's Day 1883 when he heard the worst was over. He wrote:

> My darling, I have been in such a state of mind about you ever since last Thursday ... . I got perfectly wild with anxiety and alarm ... . I could not bear the idea of your being ill without my being with you to look after you; particularly when I remembered how you use to look after me when I was ill... . What a bad illness you must have had. I am afraid you are not out of bed yet and you must be awfully weak. I am sure for my sake you will take the greatest care of yourself and not do anything imprudent. Why dearest if anything happened to you my life would be broken."[4]

He had received news of Jennie's family, and of Winston, who had been ill and at home during the school holidays. "Please thank dear Leonie for her letters to me. It has been such a comfort to me to know that your Mother and Leonie were with you. I am sorry little Winston has not been well, but I don't make out what is the matter with him. It seems we are a sickly family and cannot get rid of the doctors."

And so it went on, with Jennie saying she was wretched at causing him any worry: "Your letter made me cry – you must never worry about me again", and Randolph replying, "I am afraid you have been very ill indeed, poor little darling, and I should have been sent for. It would have done me good to look after you." As Jennie got a little stronger, their mood improved. Randolph sent her a little oyster knife for her birthday, her twenty-ninth. ("I shall not acknowledge it to the world, 26 is quite enough".) She was to join him in the south of France to complete their convalescence together. Financial problems abounded but it never seems to have occurred to either of them to modify their lifestyle in any way. Jennie reported on paying a wine bill of £246, and of having to find £500, and all that before any of the bills relating to the new house had been presented. Randolph had also spent £150 on his latest trip, more than he intended.

Jennie had a slight relapse and Dr Laking insisted she was not strong enough to travel. At the same time, though the weather was quite bad on the Riviera, Randolph's doctors told him the bracing air was doing him good and would not let him return home. She was able to pass on important political gossip to her husband, that the editor of The Times had told John Gorst that Randolph was the only man who could lead the Conservative Party, and how other senior Conservatives were "praising him up". Randolph obviously trusted Jennie's political acumen, as he advised her to have a "parting interview with Wolff … to hear what he says".

Winston had only been a little over a month at school before he came home for the Christmas holidays. Jennie was incensed to receive an invoice for a full three-month term with only £3 deducted, together with an advance billing for the first term of 1883. She wrote of this to Randolph, and made some alarming observations on Winston's behaviour.

> I send you the enclosed which is all Kynnersley has sent me as
> regards Winston. He also sends the bill £55 for next term – to
> be paid in advance – I must own I think it is rather a strong
> order to have to pay £52 for one month – As to Winston's
> improvement I am sorry to say I see none – Perhaps there has
> not been time enough – He can read very well, but that is all.
> … the first two days he came home he was terribly slangy and

loud. Altogether I am disappointed. But Everest was told that next term they meant to be stricter with him. He teases the baby [Jack] more than ever – when I get well I shall take him in hand. It appears he is afraid of me.

Winston's first report was not edifying. He was bottom in his class of eleven boys but they had had almost a year's start ahead of him. His mathematics was 'very elementary'; his French grammar 'very slight'; writing 'good but so slow – spelling weak'. The Headmaster concluded that in General Conduct he was very truthful but a regular 'pickle' in many ways at present. "Has not fallen into school ways yet – but this could hardly be expected". Arriving as it did in the midst of the ill health of both parents, this report was not treated as too alarming after such a brief start at the new school. Randolph was more concerned about the flare up of Winston's chest trouble that winter. On 5th January he wrote to Jennie, "… I am so glad to hear that Winnie is right again. Give him a kiss from me. Goodbye my darling, I think always of you". Jennie had sent Winston with Everest for two weeks to Brighton for his health before returning to school. Randolph wrote on the 16th, "Goodbye my darling, love to the children. I suppose Winston will go back to school in a few days. Give him a little money from me before he goes".

Jennie would not have been allowed to see Winston or Jack while she was so very ill with such a contagious disease. Nor would she have been welcome at St George's School in case she caused an epidemic. She had never been informed of how serious was her condition until she was over the worst. In more normal times she might have pondered why such an indulged child as Winston had become 'afraid' of his mother. He had good cause to be wary of adult authority figures. In *My Early Life* he tells of the bestial regime of floggings indulged in by Sneyd-Kynnersley. It was as bad as any in the whole British public school system and, as Winston himself observed, far worse than anything that would be allowed in a Reformatory institution run by the Home Office. The evidence provided by other boys who attended this 'model' prep school, notably the artist, Roger Fry, confirm it as a place of terror for these boys so far from home and family. Fry, as Head Boy, had to assist in the punishment:

... the culprit was told to take down his trousers and kneel before the block over which I and the other boy held him down. The switching was given by the master's full strength and it took only two or three strokes for drops of blood to form everywhere and it continued for 15 or 20 strokes when the wretched boy's bottom was a mass of blood.[5]

Today we would certainly question the sexual predilection of a man like Sneyd-Kynnersley but in Victorian England he and his ilk had a free hand with generations of upper-class youths. Winston described this awful routine, and how he hated the school and what a "life of anxiety" he led there for nearly two years, as something of a detached observer, suggesting that this happened to other boys. His letters home remained deceptively cheerful. That he uttered not one word of his troubles to either parents or Mrs Everest remains a mystery. Was it pride or embarrassment? Was it fear induced by the power figure that was Sneyd-Kinnersley? Did he think he 'deserved' punishment for being naughty, and that this was the 'normal' regime at school? Whatever teemed through that young and impressionable mind, his character was damaged by the experience. It is a blessing that Jack did not have to endure the same fate, and he developed in a quite different way as a result.

When Randolph returned invigorated from France, he was much in demand at meetings all around the country and spent a great deal of time mastering his speeches for these occasions. He would write and re-write the text, brooking no interruption while he was doing it, and then memorise the whole thing so that his delivery was all the more remarkable.

Then in March 1883 a full reconciliation with the Prince of Wales was brought about, by the tireless efforts of Randolph's friend, Sir Henry James. A dinner was arranged at 2 Connaught Place, where Jennie's famous French cook promised to provide a memorable banquet. At fairly short notice a small but select party was got together. That William Gladstone and his wife should be guests at this famous Conservative's home tells us much of the regard in which Randolph was held. The Prince and Princess of Wales arrived, perfectly on time, itself a mark of respect, and at once Princess Alexandra drew Jennie up from her deep curtsey to

embrace her and say, "We haven't played Bach for a long time!"
Winston and Jack were brought down to meet the Royals and
Edward gave them each a small gift. The dinner was a huge success.
On being offered a choice of two soups, the Prince promptly helped
himself to both. Gladstone got the conversation going and held
them all captivated throughout the meal. At the end the Prince
expressed his delight, not least because "You are not an American
food faddist, Lady Randolph". Jennie's recent brush with death
may have softened his heart towards her family and contributed to
this most welcome 'return to the fold'. The Randolph Churchill's
were immediately restored to the highest rank in society. They were
back on everybody's invitation list. Restaurants and London clubs
would compete for their patronage. The Prince also began to
bestow expensive gifts of jewellery on Jennie and she was soon a
guest at his famous country house parties at Sandringham, not
always in the company of her husband.

We know perfectly well that the Prince invited beautiful women to
his country house parties with the express purpose of seducing them
into his bed. If the Victorian era is popularly known as an age of
strict mores and prurience, this seems to have been the prerogative of
the middle-class and not of the power elite of the day. We can safely
assume that Jennie somewhat discreetly joined the long list of the
Prince's 'conquests' at about this time. We can, of course, only spec-
ulate on such intimate matters but it could well be that the dire state
of Randolph's health, his frequent and lengthy absences, and the
intense pressure of his political work had led to a breakdown in the
formerly happy physical relations between husband and wife. The
exuberant, vital Jennie, for so long the centre of attention for a large
number of handsome men of her social class, would increasingly be
driven to seek comfort elsewhere.

Randolph caused a sensation in the House of Commons, inflicting
defeat upon the Liberal government with its 'unassailable' absolute
majority. Again it was the Bradlaugh case that added to Randolph's
fame. Gladstone made the seemingly rational suggestion that atheists
should be able to refuse to swear an oath but 'affirm' their loyalty, as
could Quakers. Randolph gave one of his most devastating and popular speeches as he denounced a Bill that was not for the benefit of
the nation, but for the benefit of one man. The bill was narrowly

defeated. On the crest of a wave of popular support, Randolph's great prospects were yet again dashed by personal tragedy.

On 4th July 1883, they had dined with the Duke and Duchess of Marlborough at Blenheim Palace. The Duke had recently been very active in the House of Lords, making one of his finest speeches ever. He was in fine fettle at dinner. Jennie recalled how they received terrible news: "At eight o'clock next morning we heard a knock at our bedroom door, and a footman stammer out: "His Grace is dead!"[6] At the age of 61, the Duke had died in his sleep of a heart attack. Randolph had loved his father deeply. He never failed to greet him without an arm around his shoulder and a kiss on the cheek. He was a favourite son to both his parents. To lose his father in such a shocking and abrupt way led to another collapse in his fragile health. His doctors recommended that he go to Germany and take the healing waters and bracing mountain air at Gastein. He, Jennie and Winston, who was home from school, went there for a holiday, leaving Jack in the care of Mrs Everest at Blenheim Palace.

Jennie later recalled "we led the 'simple life' with a vengeance". On their mountain treks they more than once met the German Chancellor, Otto von Bismarck. Blandford, now 8th Duke of Marlborough, came out to join them. The 7th Duke had left all his money to his wife (for her lifetime, then it would pass to Randolph), and this left Blandford desperately short of the wherewithal to maintain Blenheim. He had finally divorced Albertha and, despite having sired a son on his mistress, began to look about for a rich wife.

Jennie returned home with Winston, leaving Randolph and Blandford to return at a very leisurely pace via Switzerland and France. She and the boys spent the summer at Blenheim, a more congenial destination now that the Dowager Duchess was no longer the chatelaine there. Winston could run riot with his favourite cousin, Blandford's son and heir, Charles Richard, always known as 'Sunny', after one of his father's titles as Duke of Sunderland. Jack, now nearly four, was able to join in some of their wild games. They stayed at Blenheim when Jennie returned to London alone, to pursue interests of her own.

Having groomed Jennie for his own sexual pleasure, the Prince of Wales now introduced her to the notorious 'Marlborough House set'. This was named after his London residence, having nothing to

do with the Marlborough family. The Prince was an opportunisti-
cally keen believer in 'free love' for his aristocratic friends. He
presided over a set where the changing of sexual partners was the
norm, and to which he gave an air of spurious respectability by suggesting that this would strengthen the marriages of the players. At
this house, and many other country houses, the maids ensured that
the bedrooms of adulterous couples were next to each other. This
was sex for its own sake. It was not meant to lead to marital splits or
divorce, quite the reverse. Neither was it meant to lead to long term
relationships and, in this respect, Jennie broke the rules. She began a
strong physical relationship with Charles, Count Kinsky, a military
attaché at the Austrian embassy, and a great horseracing friend of
Randolph. An intimate of the Prince, he was a popular hero at the
time, having just won the Grand National, riding *Zoedone*. Jennie
loved him for many years, without ever doubting her love for her
husband. Both men offered her something she needed. Jennie knew
how to be discreet in these matters and there is no reason to suppose
that Randolph knew of her adultery with Kinsky, or anyone else,
until very much later.

Winston's latest school report was every bit as bad as the first. Still
last in a class of nine, the number of times he was late for class had
soared from four to nineteen. While very good at history, his spelling
was "about as bad as it could be", in maths he "could do better than
he does", but most ominously he "does not quite understand the
meaning of hard work – must make up his mind to do so next term".
We can assume he was receiving regular beatings at school for his
transgressions, but he still uttered not a word to his parents, or to his
supposed confidante, Mrs Everest.

Sir Henry Wolff was begging Randolph to return to the fray in
Parliament, but he replied, "I am not up to it physically or mentally
... it is very melancholy here – sad recollections at every moment".
The "kind and hospitable" Blandford helped his brother by getting
him interested in running the pack of harriers based at Blenheim, and
in planning a railway extension from Oxford to Woodstock. The
family spent the rest of 1883 at Blenheim Palace, where Randolph
was a great comfort to his mother.

The only political activity he allowed himself was to play a part in
the launching of the Primrose League. On 19th April 1883, the

anniversary of Disraeli's death, Sir Stafford Northcote had unveiled a statue of him at the House of Commons, and all the Conservatives there had worn as a buttonhole Disraeli's favourite flower, the primrose. Wolff had said to Randolph, "What a show of primroses! This should be turned to account. Why not start a 'Primrose League'?" The Fourth Party had been toying with the idea of a mass membership organisation to extend the principles of 'Tory Democracy'. For that very reason, when the League was officially launched on 17th November, the grandees of the Conservative Party viewed it with disdain. But, in a stroke of genius, the founders of the organisation opened its ranks to women members, long before they would win the right to vote. Jennie and the Dowager Duchess were founder members, as was Lady Salisbury, wife of the otherwise dismissive leader of the party. While only 957 people joined in 1884, the number grew to 11,366 in 1885, and then, inspired by the Irish Home Rule struggle, rocketed to 237,283 in 1886, and 565,861 in 1887. It peaked at over 1.7 million in 1906. Jennie played a leading role in the League, and it would become the power base for Randolph's great struggle with the old leadership of the Conservative Party.

The final school report for 1883 showed some improvement, with Winston coming in eighth out of eleven in his class. Still good in history, and improving in mathematics, all other subjects were 'fair', 'variable', 'weak' or 'elementary'. In 'Diligence' he began the term well, "but latterly has been very naughty", and his General Conduct had improved, "though at times he is still troublesome". His letters home were always cheerful, stressing how well he sometimes did in gymnastics. His letter to his father on 9th December ended affectionately with one big kiss (X), followed by lots of little kisses. At about the same time he wrote to his mother, who had obviously spoken to him sternly about his behaviour: "I will try to be a good boy". In this he reported he had received a nice letter from Jack, not yet four years old, "but I think Everest held his hand".

By that Christmas the army of toy soldiers had swelled to over fifteen hundred. By February 1884, he could report to his parents that he was "very happy indeed" and had the chance of a school prize if he worked hard. As a reward for this effort, his father sent him a fine copy of *Treasure Island*, which he read many times with great pleasure. Even this seems to have annoyed some of his tutors, who resented his obvious talent for reading not being displayed on the texts they set for him. It was a letter of 24th February 1884 that should have alarmed his parents more than it did. In the space of a few lines, written in unusually bad, cramped, handwriting, he asks three times if someone could come and see him soon. Against his signature he drew a face with sad, downcast eyes. This plea was ignored by his busy parents, who probably thought the boy was overindulged already. The report for the first term of 1884 showed considerable improvement, with a placing of fifth out of ten. The concluding remarks were, "He is, I hope, beginning to realise that school means work and discipline. He is rather greedy at meals".

Randolph and Jennie were completely distracted by the prospect of a General Election. A re-drawing of boundaries was to see Randolph's constituency of Woodstock disappear. Randolph declared himself as a candidate for the large Central Division of Birmingham, held by the popular Liberal, John Bright. While beginning to court the new constituency, Randolph also saw the triumph of his platform at the National conference of the NUCA. In the election for the National Council he came top with 346 votes, and 22 of his 30 nominees were elected. The post of Chairman was his for the taking, but he declined in favour of one of his supporters. Instead, seeing the inherent danger of a Conservative Party at war with itself, he began to make friendly overtures to Lord Salisbury. An unfortunate procedural error by one of Randolph's supporters caused Salisbury to break off talks, and Randolph offered to resign. The representatives of 300,000 Tory voters held a meeting to persuade him to stay, and also lobbied Salisbury to make their support for Randolph known. Once again *The Times* came out firmly in support of this popular hero in the Party.

During this period of intense political activity by his father, Winston improved in his lessons but his school behaviour worsened drastically. "Conduct has been exceedingly bad. He is not to be trusted to do any one thing"; "General Conduct very bad – is a constant trouble to every body and is always in some scrape or other"; number of times late, 20 – "very disgraceful". In the spring and summer of 1884 he worked more successfully, coming third in his class of nine, with his conduct being "better, but still troublesome".

Another bout of illness saw Winston sent home from school to recuperate. He would never return to that awful place. Maurice Baring, who attended just after Winston left, later recorded:

> Dreadful legends were told about Winston Churchill, who had been taken away from the school. His naughtiness appeared to have surpassed anything. He had been flogged for taking sugar from the pantry, and so far from being penitent, he had taken the Headmaster's sacred straw hat from where it hung over the door and kicked it to pieces. His sojourn at this school had been one long feud with authority. The boys did not seem to sympathise with him. Their point of view was conventional and priggish.[7]

We can see that stubbornness of spirit, that pugnacity that would serve his country well in the hour of her greatest peril during World War II. But it also developed a combative streak in his personality that would find an outlet in bullying. Feuding with authority was something he instinctively shared with his father.

From the time they had lived in Ireland Winston had suffered from a weak chest and was prone to severe bouts of asthma. The family doctor, Robson Roose, was the physician at St Andrew's home for boys in Brighton, and had considerable experience in treating children. He had his own way of dealing with high temperatures, involving the use of 'stimulants, by the mouth and rectum'. It was in the course of this treatment that he first discovered the terrible signs of the repeated beatings Winston had been enduring in silence. Peregrine said the wounds had festered. Clearly Winston had not told his great confidante, Mrs Everest or she would have brought it to the attention of his mother. The Nanny would have had no part in the undressing and putting to bed of a nine-year-old boy. It took the doctor's treatment to reveal to his horrified parents just how badly their son had been treated for some time. They immediately removed him from Sneyd-Kynnersley's clutches. No child of the Churchill or related 'Jerome' families would ever be sent there again. The treatment meted out to Winston at school had obviously been much talked of in the family for years after. Peregrine related a story that one day when Winston was already an experienced swordsman at Harrow, he decided to settle the score with Kynnersley. He set out to

Ascot, unaware that the Headmaster had died of a heart attack the year after he had left.

By happy coincidence, Dr Roose's own son, Bertie, went to a very well run school in Brighton, and he strongly recommended it. The healthy climate and moderate regime would be a double benefit to the boy. The Brighton school, actually in Hove, was run by two spinster sisters, Kate and Charlotte Thomson. Systematic flogging was not permitted there and Winston recalled that he was allowed to learn things that interested him – French, history, poetry, riding and swimming. His enthusiasm for stamp collecting was ignited there. By this enlightened method, employing kindness and sympathy, the Miss Thomsons aroused his interest in the Classics, so vital for entry into the great public schools. By another co-incidence, it was near to Roose's practice so if Winston was taken ill the doctor could be called in immediately. With Bertie Roose as a friend to help him settle in, Winston's marks improved immediately, and his letters home were more frank and open. Jennie had obviously asked him not to hide things from her and he solemnly wrote that he was telling her everything that was happening in his life. He would ask if Mrs Everest could come and visit him, with Jack. He sent his love to his brother and said he could have some of Winston's artillery from the model armies at home to play with. Jack, free from Winston's 'influence', was thriving as a child, with none of the boisterous behaviour of his older sibling.

Jennie had gone to America with her sister, Clara, to attend the wedding of her youngest sister, Leonie. The Jerome girls seemed fated to make stormy engagements, for the parents of the Guards officer John Leslie, her intended husband, had objected violently to the marriage. Despite threats of disinheritance, Leonard Jerome firmly backed young 'Jack' Leslie in his ardent desire to marry Leonie. Once again he put over the best wedding money could buy in New York. When the young couple returned to England his parents would not receive them and they had to live with Jennie and Randolph at Connaught Place for a while. The £20 a month they contributed to the upkeep of the house was a boon to Jennie's precarious finances. The Leslies soon relented and invited Leonie and Jack to Castle Leslie, Glaslough, County Monaghan, for Christmas. The gracious and musically talented Leonie made a good impression and won over her in-laws to the match. The Leslies would always remain short of money and, when their children came along, Mrs Everest would take from the attic the toys Winston and Jack had outgrown and pack them in a sack for Leonie for her children. It explains why so few of the children's toys have survived.

Randolph had fallen out with some of his Fourth Party colleagues over issues relating to an extension of the franchise, and the Tory grandees saw this as an opportunity to approach Randolph and bring him back into the fold. He received heavy hints that he would be the next Secretary of State for India, his first government post and an important one at that. Feeling the need for a rest from the strain of political campaigning, and taking India as seriously as he did Ireland, he decided to take a long vacation and study visit to the sub-continent. He wrote charming letters to John Gorst and Joseph Chamberlain of the 'let byegones be byegones' variety, and sailed for India on 3rd December 1884.

Jennie and the two boys saw him off. The next news about Winston would be all too familiar to his parents. Miss Charlotte Thomson wrote on 17th December that, during a drawing examination, some dispute arose between Winston and the boy next to him over a knife needed for their work. It ended with Winston receiving a stab wound to the chest! Assuring Lady Randolph that her son was well, Miss Thomson asked how to proceed with the other boy. He, apparently, was something of a hothead and had been sent home, but if he were formally expelled he would lose his place at a Royal Navy training ship. She sought, and received, Lady Randolph's blessing to let the matter drop, hoping that these boys would learn to "govern their passionate impulses" when they saw the consequences.

Dr Roose attended to the chest wound, which was about a quarter-inch deep, and brought him safely home to his mother. She had already written to Randolph giving him the news of the incident and, before speaking to Winston, had said "I have no doubt Winston teased the boy dreadfully". At the conclusion of the letter, written after Roose and Winston had returned, she was able to add, "as I thought he began by pulling the other boy's ear – I hope it will be a lesson to him".[8] Clearly the violence inflicted on him at St George's had left its mark on Winston's behaviour.

Randolph's response was of the 'boys will be boys' kind. "What adventures Winston does have; it is a great mercy he was no worse injured", and later, "… tell little Winny how glad I was to get his letter which I thought was very well written. I suppose he is back at Brighton now. I hope there will be no more stabbing … ." There is no sign here, yet, of a father who has lost all patience with his son. Winston wrote the most loving letters to his father, always giving news of Jack.

Randolph might have gone to India with a holiday in mind but he embarked on a punishing tour of inspections. He sent back long and interesting reports on the Indian military to Sir Frederick Roberts, one of Britain's greatest soldiers, with whom he had become acquainted before he left. He also spoke passionately about the need to bring Indians forward to take up the reins of government. He did nothing by halves and was soon as formidable an expert on Indian affairs as he undoubtedly was on Ireland.

Jennie might have been 'seeing' Count Kinsky regularly, but she loved her husband and kept up a constant correspondence with him, giving him all the news of her visits to the theatre and various parties (where Liberal ministers would chaffingly hope that Randolph was not coming back too soon), of how happy the boys were together, of what a worry Winston was. But she insisted that she was lonely without him, and that she and Leonie spent many quiet evenings together. Just before Randolph was due to come home she wrote, "Remember you promised me never to go on another such journey without taking me – Life is too short for such long separations don't you think so? … . Shall you be glad to see me?"[9]

Randolph returned from India in March 1885, and was met by Jennie and Jack. He was greeted with acclaim by the Conservative Party and kept busy with meetings all around the country. Both Winston and Jack were now fully aware of just how famous their father was. Winston told his father he would be very proud if he would write to him, and also began importuning Lord Randolph for copies of his autograph, whole pages of them. He said it was to give to his school friends and some admiring teachers. Peregrine said he was also selling them to augment his pocket money! There are certainly letters from Lord Randolph to his sons in the archives where the boys have cut out the signature for purposes of their own.

Winston flourished under the benign influence of the Misses

Thomson. His position in class improved steadily, actually coming First in Classics, and, though his health remained a little delicate, he became an accomplished rider and finally learned to swim. Unfortunately, he still managed to come last in general good conduct. His many letters invariably contained some requests for more cash, something he was always short of, for hampers, or proper riding apparel. His parents seem to have indulged him a good deal. We also notice that he no longer refers to 'Woom' or 'Woomany', but now asked after 'Everest', as any young gentleman would after a respected servant.

The absolute majority enjoyed by the Liberal government was not to survive a series of batterings in the House of Commons, often co-ordinated by Randolph. He fiercely opposed the Coercive Crimes Act that applied to Ireland and let it be known that no Conservative government would renew it. This began to detach the Irish Nationalists from their automatic support of the Liberals. Randolph had entertained Charles Stewart Parnell as a friend in his London home. Stories that he had entered a pact to grant home rule to Ireland are quite without foundation, but he certainly promised enough reform in Ireland to see the Irish Nationalists abandon Gladstone in the House. This came over an innocuous-seeming amendment to a Budget speech, and the Government slumped to a defeat by 12 votes. By the standards of the day, Gladstone had to offer his resignation to Queen Victoria, which she accepted. She invited Lord Salisbury to form a minority administration until a General Election could be called.

Salisbury asked Randolph to become Secretary of State for India, and he refused while Northcote, an enemy to progress within the party, was to be Chancellor of the Exchequer and Leader of the House of Commons. Randolph confided to a friend just how weary he was of the struggle:

> In the last five years I have lived twenty. I have fought Society.
> I have fought Mr Gladstone at the head of a great majority. I
> have fought the Front Opposition Bench. Now I am fighting
> Lord Salisbury. I have said I will not join the government
> unless Northcote leaves the House of Commons. Lord
> Salisbury will never give way. I am done.[10]

So great was Randolph's popularity in the party and the country, that Salisbury conceded to him. He elevated Northcote to the House of Lords, and made places for Wolff and Gorst at Randolph's insistence. Disraeli's prediction about Randolph's future had been vindicated to the letter. He now entered the government on a salary of £5,000 per annum, a very considerable sum in its day, and the first real money accruing to the family that was not the subject of some ruinously expensive loan. Jennie would have been thrilled at this advancement; his sons were simply bursting with pride for him.

Politics had become his *raison d'être*. He was driven by a need to achieve important things in his life, perhaps aware of the short life span prevalent among the males in his family. At the expense of his health and personal relationships, he drove himself hard, 'sustained' by insomnia, strong coffee and tobacco.

CHAPTER 5

A Shooting Star Burns Out
1885–1886

In another convention with which we are unfamiliar today, new
Ministers of the Crown had to resign their parliamentary seats and
fight them in a bye-election. Randolph had so completely immersed
himself in the work of the India Office that he wrote an address to his
Woodstock constituency explaining that he would not be able to
campaign amongst them. Instead Jennie became the leading light of
his re-election effort, together with his sister, Georgiana Howe, and
leading Conservatives such as Wolff, Curzon, Milner and St John
Brodrick. Jennie revelled in the bustle of electioneering, and she was
very good at it. She and Georgiana covered the whole constituency in
a horse-drawn carriage decked out in Randolph's racing colours of
pink and brown. A local rhymester made a popular jingle about the
election that referred to the prowess of "that Yankee lady". Another
of Randolph's senior Liberal friends, Sir Henry James, teased her that
"arch looks", speeches "from my heart" and "the graceful wave of a
pocket handkerchief" would all have to be looked at in light of the
Corrupt Practices Act of 1883! Winston was enormously proud of
his father, and even the five-year old Jack was excited by all the activity. Randolph wrote to Jennie: "If I win, you will have all the glory".
And glory there was when, on 3rd July 1885, the declaration gave
Randolph 532 votes to the Radical's 405, double the majority of the
1880 election. Jennie herself gave a victory speech at the Bear Hotel,
Woodstock, and the Prince of Wales sent his congratulations, sin-
gling out Jennie's speeches as of special significance.

Randolph worked very hard to cope with the tremendous amount
of paperwork generated by his new department of state. He worked
long hours to master each subject before taking matters to council
meetings. He was an enthusiastic supporter of railway construction
in the sub-continent, and also had to wrestle with the defence issues
raised by Russian expansion in Central Asia up to the borders of

Afghanistan. He was able to appoint his new friend Sir Frederick Roberts as Commander-in-Chief India. In November 1885, he authorised a British invasion of Burma, where King Theebaw operated a most hostile regime against British interests and subjects. When Theebaw was dethroned and his people rejected a protectorate, Burma was annexed to the British Empire forthwith.

He also demonstrated his independence of spirit, and radical indisposition towards the over-privileged, by denying a senior army command to the Duke of Connaught. The Queen had made it known that she would like Arthur, her third, and favourite, son to be made Commander-in-Chief of the Bombay District, a splendid command in the Indian Army. Lord Salisbury expressed his approval, and wrote over the head of the relevant minister (Randolph) to the Viceroy, Lord Dufferin, for his opinion. Randolph pointed out that a Secretary of State could not be expected to perform his duties if others bypassed him and ignored his advice. He had already advised against an appointment that smacked of nepotism and he promptly offered his resignation if his advice was to be so ignored. Salisbury could not afford the sort of political scandal this would have caused, and was obliged to tell the Queen that her son would not be offered the post. Randolph could not have known that, in the future, this incident would earn him the enmity of Jennie's sister, Leonie, who would take her revenge in the telling of many stories to the great detriment of his character and reputation.

These were the busiest days of Randolph's political life, and the amount of work he got through astonished all who knew him. He was, as ever, deeply embroiled in all aspects of Irish reform. He strove to keep the Irish Nationalists 'on side' with his government through some difficult times with the Orange Loyalists, who saw every concession to the Irish as some sort of betrayal. He was always in demand for giving speeches to Conservative organisations around the country, and, in September 1885, Lord Salisbury wrote to advise him on the enormous strain he was under. He took a long holiday, fishing in Scotland, where he was able to entertain Roberts, and learn more of India's military problems, before the General left to take up command there. Randolph had little time during these politically turbulent years for visiting Winston at school. He was a member of the Orleans Club in Brighton, where he would meet up with his political friends for discussions. Sometimes he had time to call into the school to visit Winston. However, the boys looked upon their father as a great politician, and Jennie saw him as the future Prime Minister, and expected to be the first American lady into No. 10 Downing Street. Sacrifices had to be made.

Meanwhile Jennie was very active in charitable work, focussing especially on Lady Dufferin's Medical Fund for Women, which in turn supported the work of the National Association for Supplying Medical Aid to the Women of India. Randolph wrote to her from Scotland, praising her work, and putting her in touch with the editor of *The Times*: "I should advise you to get hold of Mr Buckle and fascinate him, and get him to write you up". In December, Queen Victoria honoured Jennie's work by personally bestowing on her the insignia of the Order of the Crown of India. After kissing the Queen's hand, Jennie stood in a fine black velvet dress, so heavily embroidered with jet that the Queen struggled with the medal and drove the pin into Jennie's chest! Jennie cherished the pearl and turquoise cipher on its white-bordered, pale blue ribbon, and it features in many photographs of her in evening dress.[1]

In the summer of 1885, Jennie had determined that Winston must do better at school, and she told him that she had engaged a governess for the holidays, who would give him some lessons every day as he was being groomed for one of the public schools like Eton or Harrow. His reply can only be described as insolent. He declared that he had never had to work through the holidays before, that it was "against his principles", and that even one hour a day would hang like a dark cloud over him and quite spoil everything. His protests were in vain and, even when they went away to the Isle of Wight, the governess was there to continue his tuition. Watching the Regatta, and driving himself about in a little donkey cart were, apparently, no compensation for the relentless strictures of the 'unkind' governess, "so strict and stiff". He actually looked forward to returning to school in September. He was now lionised at school as the son of such a famous politician, something he had never enjoyed at St George's.

The General Election was finally called for November 1885. Randolph now campaigned for the Central Birmingham seat, against the formidable John Bright. But he also spoke all round the country for the Conservative cause. When he paid a fleeting visit to Brighton, and failed to call in to the school, Winston sent a wounded letter to him, supposing Randolph was too busy to see his son, announcing that his stamp collection stood at 708, and that he badly needed a new album. His 'mild request' for seventeen shillings and sixpence was in the nature of a fine on an errant parent, and one that was willingly accepted by an affectionate father.

Randolph narrowly failed to win Central Birmingham, despite help from Jennie and his mother. But in the unfamiliar (to us) way that elections were run in those days, Randolph was able to travel to London next day and accept the nomination for Paddington South, where a Tory candidate stood down in his favour. He was promptly elected with two-thirds of the vote. Because the Liberals could no longer automatically rely on the Irish Nationalists (who had secured 85 seats), they declined to form a new government, though they had won the election. Salisbury continued to head a minority government. It was soon defeated in the House of Commons and Gladstone would form a new Liberal administration by the end of January 1886. The Irish Home Rule question moved to the front of the political agenda. Randolph joked that he would lead the Opposition for five years, serve as Prime Minister for five years, and then die. In one respect only, he proved correct. The loss of his ministerial salary so quickly was no joking matter. Winston was now of an age, and his reading ability was so good, that he could follow his father's political activities in the newspapers.

Jack was now six years old, and we can deduce from a letter to him from Winston (10th February 1886), that he was doing well at his lessons at home. The letter had several lines in French, congratulating Jack on the improvement in his writing, and giving news of the recent riot by unemployed workers in Trafalgar Square, illustrated with a suitable drawing. Winston admired Jack's drawings of cannon firing, and advised him to work hard at home, to avoid having to go to school for as long as possible. Winston was obviously maturing at Brighton, and showing a commendable interest in Jack's development. He clearly wanted to spare him the 'ordeal' of going to school. He even promised to teach his younger brother the rudiments of Latin on his next stay at home. Mrs Everest regularly brought Jack down to Brighton for short breaks, and the boys loved each other's company.

Randolph's love of the Irish people, and his passionate fight for reform in Ireland's affairs to make her a fully functioning and prosperous part of the British Empire, was entirely subordinated to his desire to keep Ireland within the United Kingdom. As soon as Gladstone brought forward a Home Rule Bill, Randolph rushed over to Belfast to address the Protestants of Ulster as they organised against the proposals. At a huge public meeting in Belfast in February 1886, he appealed to the loyal Catholics of Ireland to stand with the Protestants for the union with Britain. The speech was a call to prepare to resist the imposition of Home Rule and was inflammatory. Despite Salisbury congratulating him on a speech "to which no Roman Catholic could object", communal violence broke out in the north of Ireland and innocent men and women were killed and injured. In a subsequent letter Randolph coined the slogan, "Ulster will fight, and Ulster will be right", and a great deal of blood was shed because of it. He and his political associates never accepted any responsibility for the violence. He continued to devise Irish legislation specifically designed to entice the support of Irish Catholics, and to undermine the Irish Nationalist Party.

At Brighton School, Winston contracted pneumonia, and was in peril of his life. The remarkable Dr Roose, with a dedication that sprang from his admiration for Randolph's politics, cancelled all his London appointments, and moved into a room next to the sick child, to monitor his condition and nurse him through the crisis. Randolph and Jennie rushed down to Brighton but initially were not allowed near their son, and stayed nearby in the Bedford Hotel, communicating by frantic notes with the doctor. Between the 12th and 17th March, Winston's temperature edged up and up, peaking at 103.5 degrees, before he pulled back from the near-fatal crisis. Randolph's increased consumption of strong cigarettes and coffee at the Orleans Club, as he waited hourly for news of his son, can have done nothing for his own delicate health. As Winston gradually recovered, a flood of relieved congratulations ensued from all the great names in British society. The Prince of Wales was reported to have halted a line of audience in order to ascertain how 'Winny' was progressing. To cope with this new assault on Randolph's nervous disposition, Roose recommended the taking of digitalis in small doses as a sedative. We now know that he took excessive amounts of the medicine, doing further damage to his heart.

Throughout this personal anxiety, the political situation continually called upon Randolph's time. When the Home Rule Bill was published in March it led to the historic split in the Liberal Party, when Joseph Chamberlain led the 'Liberal Unionists' in a defection that would eventually see them join the 'Conservative and Unionist Party'. Because of the party split, Gladstone lost the vote on Home Rule by 341 to 311. In that extraordinary year, 1886, another government fell, and another election was called.

At Easter Jennie went on holiday to visit Leonie in Ireland, while Randolph went to Paris for a few days to the races and the theatre. Amongst the friends staying with him was none other than Charles Kinsky, who continued a warm friendship with an unknowing Randolph throughout his 'special relationship' with Jennie.

Back in England for the election, the ever-popular Randolph made as many speeches in Birmingham and Manchester as he did in his South Paddington constituency, and before the ballot he took himself off on a fishing holiday to Norway, knowing that Jennie would fight the campaign for him and keep him abreast of all the news. He wrote to her on 19th July: "This is doing me a lot of good. I felt very seedy leaving London, and it took me some days to get right ... . I expect the Tories will now come in, and remain in some time. It seems to me we want the £5,000 a year badly. But really we must retrench. I cannot understand how we get through so much money." This constant worry over money, caused, quite simply, by both Randolph and Jennie recklessly spending far above their guaranteed income, and trying to balance their books by more and more expensive borrowings, would lead to something of a marital crisis before the year was out.

Winston recovered well, and was able to congratulate his father on his election[2], and to his mother he declared that he was "bankrupt and a little cash would be welcome". Letters to Jack discussed their model armies, and how they would build barricades together in the summer holidays.

After a huge electoral victory[3], Salisbury returned as Prime Minister and asked Randolph to be the Leader of the House of Commons as well as Chancellor of the Exchequer. Mindful of the welcome salary, and ignoring the urgent advice of his doctors, Randolph accepted this public recognition of his powerful status within the Conservative Party. He was now openly talked of as the next Prime Minister, though still only 37 years old. Both Jennie and his mother could hardly contain their excitement as he edged closer to the highest office in the land. His closest friends noted an alarming increase in his already excessive smoking. One Liberal friend asked Randolph how long his leadership would last. "Six months", he replied. "And after that?" his friend enquired, to which the reply was, "Westminster Abbey!" (after a fine funeral we may assume). These jokes about his slim chances of a long life take on a special poignancy if we remember the record of males in the Marlborough line.

Parliament sat from 19th August 1886, and Randolph took no summer vacation to be with his family, apart from the weekends. He worked hard instituting financial reviews of all the spending departments of government. As Leader of the House he dedicated himself to a programme of reform in Ireland but the Irish Nationalists would not forgive him for his role in defeating Home Rule, and opposed him bitterly at every turn.

Jennie 'perceived' that Randolph was acting in a cold and distant manner towards her, and this coincided with her friend, Lady Mandeville, spreading gossip about town that Lord Randolph had taken a mistress. Despite her long standing sexual relationship with two other men that we can be sure of, Jennie took this very badly and, in an extraordinary exchange of letters, asked her mother-in-law if there was any truth in the story and what should she, Jennie, do about it. The Dowager Duchess could not resist suggesting that Jennie's own life style contributed to the stories going about, and she strongly advised her not to add fuel to the flames by talking of her 'troubles' to her so-called friends. On 8th September, she wrote:

Dearest Jennie,
... I pray you do not breathe thoughts of Revenge against *any one*. It will bring you no blessing. Accept your present worry and anxiety patiently and strive to dispel it by the exercise of DOMESTIC VIRTUES!! looking after the Children and the new cook etc – avoiding excitement and the Society of those Friends who, while ready enough to pander to you, would gladly see you vexed or humbled, as they no doubt are jealous

of your success in society... . If you do not go to Scotland with
him, dear Jennie, do come and vegetate quietly here. Bring Jack
and we will try to make you as happy as possible. I am sure it
will show R. you care for him, and he has a good heart and
will give you credit for it ... . And meantime, though it is a
humdrum task, try to make yourself so essential to him that he
must recognize it ... . You must now sacrifice yourself and
your pleasures and give yourself steadily up to the task –
perhaps for many a day. I have no doubt of your success for I
know in his Heart he is truly fond of you – and I think I ought
to know.[4]

Jennie fired off three letters in forty-eight hours in response to this
advice. Clearly she was very agitated about the situation and the
Dowager Duchess replied, asking her to be calm, chiding her 'impetu-
ous disposition', and offering to speak to Randolph. "Perhaps he is
full of other things. I *cannot* believe there is any other woman".
Randolph's notes to Jennie at this time were fairly curt and businesslike, with the many expressions of love she had been used to, if
not entirely absent, then relatively scarce. The strain of parliamentary
duties had induced in Randolph some temperamental outbursts that
even the closest of friends had commented upon with some anxiety.
We can only wonder if the domestic peace at Connaught Place had
been disturbed by similar outbursts of rage over the state of the household expenses. Modern medical opinion now suggests that Randolph
may have suffered from a bipolar disorder, possibly genetic in origin,
that would manifest itself in wild mood swings under too much pressure. It can border on manic depression during stress, and must have
made him difficult to live with sometimes. Jennie's 'affair' with
Kinsky was periodic. Her sisters said he was never true to her and
took other women to his bed, one of whom was said to have been
Daisy Warwick. It was only in later years that Jennie would become
dependant upon Kinsky to the point of considering marrying him.
    The Dowager Duchess wrote a firm letter to Jennie on 26th
September, in which she explained that she had had a long talk with
Randolph, occasioned by his needing to ask for her signature on yet
another huge loan to settle (purely temporarily) their chaotic financial state. These new loans were used to settle those loans falling due

for repayment, to pay off some of the most persistent tradesmen and creditors, and to try and leave some little capital to meet future needs. The Dowager Duchess complained to Jennie that this was the first she had heard of their money worries. She had tried to get Randolph to curb his extravagance and he, no doubt recalling that unfortunate letter he had written before his wedding, had said how much he had expected to rely on Jennie to manage that side of things in their marriage. His mother would not have been slow to remind him of it. The Dowager Duchess begged Jennie to "give up that fast lot you live with, racing, flirting and gossiping … . You will be happier I know if *once* you break off with the past and live for a better and more useful existence". She again re-assured Jennie that she had "no cause for jealousy", and urged her to stop discussing her private affairs at social gatherings, as the stories made their way all around Society and back to Blenheim.

Jack and Mrs Everest accompanied Winston back to Brighton after the holidays. Winston wrote to his mother that Jack sent her 'millions' of kisses, "And I send you double!" Winston was thriving in this kind atmosphere, with lots of healthy activity like swimming and riding. He was even trying for a Classical prize.

Randolph so exhausted himself in his work that he went off with a friend, Thomas Trafford, for a tour of Europe, taking in Paris, Berlin, Dresden, Prague and Vienna, travelling incognito as 'Mr Spencer'. From the latter place, where he again socialised with Charles Kinsky, he wrote to Jennie, on 12th October, a letter showing how famous he had become and how the close attention of the press to celebrities is not a new phenomenon:

> I am hopelessly discovered … . At the station yesterday I found
> a whole army of reporters, at whom I scowled in my most
> effective manner. Really it is almost intolerable that one cannot
> travel about without this publicity. How absurd the English
> papers are! Anything equal to the lies of the *Daily News* and
> *Pall Mall* I never read: that *Pall Mall* is most mischievous … .
> The reporters have been besieging the hotel this morning, but I
> have sent them all away without a word. … This pottering
> about Europe *de ville en ville* suits me down to the ground, if it
> were not for the beastly newspapers.[5]

His letters were friendly without being effusive, and he described how he was sending back presents of Bohemian glassware that he hoped she would like. Jennie had finally suggested to the Dowager Duchess the name of the alleged mistress, Gladys, Lady de Grey. The Dowager Duchess replied firmly, "I still believe you have you have no cause for jealousy of that Lady". Gladys de Grey was a good friend of Randolph's and he often discussed the politics of the day with her, but there was no basis for the lurid tales circulating about them. At house parties with the Prince of Wales at Sandringham, with the Queen at Windsor Castle, and with the Salisburys at Hatfield House, everyone was commenting that either Jennie or Randolph looked ill or 'out of sorts'. The whole of Society was wondering what would happen next. Nobody could have guessed how the rise and rise of Lord Randolph could come to such an abrupt end.

Randolph really shook up the Treasury, whom he denounced as "a knot of damned Gladstonians". His first great budget was a profoundly reforming document. Slashing away at many wasteful aspects of finance, and increasing death duties, stamp duties and taxes on luxuries, he planned to produce a surplus of government income over expenditure, helping local government with grants and cutting income tax from eight pence to five pence in the pound. The government departments that would feel the biggest cuts were the Army and the Navy. Randolph was always incensed at the way governments seemed to embroil themselves in 'foreign adventures' and these curbs on the armed forces were one way of limiting such policy. From late October to December 1886, he was bombarded with complaints from his colleagues over his stringent policy. Salisbury indicated that the Army and Navy budgets would have to be maintained; Randolph replied that he could not continue to serve unless they both made significant cuts.

Randolph embarked on the last great political gamble of his life. On 20th December 1886, after a meeting with Queen Victoria at Windsor Castle, he returned home and wrote out a letter of resignation, and sent it to Lord Salisbury. He later explained that he had intended this to force Salisbury into a serious discussion of the issues raised by the Budget. It seems he mentioned it in passing to Lord George Hamilton, First Lord of the Admiralty, whom he met on the Windsor train, and he informed his old friend, Henry Drummond

Wolff. He even slipped out of the theatre the night before during the interval, to hand a copy of the letter to the editor of *The Times*. He did not, apparently, tell either his wife or his mother, both of whom were astonished to learn second-hand of this blow to their ambitions (and finances) when they read it next morning in the newspaper. Jennie was too crushed and miserable to ask for an explanation.

Clearly, he expected Lord Salisbury to concede the point that Randolph had pledged in public to carry through this budget and that he could not, in all conscience, remain in office if his own government would not support him. He badly misjudged Salisbury's reaction. The Prime Minister circulated the letter to Cabinet colleagues and, on 22nd December, replied that he could not support cuts in military expenditure in what he considered to be dangerous times. However much he knew that Randolph's resignation would be injurious to the government, he would stand by the financial demands of the ministers for the Army and the Navy.

Randolph replied that he thought the Conservative government's foreign policy was "at once dangerous and methodless". That Salisbury had accepted his resignation without so much as an interview, he took as a calculated blow at Tory Democracy. Having resigned at Christmas, he would have no opportunity to explain his reasons to the assembled House of Commons. It would be very little consolation to him that all the cuts he had demanded were, in fact, carried out in the next session of Parliament. If he had calculated that he could face down Lord Salisbury, he had made his most serious error. Standing by his principles led to a ruinously costly loss of office.

In a letter to Lord Salisbury, after Randolph's death, the Dowager Duchess revealed how utterly devastated her son was at the way Salisbury accepted the resignation without further discussion. She had gone to Salisbury, personally, and begged him to relent but "your heart was hardened against him".

CHAPTER 6

A Happy Family Again?
1887–1889

The year 1887 could hardly have started any worse for Jennie. Fearing for the state of her marriage, and reeling from the disappointment of Randolph resigning high office without having the decency to inform her, she received on 14th January a shocking letter from Arthur Brisband, the London correspondent of the New York *Sun* newspaper. He asked if there was any truth in an article he had received for publication that she and Lord Randolph were to separate. He sought an interview to clarify matters, and explained that he had tried and failed to speak to both Lord Randolph and Jennie's father, Mr Jerome, about it.

Jennie handed the letter to Randolph that very day, and he fired off a blistering reply, wondering how an American gentleman could circulate statements so utterly false, libellous and unfounded about a compatriot. Mr Brisband immediately wrote back explaining that he had tried to see Lord Randolph himself and, on being told he was out of town, had only written to Lady Randolph to prevent the story being printed without their comment. He stopped another paper from running the gossip, and insisted that he was helping a lady and a compatriot to avoid scandal.

This came as 'a wake up call' to them both. Randolph realised that the frenetic energy he had expended on political work had come at a heavy price to his family. He told Lord Rosebery "I would not live the last four years again for a million a year". Jennie was re-assured by Randolph's response to the talk of their separation, and all her letters to him are once again filled with deep affection. They continued to live much as they had done before, often apart, but both remained in love with each other and committed to their marriage and their children. Small wonder that Jennie would later reminisce, "How dark those days seemed!"

Once out of office Randolph came to see what a burden his relentless work had been. In search of fresh air, and to calm his shattered nerves, he went off in February on a tour of the archaeological sites of Algeria, Tunisia, Malta and southern Italy. Jennie kept up a stream of correspondence giving him all the news she gathered at the many parties and dinners she attended. She defended him loyally against the many gibes she had to listen to. The Prince of Wales had called on her and stayed for an hour, kissing her hand and declaring himself their 'best friend'.

There was always news of the children. Jack's seventh birthday was noted ("How time flies"), and Winston had been to a pantomime in Brighton, where he had rounded on a man who hissed a reference to Lord Randolph, saying, "Stop that row, you snub nosed Radical!" Randolph was so delighted by this display of filial loyalty that he asked for Winston to be sent a sovereign. Jennie was invited to dine with the Salisburys, and she was made very welcome there. Lord Salisbury spoke to her for an hour, in a shy and nervous way, but obviously wanting to be friendly. Randolph was only mentioned when Jennie spoke of his travels; Salisbury said he was glad he was getting a rest, as he knew his nervous system had suffered under the stress of his work. Jennie loyally suggested that Randolph's brain worked so rapidly that he arrived at conclusions six months before most other people. In her account of this meeting to her sister, Leonie, Jennie did say how exasperated she was that Randolph had thrown everything away in a gamble that had backfired at just that moment when he could have achieved anything he desired, a thinly veiled reference to No. 10 Downing Street. But she also stressed that their relationship had returned to its normal loving self and "I ought not to regret the crisis".

Many Conservatives, and even more Liberal Unionists, thought that the loss of Randolph was a fatal blow to their hopes of re-election. But Jennie had to report that there was "much that is disagreeable here – where people are as venomous & ill natured about us as possible – But you are good to me & I trust you utterly, & don't care twopence what they say – Enjoy yourself as much as you can & come back well, ready to fight the whole lot – And if you are only glad to see me, & understand how much I think of you & all that you are to me – I shall be quite happy".[1]

Randolph's replies often asserted that he did not give politics "two thoughts", and probably spoke from the heart when he wrote, "If people only knew how little official life really attracts me, they would judge one's actions differently". But his later letters wondered if the "old gang" would soon be played out, and if "the young lot" would get their turn. He advised Jennie on which politicians to keep in with. He could not shake off the excitement of political life and still thought he had something to offer.

Randolph returned from his holiday at the end of March 1887, and resumed his seat in the House of Commons in April, in time to see a budget pass that accepted the cuts in military spending that he had sacrificed his career over. He spoke at three huge public meetings that month, in Paddington, Birmingham and Nottingham, showing that he had lost none of his popularity with the people. He affirmed his loyalty to the Party and began a campaign for efficiency in government spending. He continued to be a thorn in the side of the Conservative hierarchy. At meetings he would see local dignitaries refuse to share the platform with him, but the large crowds adored him more and more.

Winston's letters from Brighton were full of good news, of his progress at sports (football and cricket), and his assertion that he was "blessed with that inestimable treasure, good health". He was playing Robin Hood in an opera, and his friend Bertie Roose was Maid Marian. He mounted a great campaign to be allowed leave from school to attend Queen Victoria's Golden Jubilee, though the chief attraction seemed to be a chance to see Buffalo Bill's Wild West Show. His uncle, Moreton Frewen, a friend of Buffalo Bill himself, had stirred his imagination with stories of the exciting show. Young Jack entreated his mother daily to let 'Winny' come home for the celebrations. Miss Thomson was not keen on the idea, but Winston assured his mother she would allow it if asked, and he cleverly deployed the 'threat' to his health if he were to be disappointed in something on which he had so completely set his heart. Not only did he see Buffalo Bill's show, he got to meet the great man, was able to enjoy the Golden Jubilee in London, and was invited, with his mother, onto the Royal yacht, *Britannia*, to be introduced by the Prince of Wales to his son, Prince George. In some respects Winston had not changed much, as we see him, following his return to school, writing an abject apology to Jennie for his bad behaviour while at home, and hoping that it will not cloud his pleasure during his summer holidays. The following letters all stressed how well he was doing in his lessons. Amongst the requests for autographs of both his mother and father, and, of course, for more cash, there was the news that he and another boy had applied to join the Primrose League locally, and he asked if he could join his mother's Chapter of the League in London. How could she deny him anything? However, his complaints about having to endure another tutor during the holidays met with a very stiff reply from his mother to do as he was told, to which he reluctantly agreed.

Mrs Everest took Winston and Jack to Ventnor, on the Isle of Wight, to commence their summer holidays. Their mother and father joined them there, for Cowes Week. At one party the Prince of Wales gave each of the boys a beautiful gold tiepin, set with a diamond. In a letter to his mother, Randolph reported that the Prince had invited him to visit him at his London residence, for private political discussions. In the same letter he had to report that Winston had already lost his tiepin, and the Prince had most graciously supplied him with another. It speaks volumes about the respective characters of Winston and Jack to know that Jack kept his tiepin carefully all the days of his life, in its original box, and handed it on to his son, Peregrine.[2] We cannot speak for the second gift to Winston.

Later that summer, Randolph was making enquiries about a school for Winston. The boy had been preparing to go to Winchester, but Randolph's brother-in-law, Edward Marjoribanks, introduced him to the idea of Harrow. A letter to the Headmaster, the Reverend J.E.C. Welldon, elicited a warm response, saying they would be delighted to find a place for Lord Randolph's son:

My dear Lord,
I wish to thank you for your letter respecting the admission of your son to Harrow school.
I shall look forward with much pleasure, & hope I may be useful to him, when he is here.
You may rely on my placing him in a House where his health will be carefully watched, if I cannot find room for him immediately in my own.[3]

Dr Roose later said that Harrow-on-the-Hill would be a particularly healthy location for a boy like Winston with a weak chest. Winston wrote and thanked his father for the choice, as the entrance exams for Winchester were the harder of the two. Jennie took Winston back to Brighton for his last term of 1887, and was pleased to see him settle in well. He came top in History, Ancient History, Bible History and Algebra, and second in Geography and Arithmetic. He would win prizes for English and Scripture by the end of the year. He took up boxing, and was doing well at riding and swimming. He still managed to come last, or nearly last, in Good Conduct.

In September 1887, aged seven years and seven months, Jack began boarding at Elstree Preparatory School, in Hertfordshire. His earlier fair hair had turned dark and curly like his mother's, and he was tall and slim, blue-eyed, and very like his father at the same age. If there has been less to say about him until now, it is because he was a very well behaved child, of a placid and serious disposition, already in thrall to his adored older brother. He had worked diligently at his lessons at home and, spared the horrors of Winston's first school, he would flourish academically. From his years at school some three hundred letters to his parents have survived, and although not many of Jennie's or Randolph's replies seem to have been preserved, the nature of Jack's letters show that she was in regular contact with her boys by post and visits. As ever, she kept Randolph abreast of his younger son's progress from his letters home.

The early letters, as may be expected, were a little homesick. "Do you miss me much? I do you. I hope Papa is quite well give him my love and a million kisses, also to you". This showering of affection on their parents was the hallmark of both boys in their letters home. However happy he was at school, Jack still counted the days to getting home: "My dear mama, I got my hamper on Wednesday. I hope you are quite well. I am very happy. There are only 5 more weeks before the holidays. The exams are going to begin very soon". His dear 'Woom' was never far from his thoughts as, after a trip with her to Brighton to see Winny riding, this kind little boy wrote to Jennie on 20th October: "Please dear Mama will you send Womany some money very soon as she is very low down indeed".

Despite their precarious finances, Randolph made an investment in September 1887, spending 300 guineas at the Doncaster Sales on a

1. Lord Randolph Churchill c. 1874

2. Miss Jeanette Jerome c. 1874

3. Lord Randolph Churchill, at the
height of his power.

4. Lady Randolph Churchill, at the height
of her beauty.

5. Randolph as a child.

6. Winston as a child.

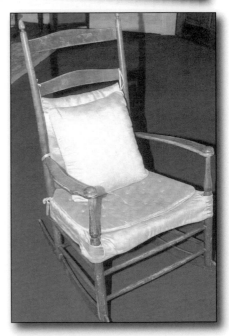

7. Jack as a child.

8. The 'Jerome' rocking chair (p.29), now at Blenheim Palace.

9. Randolph and Jennie, soon after the birth of Winston.

10. Winston, aged 10; Jack, aged 5.

11. Jennie in her riding habit, Ireland 1877.

12. *L'Abbesse de Jouarre*, painted by Emil Adam, Newmarket 1889.

13. *Left to right:* Jack, Jennie and Winston.

14. Jennie and her boys, Winston *(front)* and Jack *(standing)*.

15. Jennie walking out with the Prince of Wales, Tower of London c. 1896

16. Jennie making free with the Prince's headed notepaper.

17. Jennie as the Empress Theodora, 1897.

18. George Cornwallis-West, 'the most beautiful man in England'.

19. Winston in the South
African Light Horse, 1900.

20. Jack in the South African
Light Horse, 1900.

21. Jennie working in her office aboard
The Maine, 1900.

22. Jennie and Jack, recovering from his
wound, *The Maine*, 1900.

23. The officers of the Oxfordshire Hussars. Winston and Jack on the left of the back row.

24. The 'family regiment': Colonel The Duke of Marlborough, KG, PC; Major Viscount Churchill; Major W. Churchill, MP; Major J. Churchill.

beautiful black mare. He named her *L'Abbesse de Jouarre* after a French novel Jennie was reading at the time. The family all followed the fortunes of 'The Abbesse' on the racetrack, and the race-going public who could not pronounce the name, also took an interest in the popularly known 'Abscess of the Jaw'. Randolph decided to take Jennie away on a long holiday, to enjoy each other's company, to escape the political treadmill and to raise their prestige overseas. With the backing of the Prince of Wales, they made a highly publicised visit to the court of the Tsar and Tsarina of Russia. In December they visited the boys before they left, giving them generous gifts of money, though Winston, perhaps fairly enough, made it quite clear that he did not approve of being 'abandoned' for Christmas. Randolph had gone down to Brighton School to see Winston. The Miss Thompsons were in such admiration of him that they gave all the boys a half-holiday.

On arrival at St Petersburg they were received exactly like visiting royalty. Before they could leave for Moscow, Tsar Alexander III immediately invited them to the Gatschina Palace, which Jennie described as Russia's Windsor Castle. Each had a private audience, Randolph with the Tsar, Jennie with the Tsarina. She wanted to know everything about society, fashion and political life in England, and showed Jennie the many beauties of the palace. The Tsar received Randolph with great affection and, over shared cigarettes, got on to the serious matter concerning him. He wanted Randolph to know, and presumably to convey home, that Russia was absolutely no military threat to Britain and its Empire, contrary to many stories in the newspapers. The Tsar always impressed visitors with his sincerity and open, friendly character.

They were so completely lionized by St Petersburg society that Jennie would complain that she could do no sight seeing. Every day they were the guests at some aristocratic party – troika drives in the country or skating by day, balls and dinners, theatre and the opera by night. Randolph kept up a stream of amusing and highly informative letters to the Prince of Wales, assuring him of the great friendship towards Britain expressed by the dignitaries he met.

The Dowager Duchess had caused a furore at Christmas by writing to ask if she could have Winston for a week. She had nothing against Jack but she did not like Mrs Everest at all. Winston appealed directly to his aunts, Clara and Leonie, against this disruption of his holiday plans and separation from Jack. They refused his grandmother's request, to her great annoyance. She wrote in high dudgeon to Randolph that she would "trouble no more about my grandchildren". She was fated to get her way in unusual circumstances. Soon after a very happy Christmas at Connaught Place, Mrs Everest was taken seriously ill. Dr Roose thought it was diphtheria, and both boys were immediately taken to Blenheim after all. The boys had other playmates there, and a governess. Between Blenheim and their grandmother's London residence in Grosvenor Square, the boys enjoyed many visits to pantomimes and the theatre. But we get the impression that she was glad when Winston went back to school, writing to Randolph on 23rd January 1888:

> I do not feel sorry for he is certainly a handful. Not that he
> does anything seriously naughty except to use bad language
> which is bad for Jack. I am sure Harrow will do wonders for
> him for I fancy he was too clever and too much the boss at that
> Brighton school. He seems quite well and strong and very
> happy – Jack is a good little boy and not a bit of trouble ...[4]

Winston was able to write to his parents that Mrs Everest was not so ill as at first feared. It was "more Quinzy than Diptheria". He solemnly reported that he was glad she had not died.

After a fabulous New Year's Eve party in St Petersburg as guests of the Tsar and Tsarina, Randolph and Jennie went on to Moscow. Here they were able to do more private visits to galleries and museums, though their every move was still featured in the press and the invitations to social gatherings were plentiful. They left Russia for a ten-day visit to Berlin. They were joined by their mutual friend, Count Kinsky. Again a round of holiday visits to palaces, galleries and museums was interspersed with some grand social events. They were invited to a royal command performance at the opera, and were formally introduced to the Emperor Wilhelm and his court. Jennie shrewdly noted that "everything military was in the ascendant". They called in at Paris for a few days before returning to England by the end of January.

Jack was well settled into Elstree School. On his eighth birthday

(4th February 1888), he wrote to his mother asking her to come down and see him, with the very specific instruction to "bring a hamper and 2 tins of sardines". However many times Jennie visited her boys, it was never enough for them. Mrs Everest was a very regular visitor, bringing hampers of food, sweets, clean or new clothes, and the ever-needed cash pocket money. Peregrine said it was remarked at Elstree with what care and attention Jack greeted her and walked with her around the school.

In his last term at Brighton, Winston worked hard to prepare for the Harrow entrance examinations. He acknowledged that he was poor in Greek and only marginally better at Latin. One of his letters makes clear that Randolph had written to him with some good advice on how to handle the exams. Winston accepted that he should do the most 'paying' questions first (those carrying the highest marks), and tackle the others later. It is from small details like this that we can challenge the more extreme writers that suggest that Lord Randolph took nothing whatsoever to do with his sons. Similarly, Winston's account of the exams themselves, taken on 15th March 1888, is open to question. Admittedly he had just had an attack of mumps and was not in the best of health. But for him to say that he couldn't answer a single question on the Latin paper, which he merely adorned with an inkblot and several smudges, sounds rather like an amusing story told for effect. Miss Charlotte Thomson had accompanied Winston to Harrow, where she dined with Dr Welldon. She would have told the Headmaster that Winston had been translating Virgil for more than a year, and Caesar for much longer. She did note that he was extremely nervous on the day of the exams, getting quite upset and telling her that he had never translated Latin into English. As she had supervised his work at the small school in Brighton, she knew that this was simply not the case. Given the state of his health, and his nervous disposition on the day, he may have put in a poor performance, but Dr Welldon, assured by Winston's teacher that he was capable of good work, and very much in admiration of Lord Randolph, would let very little stand in the way of the young Churchill passing into Harrow Public School. Randolph visited Winston at Brighton to tell him just how pleased he was that he had passed.

He went up to Harrow on 17th April and, with his cousin, Dudley Marjoribanks, and two boys from his year at Brighton School there, he settled in quickly. Harrow was an expensive school. At £80 a term, plus £38–40 board, it was "amongst the highest of public schools, nearly double some of their competitors. Boarding was pricey and all additional but often-compulsory activities, including music, games, specialist science and workshop were paid for separately. On top of that came uniform and inevitable expenses on clothing and laundry, let alone food to supplement often spartan rations and pocket money."[5] Randolph and Jennie were perfectly used to Winston asking for more money, but their straightened finances were assailed by a succession of urgent demands for cash to cover subscriptions and (compulsory) gifts and charitable donations. Winston suggested that all the other boys seemed to have much more pocket money than he, and reminded his mother that she had promised he "should not be different to others".

Lord Randolph had written to Welldon pointing out Winston's delicate health. We can also surmise that Jennie told him something of the terrible treatment at St George's. Welldon personally saw to it that Winston was taken into a special House run by Mr Davidson, where he would be coached along gently until he was ready to enter Welldon's own House. Academically he was put into the bottom class of the school, the third division of the Fourth Form. He excelled at English and History, always struggled with the Classics, but did notably well at Mathematics. By the end of 1888, he was tenth overall in a class of thirty-one, and was second in mathematics and modern languages. Academically he often achieved much more than he liked to admit to in his later writings.

Most significantly for his future career, he took the first opportunity to join the school's Rifle Corps, in May. Before he even had his uniform or had begun training, he was engaged as an 'ammunition carrier' in a mock battle with another cadet corps. He proudly told his father that he was competing for an English prize and had to learn a thousand lines of Macaulay. Sadly there was a malaise at the heart of this seemingly good news. On 12th July, Mr Davidson wrote to Jennie a long and heartfelt letter, setting out their concerns:

> After a good deal of hesitation and discussion with his form-master, I have decided to allow Winston to have his exeat: but I must own that he has not deserved it. I do not think, nor does

Mr Somervell, that he is in any way *wilfully* troublesome: but his forgetfulness, carelessness, unpunctuality, and irregularity in every way, have really been so serious, that I write to ask you, when he is at home to speak very gravely to him on the subject.

When a boy first comes to a public school, one always expects a certain amount of helplessness, owing to being left to himself so much more in regard to preparation of work etc. But a week or two is generally enough for a boy to get used to the ways of the place. Winston, I am sorry to say, has, if anything got worse as the term passed. Constantly late for school, losing his books, and papers, and various other things into which I need not enter – he is so regular in his irregularity, that I really don't know what to do: and sometimes think he cannot help it. But if he is unable to conquer this slovenliness, (for I think all the complaints I have to make of him can be grouped under this head, though it takes various forms); he will never make a success of public school. I hope you will take the opportunity to impress upon him very strongly the necessity of putting a check on himself in these matters, and trying to be more businesslike. As far as ability goes he ought to be at the top of his form, whereas he is at the bottom. ... I thought it would do him good to spend a day with you, and have therefore let him go: but unless he mends his ways, he will really have to be heavily punished and I cannot help thinking he does not deserve any special treat during the exeat! I have written very plainly to you, as I do think it very serious that he should have acquired such phenomenal slovenliness. ... He is a remarkable boy in many ways, and it would be a thousand pities if such good abilities were made useless by habitual negligence.

I ought not to close without telling you that I am very much pleased with some history work he had done for me.

I am afraid this is a very long letter, but my excuse must be my interest in the boy.

Clearly Jennie had expressed an objection to corporal punishment, and Winston had been treated leniently so far, but he had tried the patience of his teachers to the limit. She must have given him a good talking to because his performance improved somewhat, and he won the prize for a word-perfect recitation of 1,200 lines of Macaulay from memory.

There was good news about Blandford that summer. In America he had married for the second time, Lillian Hammersley, a rich widow who would bring much needed cash for the upkeep of the ailing Blenheim Palace. Winston and Jack called her aunt Lily or the Duchess Lily.

For the summer holidays, Mrs Everest took the boys to stay with her married sister and husband, Mary and John Balaam, in Ventnor, on the Isle of Wight. They loved these jaunts out with 'Woomany', as she was still affectionately referred to at home, and their days were filled with good, healthy exercise. John Balaam, chief warden at the high security Parkhurst Prison, was able to regale Winston and Jack with stories about criminals and their adventures. Everest, whilst still on duty, could also be on vacation with her relatives and it was a happy arrangement for all. Winston could report to his mother that 'Jackey' went to bed saying, "Well I think that *has* been a successful day". He thought that he and Jack ate "about a ton a day". A stay at Blenheim Palace rounded out their holiday.

On returning to Harrow, Winston found himself denied a 'remove' (promotion to a higher class) that he might otherwise have expected. This was clearly a punishment for general bad behaviour. But in a special study of three Shakespeare plays, Winston came fourth out of twenty-five boys, and his letters home insisted that he was working diligently.

Since their return from Russia, Jennie and Randolph were enjoying a renewal of their close relationship. The break from politics had done Randolph good. Jennie fondly remembered how, together, they took great interest in the races and, with advice from Lord Dunraven, made some shrewd purchases of racehorses that would perform well and earn useful prize money. Jennie described 'The Abbesse' as a gallant little thing, having a great heart in a small body. Her unprepossessing size meant that she often competed at very favourable odds. She won the Prince of Wales Handicap (a £1,000 prize), and the Portland Plate (£775). How ironic that Randolph should be away on a fishing trip in Norway in November 1889 when the little beauty won the great race of her life, the Oaks at Epsom, at odds of twenty to one, netting a prize of £2,600. In 1890, Randolph entered her for the Manchester Cup, against the advice of his trainer, and she romped home in first place, winning £2,202[6]. He had received an Honorary Doctorate of Law from Cambridge University in June 1888. A short holiday in August in the beautiful south of France was especially invigorating. Life was good.

By his fourteenth birthday (November 1888) Winston had a fine collection of soldiers, all perfectly organised into a British infantry division and a cavalry brigade, with the correct artillery. Sir Henry Drummond Wolff noted a deficiency in the wagon train and generously supplied the models to make good this important aspect of military organisation. Jack was a regular playmate, with his own collection. By a 'Treaty for the Limitation of Armaments', devised by Winston, of course, Jack was restricted to only coloured troops, with no artillery at all! Soon after his birthday, Winston was marshalling his army at Blenheim when his father paid him a visit. After a detailed inspection of some twenty minutes, Lord Randolph asked his son if he would like to go into the army. Winston immediately replied that he would, and his career was decided upon.

Was Randolph giving Winston the chance to follow a career that clearly interested him, or was he in despair that the boy would ever achieve anything at school that might get him into a university to further his education and career choices? Perhaps he observed in these perfectly arranged regiments of toy soldiers the flare of the famous 1st Duke of Marlborough. Contrary to some opinion, Randolph did all he felt able to do to see that his two boys got off to a respectable start in life. Many years later, Winston would write that his early appreciation of his father's encouragement to go into the army was tempered by the knowledge that it was only because he thought he was not clever enough to go to the Bar. One might wonder what sort of malicious spirit would tell a young man such a thing about his father.[7]

Randolph wrote to Dr Welldon conveying this important news, and certainly visited Harrow soon after to see Winston and his teachers at the school. Christmas was spent at home at Connaught Place. The boys so over-indulged themselves, eating too much and singing themselves hoarse, that they were both quite ill. Jack recovered quickly and was taken to see the circus. Winston had a prolonged sore throat and a slight fever, and confessed to being "horribly bored & slightly irritable", made worse by the "awful rot" of having to spend part of one's holidays in bed. A short break with Mrs Everest in the bracing air at Ventnor prepared the boys for their return to school at the end of January 1889.

Jack's letters were always, if sometimes unintentionally, amusing. In the autumn of 1888 the whole country was aghast at the series of murders in London's Whitechapel district attributed to the notorious 'Jack the Ripper'. Though the murders seemed to have stopped, they were still a hot topic of conversation, and Randolph may well have discussed them with his friend, Henry Mathews, the Home Secretary, at home over Christmas. Like any boy of his age, Jack would have been all agog at these sensational events. That they continued to fascinate is illustrated by Jack signing off his letters in February 1889, as "Jack, not the Ripper". In March he wrote a classic schoolboy letter to his 'Dear Papa'. "I hope you are quite well. It has been snowing more. You will be glad to hear that I got 20 marks for gymnastics. I have not one thing to say. I remain. Jack". He was always aware of his father's troubled health and almost every letter contains some reference to it: "How is Papa", "I am glad to hear Papa is better", "Give Papa my love". At one stage Randolph must have been concerned for Jack's health because the boy wrote a special letter to his father: "I am writing because I think that you will think I am not well". He sent regular and detailed reports on the school sports teams. His letters contained as much news of 'Winny' as they did of himself, but he was able to report that he was already fourth in his class. His reading ability improved apace and Jennie sent him the *London News* and the *Daily Graphic*, and took out a subscription for him to the monthly *Strand* magazine. He was well informed in current affairs, the racing world, society gossip, and, of course, his father's political work.

At Harrow, Winston remained in Mr Davidson's 'small' House but did get his Remove to the second division of the Fourth Form, some recognition for his improved efforts. He came second in the tasks set for the holidays. The winter was again hard on his general well-being and he was often ill, missing classes because of it. If Winston complained that his mother 'never' came to see him, we know from a letter of Jack's to his mother that "you had gone to Harrow". In March Winston was in another great mock battle with the Rifle Corps, in which they were defeated "because we were inferior in numbers & not from any want of courage". He had bought a drill book, was studying hard for the examinations to become a Corporal, and was proud to have been part of a Guard of Honour for a visit by Princess Louise. Randolph wrote to ask Welldon if he could take Winston into a 'big' house, and Welldon replied that it was already arranged that Winston would be so promoted after Easter. Once settled in, with its new lists of demands for 'essentials' to furnish the room he shared with two other boys, he was delighted when his father sent him the money for a new bicycle. In September he would enter the Army Class at Harrow and begin his serious preparation for entry into Sandhurst. His usual conduct of doing well in some subjects and frankly shirking in those he disliked led to Dr Welldon putting him 'on reports' for a long period. This meant that his work was reported on every week by all his tutors, and he was called to account for failings. It was an onerous life and Winston asked Jennie to visit the school and "jaw" Welldon about it. She did pay the visit but almost certainly agreed with the need to make Winston do as he was told.

In the House of Commons Randolph was still a popular speaker, and in July he gave one of his most charming and witty speeches in support of more money from the Civil List for the children of the Prince of Wales. He received many letters of congratulation for his performance. But soon after this success, he returned home one day earlier than expected and found Jennie alone in his house with the Prince of Wales. Randolph was furious at this breach of etiquette and angrily ordered the Prince out of the house. Jennie may well go off to Paris, ostensibly to visit her mother, but to be often seen in the company of Charles Kinsky, but there were limits of decorum beyond which Randolph would not allow her to stray.

On more serious issues, Randolph was giving some of his greatest speeches, getting deeper and deeper into conflict with the leadership of his party. Out of compassion for the plight of the industrial working class, he joined the campaign for temperance reform. By taking on the power of the brewing magnates, a central support of the Conservative Party, he ensured a new wave of enemies, and attacks on him in the press. He kept up his demand for the Irish people to be accorded full and free status within the United Kingdom. He drew up plans for local government and land purchase reform, and would have spent a hundred million pounds on his programmes (five to seven billion in today's prices). Racial prejudice against the Irish incensed him:

> I have had some experience of the Irish people, and I have lived
> amongst them for some years, and that I have always found
> them a very pleasant people and a very amiable people, and
> very easy to get on with if you take them the right way … . I
> hope … earnestly and … strongly, that I may live to see the day,
> … when the Irish shall not only be prosperous, but free – free
> in the full and proper sense of the word – free as the English, as
> the Scotch, and as the Welsh are free … .'

Friends warned him he was going too far. Joseph Chamberlain was a particularly harsh critic of his "crazy quilt" of policies, accusing him of being a "carpetbagger" of other men's ideas.

He had an unofficial agreement with Chamberlain that, when the Central Birmingham seat became vacant, Randolph was to be the Conservative and Unionist candidate. When John Bright died in March 1889 a bye-election was called and the Birmingham Conservatives invited Randolph to put in for the seat. He was stunned to find Chamberlain utterly and implacably opposed to his candidature, and he was put under such pressure by Party officials that he backed away from the fight. Jennie was incandescent with rage. She was so sure that Randolph could still achieve great things in politics, and was so convinced that the people of Birmingham would have turned out for him, that she rounded on him when he agreed with the "old gang" that he should not press his suit. She accused him of "showing the white feather for the first time in his life". This supposedly frivolous wife clearly retained considerable ambitions for her husband.

CHAPTER 7

Looking for Gold
1890–1892

In March 1890, Randolph showed signs of serious illness, but also fought one of his most principled and selfless campaigns. In April 1887, *The Times* had printed a facsimile of a letter that purported to show Charles Stewart Parnell's involvement in the Phoenix Park Murders of 1882. Parnell denounced it as a forgery but did not sue for libel, as he had no confidence in winning his case before an English jury. When another Irish MP began proceedings against *The Times*, no less a figure than Sir Richard Webster, the Principal Law Officer of the Crown, defended the newspaper. He used the case to introduce still more incriminating letters allegedly signed by Parnell. The Government refused a Parliamentary Select Committee of Inquiry, and set up a commission of three judges with statutory powers to investigate the letters in July 1888. Randolph denounced the illegality of the Government's proceedings, and the outrageous use of judges in an overtly political matter. After a ludicrously long drawn out affair, the whole case collapsed in ridicule when a man named Pigott was exposed as the forger. Five days later Pigott died at the hands of a pistol-wielding assassin.

It was March 1890 before the Special Commission reported to the House. A friend of Randolph's moved an amendment in the House that would have formally criticised its conduct. Randolph knew that to support this motion would renew the criticism aimed at him in the press. He asked his friend, Jennings, to withdraw the amendment but it was not to be. He rose on 11th March and, while not addressing the amendment directly, spoke for an hour in attacking the breach of constitutional procedure that had just come to its shameful conclusion. The House had to collectively grit its teeth as he relentlessly and forensically exposed the sorry workings of the Commission. Once he paused and asked for a drink of water. Such was the palpable resentment all around him that no one moved to help. He asked again, and a young Tory MP, a Mr Baumann, went for the water. As he returned the bloc of Irish Nationalist members cheered him, and gratefully taking the proffered glass, Randolph said to Baumann: "I hope this will not compromise you with your party". The implication was there that he no longer considered it his party. All these years of investigation, and it came down to "a man, a thing, a reptile, a monster – Pigott!" Randolph sat down utterly exhausted, drained emotionally and feeling quite ill. It was his final break with the Conservative Party.

How the Government must have rejoiced as, at the moment of its greatest humiliation over the forged letters, Parnell was dragged through the divorce courts over his relationship with Mrs Kitty O'Shea. In the eyes of Catholic Ireland he was destroyed once and forever as an adulterer.

In the first term of 1890, Winston got his Remove to the first division of the Fourth Form. It is clear, despite the lack of surviving letters that Lord Randolph was in regular touch with him, as many of Winston's letters to his father are in the nature of a reply to a communication. Thus on 26th February, he thanks him for a postal order received safely, asks if he could come down and resuscitate the Conservative Club at school, discusses some of Randolph's recent political speeches, and ends with a cheery note, "Don't trouble to write because you are so busy".

From Jack's letters we can see that the whole family were in regular touch with each other. Letters back and forth between all parties – Randolph, Jennie, Winston, Jack and Mrs Everest – were all shared and read between each other. There are often reminders to return letters once read. Like Winston, Jack kept his parents regularly informed of how well he was doing at school, usually with a reminder of how low his finances were that particular week! A little note just before a birthday (in February) was always useful: "Dear Papa, I am quite well. I am ten on the fourth of this month ... two more years till I can go to Harrow. I must work up. It is a very short term, but it is very cold. I am getting on in writing. I hope you are enjoying yourself. I will write some other time, so goodbye. Your affect. son, Jack S.S. Churchill". The next letter is by way of thanks for the birthday present, assuring his father that "I have not spent a shilling yet", and he was saving the rest for the holidays. Another typical letter shows how this subtle manipulation of the parents was conducted:

> Dear Papa
> I am quite well and happy and hope you are the same. My
> money is very low. I send you my two [school] lists. I am sorry
> to say Ringworm has broken out here … their [sic] are only
> two cases of Ring-Worm here. Nothing to be afraid of.
> As I said before *my money is very low.*
> … I have been top of my form 3 times,
> I remain
> Jack[1]

Jack, already consistently top of his form, was very popular with his schoolmasters, who had clearly marked him out as a boy of great promise. When a Mr Meryick invited Jack to stay with his family in Somerset for a few days at Easter 1890, Jack implored his mother to agree. "It is the same man as wrote to me in the holls [holidays] who you thought rather a nice man".

Randolph made a point of 'sharing his winnings' with the boys, particularly following some of the triumphs of 'The Abbesse'. On 3rd May Jack wrote:

> Dear Papa
> I am so glad you put something on the Abbesse as you say.
> Thank you so much for sending me £3. It is a lot.
> I have been top of my form 5 times. I send you the lists.
> I am working very hard…I am very happy and well…
> I hope the Abbesse will win a few more races before she's
> done.
> It is very nice weather here all the same…
> I remain
> Jack S. C.

The enclosed lists showed that Jack was top of the form with 300 marks, 35 ahead of the boys who came joint second. On 15th May he was top by 96 marks.

Now Randolph had also sent Winston £5 as his share of the

winnings. On 12th June Jennie had to write her son a very stiff letter, sent via Mrs Everest:

> I have much to say to you, I'm afraid not of a pleasant nature.
> You know darling how I hate to find fault with you, but I can't
> help myself this time … . your Father is very angry with you
> for not acknowledging the gift of £5 for a whole week, and
> then writing an offhand careless letter.

This brought to a head the dissatisfaction that his parents were feeling with the fifteen-year old Winston. He had been kept back from one examination because his work wasn't up to standard. Then, on 1st June, he wrote a long and carping letter to his father about the drawbacks of the Army Class. It is a frank letter, and is not the sort of thing a boy who was afraid of his father would write. He complained that the Army Class meant a lot of extra work, in the evenings and during weekends and half-holidays. Boys in that class tended to fall behind in their general school placings because of the extra studies. He didn't like the idea of having to go to a 'crammer' for the forced extra tuition to get through the Sandhurst entrance examinations, and suggested instead going into the militia. This was an 'easier' route to obtaining a commission in the army.

Jennie gave free reign to the disappointment they both felt:

> Your report which I enclose is as you will see a *very* bad one.
> You work in such a fitful inharmonious way, that you are
> bound to come out last – look at your place in the form! Your
> Father & I are both more disappointed than we can say, that
> you are not able to go up for your preliminary Exam: I daresay
> you have 1000 excuses for not doing so – but there the fact
> remains! If only you had a better place in your form, & were a
> little more methodical I would *try* & find an excuse for you.
> Dearest Winston you make me very unhappy – I had built up
> such hopes about you & felt so proud of you – & now all is
> gone. My only consolation is that your conduct is good, & that
> you are an affectionate son – but your work is an insult to your
> intelligence. If you would only trace out a plan of action for
> yourself & carry it out & be *determined* to do so – I am sure

you could accomplish anything you wished. It is that
thoughtlessness of yours which is your greatest enemy. Your
Father threatens to send you with a tutor off somewhere for
the holiday – I can assure you it will take a great deal to pacify
him, & I do not know how it is to be done. I must say I think
you repay his kindness to you very badly.

Inevitably, his conduct was now being compared, unfavourably, with
the ten-year old Jack:

There is Jack on the other hand – who comes out at the head
of his class every week – notwithstanding his bad eye.[2]
   I will say no more now – but Winston you are old enough to
see how serious this is to you & how the next year or two &
the use you make of them, will affect your whole life – stop
and think it out for yourself & take a good pull before it is too
late. You know dearest boy that I will always help you all I
can.
Your loving but distressed
Mother.

Today's child psychologists expressly warn parents not to make this
kind of comparison. It is held to be particularly damaging to the
psyche of the sibling under criticism. It leads to fears of affection
being lost, or transferred to the 'favoured' sibling. We shall witness
other, and more severe, comparisons being made by both Randolph
and Jennie, holding Jack up as a model to be followed by the elder
brother. We can only wonder at how this affected the relationship
between the boys. It remained outwardly loving, but it cannot be
denied that Winston could, on occasion, 'airbrush' Jack out of his
life.
   The errant son wrote a very apologetic letter, admitting "I have
been rather lazy", and that while 'on reports' his work was bound to
improve. He said Jennie's letter had "cut me up very much", and he
promised to work very hard before the summer holidays came
around.
   The holidays were taken at Banstead Manor, conveniently close to
the Newmarket Races, which the family had rented for several

months. This was a sign of their improved finances. 'The Abbesse' had made a tidy profit, and Randolph was elected to the Jockey Club because of her string of victories. It also bordered on Charles Kinsky's country estate. This was a long and glorious holiday, with lots of visits from family and friends, including Kinsky, a great favourite with the boys. He set up a target range and began to teach them to shoot. The boys also formed, and operated successfully, a 'model farm'. It included horses, ponies, dogs, puppies, rabbits, hares and a number of hens that proved to be good layers. It was quite the norm for Randolph and Jennie to spend time separately, visiting other friends or race meetings during the holidays. Randolph took the boys on a long visit to the Astors at Cliveden. Jack wrote to his mother: "We are at Cliveden, we have got rooms; well, if the house had been built for us, they could not be better". Randolph, a man routinely and thoughtlessly described as not liking children, wrote that he had taken Winston and Jack, together with Jack Leslie (Leonie's son and his Godson, later Shane), and John Milbank (Winston's friend from Harrow), on a trip up river: "We made an expedition up the river to Oxford, sleeping the night at Wallingford. We nearly got as far as Abingdon the next day. The boys enjoyed it. Jack has at last got a pony to ride and had his first ride this morning. He is seemingly pleased."[3] Jennie returned to Banstead to finish the holidays with the family.

Back at school for the autumn term, Jack continued his regular stream of chirpy letters, commiserating with his "dear papa" when 'The Abbesse' did not win ("I hope you did not lose anything"), thanking "dear Mama" for a gift of figs, and generally enquiring after the well-being of his menagerie of dogs, ponies and rabbits.

Winston was in trouble again at Harrow, but the incident reflected well on his forming character. News got back to Jennie that he was getting very bad reports from one master, and she had let it be known that she was mightily displeased with this development. He wrote to explain that he was working very hard, but had fallen in with one master "whom I hated & who returned the hate". He complained directly to Dr Welldon, who immediately stepped in and transferred Winston to the care of masters who got good work out of him. Jennie was able to write to Randolph, who was on another trip for the sake of his health, 23rd November:

I went to Harrow on Thursday & had an interview with
Welldon – who told me he thought Winston was working as
hard as he possibly could & that he would pass his preliminary
exam. – It appears that Winston was working under a master
he hated – & that one day the master accused him of a lie –
whereupon Winston grandly said that his word had never been
doubted before & that he would go straight to Welldon –
which he did. Welldon quite approved, took him away from
the master, & now he is with one he likes & works very well
with – I thought him looking pale, but he was very nice & full
of good resolutions which I trust will last.

It was clear that Welldon, out of his high regard for Lord Randolph,
was going to a good deal of trouble to see that they got the best out
of young Winston. The boy really was working hard, especially at his
drawing, an important subject for military cadets. Jennie was less
pleased to see he had taken up the smoking of cigars, given the health
problems his father had with cigarettes.

Once again, Randolph was advised to holiday in warmer climes
for the winter 1890–91. He set out with two friends, via Monte
Carlo and Rome, for Egypt. Jennie's letters kept him informed of the
political situation. From Rome, on 3rd December, he wrote: "Your
nice long letter was very pleasant to receive. I should like to get them
very often." In this he could not help relishing the disarray caused to
the Home Rule party by the latest news about Parnell. The slow sailing along the Nile was a tonic to Randolph, and he would have loved
to share its pleasures with his wife. He wrote on 28th December:

It was very pleasant on waking up this morning to find a
bundle of letters from you and others … . I cannot tell you
how pleasant it has been; one day more perfect than another,
and yet the heat has never been oppressive. The days slip by …
We are enjoying ourselves immensely. Life on the Nile is
ideal. The scenery would be monotonous if it were not on so
vast a scale; but as it is, one never tires of it. Certainly this is
the only place to pass the winter if fine warm weather is
desired … . I must say I wish you were on board this boat – a
week of this weather and rest would make you as strong as a

horse. Perhaps next winter, if we are alive and well, we may do
it together... .

He sent back news of all the wonders of Ancient Egypt that he saw,
and was clearly improving a lot with the prolonged rest. In January
1891 a letter to his mother tells us much of his character: "I received
a letter from a man offering me the Chairmanship of a ruby and sapphire mine in Montana, with a salary of £2,000 a year guaranteed for
5 years – so if I wanted to sell myself I would get a good price. I
declined".[4]

The family's winter holidays were spent at Banstead Manor. Mrs
Everest took Winston and Jack there ahead of their mother's arrival.
She reported to Jennie how well Winston seemed after his end of
term exams relating to his preparation for entering Sandhurst. They
settled in quickly, and the boys enjoyed lots of healthy outdoor activity, especially riding. Jennie was quite glad of the excuse not to spend
another Christmas at Blenheim. When the exam results were
announced in January 1891 Winston had done well. Out of 29 candidates at Harrow, twelve had succeeded, and Winston came fourth
in that group. An overjoyed Jennie sent the good news to Randolph,
now on his way home from Egypt. She thought the present of a gun
would be a reward for him, "He is pining for one, and ought to have
a little encouragement".

Jennie had her own share of troubles to cope with. Her father, now
living in England, was seriously ill. Mrs Jerome, Clara, and Jennie all
took turns to sit all night with him, until he began to get better.
Winston wrote some loving letters to his mother, hoping that his
"Grandpapa" would recover but also concerned that she should not
exhaust herself in looking after him. – "you have enough worries
without getting ill".

Randolph was back in England in February 1891, when he penned
a heartfelt letter to his Paddington constituency that summed up his
political stance to a remarkable degree:

I have always been more or less an independent member. From
the year 1874, when I entered Parliament, to the year 1880 –
during the time of Lord Beaconsfield's Government – I felt it
my duty on more than one occasion to vote and speak against

the powerful Government, and at times when in certain circles
in London even to whisper a doubt as to its wisdom was
considered almost treasonable. From 1880 to 1885 I pursued a
course of Parliament of the greatest freedom and independence.
More than once I went my own way not caring much whether
anyone followed; but I hardly think there are those who will
assert that my action from 1880 to 1885 did injury to the Tory
party. I have been unable even of late years to divest myself of
my independent character. Lord Melbourne – or was it Lord
Palmerston? – once characterised an independent member of
Parliament as a member who could not be depended upon.
Well, this much is certain. If I am called upon to support a
reactionary and antiquated policy, then I am not to be
depended upon. ... If I am called upon to support an aggressive
policy or a policy of large expenditure, then I am not to be
depended upon. But if I am called upon to abide by pledges I
have given on any platform or in any published letter or to
support the political principles I have advocated, since I
entered Parliament, then I can confidently point out to you my
past career as a proof that I am to be depended upon – more,
perhaps, than any devoted partisan of the present Government.

He now felt under no obligation to stand by the Conservative Party
in the House of Commons. Instead he raised a new loan of £5,000
from Lord Rothschild and set off at the end of April 1891 for
Southern Africa to look for gold. Rothschild protected his investment
by supplying a fine mining engineer, Mr Perkins, to the expedition,
which was led in the field by the experienced Major Giles and, in
Hans Lee, had one of the best hunters in Africa to guide it and supply
a plentiful diet of fresh meat. They trekked into Mashonaland, risk-
ing attack by Matabele tribes and wild animals. This was a very
rugged journey, crossing difficult, largely unexplored country. It is
not the sort of journey to be undertaken by a man almost terminally
riddled with syphilis, as some would have us believe.

The Press took the greatest interest in the whole thing. His enemies
printed malicious stories and spiteful cartoons, ridiculing his efforts.
But the *Daily Graphic* commissioned a series of twenty letters from
him, at £100 each, a very generous remuneration. He sent back an

entertaining account of his travels and adventures, which kept him in
the public eye.

Jack was growing quite tall and seemingly insatiable; his letters to
his mother bombarded her with requests for hampers and fresh fruit,
all of which seem to have been supplied. If he thought his mother was
falling behind in replying to this stream of letters he would tell her so.
"I am all right. You have not written to me for a fortnight. Do write
and tell me how Papa is and the family of animals. Do write to me.
You are hidden away at Banstead. Do write and talk". This letter
ends with the word 'Do' repeated forty-five times! He once complained that she had only written to him six times in one term. He
wrote that letter in the seventh week of the term. It is from the writings of her demanding children that Jennie stands 'condemned'.

Jennie did send news of the 'farm' at Banstead quite regularly. In
particular the hens were terrific layers, and the boys tried to negotiate the sale of the eggs to boost their pocket money. On 17th May
Jack wrote to 'Winny' querying whether the sale of seventy-three
eggs could really only have raised two shillings. Their letters were full
of sports news – the results of various cricket matches and well-
informed commentaries on the big races. Jennie's letters often
contained references to races and the prospects of various horses in
which they all had an interest. Like any eleven-year old, Jack could
not resist sending a 'risky' poem to his brother:

> The boy stood on the tram way line
> The conductor rung the bell.
> The tram went to London
> And the boy went to hell.

Jennie visited Harrow regularly, and spoke with Welldon about
Winston's progress in the Army Class. He seems to have passed over
one incident in their discussions, but the frank young Winston wrote
on 17th May confessing all. He had, he explained, been in "a deuce
of a row" when he and four chums had smashed all the remaining
windows in a derelict factory. He had been one of the two boys
caught and had received a birching, the record of which is in the
school punishment book and can be seen at the Churchill Museum in
London's Cabinet War Rooms.

On 27th May (Derby Day) Winston wrote to his father, who had newly arrived in Cape Town after his trek 'up country'. The letter is full of the most detailed accounts of recent racing successes and the prospects for the Derby, the amusing story of Lord Elcho being bounced out of Jennie's dog cart, news of the productiveness of the hens, of Mrs Everest's influenza and Jack's coming top of his form again. About two-thirds of the way into the letter he related the story of the factory windows and having "got 'swished' for it" by Welldon. It was not a "serious row" as he "never even mentioned it to Mama". The letter was then put aside so that Winston could include the results of the Derby (the favourite, *Common*, won) and it concludes with "Much love and many kisses". This is not the letter of a young man who lived in fear of his father. It is frank, open and loving. The news may well have annoyed Lord Randolph, who saw in this sort of bad behaviour a repeat of his own rapscallion ways at Eton. (He, too, had been beaten for breaking windows). Randolph always regretted not applying himself more diligently at school, and may have feared that Winston was not doing as well as he ought. But then to receive such honest and affectionate letters would soften the heart of many a father, particularly one who was away from his family for a prolonged period on the other side of the world.

Like most small, live-in communities, Elstree School could do little to prevent the spread of illness once contracted. During his time there, Jack wrote of "epidemics" and "outbreaks" of measles, mumps, whooping cough, chickenpox, influenza, ringworm, eye infection or "eye disease". He caught everything that was going, and wrote of having influenza, colds, coughs, bilious attacks, and eye trouble. His glands were prone to flaring up, and he suffered from sore ears that dogged him into adulthood. Just when he was looking forward to seeing an important cricket match at Lords, he went down with the mumps. That the Headmaster himself had offered to take him is an indication of how well liked he was at the school. Jack was very ill for two weeks and then recovered rapidly. Jennie bought him a new pony as compensation for missing the cricket. From one of Mrs Everest's letters we can see how kind Winston was to him. After a visit she had:

… found him looking remarkably well in spite of the mumps. He was much better & the swelling going down. There were

about 16 boys isolated in a house called the Homestead which
Jack considered rather dry. ... He told me about the hamper &
5/- you sent him. Awfully kind of dear Winnie.

There followed a celebrated incident, often used to abuse Jennie as
a bad mother who shamelessly paraded her lover before her teenage
son. It concerned Winston writing to "My darling Jack" in which
he referred to finding his mother and Count Kinsky breakfasting
together. Most writers have failed to realise that Winston was
speaking of 18 Alford Street, the London home of his aunt Clara,
who rented out rooms, and where a large party were staying before
going to the races. Jennie and Charles Kinsky were but two of several guests at breakfast that day. Winston's letter went on to
describe the game at Lord's and a visit to a display of naval models.
The next day Kinsky took him to Crystal Palace to see the visit of
the German Kaiser. A subsequent attempt to travel on a switchback
railway led to unedifying scenes that remind us of the latent racism
in that society, and reveals a violent streak in Kinsky's character.
The pair were prevented from mounting the already full 'aerial car'.
In Winston's unfortunate words, "a half bred sort of Kaffir who
was in charge attempted to stop us". A scuffle and harsh words
ensued, until the crowd "made the scoundrel be quiet & we went
on our way angry but triumphant". Kinsky bent the Kaffir's hand
backwards, a most painful experience. Kinsky also invited the 16½
year-old Winston to join him in alcoholic drink on this boisterous
expedition.[5]
   There followed a long summer vacation at Banstead Manor. Mrs
Everest had been down to prepare the way, but had been sent off on
her own holidays because of the large party staying there for the
races. Then she and Jack arrived for the holidays. He fired off a
report to Winny about the parlous state of the fort they had built in
the grounds. The house was always full of guests. Jennie was able to
write to Randolph on 29th July, "Mama is asleep in the drawing
room, Jack playing with the soldiers and I, are in the little hall writing – you can see us! Winston is camping out with Dudley
Marjoribanks etc, I send you his letter ... ". Jennie rode out often
with her two sons, and a later note to Randolph would say, "'The
boys are very happy. Kinsky has gone out with them to put up a

target. ... Both boys ride very well – particularly Jack." Winston supervised a large force comprising his brother, cousins and estate workers to build a two-room 'den', complete with moat and draw-bridge, defended by catapults that fired apples at any attackers. Between these military adventures and the busy model farm, the Churchills, Frewens and Leslies spent an idyllic summer.

Given the long delays in postal deliveries, Winston must have been delighted to receive this letter from his father, dated 27th June:

Dearest Winston,
You cannot think how pleased I was to get your interesting & well written letter & to learn that you were getting on well. I understand that Mr Welldon thinks you will be able to pass your examinations into the army when the time comes. I hope it may be so, as it will be a tremendous pull for you ultimately. I have been having a most agreeable travel in this very remarkable country. I expect that when you are my age you will see S. Africa to be the most populous & wealthy of all our colonies. I suppose Mama has read you my letters & that you have seen my letters in the *Daily Graphic*, for I cannot tell you more than I have already written. You would have enjoyed an expedition I made last week for shooting purposes. A regular gipsy life, sleeping on a mattress in a bell tent, dressing and washing in the open air & eating round a camp fire. The sport was very fair & wild & there was much variety of game to shoot. Here I have been examining gold mines & investing money in what I hope will be fortunate undertaking for I expect you & Jack will be a couple of expensive articles to keep as you grow older ... .
    I suppose this will just reach you as you are going home for the holidays. I hope you will have a good time at Banstead & that you and Jack will amuse yourself well. Give him my very best love & tell him how glad I am to hear of his good place in the school. Perhaps he will write to me before long. Goodbye, take care of yourself, don't give Mama any trouble.

In a long and affectionate reply, Winston gave his father lots of news, including all about the abuse that his letters to the *Daily Graphic* from Africa were receiving from those papers in competition. He also explained that his request for "an antelope" was not, as poor Randolph had imagined, for a live one, but for a head to put up in his room at home. Further details of the magnificent uniforms of the Kaiser and his entourage followed, and a description of a letter Jack had sent him, "8 sides very well written".

A tutor was hired for part of the holiday, to improve Winston's command of the French language. He had successfully fought off a suggestion from Welldon that he go to France or Germany for part of the holidays. He had enlisted the help of his father, who had offered to get a German scullery maid at Banstead for the purpose. In a reaction to all the hard work he was being subjected to, Winston even hinted that he was already done with the Army and wouldn't mind going into the Church.

On returning to school both the boys were ill, with "bilious attacks". Jennie was sure they had exhausted themselves during their frenetic holidays. Jack wrote to his mother, "Don't tell Woom because she will think I am dying".

Jennie was in serious discussion with Welldon about Winston's future. The Headmaster was insisting that the Christmas holidays be used to get some grounding in German, preferably by a stay in that country. Jennie needed Randolph's help and advice. She wrote from Connaught Place on 25th September:

> Winston conveniently worked himself into a bilious attack and had to stay on a couple of days. On the whole he had been a very good boy – but honestly he is getting a bit too old for a woman to manage. After all he will be 17 in 2 months and he really requires to be with a man. I send you Welldon's letter. You will have time to answer me before I decide anything. Of course it will be hard upon him not spending his holidays at home – but after all I shan't know what to do with him, and it will be impossible for him to pass his exam if he does not get a smattering of German … . Winston will be all right the moment he gets into Sandhurst. He is just at the 'ugly' stage – slouchy and tiresome. I managed to get a very nice little man from Cambridge – very clever spoke 12 languages. He might be made use of later to travel with him. It will be all the better for

Jack to be without him – the difference in their ages is
beginning to tell and poor Jack is quite worn out rushing about
after Winston ... .

Money was becoming a worry again. Horses could not be depended
on to win races, and they were expensive to stable and feed meanwhile. They were back to relying on Jennie's income from the rented
property in New York and the occasional gift from her father. School
fees were a serious drain on their finances. "How I long for you to be
back with sacks of gold" was a heartfelt message from Jennie to her
absent husband.

Mashonaland failed to produce any new gold deposits. The party
returned to Cape Town to reorganise and then set off for
Johannesburg. Here the engineer, Perkins, came up with some new
ideas about deep level mining and the speculators soon struck gold,
literally and richly. From his share in the venture, Randolph would
eventually acquire gold shares to the value of £70,000 (some £4 million today). Hearing that Arthur Balfour had accepted the office of
Leader of the House in his uncle's government, Randolph wrote to
Jennie on 23rd November, stressing his complete disillusion with
politics, and his yearning to get home:

So Arthur Balfour is really leader – and Tory Democracy, the
genuine article, at an end! Well, I have had quite enough of it
all. I have waited with great patience for the tide to turn, but it
has not turned, and will not now turn in time. ... I feel sure the
other party will come in at the next election. ... No power will
make me lift hand or foot or voice for the Tories, just as no
power would make me join the other side. All confirms me in
my decision to have done with politics and try to make a little
money for the boys and for ourselves. I hope you do not all
intend to worry me on this matter [politics] and dispute with
me and contradict me. ... I am quite tired and dead sick of it
all, and will not continue political life any longer. I have ...
many things and many friends to make me happy ... It is so
pleasant getting near home again. I have had a good time, but
now reproach myself for having left you all for so long, and am
dying to be again at Connaught Place.

Winston's extravagance and constant requests for more money were proving very irksome to his mother, and even to the devoted Mrs Everest. In a series of letters in the autumn of 1891 she came as close as ever she did to scolding him for the amazing rate at which he got through money. She explained that working-class families of six or seven got by on less money than he spent in a week. Inevitably he was again compared unfavourably with Jack, who managed his money more successfully.

Jack took up photography towards the end of 1891, an interest that stayed with him all his life. From the moment the boys went back to school they were calculating how long it would be before they could get back to their adored mother, to 'Woom', to their ponies and farmyard menagerie. It is hard to equate all this, and the stream of demanding letters from both, with the image in *My Early Life* of children neglected by selfish or indifferent parents. Jennie did seem to be losing patience with Winston's endless extravagance however, and also resented him sending 'orders' to her cook to send him cooked chicken and duck without asking his mother first.

A crisis at Harrow arose as Winston absolutely refused to go and stay with a French family over Christmas. Welldon got very angry and said, "very well, then you must give up the Army". Jennie, in a letter of 8th December, was unforgiving:

> My dear boy, I feel for you in every way & can quite
> understand your anxiety & desire to be at home for Xmas, but
> quite apart from other considerations, the tone of your letter is
> not calculated to make one over lenient. When one wants
> something in this world, it is not by delivering ultimatums that
> one is likely to get it. You are old enough not to play the fool,
> & for the sake of a few days pleasure, give up the chance of
> getting through your exam: a thing which may affect your
> whole life. You know how anxious Papa is that you should go
> to Sandhurst this summer – I have received a letter from him
> this morning, dated 7th Nov in which he says 'Please tell Mr
> Welldon that I gladly agree to any arrangement which he may
> be kind enough to make for Winston's studies during the Xmas
> holidays'. He also says 'I have such a nice letter from Winston
> please thank him for it & give him my best love'.

A week later, she was even more displeased:

> I have only read one page of your letter and I send it back to
> you – as its style does not please me. I confess after our
> conversation the other day I did not expect you to go back on
> your word, & try & make everything as disagreeable for
> yourself & everyone else as possible.

It almost goes without saying that Jack never behaved in this manner
when his turn came to go overseas for language tuition. Winston's
egotistical behaviour, when he should have been concentrating every
effort to succeed in the Army Class, was truly reprehensible.

Financial constraints saw Banstead Manor given up in October,
and, to Jennie's great chagrin, she had to let 2 Connaught Place for
the winter and move in with her mother-in-law, at 50 Grosvenor
Square. To Randolph she pines, "I know beggars can't be choosers
but I feel very old for this sort of thing … . I shall be glad to get you
back … I feel rather low and lonely at times".

Winston was sent to France for Christmas, to improve his language skills. His letters home seethe with resentment, about the
"queer food", the cold, the lack of good company. "I count the
hours". And he was out of England when his father finally returned
from South Africa, a richer man than when he left.

CHAPTER 8

One 'Handful'; One Model Child
1892–1893

Jack was able to accompany his mother to meet Randolph when he landed at Southampton on 8th January 1892, bringing with him the antelope's head for Winston. In an excited letter to Winston, Jack described how the press were there in great numbers to see him back in England. *The Globe* reported that Lady Randolph "nimbly ran across the dock" to greet him. He seemed in vigorous good health, but had grown a beard that did not find favour with his nearest and dearest. Jack described it as "horrid", and drew a picture of his papa with it in his letter to Winston. Jennie called it "a terror" and thought she might have to bribe him to shave it off.

Randolph's gold shares showed a steady growth over the next three years and would eventually be valued at £70,000. He was able to settle some of the more pressing loan repayments and bills. These funds greatly boosted his estate, and enhanced the terms of his will (made in 1883), whereby a Trust Fund was set up to maintain Jennie and his sons after his death. The provisions were extended to make allowances, after the boys were married, for their children. This, from a man whom we are asked to believe cared little or nothing for his own children. Jennie would administer the proceeds of the Trust Fund. As our research developed we made the astonishing discovery that she kept these provisions completely secret from her sons, leaving them to think their father had not made proper provision for them, and that they were entirely dependent on her for support.[1]

On learning that his parents intended to take a holiday in Paris together, Winston asked if he could extend his stay in France by a week to join them. Randolph made it quite clear from the outset that he was expecting much better things from his elder son. He wrote on 15th January, reminding Winston of his own disappointment at not doing better at Oxford:

Dearest Winston,

I was very glad to get your letter this morning. I think I will
not try and get you an extra week because really every moment
is of value to you now before you go up for your examination
in June. The loss of a week now may mean your not passing,
which I am sure you will admit would be very discreditable &
disadvantageous. After you have got into the army you will
have many weeks for amusement and idleness should your
inclinations go in that direction, but now I do pray you my
dear boy you make the most of every hour of your time so as
to render your passing a certainty.

I remember when I was going up at Oxford for "final
schools" I took something of an extra week & consequently
altogether neglected what was called "special subjects". The
result was that I just missed the First Class degree and only
took a Second, & I have often thought since what a fool I was
to lose the chance of a First for a few hours or days
amusement. If you return Monday as I understand you will, we
shall have a few days together before you return to Harrow,
and after that the Easter holidays will soon be upon us, tho I
must say I hope you will work like a little dray horse right up
to the summer examination, only about four months off.

As it happened, the sudden death of the Duke of Clarence from
influenza put all Society into mourning and the Paris trip was postponed. In a letter to his mother, Randolph made some observations
about the behaviour of the Prince of Wales that reflects upon his own
moral standards, and is clearly not noticed by the many writers who
casually assume he was an unfaithful husband. "How very sad is this
death of the poor Duke of Clarence. I hear they are heart broken at
Sandringham. Perhaps this grief now may bring them together more
[the Prince and Princess of Wales] and put a stop to importunate
affairs."[2] Following his return from South Africa, Randolph suffered
mood swings and Jennie found him difficult to live with. There were
many arguments and their domestic situation had all but broken
down. Later in 1892, another letter from Randolph to his friend,
'Natty' Rothschild, reveals something of their relationship: "I suppose you know she is living with Freddy Wolverton". We know that

he did not mean that Jennie had literally moved out of the marital home, but it is a frank acknowledgement, for the first time, that she sought sexual gratification elsewhere. Frederick, Lord Wolverton was a handsome young aristocrat who seems to have seized his chance during a cooling off between Jennie and the wayward Kinsky. It seems likely that Wolverton was encouraged in this by the Prince of Wales, who was anxious to see Jennie divided from Kinsky, leaving her free for his own attentions. Clearly Wolverton had no long-term interest in Jennie, as he was already engaged, and married another in January 1895.

Winston returned to school and did apply himself to his work, getting a Remove, but not the 'Double Remove' he had hoped for. He also took up fencing and proved very good at it, soon rising to be school champion. He won a fine cup, and was by far and away the winner, "Absolutely untouched in the finals". Randolph was delighted that Winston had done so well, and wrote on 25th March, "Dearest Winston, I congratulate you on your success. I only hope fencing will not too much divert your attention from the army class. I enclose you £2 with which you will be able to make a present to y[ou]r fencing master. Jack came up the other day looking v[er]y well & fit…". Winston bought "a rather nice cloak" for his Instructor, and concluded his next letter with the usual request for more pocket money. Sadly, this brought a riposte from his father that must have come as a shock:

> I send you a P.O. £1, but you are really too extravagant. Do you mean to say you spent the £2 I sent you on the present to your fencing master. If you were a millionaire you could not be more extravagant … . I think you have got through about £10 [£500–700] this term. This cannot last, & if you are not more careful should you get into the army six months of it will see you in the Bankruptcy Court. Do think this over & moderate your ways & ideas.

A lengthy explanation about the expenses accruing at Harrow, especially in the line of extra food, amounting to a pound a week, would not have endeared Winston to his irate father.

When Jack returned to Elstree he stated with the utmost confidence that he would take the entrance exams for Harrow later that year. Even Mr Sanderson thought this attempt, a full year ahead of schedule, was a bit premature. Jack had his usual bout of winter illnesses, and chickenpox hit the school. This led to Jennie cancelling a visit to see him, which disappointed Jack greatly, but was probably the responsible thing to do. Randolph, perhaps putting more faith in Jack's future development than in Winston's, was keen for him to go up to Harrow as soon as possible and wrote to Dr Welldon accordingly. On 12th May, Welldon replied:

Dear Lord Randolph,
Mr Sanderson was no doubt right in saying, that your younger boy, if he enters the School in September, will be somewhat below the usual age at which boys enter. I understand that you wish to send him then, and I have kept a place for him. I shall therefore look for him at the examination in July. Of course I cannot offer an opinion on his fitness in point of character for public school life but of that you will judge.

Randolph resumed his seat in the House of Commons in February 1892, and his demeanour was remarked as silent and reserved. He was, nevertheless, still the centre of attention whenever he appeared. He had promised his South Paddington constituency that he would stand again as their candidate but many larger party associations made it clear that they would guarantee his election in any number of places. He had been thinking deeply about the social changes in Britain. He recognised the growing power of organised labour, and saw that they were ill served by the Liberals. A delegation of coal miners had once aired their grievances to both Prime Minister Gladstone and Randolph, and they openly declared they got far more satisfaction from the Conservative lord than the Liberal premier. "Labour ... has against it the prejudices of property, the resources of capital, and all the numerous forces – social, professional, and journalist – which those prejudices and resources can influence". It was the duty of the 'Constitutional Party' to tie the legitimate claims of the workers to reform within the constitution. If the existing parties did not address the issues concerning the working-class, then that class would form its own political organisation and seek representation in the House of Commons in its own interest. Randolph still aspired to make the Tory Party (an historic name he was proud of) to be the people's party, a "party of broad ideas and of a truly liberal policy". Later in 1892, he would miss three important race meetings in order to vote in favour of the mineworkers in the Eight Hours Bill. "I do not think I would do this for the Monarchy, the Church, the House of Lords or the Union".

Winston confidently predicted he would pass the Sandhurst entrance examination in June. He added the rider, "If I don't it will not be any fault of mine". Whose fault, we might ask, would it be? A string of carefree weekends, often spent visiting London, led to letters now suggesting that if he didn't get through in June, he certainly would in November. It sounds as if he was expecting to fail, because he had not worked hard enough, and was trying to prepare his parents for the eventuality. He kept up his 'reasonable' requests for cash from his father, while receiving sums regularly from his mother, his grandmother, Mrs Everest and his aunt, Lady Wilton.

A General Election was called for July 1892. Randolph did not campaign much in South Paddington, having reached an unofficial agreement with the Liberals that, if they left him alone there, he would not address Conservative rallies elsewhere in the country. He had no strong inclination to officially assist a party that had boycotted and slandered him for the best part of five years. In his election address he made the point forcefully of his desire "to meet with all legitimate sympathy and good-will the newly-formed but very articulate and well-defined demands of the labouring classes". He was returned unopposed while the Tories crashed to defeat. Gladstone formed yet another Liberal administration, and promptly recessed for the summer.

It would not be long before the Conservatives would turn again to Randolph, still hugely popular with the rank-and-file members in the country, to lead a renewal of their fortunes. It was tragic that this coincided with the onset of the disease, a tumour on the brain, which would gradually incapacitate him and lead to his early death.

The results of the Sandhurst entrance examinations were a disappointment. Out of 693 candidates, Winston came 390th, a full 300 places below those who passed. He was short by 1,500 marks overall. He did well in English History, French and English Composition.

The saving of him, where his father was concerned, was an encouraging note from his Army Class tutor, Mr Moriarty, saying that his marks and place were "very creditable for your first try", and that if he worked sensibly and tried to keep up in the next term, he should pass at the next sitting. Welldon was deeply upset and said he would speak to Winston when he returned to school. It was no good working in "fits & starts but with regular persistent industry". His confidence that Winston could achieve better things was all that prevented him telling Lord Randolph to take him out of Harrow forthwith and send him to a 'crammer'.

Randolph wrote to his mother with the bad news. But "two very kind and encouraging letters" from his tutors gave him hope that Winston would do better in November. "If he fails again I shall think about putting him in business. I could get him something very good either through Natty [Rothschild] or Horace [Farquharson] or [Sir Ernest] Cassel". This was a dire threat indeed, in an age when the sons of aristocrats could still afford to look down on those who toiled in banking or stock-broking. It would have been a last resort after failing in anything more honourable, but it is highly unlikely that Randolph would have made good his threat. It would never have been considered for a moment where Jack was concerned.

Randolph was gradually beginning to suffer the onset of his final illness. He was, as always, 'living on his nerves'. Winston had been trying out his new shotgun, and fired at a rabbit in the garden, close to where his father was resting. Randolph flew into a tremendous fit of rage, entirely in keeping with a sufferer of a bipolar disorder, which demonstrably distressed Winston. Randolph relented and spoke reassuringly to his son. Winston later remembered the conversation as one of the longest and most pleasant he ever had with his revered father. They spoke of school life, of going into the army, and "the grown-up life which lay beyond". The strain of the continual abuse Randolph took in his political life was evident. "Do remember things do not always go right with me. My every action is misjudged and every word distorted ... . So make some allowances".

It almost goes without saying that Jack passed his entrance exams into Harrow at his first attempt. In September 1892, at twelve and a half years old, he had entered the school a year ahead of normal, and was easily the youngest boy there. To his great delight, Dr Welldon agreed that Winston and Jack could share a room. Jack's first letter to Jennie reported that Dr Welldon had said to him "... if I worked like Winny did his first three years here, it would turn his hairs white". That remark must have come from the heart of this long-suffering Headmaster. By some administrative error, Jack arrived too late to take an arithmetic test. Undismayed, Jack was able to tell his father in his first letter that he sat, and passed, the exam the next day. He was given the same tutor as Winston, and all his letters said how kind and helpful his brother was to him. Jack took to the school life like a duck to water, and was soon forging ahead with his studies. He was rewarded with the gift of a fine gold watch by his proud father, who wrote on 25th September:

> Dear Jack
> I was very pleased to get your nice letter and to learn that you had settled down comfortably in your new quarters. You will get the watch in a few days. I hope you will take great care of it as it is a valuable one. You must wind it carefully and slowly, never in a hurry and never hard. Don't forget always to wind it up every night. I was delighted to hear you got through the Arithmetic paper. That Newmarket Schoolmaster was rather useful I expect ... . Your mother writes that it is very pleasant up in Scotland and that she feels better for the change.
>   With my best love to Winston.
>   Your affectionate father[3]

This early letter to Jack at Harrow is preserved with Randolph's signature cut out. The boys always made capital of their famous father's 'valuable' signature. While Jack began in a class of thirty-two boys, all a year older than him, he was soon placed twentieth in the form, and was coming top in 'Essay'. Jennie wrote from Scotland to Winston, hoping he was working hard, assuring him that she felt much better, and thanking him for looking after Jack, and for making their room so nice for them both.

    Randolph did not neglect the boys while he was fishing in Scotland. He sent them generous hampers, and responded readily to their constant demands for money. Even the careful Jack was finding Harrow very much more expensive than Elstree, and his letters became every bit as money-orientated as Winston's. Typically, Jack immediately began an accounts book, and kept an accurate record of income and expenditure. It was a great boon to be able to share a room with his older brother, and he was spared many of the rigours of the 'fagging' system that made new boys perform menial services for the seniors. Before long, however, the studious Jack saw the drawbacks. One letter suggested that Winston could be a noisy and disruptive companion. Telling his mother that Winston was going off for a medical examination, Jack concluded: "so I shall expect a quiet day. (I am longing for it); I do not get much peace when he is here". While Jack continued to adore his elder brother, he was developing a sufficient sense of his own self worth to see some failings in Winston's behaviour.

On her return from Scotland, where she had felt much better, Jennie was suddenly in a great deal of pain and, for a while, her doctors were very concerned for her. One modern writer has implied that she was suffering from a sexually transmitted disease, supposedly acquired during her frequent trips to France.[4] This is completely unnecessary, as Dr Roose had called in the gynaecological specialist, Dr Thomas Keith, who has left perfectly clear reports on Jennie's condition. He diagnosed an "irregular tender swelling about the size of a hen's egg" behind the uterus – "an enlarged ovary and tube or boil or both". It was very painful and too dangerous to operate upon. She was in such a bad way that Randolph wrote to the boys to warn them of just how ill she was. After two weeks of extreme discomfort, she did respond to complete rest and medication.

Randolph hoped that Winston would work hard to please his poor mother. Winston's letters back were not encouraging. He began to doubt his chances of getting through the next exam, and complained of headaches and eyestrain. He was working himself up into a state of nervous excitement as the exams drew near.

In a letter to FitzGibbon, Randolph said he was living quietly, "mainly occupied in reading books of one kind and another". He dismissed the fanciful idea of some Tories that the Liberals would soon be turned out of office. "At any rate, beyond opposing their Home Rule Bill, I shall do nothing to bother them, as I greatly prefer them to their predecessors". The break with official Conservatism could hardly have been greater.

At a time when his wife was ill, and he felt less well day by day, another terrible blow was the sudden death of his brother, Blandford, at the age of 48, from a heart-attack. This further example of the fragility of the male line in his family must have haunted Randolph's thoughts on his own mortality. Blandford's son, Charles, (Sunny), became the 9th Duke of Marlborough. It was no comfort to know that, for the time being, Randolph was next in line to the title.

Just as Jennie was recovering, the doctors advised Randolph to go off to the South of France for the sake of his health. Before he left he had a nice letter from Winston, giving the news that Jack had set a new record at Harrow, for having received not one single line of punishment for the whole of his first term. (Neither was he ever punished for any misdemeanour during his whole time at either Elstree or Harrow). Randolph received an interesting letter, dated 28th November, from Dr Welldon, praising Winston's work but warning that it might have come a bit too late:

> His work this term has been excellent. He understands now the need of taking trouble, and the way to take it, and, whatever happens to him, I shall consider that in the last twelve months he has learnt a lesson of life-long value.
>
> The two disadvantages under which he lies are that he was not well grounded, when he came here; hence he is still not safe against bad mistakes; and that he partially wasted the beginning of his public schooldays.
>
> Still, when this is said, I am of the opinion that he is now well up to the level of passing into Sandhurst according to the standard which has been usual in past years. We are aware however that the level tends to rise and that, owing to the change which is being made in the age of admission, it is likely to be very high this time. At the next examination it will be normal again.
>
> On the whole so far as I can judge from my own observation and the reports of his master, I should say he has a very fair chance of passing now and is certain to pass in the summer if not now.

Welldon was inferring that, however much Winston improved there, Brighton School was not a recognised preparatory school for aristo-

cratic boys, and had done little to help him get the best out of the
great public schools. It would be encouraging to think that the need
to help Jack at school, who was settling in and doing so well, might
have regulated Winston's errant behaviour to some degree.

A holiday at Monte Carlo did Randolph some good, but it was
over that winter of 1892–3 that he began to show the physical signs
of the tumour developing in his brain. He suffered from vertigo, palpitations, and numbness of the hands, all of which would get steadily
worse. Eventually his wonderful memory and his sense of hearing
would both be affected. We gain an insight into Randolph's true feelings for his sons in a quite independent letter from Lady Wilton, who
saw him in Monte Carlo, to Winston. Randolph had obviously been
discussing the boys and their futures with her:

> Your Father is well & resting quietly here – I think your
> Uncle's death was a great shock to him. I am sure he will do
> everything for your future career & happiness. – & he is *so*
> kind & good…My love to Jack when you write to him.
>
> Dear Winston, I enclose the small sum of £2 for your *tiny*
> expenses.

During the winter holiday, while Randolph was staying in Dublin
with Gerald Fitzgibbon, Jennie, the boys, and the Dowager Duchess
were offered Canford Manor, the house of Lord and Lady
Wimborne, near Bournemouth, for the month of January 1893. Lady
Wimborne was Randolph's sister, Cornelia. Playing a boisterous war
game in the grounds, Winston found himself trapped on a bridge by
his brother at one end and a cousin at the other. It was not in his
nature to surrender, to Jack or anyone else, so he climbed over the
bridge and leapt for the nearest pine tree. He missed and fell thirty
feet. Jack rushed to his mother, crying, "He jumped over the bridge
and he won't speak to us". It was three days before Winston recovered consciousness. Randolph rushed back from Dublin, and
collected one of the finest surgeons in London, as he sped towards
Bournemouth. Besides concussion, Winston suffered a ruptured
kidney and injury to his right shoulder. It is thought the fall had very
long term consequences for his overall health. The doctors ordered a
long rest from hard study or vigorous exercise.

Later in January, Winston learned that, despite a general improvement in his marks across the board, he had again failed the entrance exam for Sandhurst. He had been 203rd out of 664 candidates, but the level of the pass marks had been raised and this added to his difficulties. Winston was "awfully depressed" but Welldon was very encouraging. If he kept up his work, and there were no further changes in the pass requirements, he should get through at the next attempt. He sounded out the best of all the 'crammers', Captain James, ex-Royal Engineers, whose famous school in London, known as 'Jimmy's' had a wonderful record for divining the questions before an exam and preparing his pupils to pass successfully.

The extra tuition would be very costly but Randolph would spare no expense or effort to see Winston into the army. Captain James agreed to take on Winston, and Randolph visited him to discuss the requirements, and wrote to the Military Secretary at the War Office to see if Winston was eligible for a commission in the Household Cavalry.

Jack returned to Harrow alone, and got on with his work. He was invited to join the Rifle Corps but very sensibly said he would wait and see if he could use Winston's uniform, as he knew it to "cost such a lot". What he did have to cope with was an enormous demand relating to unpaid bills left by Winston. He wrote forcefully to his brother detailing all the expenditures he made on his behalf, often settling for items in cash, so that the school authorities did not find out about various breakages that Winston was liable for. Jack was clearly maturing quickly. An enforced absence from Winston seems to have coincided with some his best work at school.

While Winston convalesced at Brighton, he did make some effort to continue with his studies, having to re-do his history notes as the Sandhurst syllabus had altered. Jack, already low with the usual winter ailments, was sent away from Harrow when scarlet fever struck the school. Mrs Everest took him to Margate, where the sea winds 'blew away' his coughs and colds. It was a dreary place in winter, and neither of them enjoyed it much. Jack tried to buy one of the new type writers in the shops, so he could write to his adored brother in the latest style. Mrs Everest reported that "such articles are quite unknown in this outlandish place". On his return to

Harrow, Jack roomed with two new boys. One of the masters wrote to Winston, saying how popular Jack was at the school. "Everyone likes him, as indeed no one could fail to do".

At the end of February 1893, Winston went to Captain James to begin 'cramming' for the next Sandhurst entrance exam. By 7th March, James found it necessary to write to Lord Randolph:

> I have issued orders for your son to be kept at work and that in
> future he is to do the full hours. I had to speak to him the other
> day about his casual manner. I think that he means well but he
> is distinctly inclined to be inattentive and to think too much of
> his abilities. These are certainly good and if he does as he
> ought he should pass very well in the summer, but he has been
> rather too much inclined up to the present to teach his
> instructors instead of endeavouring to learn from them, and
> this is not the frame of mind conducive to success. I may give
> as an instance that he suggested to me that his knowledge of
> history was such that he did not want any more teaching in it!
> I think you will agree with me that this is problematical. I have
> no doubt that between the two of us we can manage him well
> enough and I am glad to have received your letter of today. ...
>   The boy has very many good points in him but what he
> wants is very firm handling.

Winston, nearly eighteen and quite good-looking, could be very charming. At Easter, Blandford's widow, the Duchess Lily, wrote to Randolph: "I am glad to have Winston with me for I have grown really fond of the boy. He has lots of good in him and only needs sometimes to be corrected, which he always takes so smartly and well." Lady Warwick made an acute observation on how Jennie handled both her sons:

> In those days, people could not see any definite principle
> behind Jennie Churchill's upbringing of her sons, ... They did
> not realize that she was developing in them qualities, which, in
> the ordinary course, take years to show themselves. She always
> found time to encourage her boys to express themselves I
> still chuckle when I remember how, as a schoolboy, he

[Winston] would comment to his face upon the view of such a politician as Lord Hartington.[5]

These political distractions did not impress Captain James, who wrote again on 29th April, to Lord Randolph:

I am sure you will feel that I am impelled by kind motives in writing to you about your son. I have no definite complaint to make about him but I do not think that his work is going on very satisfactorily. All the tutors complain that while he has good abilities he does not apply himself with sufficient earnestness to his reading. He can and will succeed if he will but give up everything to the examination before him but I doubt his passing if he does not do this. Of course I feel that at a time like the present it is difficult for him not to take an interest in current political topics, but if this be done to an extent which takes his mind away from his studies, the result is bad for the latter. I have spoken to him on the question and I hope you will give him a little paternal advice and point out, what I have done, the absolute necessity of single-minded devotion to the immediate object before him, and the extreme desirability of thoroughness and detail[ed] attention to all he attempts.

Winston would later complain that his father would not discuss politics with him, however much Winston desired it. We can see that Randolph would have considered this yet another distraction to this wayward boy. He had a finite task to perform, an examination to pass, and he seemed incapable of applying himself to it. If later authors think that Randolph was unduly harsh to Winston at this stage in his life, we can see why the father, gripped by his final illness, would get increasingly disappointed and exasperated at his son's attitude to life.

When the new session of Parliament convened in January 1893, Randolph was warmly welcomed by the Conservative leaders and invited to sit on the Opposition front bench. The new leader, Arthur Balfour, wrote in the friendliest terms to him. At a Carlton Club meeting to discuss resistance to a new Home Rule Bill, Randolph kept quietly in the background until a great clamour went up for him to come forward. He declared his willingness to serve to the best of his ability under his old friend, Balfour. He attended private meetings of the Unionist leaders held at Devonshire House, and participated in the policy-making process of the Opposition. He began a demanding series of public speeches all around the country, fiercely denouncing Home Rule. He was as popular as ever. Could a sense of his own mortality have induced this return to the political life that he had apparently abandoned so gladly? Finally the Bill came to Parliament for its First Reading. There was great excitement in the House as Randolph rose to make his first major speech for some years, on a subject of which he was the master. It was a shock to his many friends and colleagues. He was pale, his eyes protuberant, his hair much receded, his beard wild, his hands trembling. Gone was that wonderful memory. He had to read from eighteen pages of notes. But the speech itself was cogent, closely and carefully reasoned, and full of 'Randolphian' witticisms. It was the best of the whole debate. Later the Party asked him to close the debate on the Welsh Church Suspensory Bill. He was in marvellous form. All his old vigour was restored, and he ended by putting aside his notes and excoriating Gladstone in a fierce and sparkling attack that recalled the great days of the Eighties. If his physical health was in decline, there was nothing wrong with his great mind, yet.

In April he wrote to FitzGibbon, "I have not been very well lately, and the last three days have had a dreadful cough, which would quite have incapacitated me from speaking. I hope now it is yielding to treatment ... ." In May and June he made ten major speeches in ten cities. Towards the end of the session, on 29th July, there was extraordinary disturbance in the House, where the Opposition refused to follow its leaders into the 'No' lobby until some arcane item of procedure was dealt with. For a man who would soon be denounced as 'raving mad', Randolph wrote to the Speaker with the most calm and rational explanation of how a bit of 'routine' House of Commons name-calling had got ridiculously out of hand. He ended the session at the height of his renewed power in the party, a major spokesman, a force for progress, and candidate for a great safe seat.

Randolph must have found the time to talk to Winston about his work, for Captain James was able to report on 19th June:

Without saying that your son is a certainty I think he ought to pass this time. He is working well and I think doing his best to get on but, as you know, he is at times inclined to take the bit in his teeth and go his own course.

I believe, however, I have convinced him that he has got to do what you wish him to do, and I have lately had no cause to complain of him.

It would not do to let him know what I think of his chance of success as with his peculiar disposition this might lead him to slacken off again. ...

Jennie had been to Harrow to see Jack and heard the highest praise of him from Dr Welldon. On 5th June a proud father wrote to Jack, "Thanks for your charming letter. I got a capital report of you today. I will come down Saturday [crossed out] Friday if Mr. Welldon likes I will stay for evening service as I should much like to hear his evening sermon." Jack received a new clock and a new camera as rewards for his good work. He soon wrote to his mother about another visit from his father:

I took Papa for a walk on Sunday, and we had some tea he went to chapel and I think that he liked Welldon's sermon. I went to see him off at the station. He told Welldon that Winney had been working very hard and he thought he was going to get through. I suppose the examination has begun.
... I should like so much to go to Switzerland for the holiday, has Papa found a tutor?

Randolph and Jennie took their summer holiday together at the German health spas around Gastein. Following strict doctor's orders, they led a quiet and healthy life together, taking the waters, going for long walks and longer drives in the fresh mountain air. Jennie was quite keen to share this rigorous life style in order to lose a little weight. Prince Bismarck called upon them and enjoyed a conversation, in English, about the health resorts, some current foreign news, and how a great country like Britain could be governed by someone as 'unmanageable' as Mr Gladstone. Jennie wrote a cheerful letter to Jack, on 9th August 1893:

Dearest Jack

I hope you are still continuing to enjoy yourself and are
keeping well – I was very glad to get your letter the other day –
what a tiresome journey you must have had – Mind you write
often and tell me all you do and see – I enjoy you being in
Switzerland I have never been there – I hope you do not
overtire yourself? The weather is lovely here … – You know I
love the sun and can never find it too warm – We met and
dined with the "Great Bismark" last night – It was very
interesting and I got on very well with him – He smoked a pipe
a yard long! Papa is much better I think the place suits him.
Give my best love to Winny.

    Your loving Mother JSC.

Before he left for Germany Randolph had gone to a good deal of
trouble to organise a six-week European holiday for his sons. He
engaged the services of a young Eton master, Mr Little, to travel with
Winston and Jack. Together they devised an interesting itinerary,
involving a good deal of walking in Switzerland, with plenty of
opportunity for them both to improve their language skills. Mr Little
injured his leg quite early on in the trip, and this left the boys to
themselves for part of the time. There occurred a most extraordinary
incident, about which Winston seems to have remained 'in denial'
ever after. In *My Early Life* he related that he went boating on a lake
with 'another boy' in Switzerland. They got out of the boat for a
swim and subsequently got into difficulty when the boat began to
drift away from them. As the younger boy desperately struggled to
stay afloat, Winston struck out for the boat, recovered it and
returned to save the 'other boy's' life. Far from his taking any credit
for this action, it remained a complete secret until published in 1930.
It was only in conversation with Peregrine Churchill that we learnt
that the other boy was Peregrine's father, Winston's brother, Jack.
Why was Winston not able to say as much in 1930? His own father
and mother were long dead and could not, as they certainly would
have done in 1893, bring him to book for this dangerous escapade.
Was he ashamed of having put his brother at risk, or was it more
important to make the story only about himself and his brave deed?
Jack never made any reference to the incident, apart from telling his

son about it many years later. He would never say anything that reflected badly on his adored elder brother.

Winston had good cause to fear the wrath of his parents at that particular time. He had scraped into Sandhurst at his third attempt, and had made the error of writing a very self-congratulatory letter to his father. Randolph's violent reaction to this letter is often held against him as evidence either of incipient insanity, or 'proof' that he held no great affection for his son. What we have is the bitter disappointment of an ailing man, who felt let down by his elder son's poor record, and who faced ever greater expense to see him into an inferior arm of the services. He had failed to qualify for the infantry, and was consigned to the less-demanding cavalry. This letter of 5th August from Randolph to his mother explains all:

> I cannot think highly of Winston's [result]. He missed the last place in the infantry by about 18 marks which shows great slovenliness of work in the actual examination. He only made about 200 marks more than last time, I think not so many even as 200. He has gone & got himself into the cavalry who are always 2nd rate performers in the examination and which will cost me £200 a year more than the infantry would have cost. I have told you often & you never would believe me that he has little [claim] to cleverness, to knowledge or any capacity for settled work. He has great talent for show off exaggeration & make believe. In all his three examinations he has made to me statements of his performance which have never been borne out by results. Nothing has been spared on him; the best coaches, every kind of amusement & kindness especially from you & more than any boy of his position is entitled to. The whole result of this has been ... to prove his total worthlessness as a scholar or a conscientious worker. He need not expect much from me. He will go up to Sandhurst when for the first time in his life he will be kept in order & we shall see whether he can stand military discipline. If he can he may rub along respectably. I shall try & get Brabazon who has a regiment of Hussars to take him & after 2 or 3 years shall exchange him with the infantry. Now this is all truth & it is better to look facts in the face. When he is at Sandhurst I wont have any

running backwards & forwards to London. He shall be kept to his work so that he may acquire the elementary principles of a military education.

I will not conceal from you it is a great disappointment to me. I never had much confidence, James's 2 or 3 revelations as to his manner of working & his attitude to the tutors stopped all confidence. But I did hope seeing the chances he had he would show a considerable improvement on his last examination but one. There was much less competition in his last and the result was much worse & much more discreditable in a relative sense for Winston. Now dearest Mama goodbye; the above is only meant for you alone & need not be communicated to any of the family. After all he has got into the army & that is a result which none of his cousins have been able to do, but still that is a very wretched & pitiable consolation.

Randolph had approached the Duke of Cambridge himself, one time Commander in Chief of the British Army, to secure a commission for Winston in the elite 60th Rifles, of which the Duke was Colonel in Chief. All this had turned to dust. His letter to Winston a few days later was a stiff rebuke, fully expressing the exasperation with this young man that had been building up for years:

My dear Winston,
I am rather surprised at your tone of exultation over you inclusion in the Sandhurst list. There are two ways of winning an examination, one creditable the other the reverse. You have unfortunately chose the latter method, and appear to be much pleased with your success.

The first extremely discreditable feature of your performance was missing the infantry, for in that failure is demonstrated beyond refutation your slovenly happy-go-lucky harum scarum style of work for which you have always been distinguished at your different schools. Never have I received a really good report of your conduct in your work from any master or tutor you had from time to time to do with. Always behind-hand, never advancing in your class, incessant complaints of total want of application, and this character which was constant in your reports has shown the natural results clearly in your last army examination.

With all the advantage you had, with all the abilities which you foolishly think yourself to possess & which some of your relations claim for you, with all the efforts that have been made to make your life easy & agreeable & your work neither oppressive or distasteful, this is the grand result that you come up among the 2nd and 3rd rate class who are only good for commissions in a cavalry regiment.

The second discreditable fact in the result of your examination is that you have not perceptibly increased as far as my memory serves me the marks you made in the [previous] examination, & perhaps even you have decreased them, in spite of there being less competition in the last than in the former examination. You frequently told me you were sure to obtain 7000 marks. Alas! your estimate of your capacity was, measured arithmetically, some seven hundred marks deficient. You say in your letter there were many candidates who succeeded whom you knew; I must remind you that you had very few below you some seven or eight. You may find some consolation in the fact that you have failed to get into the '60th Rifles' one of the finest regiments in the army. There is also another satisfaction for you that by accomplishing the prodigious effort of getting into the Cavalry, you imposed on me an extra charge of some £200 a year. Not that I shall allow you to remain in the Cavalry. As soon as possible I shall arrange your exchange into the infantry regiment of the line.

Now it is a good thing to put this business very plainly before you. Do not think I am going to take the trouble of writing to you long letters after every folly & failure you commit & undergo. I shall not write again on these matters & you need not trouble to write any answer to this part of my letter, because I no longer attach the slightest weight to anything you may say about your own acquirements & exploits. Make this position indelibly impressed on your mind, that if your conduct and action at Sandhurst is similar to what it has been in the other establishments in which it has sought vainly to impart to you some education. Then my responsibility for you is over.

I shall leave you to depend on yourself giving you merely such assistance as may be necessary to permit of a respectable life. Because I am certain that if you cannot prevent yourself from leading the idle useless unprofitable life you have had during your schooldays & later months, you will become a mere social wastrel, one of the hundreds of the public school failures, and you will degenerate into a shabby, unhappy & futile existence. If that is so you will have to bear all the blame for such misfortune yourself. Your own conscience will enable you to recall and enumerate all the efforts that have been made to give you the best of chances which you were entitled to by your position & how you have practically neglected them all.

I hope you will be the better for your trip. Your mother sends her love.

Your affectionate father
Randolph S.C.

Winston might well reply that he was very sorry indeed that his father was displeased with him. He promised he would improve in both work and conduct at Sandhurst, and that his low place at passing in would be much improved upon by the time he was ready to 'pass out'. Randolph had addressed Winston man to man for the first time and it had the desired effect. At Sandhurst, Winston would do well.

CHAPTER 9

Settling the Boys' Future
1893–1894

Jennie went to stay in Paris for three weeks with her mother. On his return from holiday in Germany in late September 1893, Randolph resumed a punishing schedule of political meetings throughout October and November. While the party leadership had been thinking of restoring Randolph to the front bench, and offering him high ministerial office, the truth is that he was so ill that his public performances were a tragic shadow of his former greatness.

Winston had returned to London, leaving Jack and Mr Little to complete their holiday. He was to report to Sandhurst on 1st September 1893, having found a letter from the Military Secretary awaiting him, explaining that a number of cadets had failed to take up their places, and that Winston had been promoted to the Infantry Class. While secretly yearning to join the cavalry, Winston duly wrote to his father that he might yet be able to take his commission in the 60th Rifles as Randolph had fondly hoped. He wrote a long and pleading, though carefully reasoned, letter spelling out the expenses to be incurred at Sandhurst, asking for a quarterly allowance, and promising to account for all his spending. He had learnt at least one important lesson in life.

Randolph was pleased to see the mature tone of the letters from Sandhurst, with their promises of application to the principles of the 'trade' Winston had committed himself to. The boy-become-man spoke of the lack of comfort and the strict discipline, but expressed interest in the drill and military education he was learning, and expected to improve mentally, morally and physically. Randolph responded warmly and made a £10 per month allowance, which Winston professed to be ample. He kept his father fully informed of his daily timetable, and the subjects he was studying. However, Winston's persistent requests for parental written consent to be allowed complete freedom of movement at weekends led to

Randolph expressing extreme annoyance at this suggestion that Winston would go off to London at every opportunity, instead of applying himself to that extra study that ensured success. Jennie warned Winston that his father was not pleased. Winston complained that other cadets had unrestricted leave and that he was being treated as a boy. The Dowager Duchess agreed with Randolph's obstinate refusal. Winston had to remember that he was not the son of a rich man and that he was at Sandhurst not for amusement but to distinguish himself.

Mr Little completed the holiday in Switzerland with Jack after Winston had left. In a trend we have noted before, Jack's French improved after Winston's departure. The latter was always so voluble, that Jack seldom found the chance to speak. He found the trip rather tiring and was a bit remiss in his letters home. His father wrote to him on 26th September:

> Many thanks for your letter which I received two days ago. I think your mother is a little hurt that you do not write more often to her. You ought to write regularly to her for she is very good about writing to you … . I will send you some money when I get to London for your school expenses, subscriptions etc. I have a lot of speeches to make in different parts of the country during the next two months and shall be very busy. I daresay you have had a good time in London with your Aunt Leonie. Your mother sends you her love; she will not be home till some 3 weeks or so after me … Remember me to Mr Welldon. I will try to run down to see you at Harrow some day.
>   Ever your affectionate father

Jack was back at Harrow without Winston to share a room with. His letters home expressed some loneliness and were full of the usual references to being "absolutely broke" and "I have not had any money since last Tuesday week". He was able to make visits to Winston at Sandhurst and was hugely impressed. Winston was able to return the visits to Harrow, and passed on the message that Dr Welldon was anxious to see Lord Randolph to discuss Jack's future.

It is pleasant to record that Randolph and his eldest son were getting on very well, as Winston settled into his work at Sandhurst. Randolph wrote to his mother, the Dowager Duchess, on 23rd October 1893:

> I took Winston to Tring on Saturday. He had to leave at 4.30 afternoon to get back to Sandhurst. He has much smartened up. He holds himself quite upright and he has got steadier. The people at Tring took a great deal of notice of him but [he] was very quiet & nice-mannered. Sandhurst has done wonders for him. Up to now he has had no bad & [only] good conduct [reports] & I trust that it will continue to the end of the term. I paid his mess bill for him £6 so that his next allowance might not be '*empieté*' [encroached] upon. I think he deserved it … .

Winston later recalled that his father took him to the Empire Theatre, to the races, and to Lord Rothschild's house at Tring, to join a large gathering of the leaders and 'rising men' in the Conservative Party. He later regretted that this period of warmth and friendship was cut short by his father's sudden death, and never once seems to have considered that his own wayward behaviour might have contributed to any distance between them until then. Randolph was happy to pay for extra riding lessons from a Life Guards riding master for Winston. He also took the time to warn Winston, from his own personal experience, of the perils of excessive smoking. How very gratifying for everyone that Winston did splendidly in his end of term examinations, coming twentieth in his year, with a fine all round performance that tempered the slightly negative remark on his conduct, "Good but unpunctual".

Randolph and Jennie were saving money by living with the Dowager Duchess at her prestigious Grosvenor Square house, and renting out Connaught Place. There was an acute cash shortage in the Churchill household, and Randolph had to sell some £500 of gold shares, of which £105 had to be sent to Jennie who was visiting her mother in Paris. Jennie was always very uncomfortable at being beholden to her mother-in-law. This was aggravated by the Dowager Duchess taking advantage of Jennie's absence on a trip to Scotland to dismiss Mrs Everest from their service, as being no longer needed to raise the boys. Jennie was not able to protest while living under her roof. She did find new employment for Mrs Everest as housekeeper to a bishop in Essex, and sent her small sums of money from time to time. Winston wrote a long, impassioned letter to his mother about the "cruel and mean" way Everest had been treated. Mrs Everest kept up a lively correspondence with both Winston and Jack, reminding them of birthdays, and continually monitoring their progress.

That winter Randolph's general health was not good. He took another holiday at Monte Carlo, staying with Lady Wilton. He wrote to Jack on 30th January 1894:

> Dear Jack
> Many thanks for your letter of the 25th. I am glad to hear you have got your room in order, but I am afraid you must rely on Mama for funds till I return.... I have been kept to the house by a bad cough during the last few days but it is getting better and I poked my nose out with the garden today .... 'Mama' writes me that the Paddington Meeting went off very well and that Welldon let you stay [at home] the night for it.

Jennie had addressed a meeting of the Primrose League in Randolph's London constituency, as part of her continual support of her husband's political career, and her own interest in political affairs. Randolph also asked Jack if he had begun the Army Class at Harrow yet. This is the first indication that Jack had also decided on a career in the Army. Winston was able to report, after a visit to Harrow, that Jack had indeed started with the Army Class just before his fourteenth birthday.

Jack continued to perform very well at school, always in the top three or four boys in his year. Randolph had arranged to meet Jack at Harrow and introduce him to no less a figure than Lord Roberts, the Commander in Chief of the Army. Having been instrumental in advancing the career of Roberts when he was Secretary of State for India, Randolph was 'calling in a favour'. Regrettably Randolph had set a date when he was already booked for dinner, and was not able to attend. But Jack went ahead and had a long conversation with the great general, in Dr Welldon's drawing room after supper. We can only imagine how the conversation went, as Jack left no precise record of it, but an army career was now his dearest wish. On 10th

April Winston said, after a visit by Jack to Sandhurst, that he was looking forward to going there officially.

Jennie was spending a good deal of time in Paris, ostensibly to see her mother, but equally to avoid the company of her mother-in-law. She kept up a prodigious correspondence with both her boys.

Randolph had, at last, realised that all his hectic political work was too much for him. There had been an unfortunate incident in the House of Commons, on 13th March 1894, when he had lost control during a debate and screamed abuse at his own benches, along the lines of, "You damned fools! You're playing the devil with the Tory Party and making hell of the House of Commons". Apparently members fled from the chamber in fear of assault. It was later held to be the onset of 'syphillitic madness'. It was of course, the relentless decline brought on by a fatal brain tumour. He finally accepted the advice of his doctors and gave up all official involvement in politics for the time being.

The letters from Randolph to Jack show the care and attention he paid to setting him up with a career of his choice. On 28th April he wrote, "I went to see the Duke of Cambridge yesterday and he put down your name for the 60th Rifles. I gave your name as Jack Spencer Churchill for there was a celebrated Jack Churchill many years ago". Here is a father, proud of the superlative record of his younger son, associating him with England's greatest soldier and one of the 'Great Captains' of history, the 1st Duke of Marlborough. Randolph then arranged a second meeting with Lord Roberts on 20th May 1894. First Jack would travel to Roberts' house at Grove Park, Kingsbury (about four miles from Harrow) for luncheon. Randolph would join them there on his return from a few days fishing in Scotland. Then they would travel together to Harrow School, to hear one of Welldon's fine sermons.

Both Jack and Randolph wrote accounts of the meeting to Winston, regaling him with stories about the wild behaviour of an old army horse that Lord Roberts had in harness. Jack wrote on 23rd May:

> I drove over to Luncheon (only 3½ miles) and there was shown into a very Indianfied room, he [Roberts] was out or something so I looked around and saw a sort of Butterfly case on the wall.

I went for a nearer inspection and found them to be Medals!!!! of every discription [*sic*] under the sun. VC [Victoria Cross] was among them. Then we went to meet Papa. Lord R. got in the little cart and the poney [*sic*] stood on its head, and he sat motionless, then it ran into a wall and smashed all the back of the cart, he seemed rather to like it and at last I got in and we went off alright. Papa missed his train I think or something he did not arrive till the end of Luncheon. Then he came to Harrow … . I had supper with Welldon!!!

Randolph wrote to Winston on 24th May, clearly very proud of the singular honour done to Jack, a junior boy, by Dr Welldon:

I went to Grove Park to lunch with Lord Roberts and Jack was there. Lord Roberts drove us over in his pony cart in rather showery weather to Harrow. He did not remain & would not get out of his cart as the pony could not be [left] with anyone else. He is a Waler "Service" Australian pony & not quite safe in harness. I believe he had kicked up a fine row in the morning before I arrived when Ld Roberts started with Jack to meet me at the station. He stood on his hind legs & backed the cart against the coachhouse door inflicting some damage on the back panels. When I was being driven to Harrow he started quiet enough & remained quiet for he had been pacified with lumps of sugar by Miss Roberts [Aileen, Lord Robert's elder daughter]. Well Mr Welldon insisted on Jack & I having tea in his drawing room alone, as he said he had some hard work to do. I expect thoughts on [the] sermon, which I afterwards heard & thought a very fine one. It was Trinity Sunday which gave him a good subject, I heard him much better than the last time I was there … .

Jack was greatly honoured on Sunday evening. I told him Mr Welldon would ask him to supper. But he replied that he would only be asked in after supper as Mr Welldon never asked more out of the school than the two sixth form boys who read the lessons [in chapel]. Sure enough however Mr Welldon did tell him to come into supper & afterward to sit in the drawing room till I went away at nine o'clock.

No one could remember a 'Lower boy' being treated in such honoured fashion in the history of the school, a tribute to Welldon's respect for Lord Randolph and his regard for his younger son.

Poor Winston! Just when things were going so well with his father, the attempt to conceal a small accident to some personal property led to another dreadful rupture between them. There had been one or two annoyances earlier in 1894. Just as he had done for Jack, Randolph had arranged for Winston to lunch with Lord Roberts, who might be very useful in advancing his military career. But Winston had been out on the town the night before, visiting music halls with his cadet friends. He was very late for the luncheon, which was offensive to both his father and the general. In March Randolph went to visit Winston at Sandhurst, only to be told that he was still asleep in his bed. Randolph left immediately, and it was not much use Winston writing to explain that he had asked to be roused in good time but someone had forgotten to do so. Winston wisely chose not to tell his father that he was in negotiation with Colonel Brabazon to join the 4th Hussars when he graduated. Fearing for his eldest boy's application to his studies, for which he had ample precedent, Randolph wrote a letter "in perfect kindness", a stern lecture on the need for strength of character at this crucial time:

> I have to thank you for two letters. The Bradford meeting in St. George's Hall was very fine & crowded in every corner. Mr Balfour made a very fine speech and received an enthusiastic greeting.
>
> Now I turn to another subject on which I must write seriously. You have written two letters, one to your grandmother, one to me, announcing your intention of coming up to town on Saturday. Now to this I particularly object. You have been just one day over a week at Sandhurst & you get restless & want to get away. Now this is your critical time at Sandhurst and you have got to work much harder than in the former term. If you are always running up to town every week on some pretext or other & your mind is distracted from your work besides being an unnecessary expenditure of money. Now I am not [going to] have you this term come to London

more than once a month, and I give you credit for not coming to London without my knowledge. Now it is no use your telling me there is nothing to do on Sunday, because you can do work on Sunday instead of loitering about as I expect you do & getting through no work. I remind [you] that in your holidays you rode in Knightsbridge riding school & that practice placed you ahead of the other cadets.

The same result will arrive if you devote on Sunday at least 3 hours of real study. You will have that advantage of extra knowledge over those cadets who take their leave for Saturday & Sunday, or who do nothing all day. You not only gain Sunday but you gain some two hours extra on Saturday. Now all this may seem to you very hard & you may be vexed and say that 'all work & no play makes Jack a dull boy'. But it is no use complaining about what I tell you to do, for if you act as I advise you, you will excel at Sandhurst and the sacrifice of your taking your leave so frequently will be amply rewarded, and I shall be ten times more pleased with you than if you resumed your habits of coming to London many times in the term.

You are 20 & in November 21 [Winston was in fact 19, coming 20] & you must remember always that you are a military cadet and not a Harrow schoolboy. Now is the time to work & work hard; when you are in the regiment your work may be slightly relaxed, by the performance of regimental duties. But even then if you desire to be thought smart & well trained & well informed about all the details of your profession you should still carefully keep up all your Sandhurst acquirements. Why do I write all this. Because when you go into the army I wish you to make your one aim the ambition of rising in that profession by showing to your officers superior military knowledge, skill & instinct.

This is all written in perfect kindness to you. If I did not care about you I should not trouble to write long letters to you. I shall always take a great interest in you & do all I can for you if I am certain you are wrapped up in your profession. You need not answer this letter. I only want you to think over it and agree with it.

Winston did reply a week later (20th April 1894), assuring his father that he was working very hard, including the weekends and at a voluntary extra class in signalling. Regrettably for him this letter arrived just as his father discovered a deception on Winston's part. On the tenth anniversary of the death of the 7th Duke of Marlborough, Randolph had given his father's treasured gold watch to Winston as a gift, and a sign of the new respect he had for him as an adult. Twice Winston had to send the watch to the makers, Dents, for repair. Once it had been knocked from his hand by a running by-passer; the second time was more careless. Bending over a stream to pick up a stick, the watch fell out of a pocket into the only deep part of a relatively shallow stream. He went to extraordinary lengths to recover it, diving into the pool, having it dredged and, finally, hiring a squad of twenty-three infantrymen to completely divert the stream from its course (at a personal cost of £3, which he later brought to his father's notice). Sending it again for repair, he hoped his father would never know of the mishaps. The broadside he received, dated 21st April, must have been a blow:

> I have received your letter of yesterday's date & am glad to learn that you are getting on well in your work. But I heard something about you yesterday which annoyed & vexed me very much. I was at Mr Dent's about my watch, and he told me of the shameful way in which you had misused the very valuable watch which I gave you. He told me that you had sent it to him some time ago, [in March], having with the utmost carelessness dropped it on a stone pavement & broken it badly. The repairs of it cost £3 17s. which you will have to pay Mr Dent. He then told me he had again received the watch the other day and that you told him it had been dropped in the water. He told me that the whole of the works were horribly rusty & that every bit of the watch had had to be taken to pieces. I would not believe you could be such a young stupid. It is clear you are not to be trusted with a valuable watch & when I get it from Mr Dent I shall not give it back to you. You had better buy one of those cheap watches for £2 as those are the only ones which if you smash are not very costly to replace. Jack has had the watch I gave him longer than you have had

yours; the only expenses I have paid on his watch was 10/s for cleaning before he went back to Harrow. But in all qualities of steadiness taking care of his things & never doing stupid things Jack is vastly your superior.

Your v[er]y much worried parent
Randolph S. Churchill.

The praising of Jack over Winston was inevitable, as he was consistently 'outperforming' Winston in his childhood development. When the watch was finally repaired it was given to Jack as a present to rub home the point. However, Jennie was able to write to Winston a comforting note, suggesting that Randolph's annoyance was tempered with a little understanding: "Papa wrote me all about it. ... However he wrote very kindly about you so you must not be too unhappy. ... Oh! Winny what a harum scarum fellow you are! You really must give up being so childish". And Randolph did buy a new watch for Winston. The choice of a 'Waterbury' might have been an ironic reminder of the fate of its predecessor. Well might Winston be wounded by these outbursts, and feel that his father was a stern and distant figure, but that is to ignore the innumerable acts of kindness and the deep paternal concern shown towards him by Lord Randolph. It also avoids the issue of Winston's consistently poor performance, and bad behaviour, at all his schools. Exasperation towards his conduct, especially when compared to the model behaviour of Jack, was entirely understandable in the circumstances.

By May, Randolph was writing friendly letters to Winston, and was pleased to see him dining out with serving colonels in the army. He might not have been so pleased to have seen the letters Winston was writing to Jennie, explaining at great length his desire to join the expensive 4th Hussars, with its posting to India coming up, and the faster promotion in the cavalry.

Randolph's doctors were very concerned about his general health, and were recommending a withdrawal from public life. Randolph was actually enjoying a slight revival and was making some excellent speeches at large public meetings. He was very proud of Jack's record at Harrow, and made a point of attending the annual Speech Day at which the Prince of Wales was guest of honour. After a good win at the Derby, backing Lord Rosebery's horse, *Ladas*, he sent Jack a gift of £2.

Violent mood swings were a symptom of Randolph's worsening health. In a letter of 19th June to his father, another importuning plea, this time for his own bank account to be regularly supplied with money by his cash-strapped parents, Winston addressed it to "My dear Papa". Randolph was incensed at this childish opening, preferring the more adult "My dear father", and denounced the letter as "stupid" and "idiotic". Another damning comparison with Jack was made:

> I do not comment on this letter so delicately expressed about matters of money further than to observe that Jack would have cut off his fingers rather than write such a very free-spoken letter to his father.

Randolph was now so ill that his performance in the House of Commons was a subject of public comment. His great oratory was a thing of the past. His speeches were sad to behold – halting, forgetful, punctuated by long silences. He finally accepted medical advice to give up public life. Instead he decided upon a world cruise of one year's duration to restore his health. His doctors were not convinced this was a good idea, but agreed when he said he would take Dr Keith along for the whole trip. Thomas Keith was a very experienced doctor, well known to the family, and, interestingly, something of a tumour specialist, which is probably why Dr Buzzard recommended him. Buzzard did not seem to know what was wrong with Randolph, having not attended him for two years previously.

Jennie gave up her place in society to accompany her husband on this important journey. She also 'gave up' her long-term lover, Count Charles Kinsky. He had, somewhat insensitively, asked Jennie to divorce her sick (and dying) husband of twenty one years, and go off to his new posting at Brussels with him, there to be married. Kinsky was heavily in debt, and would have been cut off by his father. Did he think they could live on Jennie's £2,000 a year from the New York property? A divorce for someone as attuned to the importance of social standing in Victorian Britain as Jennie was out of the question. The break with Kinsky was absolute.

As part of the serious preparations for the trip, the Churchills sold their house in Connaught Place, some gold shares, and their share in the great horse, *L' Abbesse de Jouarre*. The most pressing bills were settled and there were funds enough for what would be an expensive trip when doctors, maids and valets were included. A farewell dinner was held by family and friends in Randolph's honour. Winston was at first refused permission to leave Sandhurst for it, but Randolph cabled a personal appeal to the Secretary of State for War to obtain a special dispensation. He was not going to part from his son on anything other than friendly terms.

CHAPTER 10

The Last Journey
1894–1895

They left on 27th June 1894 for New York. They were met there by
Jennie's cousin, William Travers Jerome, and were soon the centre of
attention in New York City society. The *New York Times* reported
that at one great banquet Jennie invented a new version of the
Manhattan Cocktail. Family legend says it was influenced by one of
Randolph's many cough medicines. From there they travelled to Bar
Harbour in Maine to relax in the bracing New England air.

Jennie sent a letter to Jack on 10th July:

> I wonder how you are getting on? I hope Winston sent you my
> letter from New York.
>
> It was so hot and noisy there – we were very glad to come
> away. But all the places are so far from each other in America.
> This is 18 hrs. by sail from N.Y. It is a most lonely spot right
> on the Atlantic and great high mountains. The air is wonderful
> and ought to do Papa a great deal of good. I think we shall
> stay 3 weeks, of course it is very dull, not a soul or kindred.
> We take long drives – each a great ordeal. Mr Keith and I
> walk. I miss you and Winston and feel very far away. I hope
> darling that you are well and happy and working. You will be
> going to Lords this week. I hope you will write to me all about
> it. If you need any money you had better write to
> Grandmamma Marlborough. She will give it to you for me.
> Send this to Winston, and give him my love. I hope to be able
> to tell you that Papa is much better in my next – Anyhow this
> will give him a good chance. Mind you write I think of you.

On 17th July Jack wrote a long, effusive letter to his mother, full of
news about school, family, and the holiday in Switzerland that had
been arranged for Winston and Jack together:

I have got a lot to tell you, of what has happened since you went away.

I suppose you saw in the papers about speech day here.

The Prince was very nice and came to my room and recognized the little tie pin, which he gave me 7 years ago at Cowes.

There were a lot of people here Lord Houghton, Lord Roberts who was very nice, Mr Chaplain, Earl Spencer, Lord and Lady Rothschild and General Ellis who was equerry, Uncle Edward was down too with Dudley. Luckily it was a very fine day and everything went off very well. Especially Mr. Welldon's who went strutting about all over the place, very proud of himself.

I have just come back from Lords exeat, I had a very good time on the whole. Unluckily it rained the whole of Friday so there was no going to see the match. But on Saturday I went on Lord Londonderry's coach and had luncheon … .

Winston told me he had had another letter from you and that you were drinking many American drinks! Grandmama read me Papa's letter. I am so glad he is so much better. What a pity you didn't have a nice voyage .. .

Today fortnight we go for Switzerland. Did not Papa say he would give Winston £10 and me £5 besides the £200 for Mr Little??

I have no more news, write and let me know what happens.

When we get in Switzerland we will write Illustrated letters with photos.

I remain
your loving son
Jack S. Churchill
Please give my best love to Papa.

Jennie was usually optimistic in her letters to the boys, but to her sister, Leonie Leslie, she was more candid about some of the difficulties of the trip:

R. is not as well as he was at Bar Harbour. Of course the journey has told on him – but I feel it is always going to be so.

As soon as he gets a little better from having a rest and being quiet he will be put back by this travelling – and *nothing* will deter him from doing what he likes. ... Keith thinks that R. will eventually get quite well, & I think so too – if only he would give himself a chance. He is very kind & considerate when he feels well – but absolutely *impossible* when he gets X [cross] & excited – & as he gets like that 20 times a day – you may imagine my life is not a very easy one. Then Keith gets '*enervé*' and worried. Our plans as far as we can make them are to go from Vancouver to San Francisco & to sail for Yokohama the 24th August. R. won't take any thought or consideration of the war [between China and Japan] because it does not suit him & 'pooh poohs' any danger or inconvenience. I confess I think it will all be settled before we get there.

Arriving in California, they were feted as visiting celebrities. The press hounded them everywhere. One woman journalist thrust herself into Jennie's hotel room and, on being ordered out forthwith, burst into tears. Jennie took pity on her and granted an exclusive interview. It was from there that Randolph wrote a most interesting letter to Sir Edward Hamilton, Gladstone's private secretary. It shows the extraordinarily close relationship Randolph had with the leaders of the Liberal Party, and how he freely discussed their policy with them. He even made suggestions about Gladstone's health. This twelve page, legible, hand written letter was found in the private papers of Peregrine Churchill, and has never been used before in any publication. It is not the work of a man supposedly dying in a 'syphilitic madness':

August 20 1894
Hotel Delmonte California

Dear Eddie Hamilton

I was overjoyed to get your letter from West Park the other day of the date of the 20th July. It reached me at San Francisco on 14th August. Well you say you are well out of the budget, and I gather that you think Harcourt will derive political advantage from retiring from the Government and supplanting and effacing poor Rosebery in the Govt. On all this I disagree with you; the moment the man is out of the cabinet he is lost, he is not a bit worth more than any other member of Parliament. Labouchere, Storey, Dilke, and a lot of those radicals could answer or attack him with the greatest ease. Imagine the pull which Arthur Balfour, Goschen, and above all, Joe [Chamberlain] would have over [him] and how they would kick him to pieces.

Another suggestion of mine is that Asquith and Morley would be leaders, Asquith presumably leader. What a wretched position would be Harcourt's. He would not hold up for 6 weeks – where would he sit. My opinions are and have been for a long time that Harcourt is sown up. He has no political energy cannot remain in the house for long, always has to wear spectacles and having seen a great deal of him personally and considering myself to have a very good parliamentary judgement on the strength of men in Parliament and specially ministers, I lay down positively that Harcourt is finished and that if he leaves the Govt. that for him there is no return.

Now my dear Eddy you praise the budget and you are of opinion that other succeeding Chs of Exchq [Chancellors of the Exchequer] will be much attached and quite converted. Well the only chancellor that would try and maintain that Budget would be Goschen. That I know for certain. He told me what amounted to this that that budget could never be altered. But the prevailing opinion of the Unionist Party is that when they come into power that Budget will be revised and largely for Goschen is only one among many, the overwhelming majority of the Unionist Party in the House of Commons strongly reinforced by the House of Lords will support that policy. Certainly if I am back in time and restored to ordinary health I should leave no stone unturned to recast it.

I greatly regret your rather discouraging account of Mr Gladstone. I thought when I went to see him at Dollis a day or two before I went away, and when he showed me his eyes I could make out very little. An old man like Mr. Gladstone in cases of that kind always fails to avail himself of the greatest

skill of the profession. I will venture to say that for performing
great operations on great people Dr. Nettleship was little
known. I have never heard in my life of bandages being
removed in 3 days I think. The great practitioners 3 weeks
bandaged in a dark room. Nettleship is found out at once. His
first operation has been unsuccessful, he now proposes I read
in a paper that Nettleship means to restore the old disused eye
that was injured by strong use of atropine, and to gain strength
for the other eye which has been operated on after a little time.
Fact of the matter is the cardinal error was calling Nettleship
instead of that incomparable Critchett for whatever Critchett's
other faults might be and I do not deny them, but in all
London he has not got a rival for cauching for cataract.

Now I pass away from all these things and I tell you some of
my news. I didn't stay long in New York. We occupied the
seventh Floor at the Hotel Waldorf for the purposes of
thorough draft. But we breakfasted noon and dined at ½ seven
in the saloon. This is ventilated not only by an enormous
cupola being moved off at the top, but also by electric
ventilators which made the wind by a powerful fan and was
very refreshing. I have never known such cooking in New York
as at the Waldorf and Delmonico's has been almost minimised
by it. The appartments [sic] were comfortable and as we
stopped two days and departed on the morning the 7th July for
these 2 days 494$ was the bill. The Beneficance of Mr.
Chancey Depew came down upon us. He is President of the
New York Central [Railway]. I wanted to go to Bar Harbour
in Maine and did not know how to get [there] and my party
were not favourable to the project. But Chauncey Depew put
his private car at our disposal and it was hung onto the Boston
& Maine train and we arrived at the station for Port Desert
which is the station for Bar Harbour steamer on the morning
of the next day the 8th. The black cook and the black
Majordomo were as gentlemanlike as any Christian and the
food was excellent. So we got to Bar Harbour. It is on an
island which faces among other things like other islands the
Atlantic Ocean. There is no doubt it is a most bracing place,
weather variable, sometimes very hot some times coldish wind

and once or twice heavy rain but on the whole it will certainly [be] a place to do one good. We stopped at the Malvern Hotel close on 3 weeks. Then after many troubles with respect to our journey by the Canadian Pacific after having been plundered and persecuted by his myrmidons and himself I found myself and my wife and Dr. Keith and the servants in a Pullman car attached to the end of the train for which Sir William Van Hone in addition to 50Dlrs [Dollars] a day for the Pullman to Vancouver and back which he saddled me with he ran me what brought the whole charges to some $2000. Never such a rascal: and I had letters for Lord Rothschild and also Sir Henry Irving to the rascal! However I got to Vancouver having my car detached at Banff which stands 4000 feet up it's a very beautiful place in the centre of the valleys of the highest Rocky Mountains. We stayed there three days and the scenery was lovely and driving and boating on the Saskatchewan were both ideal. We got in [to] Vancouver in a journey of a day and a half. The next day we reached Victoria the capital of the Island of Vancouver. We looked about the island which has fine timber and fine larch.

We spent an afternoon with Admiral Stephenson Commander of the *Royal Arthur* a first class cruiser and who used to be at the Cape of Good Hope when I was there and other commands and has well settled down Chief in Command here. On the 11th we took passage on an American Pacific Coast Steamer. Poor sort of vessel, accommodation rather rough, Captain in character but not a bad fellow; breakfast 8–9 AM luncheon 12.35 PM dinner 5.25 PM and nothing after that till the following morning.

We were glad to get off it and settle down in the Palace Hotel. This is a good Hotel. Good rooms excellent restaurant. San Francisco has at this time of year a most unpleasant climate. In the morning fog cold wind of the worst kind about noon the sun comes out. But he does not often do much good for he is accompanied by much wind and is succeeded at 5 in the afternoon by colder winds which last all through the night. However we managed to do some business of one kind or another amongst it being rather well photographed both my

wife and myself. On Friday 16 we took off ourselves over by
train some 50 miles from the capital of California to a place
called Hotel Del Monte which is really sprung up out of the
old town of Monte Rey. This is a splendid hotel not only in
size but in the beauty and extent of its gardens and grounds.
There are some beautiful drives here, one of which is called the
eighteen miles drive. You practically make the circuit of the
peninsular on which all this land is situated and it is a lovely
drive for it compasses sea and land in their grandest form. The
greatest sight are the old cypresses which have no equal for
number or fine growth and when exposed to sea gales their
curious crouching and creeping which protects them. I drove
over a whole mile of these trees of every shape and form. In old
days seeds have been taken away for England and for
Australia. But the Cyprus grove is one of the finest things I ever
saw.

Now my dear Eddie I must have wearied you. We go back
on the 23rd in another American Pacific Steamer and arrive at
Victoria in Vancouver on 25th. On the afternoon of the 27th
we sail in the Empress Line, the fine line that goes to Japan in
succession with the Pacific Railway and I hope to have a
pleasant and prosperous voyage. We shall probably arrive on
the 14th or 15th [of September].

Your ever faithful friend
Randolph S.C.'

They sailed to Yokohama in Japan, and toured a country expecting
victory in its war with China. With all things Japanese very much in
fashion, Jennie enjoyed some serious shopping, buying silk material
to make clothes when she returned, and treating herself to silk
kimonos and underwear. She also bought a silk screen, silk paintings, two dozen doyleys, two fans, and a silver teapot. They had
their photographs taken, and no expense was spared in having sixteen copies made, some of which Jennie sent home to Winston and
Jack.

The boys had enjoyed another holiday in Switzerland under the
care of Mr Little. They had travelled via Antwerp and Brussels,
where Charles Kinsky was "very kind to us", according to Winston's

letter. Winston had to return to Sandhurst at the end of August; Jack was back at Harrow later in September. He wrote to his father on 28th September:

Dear Papa

I have just settled down again at Harrow, and stay here for twelve weeks ... .

I then came on here in the evening and for the first time I did not care a rap about coming back I do not know why because I had had a most pleasant holiday as I had travelled, climbed, rowed, rode, shot and fished a very little. But still I did not care a bit.

Mr Welldon received me with open arms and of course asked a great deal about you, he had been I believe rather ill during the first part of the holidays but now he is back at his work again looking just the same ... .

I think the photos Mama sent are very good indeed although I do not care very much for the one of you both together ... .

I suppose this letter can't get to you for five weeks, I don't know what the right address is ... .

Every body is quite well and I have no more news to tell you ... .

I remain
your loving son
Jack S. Churchill

Jack obviously cast a photographer's eye over the pictures sent home and was self confident enough to pass judgement on "the one of you both together".

Winston was doing well at Sandhurst and confidently looked forward to his finals. With his parents away he certainly took advantage of every opportunity to get up to London and enjoy himself. The music halls were a great attraction for the Sandhurst cadets and Winston took to mooning after a musical comedy actress, Miss Mabel Love. He regales us in *My Early Life* with stories of leading protests against the 'prudish' plan to close off the bars at the Empire, Leicester Square from the main part of the theatre. This was, apparently, the first independent essay into 'politics' by the twenty-year-old cadet. All this toing and froing to town led to the pawning of the gold watch his father had bought him, disguised to earn sympathy under the pretext that he needed the money to buy food.

Randolph and Jennie had taken a rather risky trip to China, trying to get from Hong Kong upriver to Canton. They were not able to get that far and returned to Japan. Jennie wrote to Winston, revealing something of the strain she was under. "It seems such ages that we have been away – I can't imagine how I shall be able to hold out a year! I think Japan has done your Father good – altho' he is not as well as I could wish – For a fortnight he has been *much* better and then again today without any reason he is not so well … . Goodbye my darling Winston mind you keep straight in every way. I *count on you*. Bless you darling I can't tell you how miserable I am, often – so far away from you all – but I shall feel nearer when I am in India & perhaps things will look brighter".

Dr Keith had written to Dr Roose in England an alarming note: "I have lost all control over your patient. He intends to take a journey tomorrow that I distinctly disapprove of, and all I have said has been to no avail." Randolph was now suffering a transient paralysis of the left arm[1], but insisted on journeying on, via Singapore, to Burma and India. His health took a severe downward turn. Keith again wrote to Roose: "This has been the worst week since leaving home by a great deal. Lord Randolph has been violent and apathetic by turn … I have warned him again in the most solemn manner that I entirely disapprove of Burma, but with no effect … ." Winston finally heard the truth about his father's poor condition from Dr Roose. Randolph insisted on visiting Burma, with which he had such historic links. They were put up in the Government House at Rangoon. It was here that Jennie received the distressing news that Charles Kinsky was already engaged to be married to another. He had, wisely, chosen an attractive, 21 year old, wealthy heiress, the Countess Elizabeth Wolff Metternich zur Gracht, a cousin of the beautiful Empress Elizabeth of Austria. In a strange act of desperation Jennie wrote and asked her sister to intervene: "Leonie darling use all your cleverness & all your strength & urge him to put off his marriage".

Jack wrote to his father in November:

Dear Papa

Winston has just sent me a letter which he received from
Mama dated October 11th, when you [were] leaving Japan.
She says my letters "are few and far between" all I can say is
that is not my fault. I have written every week and when you
were in Japan sometimes twice a week to you since Winston
left me in Switzerland that is to say since the end of August ... .

Here at Harrow we are cursing our founder for having built
Harrow on a Hill, because Eton being in a valley is under
water and the boys have all gone home, to show what it is like
one Eton boy swam the whole of the High Street!!! ... .

You have only been away 5 months and a bit, almost "half
time". I don't know how we shall get through the rest of the
time without you it certainly can't be longer than the last five
months have made themselves. This will be the first Christmas
when you both have been so far away, one Christmas you were
in Russia but that was only a step from here. You seem much
closer to us now perhaps it is only because we have heard the
names of India more often than those of Japan ... .

I have nothing more to tell you.

Thank Mama for her letter very much as it was for both of
us?

Good bye dear Papa
Give my best love to Mama
I remain
Your loving son
Jack S. Churchill.

A subsequent letter made clear the strain this trip was on the whole
family, when young Jack wrote, "To think I have not been really
happy for nearly 6 months since you left. O how I wish I could
express my thoughts and soul as regards you and dear Mama but I
can't and if I try I only write bad English".

Randolph would have been gratified to receive a warm letter,
dated 27th November, from Dr Welldon about Jack's progress at
Harrow. It was markedly different from the sort of letters he usually
received concerning Winston:

I hope I may be so fortunate as to send this letter in time to catch you at Calcutta. It has occurred to me that you would be glad to receive some account however brief, of Jack and of his doings.

He is very well in health, and is growing fast. Next term it will be necessary for him to substitute a tailcoat for his jacket. His conduct in the House is excellent; there is no better boy, and I think you may look with very great satisfaction upon his character. At the beginning of this term he was moved into a higher form, and the work done in this form has been hard for him, especially as (like Winston) he has so much more capacity for History and English subjects than for Classics. However he is young, much younger than the majority of boys in his Form.

You may have read in the newspaper that the rainfall in November has been excessive and has resulted in floods which have at Eton brought the School life temporarily to an end. One Eton master took refuge upon Harrow Hill as upon Ararat.

The accounts of your Lordships health have not been all that your many friends could desire. I earnestly hope your long journey may do good. It is with the view of cheering you on that journey, so far as I may, by a good report of Jack, telling you how well I am satisfied with him, that I have ventured to write you these few lines.

Allow me to send my best regards to Lady Randolph.

It was now obvious to Randolph's doctors that he was dying and nothing more could be done for him. A lead-lined coffin was brought onto their ship, signifying the finality of the diagnosis. Despite Randolph's protests, the world tour was cut short after six months and they returned via Egypt and France. Jennie told her sisters the truth about the serious situation, and even considered inviting Randolph's mother to join them in the South of France in case he would not make it back to England. She told Winston on 1st December, that his father was not long for this world. She softened the blow to Jack, writing, "'I wish I could tell you that Papa is better – but I am afraid he is not. Perhaps if he remains quietly in one place he will improve. I feel this is a very poor return for your nice long letter but we are just approaching Suez and the ship is in a thunder-storm. We are going to Cairo for 3 days – then to Alexandria where we get on a French ship and go to Marseilles which we ought to reach on 20th."

Jack wrote his last letter to his father on 21st December, with news of school and family. He concluded, "We are expecting a telegram any minute from you to say you have arrived at Marseilles. Of course you have heard about Winston coming out 2nd in the Sandhurst riding it is supposed to be a smart thing to do. I think he owes most of it as well as everything else, to you. I will write again to you soon. Goodbye dear Papa. Lots of love. I remain . Your loving son. Jack S. Churchill."

How entirely in character that Jack should recognise the debt that both boys owed to their father. Unlike Winston, he recognised the many and consistent acts of kindness and support their father had provided to them both.

The Churchills arrived back in London on Christmas Eve, 1894, and moved in with the Dowager Duchess at 50 Grosvenor Square. Randolph was exhausted and, according to Winston, "as weak and helpless in mind and body as a little child". He was nursed constantly by Jennie and several health professionals. He rallied slightly in January, enough to receive many visitors, with whom he conversed freely. His nights were very disturbed, when he would writhe in pain and call out in a deranged way. The press gave daily coverage to his condition through a dreadfully cold, wet January 1895.

In his last days he would have received great comfort from Winston's excellent performance at Sandhurst. A splendid set of marks placed him twentieth in a class of 130 cadets. He was easily the top placed cavalry cadet. His conduct had been 'Good', with no hint of the usual lack of punctuality. He seems to have heeded his father's advice and got down to some hard work in his last term.

In January, Kinsky married the Countess Elizabeth. Jennie, some-what irrationally, felt a sense of betrayal, having foolishly thought that her lover would be waiting to marry her at Randolph's death. She wrote to Leonie in Ireland, "Don't dream of coming over at pre-sent & until it suits you … . I am really in a much better frame of mind … as regards this wedding … . He [Kinsky] and I have parted the best of friends and in a truly *fin de siècle* manner … . He has not behaved particularly well & I can't find much to admire in him but I care for him as some people like opium or drink although they would like not to … ."

On 23rd January, in the middle of a snowstorm, in sub zero temperatures to the extent that the Thames had frozen, Randolph sank into a coma from which he would never awake. At 6.15 am the next morning, he died in his sleep. His wife, his sons, and his mother were all with him at the end. He was three weeks short of his forty-sixth birthday, another brief life for a Marlborough male.

Jack sent a telegram to Dr Welldon at Harrow, and received a moving reply by return:

> It is especially sad for you and Winston and saddest of all for your mother … . To me it will seem that I am tied to you, now and ever, by a special bond of interest and affection because of this great sorrow that has happened during your school life.

A great funeral was held at Westminster Abbey, with crowds thronging the streets, and politicians of all ranks and parties at the service. Randolph had asked to be buried, not in the crypt at Blenheim Palace, but with his deceased brothers at Bladon in St Martin's churchyard. All of Woodstock was there, with large delegations from the Birmingham Conservatives and from Ireland.

It is so universally propounded that Lord Randolph Churchill died after suffering from syphilis for many years that we need to discuss his final illness, and some of the sources for the stories circulated about him.

Winston's biography of his father stated that he died of "a rare and ghastly disease". The cause of death, as stated on Randolph's Death Certificate, was "bronchial pneumonia from paralysis in the brain". The charge that he died of syphilis only appeared in print in 1922, in a book no on would publish in Britain (of which more later). This seems to have opened the floodgates of speculation. Was Randolph infected while at Oxford, by student pranksters getting him drunk and bedded with 'an old hag'?[2] How, then, would his new wife and first child have remained uninfected? Was he infected by a housemaid at Blenheim Palace during Jennie's first confinement? We refer you to the intimate, loving letters passing between

Randolph and Jennie after Winston's birth, that give no hint of sexual estrangement.[3] During their bouts of ill health in 1882 and 1883, Jennie's letters are all about the need for "fresh air and sun" and "a quiet mind". This is hardly a cure for syphilis. Attention is sometimes drawn to the degree to which Jennie went out in society without her husband. We know that Randolph was no great lover of dances and balls, and that the trouble with his nerves and balance, and the phenomenal work rates he set himself, led him to eschew many of the social events that Jennie loved so much. During the marital crisis of 1886, people suggested either that syphilis had taken hold or that Randolph had taken a high-born mistress. A more careful analysis of letters at the time shows the problem to have been entirely financial. Allowing that he fathered both Winston and Jack, perhaps he was infected while keeping a mistress in Paris? His frequent letters to his mother show that he was hardly ever in Paris but visited and stayed in Monte Carlo. And so it goes on and on.

From recent conversations with the Churchill family, it seems that Winston believed that his father died of syphilis contracted some time after Jack's birth. This was assumed to be true within the family and not discussed. One of the sad consequences of this is the suggestion that Jack may have been led to doubt his own paternity, and this is advanced as a reason for his passive fading into the background of the family history. We shall advance some ideas about how and why the syphilis smear was promoted, and use medical research to refute it.

In more recent years the automatic acceptance of syphilis as the cause of death is being challenged. In 1981 Roy Foster first suggested that Randolph had been misdiagnosed by his doctors, and instead referred to his "withdrawal into a mysterious illness" which, with its intimation of mortality, led to his frantic activity for political reform. Robert Rhodes James stated that syphilis was now almost the last thing anyone should think Lord Randolph died from.

The eminent doctors attending Lord Randolph were doing their best in an age that knew nothing of definitive blood tests or sophisticated neurological testing, and with no imaging techniques, such as CAT scans and MRIs. The specialist attending him was the neurologist, Dr Thomas Buzzard. He was asked by Sir Richard Quain,

Physician to Queen Victoria, to supply details of Randolph's illness for perusal by the Prince of Wales. Setting aside this extraordinary invasion of privacy, Buzzard replied with his usual description of the illness that he specialised in, 'General Paralysis':

Dear Sir Richad Quain,

I am happy to comply with H.R.H.'s wish and give you such information about Lord Randolph Churchill's condition as I think may be communicated without indiscretion. As you are aware Lord Randolph is affected with "General Paralysis" the early symptoms of which, in the form of tremor of the tongue & slurring articulation of words were evident to me at an interview two years ago. I had not seen him for a long while – a year or two, I think – previously, so that it is impossible to say how long he has been affected with the disease. But I think it likely, from what I have heard from members of the House of Commons that the articulation difficulties may have been present something like three years. You well know how much such cases vary as regards particular symptoms altho' they usually agree in leading to a fatal termination in the course of three or four years. In Lord R's case the physical signs – tremor, faulty articulation, successive loss of power in various parts of the frame have been much more marked than the mental ones which have hitherto been of comparatively slight character, grandiose ideas, however, not being absent at times & on some occasions violent of manner. These symptoms have alternated with dejection and apathy or an unnatural bonhomie.[4] You will understand, with the uncertainty as regards the occurrence of mental symptoms how important it was to get the patient away [from the Commons and out of the country].

When I saw him on the night of his arrival [home from the world trip] in town he had refused food for 24 hours and the comatose state was doubly consequent on this and the fatigue of a rapid journey from Cairo.

Under regular feeding & rest his Lordship has greatly recuperated and can now converse – recognise persons & the room in which he lies and shews a fair amount of memory of past events. His articulation, however, makes it at times difficult to understand a word that he says. He has no delusion. The condition is rather one of mental feebleness. It is quite possible, I think, that his mental condition may become still clearer if his life be spared. But just as there have been successive assaults of paralysis on different parts so he may at any time, experience others, & the occurrence of one in a vital situation might produce sudden death. His heart is very weak. Or it is possible that he may sink into a state of increasing dementia with its accompanying physical troubles – slowly ending in death. I write hurriedly, to catch the post, but I trust that I have made myself intelligible."[5]

It will be noted that there is no specific reference to any sexually transmitted disease. It is, however, well known that Buzzard, and the doctors he worked with, including Dr Roose, were enormously preoccupied with the problem of syphilis. Roose wrote a paper *Nerve Prostration and Other Functional Disorders of Daily Life* (1888), which, in Roy Foster's words "... dealt with neurasthenic diseases, which in many instances (ranging from headaches and constipation to neuralgia and epilepsy) he attributed to hereditary or contracted venereal disease."[6] Buzzard, the great expert of neurosyphilis and later stages of the disease, is reckoned to have diagnosed ninety-five percent of his patients as syphilitic.

In Buzzard's files there is a brief medical note, dated 24th December 1894:

Lord Randolph Churchill.
I saw him with Dr Roose in October 1885, but whether for the first time or not I do not know.

It was in the early summer of 1893, as shewn in my notes, if not before that I came to the conclusion that there was in all probability G.P. [General Paralysis].

His articulation became slurred, and his tongue tremulous.

He left England at the end of June [1894] for a lengthened tour abroad, taking his wife and a young doctor with him, Dr G.E. Keith.

He had been consulted about Randolph's health in 1885, but had not found it necessary to make any significant note about it at the time. In 1891, Randolph made a most arduous trip to South Africa, enduring many outdoor hardships, from which he returned richer and fitter. In January 1892 he told his friend, FitzGibbon, "My travel through South Africa was as nice an experience as anyone could have, and though I am very glad to be back I really enjoyed every hour of my journey." On 13th May 1892, Herbert Asquith, the future Liberal Prime Minister, wrote to his wife, Margo, about his friend Randolph, and how he admired "his vitality and a certain freshness in his mental atmosphere". Clearly, Randolph's terminal illness had not set in until after that date.

Randolph found out, in 1893, that Buzzard was interviewing parliamentarians to ask about his general condition, seemingly at the request of Jennie and Dr Roose, who were alarmed at his sudden deterioration. Not surprisingly, Randolph wrote to protest, and insisted that he did not feel "in bad health". He said his appetite and sleep patterns were good, and that he had heeded Buzzard's advice about moderating the consumption of alcohol.[7] Most significantly the letter said, "I have hardly ever had that numbness or difficulty of articulation, which you yourself assured me was of small importance". Either Buzzard was outrageously deceiving his patient, or he did not then see the signs of terminal syphilis. It should also be stressed that Randolph's medical reports have survived and at no time in his life was Randolph ever prescribed the then known treatments for syphilis, mercury or potassium iodide.

Buzzard's own work could have suggested an alternative source of Randolph's illness. While he would normally refer to terminal syphilis as 'General Paralysis of the Insane', he only ever referred to Randolph's condition as 'General Paralysis', leaving open the interpretation. Buzzard also researched the effects of excessive brainwork on men in public life and had deduced: "Chronic inflammation of the brain attacks persons of exhausted habits, brought on by excesses and irregular living. The patient has frequent headaches and gradual loss of health, and then gets a perversion of most of the senses, as of sight, taste, smell etc., and in fact, all the symptoms of incipient mania."

For some three years Peregrine Churchill assisted the American physician, Dr John Mather, in a study of Randolph's medical reports. They did consider the report, from an extremely unreliable source, that Randolph may have picked up an infection while at university. The genital discomfort described was not remotely similar to a primary syphilis chancre and may, just possibly if the report is considered at all, have been a mild herpes. Mather looked at the symptoms of the 1893/4 malady – mood swings, speech problems, dizziness and palpitations at the heart. Randolph was able to write cogently until his final days, as his letter to Eddie Hamilton shows. Mather studied his handwriting of the period and noted that "His script slowly becomes shaky, but never, ever, unintelligible. Until the last when he was in a coma, the thoughts expressed in writing remain rational and cogent." It was not his mind that was affected but his ability to express his ideas in words. He made his last speech in the Commons in June 1894, on the subject of Uganda, but his inability to find his words was such that his friends, Michael Hicks-Beach and Arthur Balfour, had to help him out. When Beach paid him a private visit at home, Randolph told him: "I know what I want to say but damn it I can't say it." Mather makes the point that this is not a symptom of syphilis affecting the brain, and pointed out that they are quite different, consisting of "muddled thoughts, memory lapses and profound confusion", *none* of which he found present in Randolph's medical records or the accounts of him in his last days.

Mather maintains that the "psychic seizures" which Randolph had suffered were "strongly suggestive of a variety of epilepsy found in deep parts of the brain, close to the speech area", and says that such symptoms:

> ... would be consistent with a developing brain tumour, possibly an aberration of the blood vessels ... a left side brain tumour, for which no surgery was available.

Such a condition would also have been consistent with the problems Randolph had experienced of the gradual onset of numbness, and bad circulation in his hands and feet, which would have been exacerbated by his chain smoking. Nicotine clogs the arteries, restricting the blood vessels, and hence the blood circulation around the heart. Mather wrote: "Spasms in the arteries reduce circulation which causes numbness and pain due to lack of oxygen in the tissues". He then went on to make a quite crucial point, that there was no medical record of Randolph ever having shown signs of any of the *secondary* symptoms of syphilis, "such as a rash over much of the body". Roose and Buzzard had treated Randolph for "pain" with "laudanum", and for "heart failure" with "belladonna and digitalis". The damage that two such powerful drugs could inflict on Randolph's frail constitution, along with their harmful side effects, is known today, but was not known about in Victorian times. Mather also found that Randolph's doctors had never prescribed treatment for syphilis, and concluded:

> If Dr. Buzzard had been convinced that Lord Randolph
> Churchill had advanced syphilis, he would certainly have
> treated him with mercury and with potassium iodide, which he
> strongly espoused for all neurosyphilitic patients. But Buzzard
> makes no mention of such treatments in any of his papers
> during Randolph's illness … .

Lord Randolph Churchill, never in the most robust of health, died of a brain tumour. How, then, and why, has the syphilis smear taken such a hold?

We have to look at the extraordinary connections of the first great publicist of the story, none other than the sensationalist journalist and writer, Frank Harris. We have already noted the close interest the Prince of Wales took in Randolph's illness. He, of course, was more interested in the availability of Jennie for his pleasure. (We might ask, as an aside, whether he would have been quite so interested if she was the wife of a known syphilitic). He was about to throw over his current mistress, Frances, Lady Brooke (always known as Daisy – later the Countess of Warwick). She was staying with him at Marlborough House in January 1895, when the Prince was in receipt of Buzzard's report on Randolph. Daisy, widely known as 'The Babbling Brook', and later, after she embraced socialism, as 'The Red Countess', was in possession of large numbers of very indiscreet letters from the Prince. After she was thrown over by him, for Jennie, she was in debt and looking for revenge. It is known that, in June 1914, she attempted to blackmail King George V with the threat to publish these letters in her memoirs to raise large sums of cash. Rich friends of the king arranged for the letters to be purchased and destroyed. (Some of these letters, addressed to 'My darling Daisy wife', survived and were the basis of Theo Lang's 1960 book on her life). Her agent, planning big publishing deals in the USA, was none other than Frank Harris. We can assume that he would have acquired the full news of Randolph's last illness from Daisy Brooke, and added it to the scurrilous stories that were his stock in trade. By coincidence he was also agent to Winston Churchill when he was writing his *World Crisis* in the 1920s. They had a serious falling out, probably over money, which left Harris an implacable enemy to Winston. The stories he published in *My Life and Loves* in 1922 were an act of revenge, and they were seized upon by Winston's enemies in the Conservative Party to abuse him and all his family. Lest we doubt the extent of this abuse, Peregrine remembered an incident when he was a boy at Summerfield Prep school, in 1924, aged eleven. He was taunted by the son of an MP, who said, "My Daddy says all you Churchills have revolting diseases, and are quite mad".[8] As part of his study of this whole issue, Peregrine described the situation that prevailed in the mid 1920s:

> Winston was out of favour with both the Liberals and the Conservatives and ... out of Parliament for two years. The party propaganda machines wanted to keep him out and the Frank Harris story, among others, was pertinent. ... . When Winston re-entered Parliament it was as an 'independent constitutionalist'.
>
> A pirated copy, [of Harris' book] however, found its way to the Conservative Central office and was used as propaganda depicting Winston as infected through a degenerate father and a drunkard in order to keep him out of the Conservative Party. A member of the Cabinet Office told me that in 1940 they did not believe Winston would last more than a few months because of his instability. Such is the power of propaganda! [9]

It seems the other most consistent source of the syphilis smear was Jennie's sister, Leonie Leslie, and some of her descendants. Jennie was the best looking of the Jerome girls, the first married and, consequently, recipient of the most generous settlement by their father. Clara married next and, by the time Leonie married, there was very little left for her to inherit as an allowance. Genteel poverty affected this notorious 'society snob' considerably and would not have been helped by her being in receipt of hand-me down (fine) clothes from Jennie, and hand-me-down toys for her children. A degree of jealousy hovered beneath the surface. Jennie was a titled lady from her marriage; Leonie had to wait thirty-three years before her husband inherited a title. Leonie was ever the 'plain Jane' of the Jerome girls though she was tall, with a good figure. Leonie did not like Randolph, and wrote spiteful remarks about him in her correspondence. When he resigned the Chancellorship and Leadership of the Commons in 1886, on a matter of principle, she replied to her mischievous friend, Lady Charles Beresford, "Liver or madness? Let us hope the latter, and that he will shut up before he can do further mischief". Leonie was ultra-Conservative in her political views. In her writings, Leonie belittled Jennie's relationship with the Prince of Wales, suggesting it was purely platonic. She, however, left a full account of her own very long, physical relationship with his brother, Arthur, Duke of Connaught, struck up in 1895, the year of Lord Randolph's death. Jennie had once, before this affair had begun, written to Leonie about the Duke, saying "What an ugly man he is".[10] That may or may not have caused offence, for the affair did not begin for another ten years. But what would have rankled was the great struggle Randolph waged, against both the Queen and Lord Salisbury, to deny the Duke of Connaught a major command that was vacant in the Army in India.

Leonie nursed a grudge against Randolph and gave out stories about him in revenge. We know that Frank Harris quoted her as his source more than once, including an incident on the last world voyage where Randolph supposedly brandished a gun at Jennie during one of his fits. Between the laudatory biography that Winston wrote of his father in 1906, and the lukewarm descriptions of him in the 1930 *My Early Life*, he seems to have absorbed a good deal of negative reports about Lord Randolph. If, according to Anthony Montague Browne, for most of his life Winston believed his father had really died of syphilis,[11] 'Aunt Leonie' would have been a principle source.

Her son, Shane Leslie, is also known as a source of 'Randolph' stories. It was he who thought that Count Charles Kinsky would have made a far better stepfather to Winston and Jack than Randolph was ever a father. He only saw Kinsky when on holiday with the Churchills between the ages of six and nine, and makes rather large claims based on that acquaintance. More significantly, he grew up to convert to Catholicism and became a strong Irish Nationalist, changing his name from John to Shane, wearing the Irish plaid, and even refusing to inherit the family's Anglo-Irish estates. Given that Randolph was total anathema to the 'Home Rule' movement, it is not hard to see why he too entered the lists against Randolph's reputation. This general tendency to believe every possible story against Randolph and Jennie, and in particular, to advance any number of names as possible fathers for Jack, was continued by Shane's daughter, Anita, who was a prodigious writer of books about their Churchill connections. Anita who got her stories from her grandmother Leonie, could dismiss Frank Harris' story about infection from 'an old hag' at University as a "malicious fabrication", but then went on to declare the syphilis to be a "cold fact" based on thirdhand gossip via Shane Leslie and Sunny Marlborough.[12]

Gradually informed opinion is changing about the nature of Lord Randolph's final illness. A proper understanding of his (hereditary?) generally poor health should end the unpleasant stories that he was not Jack's father, and help us to recognise that he died of an undiagnosed and inoperable brain tumour.

CHAPTER 11

A Royal Affair
Jennie and the Prince of Wales

The gross value of Randolph's estate was £75,971, about five million pounds in today's valuation. A good deal of it was required to pay off his debts though it is known that some of them were never settled. The balance, soundly invested in 'Blue Chip' companies, supported a Trust Fund for the family, administered by Jennie.[1] The regular income from the estate, in addition to the £2,000 a year she got from the rental on her property in America, should have left her quite comfortable. She inherited a payment of £500, and all the horses, carriages and household effects. If she had taken advice from Randolph's friends, the Rothschilds, or Sir Ernest Cassel, she could have sold the South African gold shares that made up the bulk of the estate to re-invest at much greater advantage. Instead the family solicitors, Lumleys, sold them immediately, in a bear market. A year later they would have sold at much higher prices. This was only the start of escalating money troubles. Without the restraining hand of her husband, Jennie's extravagance would soon take wings.

Winston also moved quickly after his father's death, claiming that Lord Randolph he had agreed verbally that he could apply to a cavalry regiment for his first commission. He got Jennie to cable Colonel Brabazon, 4th Hussars, who gave her the wording for a letter to the Duke of Cambridge explaining that there was a vacancy in the regiment, and that Winston had passed out ahead of all other candidates for the cavalry, and should not be kept 'idle' in London, but should be allowed to fulfil one of Randolph's 'last wishes'. The Duke referred the request to the Military Secretary and Winston was duly gazetted into the 4th Hussars as a Second Lieutenant by 20th February 1895.

Jack returned to Harrow, where his work slipped a little as he adjusted to life without his father. Winston wrote to him regularly. On his very first day with his regiment, he sent Jack a detailed description of his day as a subaltern, all of which Jack would have found interesting. A few days later, he boosted Jack's pocket money by buying from him a picture of Count Kinsky on his champion race-horse, *Zoedone*.

Jennie was forty-one years old, but looking as lovely as ever. She was alone with two sons to raise, and with nowhere to live but the house of her mother-in-law. But her friend and occasional lover, the Prince of Wales, moved quickly to secure her affection. On January 24th 1895, the day Randolph died, the first letter of condolence Jennie received was from the Prince at Sandringham:

> My dear Lady Randolph,
> The sad news reached me this morning that all is over ... & I felt that for his and for your sakes it was best so ... .
>   There was a cloud in our friendship but I am glad to think that it has long been forgotten by both of us[2].

Randolph was scarcely cold in his grave when the Prince changed his addresses to Jennie to: "*Ma chère*".

Jennie felt the need to get away. She obviously felt no compunction about leaving her sons so soon after the death of their father. Quite reasonably, she went to stay with her family in Paris. Jack and Leonie Leslie, with their three sons, and Clara Frewen, were all there. Not quite so reasonably, Jennie moved with the Leslies into two apartments on the fashionable Avenue Klèber, and proceeded to spend money like water as she re-decorated and re-furnished her temporary home to the highest standards. For Jennie, the next six weeks would mark a new beginning in the city of her youth. Winston wrote on 24th February that the Dowager Duchess was passing critical remarks about her extravagance. If the sudden arrival of Count Kinsky and his young bride, the Countess Elizabeth, at the nearby Hotel Bristol was at all disconcerting to Jennie, she soon found a way to put it from her mind.

In early March, her sister, Clara Frewen, introduced her to a 41-year-old millionaire, the Irish-American lawyer and Democratic Senator, William Bourke Cockran, who was a friend of Moreton Frewen's. Bourke, as he was always known, had recently become a widower for the second time, and he and Jennie embarked on a short but passionate affair. Jennie organised lavish dinners for him. They were seen bicycling together, which was very fashionable in Paris just then, and strolling arm-in-arm along the tree-lined streets. Cockran was a fine looking man and was considered one of the best political speakers of his day in the United States. Jennie and he both spoke fluent French and shared a mutual love of horses. From the letters Jennie wrote home to Winston and Jack it was apparent she was having the time of her life. On 1st March, she told Jack that Paris was "charming", that she was going ice-skating at the Palais de Glace, and, "I find I have not forgotten my various figures – Sea Breeze, etc." Jennie, a fine pianist in her own right, numbered the great Paderewski amongst her friends. She ordered Jack, to "Go to bed early and take care of yourself ... I don't like hearing of a cough ... I hope you won't get influenza ... ." Jack replied that he was planning to visit her for Easter, and she advised him to "bring knickerbockers" for bicycling, and "a pair of low shoes". Winston wrote to her on 2nd March, that he hoped to get a few days holiday, and he also planned to come to Paris at Easter, "so you must keep a fatted calf for the occasion", and said he was sending her three boxes of her favourite cigarettes, Royal Beauties.

The Prince of Wales was heading for the Mediterranean in his yacht Britannia for a sailing regatta. He arranged for Jennie to visit him on board, where their intimate relationship was resumed. He also 'visited' her at the Avenue Klèber, and the Leslies' second son, John (Shane), aged 9½ years, remembered his first encounter with the future King. The Prince arrived late, long after Shane and his elder brother were in bed fast asleep. Considering the occasion too momentous to miss, Leonie gave the nurse orders to wake the two little boys. Soaking them in *eau de cologne*, she led them into the drawing room to be presented to the Prince. They shook hands with "an enormous gentleman with a beard and a guttural voice". The Prince asked the boys what they wanted to be when they grew up, and then gave Shane what he remembered as the 'Queen's shilling' (actually a gold sovereign)[3].

Bourke Cochran asked Jennie to marry him, but she declined, considering it too soon after her bereavement, and perhaps getting used to her new independence. She had no intention of returning to America to live. More seriously, all her plans were changed by the severe illness and sudden death of her mother. Clara was looking after Mrs Jerome at Tunbridge Wells, Kent, when her health had suddenly worsened. At the end of March 1895, Jennie and Leonie made hurried preparations to return to England. Mrs Jerome died five days later on 2nd April. Jennie, always her father's favourite, had inherited his drive, imagination, and love of life. Her mother was a cold, straight-laced woman, and Jennie never got on with her and she therefore inherited nothing from her will. Mrs Jerome had not approved of Randolph as a son-in-law, or in indeed of any of her sons-in-law, having harboured grandiose notions that her daughters should have married into the French royal circle. To Jennie it meant another death and funeral in the family within a few weeks of Randolph's, and more months of deep mourning clothes. All her letters had to be written on paper edged with black, and to complicate matters her mother's coffin had to be transported to America for burial. On 5th April, the Prince wrote to Jennie from Marlborough House, extending his sympathy at her mother's passing. Over the years the Prince wrote Jennie over a hundred letters and notes and his output increased after Randolph's death.

Jennie returned to Paris, and to Bourke, for a final few weeks before parting from him. He returned to America and, in June, Jennie returned to London for good. She had not heard from the Prince in a while. He was still in the process of ending his relationship with Daisy Warwick. Jennie had no intention of eschewing male companionship in the meanwhile. She was soon seen out with a handsome, rather boyish young officer of the Grenadier Guards, the 27-year-old Hugh Warrender. Jennie arrived at Cowes Week on the Isle of Wight in August, fashionably dressed in white from head to toe, and wearing a straw boater. Jennie was loved by the press of the day, and was the subject of frequent stories. *Town Topics* ran a piece about her youthful companion, dubbing her 'Lady Jane Snatcher'. Warrender was genuinely in love with her and would have married her. There is a striking group photograph of Jennie, Leonie, Winston, Jack and Hugh, taken that week. Warrender looks impossibly young. The Prince was currently keeping the company of Lady Dudley and left Cowes early. He wrote to Jennie, on 8th September, from Hamburg, and said he hoped she had enjoyed herself at Aix les Bains, where she had now gone for a rest. Then mixing jest with jealous lust, he chided her about Warrender, wondering "where your next loved victim is?" Jennie's readiness to entertain other men without pining for the Prince was to be a feature of their relationship. The Prince wrote her only one other letter that year, on 10th November, thanking her for books she had sent him for his birthday, but better things were to come.

Jennie preferred to flit back and forth to Paris, rather than live with her mother-in-law. Finally she made the major financial commitment to buy a new house, No. 35A Great Cumberland Place, in West London. She wrote to Clara on 3rd October 1895:

> I shall go to Mintos for a few days & then to London to look
> after '35A *Greater* Cumberland Place' as the boys call it – I
> hope to get into it the end of November; but you know how
> long it takes to do anything & I am going to have it all painted
> from top to toe, electric light, hot water etc. ... . How nice it
> will be when we are all together again on our 'owns'! The boys
> are so delighted at the thought of 'ringing their own front
> door' they can think of nothing else ... .

The new house, of late Georgian design, was relatively modest compared to Connaught Place. It was tall and thin, on seven storeys with a steep staircase to the bedrooms. It was within sight of Marble Arch, and only a short distance from Hyde Park and Mayfair, and, most importantly, it was convenient for the Prince's afternoon visits. Whether by accident or design, Jennie chose to live near William Waldorf Astor's home, Lansdowne House, and their close proximity to one another would add fuel to the gossip about their relationship both in society and in the press. Jennie lavished expense on her new house, having it decorated and furnished to the highest standard, and installed her collections of antique furniture, blue and white china, glass and crystal ware, jade ornaments, and her treasured collection of crystal pigs. When she took up residence she engaged seven servants. Released once and for all from the repressive atmosphere of living with her mother-in-law, Jennie continued to enjoy her new-found freedom. Her exquisitely presented home was once again a social centre for entertaining the top tier of society.

It was in the total privacy of her own house that the sexual relations between Jennie and the Prince of Wales could flourish. From

February 1896 until the end of 1897 there was a regular stream of letters and notes from the Prince to her. (Her replies did not survive as the Prince ordered all his private papers to be burnt at his death). His notes, which follow a pattern he used for all his principal mistresses, were sent weekly and would read: "Should you wish to see me, I could call at five tomorrow". He would then visit her for dinner or tea and sex.

'Bertie', as the Prince was known to his closest friends, was 44 years old, and had a short, grey, nicotine-stained beard, but was always immaculately dressed and perfumed himself with *eau de Portugal*. His voice was husky from smoking cigars and he spoke in deep, sexy, guttural tones, rolling the letter 'r' with something of his father's Germanic pronunciation. His stature, however, was gross from gorging himself with food and drink, and his waist measured 48 inches. Early movie films taken of him going riding at his country estate show that, when he mounted his horse, the poor brute positively shuddered and stumbled under his enormous 22 stones weight. Despite his appearance, he was a royal prince and a king in waiting, and had no trouble attracting a series of high born and beautiful mistresses. Jennie could not stand her own company and craved companionship and activity, and the Prince came to the rescue to keep her amused and to comfort her in bed. Bertie had a short fuse and a terrible temper and Jennie knew how to humour and cajole him and keep him happy. It was she who nick-named him 'Tum Tum'.

It seems, at first, that the idea of Jennie taking other lovers acted as a stimulant to their relationship. Warrender was never a threat because of his extreme youth and total lack of money. The next 'fling' was somewhat different. William Waldorf Astor, one of the richest men in the world, had been widowed in 1894. Jennie embarked on a short, passionate affair with him, just as she was about to become the Prince's current favourite. On 21st February, the *New York Times* published on its front page a story that must have incensed Bertie:

> The most interesting bit of society news which has been sent by cable from London of late is the engagement of Lady Randolph Churchill to William Waldorf Astor.

It was, of course, a completely false report. Astor would have married Jennie but she would not have him, despite his billions. He was too staid a character, not sufficiently exciting for Jennie's taste. The desirable Jennie turned down more than one rich man. She once wrote to a sister that she was "no mercenary". Her favour was not to be bought. No doubt she reassured the Prince that there was no romance with Astor, and Bertie wrote to her on 27th February, thanking her for "a charming dinner". *Town Topics* would not let the matter rest and, on 12th March, published a reminder that "Older New Yorkers recall the fact that Mr Astor admired Lady Randolph before her marriage."

As the 'official favourite', Jennie was routinely photographed stepping out with the Prince at many public functions, for all the world acting as his wife. In one press photograph she is walking with the Prince at the Tower, with Leonie and her lover, the Duke of Connaught, walking behind. In June she accompanied him to Epsom to see his horse, *Persimmon*, win the Derby. Jennie was a brilliant organiser and if the Prince wanted a small, private party arranged he could rely on her to draw up the guest list and decide the menu. She knew his particular friends and his favourite foods and the kind of music he liked. After the stormy time he had with Daisy Warwick, Bertie was enjoying the company of a brilliant conversationalist who shared many of his liberal ideas. She was, of course, the widow of his trusted friend, Randolph, the Tory liberal reformer, whom he had admired as a politician. She gave him physical and intellectual comfort; he showered her with gifts, and made her a powerful figure in 'Society'. She fought to maintain this supremacy and to advance the interests of her family. Family letters made continual references to the Prince. She arranged for the Prince to meet both her sons as often as possible. An independent correspondence arose between Winston and the Prince, principally concerning his army career, in which Edward took a close interest.

In best Winston style he did manage to cause an upset. Following Cowes Week 1896, the Prince was guest of honour at a weekend party given by 'Duchess Lily'[4] at 'The Deepdene', Dorking, to which Jennie had secured an invitation for Winston. It was a great honour for a second lieutenant, and amongst the guests was his commanding officer, Colonel Brabazon. But as ever, Winston could not turn up on time, having missed his train and caught a later one. He expected to slip into dinner unnoticed but a shock awaited him. The superstitious Royal Family never sat down thirteen at table. The entire party was standing about waiting for Winston to arrive, to the great annoyance of the Prince. "Don't they teach you to be punctual in your regiment, Winston?" said the Prince, in the presence of his colonel.

All through the autumn of 1896, Jennie was either the constant companion of the Prince at country house weekends, or was receiving a stream of letters from him from Sandringham, Windsor, his private club, his yachts or his European journeys. She kept her sons informed of her travels by letter, each having to predict where letters could be sent to find her. Jack had written to her commenting on the fact that her dog, a chow, had given birth to puppies, some brown and some black. Jennie replied on Sandringham headed note-paper whilst staying with the Prince. She had, she said, given one of the puppies to the Prince who loved dogs, and Bertie had said he was going to name it after him, and call it 'Black Jack'.

While Jennie was enjoying her powerful position in society, it came at a price. She might be entertained at the expense of her admirers, but travelling about and keeping up appearances in the midst of this extravagant set was fearfully expensive. Lavish dinners at Great Cumberland Place; a famous wine cellar kept there; the necessity of an endless supply of new dresses, usually by the great fashion house of Worth. All this was paid for by a spiralling series of loans, the repaying of which was financed by yet more loans. A love of gambling, in part inherited from her father, and a joint interest with her late husband, did not help. As with all gamblers, the occasional spectacular win helped to overlook the long and dreary succession of losses. The casinos at Monte Carlo had become a fashionable haunt that Jennie would find hard to resist.

Throughout 1897, Jennie maintained her dominant position in society. The Prince had to balance his visits to her with his duties involving matters of state to which he had to attend, but despite his busy schedule throughout the year, they still saw a lot of each other. Bertie was obviously taken with Jennie's artistic interest in everything Japanese, and when he visited her in her new home he found her wearing colourful dresses or a kimono of Japanese silk, which enhanced her dark beauty all the more. She looked like a Geisha girl.

On 4th January 1897, he wrote to her from Sandringham wishing her a happy New Year and asking whether he could visit her for a "Japanese" tea. Two days later, he acknowledged that she had invited him. Other of his letters for February asked if he might come to tea "a la Geisha" or to a "Geisha tea". That April the Prince was visiting France, and wrote to Jennie on 1st April whilst on the royal yacht, *Brittania*, in Nice, asking her to recommend French plays that he should see and thanking her for a dinner. The letter was seared with a burn mark, and he apologised, "Forgive my cigarette!"

In May she was staying at Astor's Cliveden House, with both William Astor and the Prince in attendance. How she coped with two ardent lovers under the same roof is best left to the imagination.

On 2nd July, the Duchess of Devonshire held the season's ball at her London home, Devonshire House in Piccadilly, to celebrate Queen Victoria's Diamond Jubilee. It was a fancy dress affair and guests had been asked to come attired as a famous person in history. The Prince of Wales came as the Grand Prior of the Order of St John of Jerusalem, and Princess Alexandra came as Marguerite de Valois complete with attendants of the nobility. Jennie, as ever, went out to upstage every woman there. Wearing the most fabulous costume, she represented the Byzantine Empress Theodora. Many column inches in the press described 'the belle of the ball'. Jennie's gown was an expensive, flamboyant, heavily embroidered robe, copied from the mosaic portrait in the church in Ravenna. On her head she wore a crown, hung with pendants of pearls at the temples and emblazoned with diamonds. A veil of white tulle, possibly an improvisation of her wedding veil, flowed from the crown, and from her arms fluttered matching veils, studded with sparkling brilliants. Her neck was covered with pearl chokers, and her long black hair, which she normally wore up at formal occasions, was revealed on this rare occasion, flowing forward over her shoulders, almost to waist-length. In one hand she held a giant lily, and in the other the golden orb of power. Reigning supreme at least for a day, Jennie was Queen in all but name. She would later record, in her memoirs, the melodramatic end to the day: "Towards the close of the ball two young men disputed over a certain fair lady". A duel was called and the one that "got the worst of it", received "a nasty cut on his silk stocking". What she did not disclose was that *she* had been the subject of the duel, and the "young man" who had defended her honour was none other than Jack, Winston having served as his second. Jack may well have over-heard a remark about his mother he considered unfitting, and, in his fierce devotion and blind loyalty to her, he would have leapt to her defence. Mercifully, the whole thing seems to have passed off in a good humour.

In August, at Cowes Week, dubbed by Bertie 'The Wild West Show', Jennie was seen in close and friendly harmony with Princess Alexandra. The long-suffering Princess, worn out by childbearing, was perfectly used to her husband's serial infidelity and had resigned herself to sharing him with ladies of her acquaintance. The Prince wrote to Jennie often that autumn, with news of his many overseas visits. He also said he was hearing good things about Winston. Such praise of her elder son was music to her ears.

By the beginning of 1898, Jennie was in deep financial trouble and borrowing heavily to cover her immediate needs. On 24th January, the Prince wrote to her from Sandringham, discussing her proposed visit there, with Jack. Jennie had attracted another young lover, Major Caryl Ramsden, who was fourteen years her junior. He had been posted to Cairo, where an expedition was being assembled under Kitchener for the re-conquest of the Sudan. Winston was des-perate to get transferred to Kitchener's staff in Egypt, and Jennie thought she might 'kill two birds with one stone', and visit Ramsden and lobby Kitchener on Winston's behalf whilst she was there. Winston wrote that he was sure her wit, tact and beauty would over-come all obstacles. He would later describe her as the woman 'who tapped the men and opened the doors' for him. The Prince wrote to her in Egypt on 25th February 1898, saying he hoped her journey had been pleasant. Jennie had stayed with Ramsden at the Continental Hotel, Cairo, and contacted Kitchener. He had brushed aside her request, one of so many he had to deal with of a similar nature. Jennie's stay came to an end and she left for Port Said, only to find that her homeward ship had been delayed. Returning to the hotel, where she hoped to spend another night with Ramsden, she entered his room without knocking, looking to give him a pleasant surprise by her unexpected return. But it was Jennie who got the sur-prise of her life when she found him embracing the wife of the general, Sir John Maxwell. Ramsden experienced a sample of

Jennie's temper at his betrayal, and the row that she kicked up was loud enough to be heard throughout the entire hotel. It soon reached the Prince's ears, as did most gossip, and from Cannes, where he was holidaying, he let her know he had heard of her embarrassment:

> You had better have stuck to your old friends than gone on your expedition of the Nile! Old friends are best!

Immediately Jennie arrived home, Leonie called to see her and found her scribbling a reply to the Prince to even the score:

> *So* grateful for your sympathy – as your Royal Highness knows exactly *how* it feels, after being jilted by Lady Dudley.

Leonie tried to stop her posting the note lest it gave offence, but Jennie composed what she described as a wittier version and mailed it herself. Acknowledging both letters, the Prince sent Jennie an apology from Cannes, on 8th April 1898: "*Ma chère Amie* … I must ask your pardon if my letter pained. I had no idea "*que c' était une affaire si serieuse*! [it was such a serious affair]." On 15th April, he wrote and asked her to arrange a dinner at her home, and on 23rd wrote to congratulate her on its success: "I must write to thank you for your charming dinner last night … . I thought your party was exceptionally successful".

These teasing letters were masking a major shift in Jennie's fortunes. The Prince had met the Honourable George Keppel and his beautiful young wife, Alice. He soon found himself deeply attracted to her, and she, breaking all the rules concerning these things, found herself in love with the Prince. If Jennie's days as 'La Favourite' were coming to an end, she would fight to retain his affections, in a most ingenious way.

Lord Randolph once described George Cornwallis-West as the most beautiful man in England. In 1898, George was twenty-four years old, tall and handsome, a lieutenant in the Scots Guards. He would recall in his biography, *Edwardian Hey-Days*, how in June of that year, he had found himself, starry-eyed and amazed, having been invited by Daisy Warwick to a party at her castle, not knowing why he had been selected for the guest list. It was there that he met Jennie by chance, or so it may have appeared at the time. We suggest that there was more calculation on Jennie's part in this meeting.

Winston had recently befriended Colonel (later General Sir) Ian Hamilton on the North West frontier. When Hamilton returned from India, to take command of the School of Musketry at Hythe, Kent, he carried the manuscript of Winston's novel, *Savrola*, to be handed to Jennie, who would see to its publication. Having been in India for so long, Jean Hamilton knew little of English society, and Jennie was one of her first guests at their new home. Years later she recalled the events of that time in her diary:

> The day Lady Randolph and Lady Sassoon called there, [Hythe] ... Nancy [Bateman] was staying with me, and we had one or two nice boys from the Musketry School with us who had been lunching, and we were sitting grouped half in the garden and half on the low window seat ... . Winston had written so much about Ian to his Mother.
>
> I did not know at first who Lady Randolph was, and she was amazed that I should not. I suppose she thought not to know her argued oneself unknown, which I suppose was true ... .[5]

George Cornwallis-West was there with his regiment taking a course in musketry under Hamilton's direction, and it was undoubtedly at one of Jean's lunch parties that Jennie caught sight of him, and took a fancy to him. The whole of society believed him to be the Prince of Wales' illegitimate son. Perhaps the Prince's flirtation with Alice Keppel could be ended by a dalliance of Jennie's own.

George's mother, Mary Cornwallis-West, had been the Prince of Wales' first lover since she was sixteen. They had known each other long before either Daisy or Jennie knew the Prince. Mary was called Patsy in the family and, though the Prince would take many more lovers, he always retained a high regard for her. He had arranged the match between Patsy and a friend of his, Colonel William Cornwallis-West, who was over twenty years her senior. It was a marriage of convenience so that the Prince could keep Patsy as his mistress, and it was common knowledge that George was Bertie's love child. Their love nest had been 'Newlands Manor', Lymington,

Hampshire, the country home of Patsy's mother. When George was born the Prince stood sponsor for him at baptism, and his Christian name had been the choice for sons of the royal families down through the ages. His middle name, Frederick was that of the Prince's godfather, King Frederick IV of Prussia. Bertie took a great interest in George's upbringing. Writing of his childhood, George remembered the Prince being a frequent visitor at his home:

> The Prince of Wales often came, and was invariably kind to me
> and always asked to see me. Never a Christmas passed without
> his sending me some little gift in the shape of a card or a toy.[6]

George attended fishing or deer-stalking parties with the Prince on his estates. He had been educated at Eton, and had initially been destined for the diplomatic service. It had been to the Prince that he had "protested he would far rather become an engine-driver, an option which seemed not to have been considered".[7] The Cornwallis-Wests had little money at the time Jennie met George, though they would eventually own three properties that would come to him; Ruthin Castle, in North Wales, 49 Eton Place, Belgravia, London, and Newlands Manor. George's two sisters, who were also generally believed to have been fathered by the Prince, would marry men of considerable fortune and status. Daisy married the Prince of Pless, and Sheila married the Duke of Westminster. The Cornwallis-Wests assumed that George would marry a beautiful and wealthy young heiress from amongst the aristocracy, and bring much needed money to keep up his father's flagging estates. They did not approve of his association with Jennie, who was old enough to be his mother and past childbearing age, meaning the line would die out without a male heir to carry on the Cornwallis-West name.

George was fit and active, and very kind, but of no great intellect. Jennie could have had her pick of many men. She targeted George as a means of getting the attention of the Prince. If Bertie could have Alice, who was half his age, then Jennie could fatally charm a man nearly half her age. She was 44 and still beautiful, and George fell head over heels in love with her. His first letter to her – one of several hundred – was dated 29th July 1898, and was decorated with hearts: "I thought about you all yesterday & built castles in the air about you & I living together." Jennie soon found herself equally smitten and entertained him at her home, sweeping him off his feet. They spent weekends together at country houses, and then, most conveniently, George's battalion was posted to London. At this stage Jennie was teasing Bertie by her very public association with his boy. But she came to genuinely love George and tried to make him happy.

The Prince soon let his disapproval of Jennie's relationship with George be known to her. Writing to her on 21st August, from the Royal Yacht *Osborne*, Dartmouth, Devon, he told her he valued her friendship greatly and that he had decided not to write her a letter about her relationship with George that might offend her. He would have imagined at this early stage that she would soon drop George, as she had dropped other young men. The letters, dated and undated, for 1898, show an increasing annoyance over the affair, and the Prince's dislike at her fooling around with his son became apparent. Only on one occasion did he ask to have tea with her and that was probably to try and talk her out of it.

Along with other aspects of Jennie's life, things would gradually get out of control.

CHAPTER 12

Financial Worries and Career Development
1895–1897

Winston's success at Sandhurst greatly encouraged Jack in his desire for a career in the army, and he longed to join his brother. But almost immediately Winston was losing interest in an army career, telling his mother: "I do not think it is my *metier*" and that politics was "a fine game to play". This was in perfect accord with Jennie's great ambition for Winston, that he should pursue a career in his father's footsteps and achieve the great office of Prime Minister denied to her husband. According to Peregrine, when Randolph resigned as Leader of the House and Chancellor of the Exchequer in December 1886, the following January a messenger from Parliament had called at the Churchills' home, wanting to buy the official robes that he had worn as Chancellor for his successor, George Goschen. Jennie met the messenger at the door and refused to hand over the robes, telling him: "I am saving them for my son".

Winston may have been unsettled by the death of 'Woomany' [Mrs Everest] in July 1895. Regardless of how much or how little Jennie had to do with the raising of her sons, Mrs Everest had been a constant feature in their lives for many years. They always showed her the greatest respect and her death was a great sadness to them both. He had been at her bedside at the end and wrote movingly to his mother of her last moments. "Her last words were of Jack ... . Please send a wire to Welldon to ask him to let Jack come up for the funeral – as he is very anxious to do so".[1] Winston and Jack together would see that Mrs Everest's grave would be well made and cared for.

With the 4th Hussars due to go out to India for a lengthy spell, Winston was granted a 'long leave' and, without consulting Jennie, decided to go with a fellow subaltern to the Americas to see something of the country and observe the Spanish army in its campaign against rebels in Cuba. While accepting that he needed to expand his horizons, this new charge on Jennie's finances brought forth the acid comment:

> Considering that I provide the funds I think instead of saying "I *have* decided to go", it may have been nicer and perhaps wiser – to have begun by consulting me. But I suppose experience of life will in time teach you that tact is a very essential ingredient in all things.

But, making a birthday present of his ticket, she was soon contacting friends who could help Winston, notably Senator Bourke Cockran, who showed him New York and introduced him to a luxurious lifestyle and the particular pleasures of a fine cigar. This superb orator greatly influenced Winston's style of speech and he freely and generously credited him with teaching him the full use of the English language. Cockran immediately saw great promise in the young soldier and encouraged him in a course of reading to further his political ambitions.

In January 1896, Winston rejoined his regiment at Aldershot. It was during the nine months he was waiting to set out for India that Jennie and Winston, hugely encouraged by Cockran's continuing praise, finally decided that he should spend some time in the army to make a name for himself, and then go into politics. He therefore pursued political connections during his spare time in the months before leaving. He also began lobbying for a transfer to a regiment that might be doing something more interesting than serving in India – a "useless and unprofitable exile". He looked for postings in South Africa or Egypt, and soon earned the reputation of a 'medal hunter'.

In September 1896, he was obliged to sail with his regiment to India. From Bombay, the regiment moved to Bangalore, where Winston found the climate quite to his liking He shared a 'palatial' bungalow with two fellow officers, with numerous servants on hand. He resumed an interest in butterflies and gardening and fell in love, ultimately in vain, with Pamela Plowden. (She was the beautiful daughter of the British Resident in Hyderabad; later Countess Lytton).

The long and loving letters between Jennie and Winston were a solace during the tedious life of a young subaltern in India. Already on November 18th, Winston was writing to his mother of his frustration with his situation. As an MP he could "get hold of the right people"; as a soldier he vegetated to no purpose

With all her hopes for the future tied up in Winston's political advancement, Jennie began to develop a quite different strategy towards Jack. We have already seen that his exemplary record at Harrow School had won the admiration and personal attention of the Headmaster, Welldon. He discussed Jack's future with him at great length and actively encouraged him to consider following Lord Randolph's course, a university degree in History and Law, after which a career in the army or at the Bar would be open to him. He even wrote personally to Magdalen College, Oxford, arranging for Jack to sit the entrance examination, and sketched out a programme of preparatory study that included a year in France to improve his language skills and a nine-month course in Greek with a specially chosen tutor. Anxious that his possible promotion to a bishopric might remove him from this enjoyable guidance of such a fine young man, Welldon did everything he could to set Jack on a suitable path for his future.

Jack's intentions were misunderstood by both Jennie and Winston because, living with two such strong personalities, he was insufficiently demonstrative. He was only fifteen. He wanted to join the army and his late father had laid the foundations for his career as a professional soldier. It was not to be. Jennie complained that Jack was not direct enough in making his intentions clear, and Winston said of him, in a letter to his mother in November 1896, that it was very difficult to get at what he really thought. One has to wonder what it was that was so hard to understand. The previous year, Jennie had suggested to Jack the possibility of joining an infantry regiment, where she had contacts and could pull strings. When Jack demurred, she answered, 8th October 1895: "I do not wish to stand in your way if your heart is not on going into the Army". That is not what Jack meant at all; he was a natural horseman and yearned for the cavalry. It was disingenuous of Jennie to put such an interpretation on his reply.

'Jock' Colville later observed:

The character of Jack Churchill was strikingly different. Loyal, affectionate, scrupulously honourable, he was also endowed with that most endearing of qualities, natural humility. He did not share his brother's restless energy, consuming ambition, gift of eloquence or quickness of mind. He was always proud to be referred to as "Winston's brother".

Colville only knew Jack in the 1940s, after he had been obliged to work for many uncongenial years in the City of London.

Jack did make a firm decision, telling his mother: "I have decided I will go to Oxford – I just had a long talk with Welldon as to the best way to get there". In a letter to Winston Jennie discussed Jack's future:

> Jack is too mature for school life – even Welldon thought so
> … . I have been very busy arranging things for Jack. I went to
> see Welldon and had a long talk with him as to his future. I am
> much against his going in the Army. I can't afford to put him
> in a smart cavalry regiment & in anything else he would be lost
> & unhappy. Besides at the best it is a poor career. I think he
> might do at the Bar. He has plenty of ability and common
> sense, a good presence, & with perseverance & influence he
> ought to get on. The City he hates.

This last remark should have set alarm bells ringing for Jack. His enthusiasm for the cavalry was under attack in the face of Jennie's opposition, and from Winston's growing disenchantment with his own army career and his preference for politics. Writing to Jack on 7th January 1897, Winston now poured cold water on Jack's idea of becoming a Barrister, though he fully supported him in his wish for a university education:

> If you feel no desire to go into the Army, I should be the last
> person to press you to do so … . Don't think of drifting
> languidly and placidly – as your letter apparently suggests to
> the Bar … .
> I think you have great talents, Jack … but I *am* perfectly

certain that unless you start full of enthusiasm and keenness,
you will never develop your abilities ... .

... Find something *congenial* at all costs.

I shall envy you the enjoyment of a liberal education, and of
the power to appreciate the classical works.[2]

How ironic of Winston to berate Jack for "drifting languidly and
placidly" between careers, when he himself was abandoning his first
choice even before it had begun. And why would he write to his
mother, "What a strange inversion of fortune – that I should be a soldier and Jack at college", when he could not have got out of school
quickly enough to get into Sandhurst? The myth-creating tendency
began early.

Jack was now under pressure from the two people he most adored
in the world to give up the one career he truly wanted. At least
Winston approved of him going to university to increase his options
in life. Jennie was hatching another and much less conducive plan.

In another mood swing Winston wrote to his mother, in February
1897, thinking he would "stick to soldiering" after all. She would
not hear of it, having already cautioned him:

How little one hears of any of the Generals in time of peace.
There is really very little honour & glory to be got out of the
Army. A moderate MP gets better known in the country & has
more chance of success than a really clever man in the Army.

Above all, Jennie looked ahead to Winston fulfilling her political
dream and had written to him, 24th December 1896: "I am looking
forward to the time when we shall live together again & all my political ambitions shall be centred in you".

Meanwhile Jennie made arrangements to round out Jack's education. At the beginning of February 1897, she accompanied him to
Versailles and installed him with Monsieur Robineau, a French tutor,
and his family. Jennie stayed for a short while to see Jack settled in
and introduced him to some of her great friends living in France.
Amongst them were Bourke Cockran and Cecil Rhodes. In addition
to learning French, Jack would take piano and dancing lessons,
extend his knowledge of music and culture by attending concerts and

the opera, and would take horse riding lessons. He went cycling in the countryside for exercise and to see the sights. Jennie took care of paying Robineau by sending him a cheque each month for Jack's lessons and board, and she kept her son supplied with money for the other extra lessons and his personal needs, and sent him copies of the *Daily Graphic*, to keep him abreast of events in England. This is an interesting juncture in Jack's life as his future seemed to be well taken care of by his mother.

Jennie's letters to Jack were loving and full of gossip. One of the first urged:

> You must become very talkative, I wonder if you would care to do a little Latin with Mr. Robineau? … . I miss you very much but hope you will make great progress as I said darling child remember this year is the only one of your life you can give up entirely to French – Make the most of it – Do like Winston, talk incessantly!

Jack wrote to her of his impressions of his new surroundings and the progress he was making. His Roumanian riding instructor was "rather dirty", the champagne was so bad that "water is a treat after it" and as for dressing for dinner, M. Robineau "has never seen a tail coat". There was always a reminder of some money that had to be paid for something.

While carefully apportioning £3 here and £5 there to settle Jack's expenses, Jennie had to cancel a trip to visit him because of Winston's reckless expenditure in India. India was famously inexpensive and most officers lived royally on their pay. Despite receiving his £300 army pay and an allowance from his mother of £500, plus money from journalism, Winston still overspent against his account, and Cox's, the army's bankers, applied to Jennie for these overdrawn amounts. Jennie complained bitterly in a letter to Jack:

> I am very much afraid that it will be impossible for me to go to Paris next week – as I had hoped – but I am really too hard up – and Winston has been overdrawing his account and I had to meet a cheque for £50 – It is too bad of him – and I find he has anticipated the whole of this quarter – I have written him a

very stiff letter which I fear hurt me more to write than it will
him to receive ... .

The effect of these dishonoured cheques on Jennie's finances reveal
just how precarious they were. Since the death of Lord Randolph she
had been living without any restraining influence. She spared no
expense in furnishing her new London house, which she fondly imagined would be a cosy and happy home for her and her boys, and a
base to 'entertain' the Prince of Wales, as she would not have dared
bring him to her mother-in-law's house. She frequented the casinos
of Monte Carlo and the race meetings at home in a futile bid to
improve her income. The rents from the New York house left to her
by her father became just an asset against which to make ever-larger
borrowings. Just as Winston left for India she, and other family
members, fell victim to a notorious swindler, James Cruikshank. This
so-called investment adviser cost Jennie £4,000. To make Winston
understand she set out her dilemma in a letter:

> Out of 2700 pounds a year, 800 of it goes to you 2 boys, 410
> for house rent and stables, which leaves me 1500 for
> everything – taxes, servants, stables, food, dress, travelling – &
> now I have to pay money on interest borrowed – I *really* fear
> for the future – I am telling you all this darling in order that
> you may see how impossible it is for me to help you – and how
> you *must* in future depend on yourself.

Jack dutifully reported on his progress in French and music, the concerts he attended, the people he saw. Jennie was overly maternal and
protective in her replies, constantly worrying about his spelling, his
reading habits, his clothes, his ear infection, the temptations of Paris
(hardly necessary with such a well behaved boy), and sending him
letters full of adulation for Winston's heroism, every word of which
Jack relished. After yet another failure to call and see him while she
was in France, Jennie bought Jack a new bicycle. Her son would
probably have preferred her attention to her gifts. He was soon
exploring the countryside energetically and sending full reports of his
travels. The exposure to the wind did cause a flare up of his ear trouble, to Jennie's great consternation. Jack had to continually remind

her of monies that had to be paid for his tuition and board. She would ask querulously whether both she and his uncle, Jack Leslie, had not paid the £7 subscription to *The Naval Review*.

Winston came home on leave, meeting a delighted Jack in Paris. That summer, the family was together for part of the season in London. They attended the Duchess of Devonshire's famous fancy dress ball referred to in the previous chapter. Jack then returned to France to his studies, leaving behind his mother and brother enjoying themselves at the races.

On hearing of a Pathan rebellion in India, Winston reminded Sir Bindon Blood of an earlier promise to take him onto his personal staff. He was told there was no vacancy but he might serve as a correspondent and wait for one to occur. Winston set out immediately, writing to his mother from his train, asking her to obtain for him an arrangement with a newspaper that would receive his letters for payment as a war correspondent. The Indian journal, *The Pioneer*, took him on and he wrote letters to Jennie, adding greatly to her anxieties, of the need to take risks in order to get on. Later the *Daily Telegraph* employed him, thanks to Jennie's influence, to give graphic descriptions of the fighting he had been involved in. These would find expression in the book, *The Malakand Field Force*, that would do so much to bring him to the attention of the public and the establishment at home. Typically, Winston complained vociferously that he was not paid enough for the letters and was not allowed to sign his name to the column as published.

Jack was now aged 17, and Jennie simply would not treat him as an adult and let him make his own decision about his career. Despite her earlier assurances about Oxford, she had been discussing other possibilities in her letters to both Jack and Winston. She thought he might take the Civil Service exams and try for the Foreign Office. She wrote to Winston undermining Jack's academic credibility, 30th September: "if he did pass the Exams – but I fear he is not clever enough". It was an insult to Jack's intelligence to suggest he might fail, particularly since Welldon expected him to pass the entry examination for Oxford. Jennie knew from his school reports that Jack had never failed an examination in his life. Her attitude seems to have been yet another excuse for what was to come. Somewhere along the way she had conceived the idea that Jack would go into the

City as a stockbroker, like his American grandfather before him, and make a vast fortune that would solve the whole family's financial problems. That Jerome had spectacularly lost his fortune was conveniently forgotten. She had, however, to convince Winston that she was doing the best for Jack's career as, at this stage, he was not at all keen on the idea of his brother being sent into the City, though that too would change.

Jennie, now approaching her 44th birthday, was distracted by the Cruikshank case, and she had become confused and absent minded. She frequently could not remember if she had sent Robineau his money, and was late sending Jack his cheque, and her financial problems appear to have been getting the better of her. She was constantly on the move, from one country house to another, keeping up with the Prince of Wales' set. To Winston she sent some good advice:

> You have done more than well my darling boy & I am as
> always proud of you. Forgive a piece of advice – which may
> not be needed – but be modest – All your feats of valour are
> sure to come out & people will know – Let it be from others &
> not from yourself – One must be tempted to talk of oneself in
> such a case – *but resist* – Let them *drag* things out.

With his father less than three years dead, Winston meant to try and capture his old South Paddington seat, asking his mother to be alert in his interest there. In the midst of all these dramatic happenings, the case against Cruikshank went ahead. Cruikshank pleaded guilty to fraud and received a harsh sentence, two terms of four years penal servitude. A gentler side of Winston is revealed in his expressed idea that three years would have been a fairer sentence.

Finally Jack was preparing to return home from Paris in November 1897, and he wrote to his mother a most complete statement of his career preferences:

> My dear Mama,
> I can remember at Harrow one or two boys who had suddenly
> to change all their plans for their futures, I don't think you
> could easily find one who changes every year!
>   I have been "going to be" everything under the sun and as

you know I have always had a great abhorrence of being a "something in the city" with the chance of becoming nothing. I have been "going into" the army, the city, the army, the bar, the Foreign Office, or diplomacy and now I am to change again to the city.

Each time I have been told that I have lots of time, but I have no more, I am nearly eighteen and it must be settled.

It is not wholly my fault that I have changed so. I am built heart and soul for the army; but you asked me to give it up because it was expensive and not lucrative, because it might leave you alone, and because it was no 'career'. I am afraid that "many are called and few chosen" in anything.

I began to like the idea of going to Oxford, of going where Winston had not been, and even of plodding away at the Bar. But now you want me to go under the old gas lamp in the city.

The life of a cavalry officer appeals to me more; but I will do it if it is necessary and if you want me to.

Your letter did not tell me much about your "Serious financial crisis". Have things gone wrong in America? or did they get muddled in England?

Lord Vernon prophesied to me a year ago that you would either marry! or have a crisis in the next two years! I believe it is very bad indeed in England.

In the city I should undoubtedly be able to turn my French to good account, but it will take a good deal to make me do it ... .

The only part of your letter with which I agreed, was the wish that we should 'be more together' – that is at a 1000 to 3 on.

If you could imagine how much I long to come home to you at Cumberland Place, you would realise that my only wish is to please you and to do whatever you wish.

Your loving son

Jack S.C.

Jennie had put all her cards on the table before her youngest son. Pleading insoluble financial difficulties, she had induced him to abandon the career he longed for and take on the last thing in the world he would have chosen. In the end Jack would obey his beloved mother and do nothing to add to her financial difficulties. His fate was sealed by a spendthrift mother and an egocentric brother. Jennie replied, whilst still on her travels around the country, admonishing him:

> I have been so on the move I have had no time to write – Your last letter saddened me – but my darling Boy – you can be certain of one thing and that is that your happiness is the one thing I want above all others and that I will make any sacrifice necessary to ensure it – We will talk it all over later I mean before Xmas … . Darling I don't want to make any tiresome remarks but you must remember that your want of decision as regards your likes and dislikes and your choice of career has been a drawback to you – I have never heard you before really express a real desire to go into the Army – It is not too late – if you are content to have a small allowance and live on your pay – and be a major at [age] 45 on [£]600 a year! – Bless you my child don't fret all will come right for you.'

But all would *not* come right for Jack. For Jennie to say he had never expressed a real desire to go into the Army is simply not true. Had she forgotten the meeting Randolph had organised at Harrow Public School, where he had introduced Jack to Lord Roberts, (making him the envy of the school), when his army career had been agreed upon? Would she have forgotten something so important in relation to Winston's career?

Jennie's financial disarray between 1895 and 1897 determined Jack's career. It was a situation of her own making and at one stage had reached such a crisis that the bailiffs nearly moved in on her. She was constantly preoccupied with how she was going to pay her bills as she got deeper and deeper into debt. Jack was a sensitive boy, good at mathematics at school. When he was in Paris, he accounted to his mother for the money she sent him, and had kept a careful record of his spending. With his head for figures he knew, soon after his return home, that his mother could not afford to send him into the army or to Oxford. Between them Jennie and Winston spent so much money on themselves that there was not enough left to support Jack in his choice of career. But Jack seems never to have uttered a word of rebuke or attributed any blame to either of them. He was so much younger, his self-esteem was not high, nor was he sufficiently shrewd to see through them. Jennie squandered the money Jack's father had left. If she had given due consideration to Jack's prospects, she could surely have cut down her spending and turned her mind towards helping him plan a suitable career. Through her great friendship with Cassel or the Rothschilds she could have invested some money in 1895, the interest of which would have accrued to finance Jack's career. But Jennie lived for the moment, bought what she wanted, and seemed only to have woken up to the fact that she had over-spent when she had to raise another loan. Lord Randolph would have curtailed both Jennie's and Winston's spending, and put the required amount of money into Jack's career. Winston wrote his mother a consoling letter, 18th November, saying that she could always let her house; lots of places would receive "the dearest and most beautiful woman in the world".

Jack returned to his mother's empty house in London, on a bleak Friday in December. He wrote to her at the country house where she was staying, telling her he had arrived safely, and he was obviously lonely: "I beg you to come home as soon as you can". She had sent him £20 to pay his final month's expenses in France, and he enclosed a careful note of his accounts, amounting to 841 francs. The cost of Jack's year in France had amounted to approximately £240. Though Jennie had bought a family home, and incurred the expense of its upkeep, Jack was still living a lot more cheaply than either Jennie or Winston, and a fraction of the money wasted by them could have allowed him to develop his own career pattern.

CHAPTER 13

Financial Crisis and a Career Denied
1898–1899

Jennie and Jack spent Christmas at Blenheim Palace. In the New Year of 1898, three way discussions resumed regarding Jack's career. Jack had written previously to Winston in some detail of the discussions that had taken place between him and their mother. Winston was not keen on Jack being made to work in the City, and at that stage it was considered only as a temporary measure until Jennie had sorted out her finances, and recovered from the losses she had incurred by Cruikshank. In reply to Jennie's letter of November 1897, saying that she was considering sending Jack into the City, Winston had made his opposition clear. He was, he said, only prepared to go along with it on the understanding that Jack would later be allowed to go to university. With Winston so far from home, and unable to assess fully what was taking place between Jennie and Jack, he did not realise that she was in fact forcing his younger brother into the City on a permanent basis. To his credit Winston tried to help Jack as much as possible from the other side of the world, and he wrote to Jennie, 10th January 1898, disagreeing with her judgment. He clearly understood Jack's earnest desire for a university education, and even offered to raise a loan (to be repaid when he came of age) to help him.

When Jennie replied, on 13th January, she was clearly furious at being contradicted, and thought she knew best: "Everyone thinks my plan for him is the best. He will go to Germany for a year, learn bookkeeping & German, & one of these days make a fortune. He is quite reconciled to it now". Given the prevalent aristocratic disdain for gentlemen going into 'trade', it is hard to know who 'everyone' was. In its day it was hardly a proper vocation for a grandson of the Duke of Marlborough. Jack may have outwardly acquiesced but in his heart he dreaded the prospect.

Whilst this debate raged between Jennie and Winston, Welldon proceeded to complete the arrangements for Jack to go to Oxford. The amount of money that would have been required to educate Jack was not in fact very great by the standards of the day. Dr Robin Darwall-Smith, the present Archivist of Magdalen College, has assisted the authors by producing roughly the costs of living in Oxford and obtaining a degree. Even allowing for the higher expense bracket, the maximum would have been £339 per year. Lord Randolph would certainly have expected Jennie to make such a provision. Jennie herself had already estimated that Jack 'cost' her something like £300 a year.[1]

Having cajoled him into agreeing to work for Cassel, just prior to his taking up his appointment towards the end of January 1898, Jennie allowed Jack to satisfy his interest in the army by joining the Oxfordshire Hussars, a (part-time) Yeomanry Regiment that, in 1908, would become part of the Territorial Force. After a month's training, he could balance the two pursuits, working in the City during the week, and joining his regiment for further service experience at weekends and during holiday periods. Winston had suggested in a letter to his mother that as well as a university education remaining open to Jack, that he might still also have the opportunity of going into the army as a professional soldier if he chose. But to this, Jennie made her objections and her annoyance even more clear, in her reply of 13th January:

> You talk glibly of Jack going into the Army – but you know he
> would never pass the medical examination with his eyes – &
> besides how could I give him an adequate allowance? … He
> has joined the Oxford Yeomanry & will have a month's drill at
> Aldershot & his 10 days before he goes to Berlin. It will set
> him up & give him a nice uniform for all requirements. How I
> am to pay for it I do not know!

When Jack was a boy, he had been accidentally shot in the eye by a family friend, John Prescott Hewitt, at Deepdene. The problem with his eye was temporary, and Jennie was using it as an excuse to get her own way and prevent his joining the army. Jack's eye problem had cleared up, and was never mentioned again during his time in his regiment, or later when he served in the Boer War, or the First World

War. During Jack's training with the Oxfordshire Hussars, Jennie was constantly strapped for cash, and he was reduced to begging her for money to carry out the necessary exercises. The relationship between mother and son remained excellent as always, and Jack urged her to visit him in camp:

> I am going on here very well and am having a splendid time.
> Can't you come down to Blenheim next Tuesday and
> Wednesday I am sure Consuelo will be there and you can come
> and see our inspection which will be very pretty. They are
> going to ask you to the mess etc. so do come.
> I am having plenty of exercise 5 hours riding every morning.

Jennie replied from 35A Cumberland Place, and said she would endeavour to fit attendance at the inspection into her ever more hectic schedule. It must have been with a heavy heart that Jack would all too soon have to leave the excitement of the regiment to take up his job in the City.

Winston heard from his mother in a letter of 23rd January 1898, that her finances had reached crisis point. She had, she said, to find £17,000 to "buy up all the loans I have made in different Insurance offices", and that she also needed to clear up some debts. Winston replied, with a jovial, witty discussion of their mutual inability to handle money. He thought they were equally thoughtless, spendthrift and extravagant, though his extravagances were on a smaller scale than hers. He could get by on £1,000 a year[2], and could earn by writing or marrying a rich woman. He thought their extravagances were "suicidal"; at bottom they were "damned poor".

Winston's mirth, however, soon turned to annoyance, and anger, when he learnt that his mother intended the security on the loan she was about to take out to be a life insurance policy on her own life and his, and that she wanted him to guarantee £700 per annum to pay the interest. All this she had decided without consulting him, and he knew nothing until the documents landed somewhat unceremoniously on his desk, sent him by the family solicitors, Lumley & Lumley, requiring his signature. On 30th January Winston wrote from India a rather stiff business letter. He pointed out that £700 was nearly half the sum he might eventually inherit from the Trust Fund.

He would pay this "purely and solely out of affection for you", but only if she absolutely guaranteed the £500 a year he currently received "at your pleasure". This is the first indication we get that Jennie was financing her eldest son's army career quite generously, to the great detriment of Jack's prospects. She was then asked to use her influence and power over Jack, "even to threatening to stop his allowances", to make him share this annual burden when he came of age. Although Jennie stated that she needed £17,000, it appears that the loan she received was for 'only' £14,000.

At this time their mother had no intentions of paying for Jack's further education. Her income had dropped dramatically to £900 a year, because of the interest on the loan, and the debts she was paying off, and out of this sum she had also to meet her allowances to her sons. Jack, of course, agreed to these demands made on his future prospects. For Jennie he would have done it without a second thought. On the same day, 30th January, Winston wrote Jack a very different kind of letter from the one he had just written to his mother. It was nicely reasoned, and the case for Jack fulfilling his part of the responsibility was presented as caring for their mother, and was based on the principle set down by their father that they should share their inheritance equally. To do this, Jack promised to pay half of the £700 a year interest on his mother's loan, secured by a life insurance once he came of age. Winston 'jollied' Jack along by reckoning they would inherit as much as £1,800 a year each after the death of their mother.

Following a weekend with his mother and the Prince at his country home, Sandringham, Norfolk, where Jack was introduced to Cassel, he eventually, if somewhat reluctantly, agreed to work for Cassel. Jennie's financial crisis occurred just at the moment when he, with Welldon's support, should have begun learning Greek in final preparation for the entrance examination for Oxford later in 1898. Instead he would be heavily dependent on his spendthrift mother for years more, as his income as Cassel's clerk would be miniscule for some time.

Jennie could have solved her financial problems by marrying a rich man, who could have paid off her loan and settled her debts. When she informed Winston how matters stood, he had clearly weighed up in advance the possibility of the threat of a prospective step-father, and replied, 27th March: "I have also to reckon on the possibility of your marrying again – perhaps some man I did not like – or did not get on with – and of troubles springing up – which might lessen your affections for me"[3]. Jennie had made out a convincing case for herself, and Winston soon backed down: "The situation as described by your letter is appalling. As you say it is of course impossible for you to live in London on such a pittance. I hate the idea of your marrying – but that of course would be a solution"[4].

It never occurred to Jennie for a moment that she might sell her fine house and settle for something more modest and trim her extravagant efforts to maintain her place in high society in order to provide for both her sons. Instead she increasingly looked to Jack to restore their joint fortunes when he would eventually become a stockbroker.

Ernest Cassel, (1852–1921), was a financial genius with huge interests in Egypt, South America and the USA. He was an intimate friend of the Prince of Wales and was known in his set as 'the King's banker'. He certainly helped Alice Keppel rise from genteel poverty to millionairess status. How Jennie must have regretted losing her place as Bertie's favourite. She negotiated a place for Jack in Cassel's employ, hoping it would strengthen her links with the Prince and set Jack on the path to improve the family finances.

There was little hope for Jack now in achieving his own ambitions. Writing to him on 19th January 1898, Winston said he was being denied his choice of career because he was not aggressive enough in demanding what he wanted from Jennie:

> The whole thing is your own fault for not expressing decided opinions. If you had made up your mind what you wanted – insisted upon it – no one would have stopped you. As it is you will probably be making £5,000 a year and playing polo at Hurlingham when I am struggling on a pittance – as a newspaper hack. I shall come down on you like a cartload of brick.[5]

Winston's prediction that Jack's remuneration in the City would reach £5,000 a year (£350,000 today) was improbable in the short term, as were his notions about his leisure time. Jack was not able to live on the money Cassel paid him. Indeed it is not entirely clear whether he was paid at all in the beginning or was on some sort of apprenticeship until he got his own place as a stockbroker. He would work long hours in the claustrophobic heat of a City office, and would endure more harrowing conditions when he traveled overseas with Cassel on business. Winston might later boast that he had made £10,000 from a lecture tour of America. A small part of that would have made all the difference to Jack's future.

The exact date Jack started work is not known but it was probably around the beginning of March 1898, when his initial training with the Oxfordshire Hussars had been completed. Peregrine is quite adamant that his father hated the City and the demeaning work he had to undertake there. Little is known of the early months of Jack's employment. He was engaged as a clerk, but he also acted as Cassel's secretary and administrator, and his duties involved working out calculations, writing letters, organising business meetings and taking the minutes and letters in shorthand. By mid-March, Jack had set off with Cassel to Cairo on a business trip.

Winston was in great difficulties with his finances, and wrote to his aunt Leonie Leslie on 3rd May, that: "£2,000 would pay every farthing I owe in the world and more. I neither race nor drink nor gamble, nor squander my money on concubines .." One wonders, given his supposed thrift with money, exactly how Winston managed to run up such debts. To his mother, 10th May, he listed unpaid bills amounting to £1,050, none of which were paid until 1901. It is not surprising therefore that Jack's next letter from Winston (16th May) expressed delight that he was "reconciled" to working in the City and predicted that he would become an "arrogant plutocrat", enter Parliament and be charitable to "a poor old veteran pensioner". The idea that Jack might restore the family fortunes had another convert.

Winston returned home on leave, having asked Jennie to arrange two political meetings at which he would speak, one at Bradford, and the other at Birmingham. He knew he could rely on his father's name and his mother's organising skills to attract a large audience. In an endeavour to promote Winston's career, Jennie went behind Kitchener's back to Sir Evelyn Wood, Adjutant-General to the Forces, and obtained a transfer for Winston to Egypt. Towards the end of July 1898, Winston became attached as Supernumerary

Lieutenant to the 21st Lancers for the Sudan Campaign, which job he would take on at his own expense. Kitchener was understandably furious, but Winston would later write of his mother: "She left no wire unpulled, no stone unturned, no cutlet uncooked". In the Sudan, Winston saw spectacular active service. His part in the charge of the 21st Lancers at the battle of Omdurman added greatly to his fame.

Back in London again, Jack had now been working for Cassel for several months, and was not enjoying his job. He was trying to arrange to continue with his music and piano lessons but his mother and Winston were obviously using him as their errand boy, exercising Winston's horses and dealing with the family lawyers for Jennie.

In his will, the 7th Duke of Marlborough had left his money to his wife for the duration of her life time, and thereafter it was to go to Randolph. Winston wrote to his cousin, Sunny, the 9th Duke of Marlborough, 9th July 1898, regarding his and his mother's financial problems. Winston made the point quite candidly that Jennie and he had been raising loans against the day when his grandmother would expire, and Jennie would inherit the money left them by the late Duke, along with the Dowager Duchess's money. This new loan would cover payments to Jack and himself for three years. "The idea is that in three years the Duchess will perhaps have died". While it was good of Winston to make allowances for his brother, we might note here that in all the correspondence relating to the Churchills there is no record of Jack ever running up debts or taking out loans to cover them.

He would write Sunny some letters "from the seat of war" in Egypt, and went on to blame Lumley ("a damned robber") for their financial plight. Winston implied that his absence overseas left Lumley free to make extortionate charges for arranging loans. He concluded by reassuring Sunny that he "would not allow any loss to fall on you in the matter of your guarantee". He was, he said, counting on Jack Leslie as his second guarantor for the loan, and asked Jennie to "Push the matter on quickly" for him. Instead, it landed on Jack's desk to deal with and he was left seeing to the finer detail of Winston's loan, and Jack's letter continued, replying to her list of requests:

Winston's loan is in progress though they want to know the
two sureties before anything can be definitely settled.
    The rest of the things you wanted to know – I will find out
Thursday ... .

Jennie continued sending Winston's letters full of exciting tales of
war in the Sudan to Jack, which must have made his job seem all the
more dull. He was still trying to sort out her paperwork with Lumley,
following the granting of the new loan, and in paying off the old
ones. He took solace in his hobby of photography, and liked taking
photographs of his mother, and replied to her from the Bachelors'
Club Piccadilly, pointedly noting the temperature at an uncomfortable 85°:

    I am just off to Brighton for Sunday to stay with Aunt Lily.
    Thanks for Winston's letters – I return them ... .
    If he starts abusing the Sirdar [Kitchener's title as
commander of the Egyptian army] he will find himself in the
wrong box – but I hope he will not try.
    I have sent the photos to be done – you will have them
about the end of next week ... .
    I have found out about the Royal Exchange. When Lumley
paid up the loan he did not tell them to stop the [life insurance]
policy. So when the time came continued to expect the
premium, thinking you wished to continue the policy. Lumley
has at last arranged it; and about time he did it too.
    The list of payments is ready and will be sent you.[6]

Winston had not been getting on well with Kitchener. Jennie was
concerned about his continued friction with the Sirdar, who had
found out that Winston was only making a convenience of the Army
to further his political career. Winston's opinion of Kitchener was no
higher, and to his mother he said of him: "He may be a general – but
never a gentleman". Jennie replied to Jack:

    Of course, he talks like that about the Sirdar, but only to me, I
think – he wouldn't be so silly as to air his views in public.
From the Sirdar's point of view, I daresay he is right – I had

hoped W.[inston] would have made friends with him & that is
the best way of clipping your enemy's claws.

Now that she was firmly ousted from the Prince of Wales's side by
Alice Keppel, Jennie completed her seduction of George Cornwallis-
West, who was hopelessly in love with her. Jennie paraded him
before society to make a point to her former lover.

    Whilst Jennie was away, Jack was in the habit of visiting the
Duchess Lily, and her husband, 'Uncle Bill' Beresford, at Deepdene.
On one such occasion he wrote to his mother of his misery in his job:

> I am so glad you are going to stay at Newlands to day – as
> Uncle Bill has asked me to go back to Deepdene to-night and
> tomorrow night – and as I can find very convenient trains,
> which take me right into the city in the morning – I am going
> off there now.
>   It is awful here – that city is as hot as they make them and I
> feel very boiled up…
>   I got the cheque just in time before I started many thanks.
>   Goodbye – I am just off out of this stuffiness – but I am
> afraid I shall have to come back again at 8 to-morrow.

Jennie replied from 'Newlands' on a Sunday, otherwise undated, and
their letters had crossed in the post.

> I am not coming back till Tuesday – I'm afraid you will think it
> selfish of me – but it is so lovely here – and I have been asked
> to go on a yacht tomorrow for a sail … . I had a letter from
> Longman this morning telling me that they are going to edit a
> new edition of Winston's book – We might go to a play on
> Tuesday if you like – Darling boy how I wish that you were
> here – You would like it – Well Au revoir – Tuesday – Hope
> you got the cheque all right.

Jennie expected Jack to look after her male friends in London and
continue to advise her about her financial situation, and sort out the
muddles she got into. Another of her letters to him was sent from
Minto House, Scotland, circa 12th September:

Hugh Warrender will arrive tomorrow eve: You can do as you
like about which room to give him – but see that he is
comfortable – I wonder if you saw George West? – He wrote
to me from London – I hope for a letter from you tomorrow –
I trust you will be able soon to go to Lumleys – I am disgusted
never to have heard one word from him – either about
Winston's affairs or my own.

By December 1898, the Churchills were facing yet another financial
crisis which plunged Winston into a state of depression, and he wrote
to his mother (29th December) of the appalling future, expecting
years of trouble and squalor. He said that poverty produced by
thoughtlessness threatened Jennie's peace of mind and his success.

Winston seemed to think that their 'poverty' affected only his
mother and himself and none of his letters refer to the price Jack had
to pay by being deprived of an education. It is also noteworthy that
they both detested business and shied away from it as much as possible but they were not slow to impose it upon Jack.

Cassel was heavily involved in the Aswan dam project. When he
went out to Egypt in January 1899, Jack accompanied him. He had
completed a course in shorthand in order to take Cassels's dictation. Jennie knew well that Jack suffered very badly from travel and
seasickness. He wrote her an undated letter of his misery, from the
train between Passau and Vienna, in the dead of winter, but ever
sensitive to her worries he tried to put a brave face on it and soften
the effect:

We are nearing Vienna and I have had very nearly enough of
this train, which jolts terribly. We had a very good crossing to
Ostend but I did not feel very fit when I started and was sick
the whole time.

We are doing the journey most comfortably and have a
whole sleeping car to ourselves which is rather nice.

... we are now seven with seven servants. I believe Cassel
took on extra servants so that the party should not be thirteen!

We have just been through field after field of deep snow and
it is freezing here. This train rolls about so that it is impossible
to write so I shall have to end.

He wrote again, from the Savoy Hotel, Cairo, on Tuesday 2nd February, of the Barrage Ceremony and laying of the foundation stone, scheduled to be carried out by the Duke of Connaught:

> We are still here in Cairo and have not yet gone up to Assouan [Aswan] for the Barrage ceremony. The Duke of Connaught has not arrived owing to bad weather and so all the arrangements have been altered.

So absorbed was Jennie with George West that she remained insensitive to Jack's plight. Despite Winston's protests to his mother the previous year about her over-spending and borrowing, Jennie was again trying to raise a loan of £3,000, possibly the shortfall of the £17,000 she had originally wanted. Her latest fad, the magazine *The Anglo Saxon Review*, required funds, and she had written to Alfred Beit, a wealthy financier and old friend of Randolph's from their South African adventure of 1891. Her letter had been following Beit up the Nile, and took some time to catch up with him. Beit quite coincidentally was with the party that included Jack and Cassel, as they proceeded on their business trip. Jack tried to arrange the loan but did not have all the facts to hand, so he arranged for Beit to liaise with Lumley in London.

He told her the weather was "cold windy and even rain and I long for the sun to come out". He had a lot of work to do "in different ways and can very seldom get a way out". The company was boring, "There is nobody here of interest or beauty", and "I see and hear of nothing but money – barrage – and Daira Company", the latter owned by Cassel. They were starting up the Nile on the 16th February, and there was going to be "a sort of inspection of the sugar and cotton factories", also owned by Cassel, "this may be interesting but rather monotonous … . They play bridge whenever possible each game takes about three quarters of an hour – ¼ to play & ½ to abuse each other afterwards". They were due to start for home on 17th March but Cassel would not accompany Jack on the return journey, and instead was going "to his home in San Remo for a few days and I expect I shall come straight home from Naples. If he does not give me anything to bring home, I shall probably stay in Paris for two or three days, perhaps Madame de Jancourt might put me up – but that is a long way ahead". Jack's life had turned into an aimless existence, following Cassel from place to place, far away from home and family and the things he loved. However, his letter reassured his mother: "It is rather fun going and ordering two or three special trains and a steamer or two. Mr Cassel is very kind to me, he has given me his second servant and I have everything I want. ... Do you know I am nineteen the day after to-morrow". But, shamefully, Jennie had not remembered his birthday, 4th February, and he wrote again next day from the Savoy Hotel, clearly disappointed that she had forgotten to send him greetings.

They had, he said, been met at the railway station by "a lot of the Daira officials". Despite its being Sunday, Jack was still working, and at Cassel's every beck and call: "I expect Cassel will have people in here all day and I must stay in whenever he is here, so I do not suppose I shall be able to gallivant about much". His one joy was to receive letters from home, and he told her: "You need never wait for the Friday's mail as there are posts from England four times a week". They were just about to start up the Nile on a steamboat, when he received a wire from her that was very welcome. He replied, Friday 18th February, dropping a hint that he knew *she* was enjoying herself even if he wasn't:

> Many thanks for your wire it arrived just before I started up the Nile, and as I have only received 3 words since I started! I was very grateful to have it. I have read of you in the papers at balls and parties but beyond that I have not heard much from anybody... . On the way up we stop and examine the sugar factories and generally inspect the Daira properties, which is very interesting though hot and monotonous. ...
>
> I went and called on Lady Alfred who received me with open arms and a very pretty granddaughter – I evaded the arms and took to the latter.
>
> During the last few days in Cairo I had a good deal of work to do, and could not amuse myself at all though I had many very nice invitations.
>
> Cassel gave an enormous dinner the other night of 30 people. I did "galloper" and had to arrange it for him which was difficult as they were mostly foreigners.

It is too hot to write any more to-day and as I have been all day in a factory with a temperature of over 100° I do not feel very energetic.

Now do write so that I shall get *one* letter from you before I come home. The mails go 4 times a week so you need not wait for any particular Day.

Jennie had finally managed to write to Jack from London on 16th February, which letter would have taken some days to reach him. Absurdly she could not remember the date of his birthday, and thought it was 4th March. The information he had sent her *about* Beit and Lumley she had misunderstood, and thought it was *from* Lumley. Her panic was now all the greater with the threat of the bailiffs once again hanging over her. She still had not learnt her lesson from gambling and was planning to go yet again to Monte Carlo. Winston had by now resigned his commission in the Army. Jennie was trying to make plans to meet Jack on his return journey so that they could go on holiday together to Italy that would entail spending more money unnecessarily. In a long, rambling, gossipy letter she wrote:

> I felt rather a brute to have forgotten your birthday – I still think you are mistaken and that it is the 4th of March – your Father's birthday was on the 13th of Feb. Your letter of 7th interested and amused me very much. I see now that your wire meant that Beit would write to Lumley – I read it as from Lumley – I have heard nothing as yet – I hope he won't forget to write – I don't know how I have managed to keep the creditors at bay up to now – and I fear they will come upon me with a fell swoop – If I could get this money business settled – I think I would go to Monte Carlo about the 7th of March, for a fortnight – to stay with the Duchess of Devonshire – and see a little sun.

Despite the relentless pressure of work, it had a very interesting side to it that Jack appreciated, and he witnessed the initial construction of the Aswan Dam and wrote enthusiastically to his mother about it. One photograph, taken by Jack, of Cassel, who could and sometimes did double as the Prince of Wales, shows him in discussion with Daira officials in desert-like conditions, with a caravan in the background. Jack tried to discourage his mother going to the casinos: "I don't think I should go to Monte Carlo if I were you – I know what a week there costs and Rome and Naples would be just as bad – try and stay put for a little while". His parting shot reminded her that though she might enjoy herself at great expense: "I shall have to come home direct and go back to that horrid City".

Jennie had still not been writing to him often enough, she appeared oblivious to his hardships, and deluded herself he was amusing himself, and he corrected her sharply:

> I do not think much of your argument about writing – that if I
> am amusing myself I do not want your letters – it is not a good
> excuse – just you write and whether I am amusing myself or
> not I shall always be able to find time to read your letters more
> than once.

Jennie's next letter of 3rd March was sent from her home address, and the publication date of "Maggie", the nick-name (short for magazine) she had given *The Anglo Saxon Review,* was drawing near. The first edition actually appeared in June that year. Preoccupied with her new 'toy', she remained oblivious to the conditions in which Jack was working, and despite the warnings from both her sons, she was again intent on going to the French casinos. She was expecting to secure the loan through Beit, and she had asked for an extra £2,000, making £5,000 in all. Some of the money was meant to be invested in the *Review*. Despite organising a syndicate of investors, this sumptuous and expensive cultural magazine was rather a risky venture and would leave Jennie with more debts.

> I was delighted with your letter from Assouan and envied you
> the 100 in the shade – it is so cold here – I am writing this on
> the chance as I understood from you – you would have
> returned 7th – but you may prolong your stay – I mean to go
> to Paris the 1st of April for 10 days – and hope perhaps to
> have you and Winston there with me ... . I had a letter from
> B.[eit] from Constantinople – offering to advance the money –

but £3,000 instead of £5,000 which is rather a blow –
However if "Maggie" pays – it will be all for the best – Lily
M.[Lady Beresford] has been very kind and has come into my
Syndicate … . Bless you – you had better let me know when
you sail . . Take care of yourself.

Winston, having arrived home in April, had written to his grandmother, the Dowager Duchess, 26th March, giving his reasons for
leaving the army: "I can live cheaper and earn more as a writer".

The Dowager Duchess died at 45 Portman Square, London, on
16th April 1899, the day after her 77th birthday. Her passing should
have meant that Jennie inherited what remained of her parents-in-
law's money. But after Randolph's death, the Dowager Duchess's
dislike of Jennie had intensified, and now extended to Winston, possibly from the time he had stood up to her when she sacked Mrs
Everest. The American heiress, Consuelo Vanderbilt, who married
Sunny, the 9th Duke of Marlborough, recalled in her diary how the
Duchess had said to her soon after her marriage: "Your first duty is
to have a child and it must be a son, because it would be intolerable
to have that little upstart Winston become Duke".[7] In March 1897,
unknown to most, the Dowager Duchess had changed her will, cutting Jennie out without a penny, and leaving her money and the
house to her youngest daughter, Lady Sarah Wilson, who had been
experiencing financial difficulties. The Dowager Duchess's combined
estate was worth £14,800 (£800,000 today), plus the value of her
house. The only money Jennie inherited was about £2,000 which was
all that remained of the late Duke's money. This was the final blow
to the Churchills' fortunes, and the end of any chance for Jack to
pursue a career of his choice. To make matters worse, he now had to
contend for his mother's attention with her latest lover, George
Cornwallis-West.

At Cowes week in August 1899, newspaper headlines blazed out:
'British Society Astonished', as Jennie announced her engagement to
George Cornwallis-West. The Prince was furious, and George's
Colonel refused his permission to let him marry. He hinted that the
young man would soon be urgently needed by his regiment.

War in South Africa would soon give the whole family another
outlet for their energy.

CHAPTER 14

Brothers in Arms:
War in South Africa
1899–1900

Both Winston and Jack were living in London in the summer of 1899. Winston, having prepared his new book *The River War* for publication, was now vigorously pursuing a career in politics, whilst helping his mother with the *Anglo-Saxon Review*. He was on the look out for a political opportunity, which came his way somewhat unexpectedly. He had been invited to speak at a public meeting of the Oldham Conservatives, but two days prior to the meeting, Oldham's senior MP died, and Winston was asked to stand for election for the vacant seat. After a good campaign, with Jennie's help, Winston made the tactical blunder of attacking the Government and Tory Party position over a Clerical Tithes Bill. He was beaten into third place by the two successful Radical candidates in this two seat constituency.

After Winston's narrow defeat he was encouraged to try again by his party leader, Arthur Balfour. Balfour noted that Winston's sudden declared aim to vote against the government on a church issue that was annoying his Lancashire electorate was somewhat opportunist. "I thought he was a young man of promise, but it appears he is a young man of promises". But in no time at all a crisis had arisen between the Boer republics in South Africa and the British government over the lack of voting rights for the huge number of non-Boer workers on the goldfields (the 'Uitlanders'). The British ordered extra troops to South Africa from India as the crisis deepened. In September 1899, Winston was pleased to receive an offer from Harmsworth's *Daily Mail* to be their war correspondent. He referred this offer to his old friends at the *Morning Post* and used it to secure a lucrative position as their war correspondent.

He sailed on the *SS Dunottar Castle* on 14th October, accompanied by a good supply of wines, spirits and limejuice cordial. On the same ship was General Sir Redvers Buller, VC, going out to take command of the army in South Africa. There were few in late-Victorian Britain who did not think that the 'insolent' Boers had made an impossible demand that Britain withdraw troops from South Africa, a forty-eight hour ultimatum that had to be rejected if Britain was ever to hold its place amongst the great powers. Expecting to take up an old offer to be found a place on Buller's staff, Winston pulled what strings he had to hand to secure a regimental commission, to no avail.

Winston's greatest fear was that the war would be all over before he got to the front. A passing ship gave the news that, although Britain's General Penn Symons was killed in action, the Boers had been defeated in three battles. This news did not tell the whole story by a long way. Winston could not know that his friend and mentor, Colonel Ian Hamilton, had won a signal victory over the Boers at Elandslaagte, but this had not been enough to prevent a British army being closely besieged in Ladysmith as the mounted armies of the Boers swarmed across the borders into British South Africa. With two other journalists, Winston left the ship at Cape Town and used rail and boat to get into Natal four days ahead of Buller. He immediately set off for Ladysmith, having hired a special train, but got no further than Estcourt, for the Boers had blocked the line.

It was at the suggestion of Captain Aylmer Haldane, 2nd Gordon Highlanders, another old friend from army days in India, that Winston was taken along on an armoured train making a reconnaissance out towards Colenso. The force set off on 15th November 1899. On its way back the Boers ambushed it and three trucks were derailed, one of them blocking the line and preventing the safe passage of the engine, tender and two other trucks. Haldane commanded the infantry in its efforts to suppress the enemy fire, while "Mr Churchill, the special correspondent of the *Morning Post*" endeavoured to clear the line. Winston displayed great personal courage under fire whilst encouraging soldiers to manhandle the blocking truck enough out of the way for the engine, carrying a number of wounded men, to get away. Having seen the engine safely away, Winston returned to the fray and was thus made prisoner with two officers and fifty soldiers as the Boers closed in. All eyewitnesses agreed that, if he had been a soldier at the time, he would have merited a Victoria Cross. According to Haldane, Winston immediately saw the incident as a huge boost to his fame and glory and even predicted that it would see him into the House of Commons. He went into captivity at Pretoria on a perverse wave of euphoria.

The news flew around the world by cable; his mother knew of his capture by the very next day, and Jack cabled her on the 17th November, reassuring her he had heard that Winston was not wounded and had been splendidly brave. Winston wrote to Jennie suggesting that, since he was only a correspondent, the Boers might not keep him captive. By the time that letter reached London on New Year's Day 1900, he had already escaped! The Boer commanders had insisted that Winston had taken an active part in the defence of the train and should therefore be treated as a prisoner of war.

The sixty British officers held prisoner at the State Model School in Pretoria wanted to escape and set free some 2,000 British soldiers held in a prison camp nearby. The senior officers vetoed this bold scheme as being altogether too hazardous. Individuals and groups of officers began their own plans and Haldane, Winston and an Afrikaans speaker of the Imperial Light Horse, tried to get away on 11th December but were frustrated by the closeness of a Boer sentry. As the other two turned away, Winston made one more try and got over the wall and dropped down into a garden unseen. Haldane urged him to make a run for it.

In a story made famous by Winston himself, and more recently told in vivid and immaculate detail by his grand-daughter, Celia Sandys[1], he decided to strike out for the nearest railway line, with a view to jumping a train to get away to Portuguese East Africa. With the greatest good fortune at the first house he approached, with an unlikely story of being a doctor who had fallen from a train, he fell in with the thoroughly loyal British manager of the Transvaal and Delagoa Bay Collieries, Mr John Howard. By Howard's reckoning it was the only house for twenty miles where he would not have been immediately handed over to the authorities. With the help of other British patriots in the area, Winston was first hidden in a deep mineshaft.

By 18th December the Boers had posted his description, with a £25 reward; he was wanted 'dead or alive'. Next day his friends smuggled him on board a train bound for Laurenco Marques. He was provided

with a revolver, food and drink for the journey. Once inside neutral
Portuguese East Africa, Winston passed through the British
Consulate, was brought up to date with the 'Black Week' of defeats
suffered by the British Army, and sailed for Durban. On 23rd
December 1899, he landed to a hero's welcome. He wanted to return
to the seat of the war immediately and took train for
Pietermaritzburg to join Buller's forces. On Christmas Eve he rested
just a few hundred yards from the spot where he had been captured
on 15th November.

Buller had granted Winston, whom he thought a "really fine
fellow", a commission as lieutenant in the South African light Horse.
To his great delight and good fortune Buller did not require Winston
to give up his paid employment as correspondent for the *Morning
Post*. Since the rule that barred serving officers from acting as paid
correspondents for the newspapers had been promulgated expressly
to prevent a repetition of the position Winston had found himself in,
during the Nile campaign of 1898, Buller was being more than generous. Winston wisely offered to serve without pay.

As soon as Buller had arrived in South Africa he had recognized
the need for more mounted infantry to help offset the Boer superior-
ity in that arm in this most mobile of wars. He sanctioned the raising
of two regiments, Brabant's Horse and the South African Light
Horse. Referring to the latter, *The Times* history of the war said:
"The quality of this corps, composed mainly of South Africans, but
with a free sprinkling of other colonials, Texan cowboys and British
yeomen, was excellent".[2] Because the district was considered 'dis-
loyal', the Stellenbosch Mounted Infantry had not been mobilised for
the war. Now the whole unit volunteered *en masse* for the SALH, as
did large numbers of the best men of the Cape volunteer infantry.
Recruiting began on 8th November 1899, and the first three
squadrons were ready by 15th December for active duty at the battle
of Colenso.

The first regiment was commanded by Lieutenant Colonel The
Hon. Julian Byng, whose school and army nickname of 'Bungo' was
simply to distinguish him from his two soldier brothers, 'Byngo' and
'Bango'. He was an outstandingly good soldier and went on to
become one of the great British Army commanders of the First World
War, famous for his leadership of the Canadian Corps and the storm-

ing of Vimy Ridge in 1917. He employed Winston on the regimental staff as an assistant adjutant, which left him enough free time to take on various roving commissions in addition to his normal regimental duties.

One of the first major pieces Winston wrote for the *Morning Post* was an impassioned appeal for more Englishmen to come forward and join the Light Horse. One of the first to respond was Jack, for whom Winston secured a lieutenancy through Colonel Byng. Winston cabled Jack that Byng was offering him the command of a troop in the South African Light Horse. Jack sent his acceptance by return. On the 29th December 1899, he wrote to his mother from her home address, and on the notepaper of her *Anglo-Saxon Review,* with the news that he would leave on 5th January for the war. He could not conceal his glee as he wrote:

> I have thrown over the Yeomanry, who are rather annoyed but
> have promised not to stand in my way. They were so vague,
> they did not know when we were going to start or what we
> should do when we got out and I could only see the prospect of
> waiting about here for about two months and then after all
> perhaps not going. This post in the Light Horse gives me a
> chance of being at the front in five weeks and so I have taken
> my berth, ordered my kit and am off. There may be some red
> tape which will stop me at the last moment – but I think I shall
> be in Cape Town almost as soon as you – I sail on the
> *Carisbrooke Castle.*

He closed his letter in haste as he had to "fly off and buy some more brown things".

The whole Churchill family was rallying to the country in its hour of need for Jennie was also en route with the hospital ship *Maine*, a splendid gift from an American millionaire as a gesture of Anglo-American solidarity. Jenny may have thought she was flying to the side of her dear George, who had been posted to South Africa, but he had already been invalided home; their ships may have passed each other on the high seas. Jack was able to join the ship at Cape Town and travel with his mother to reach Durban by the end of January 1900. He told Jennie that she was arousing some jealousy, and that

Georgiana Curzon, Lady Howe, was trying to organise a Yeomanry ambulance for service in South Africa. Winston and Jack's cousin, Sunny Marlborough, was going out as a Yeomanry officer to take up a staff appointment; his young son was the only Churchill male not in uniform.

After defeat at Spion Kop, Buller tried to push infantry over the Tugela River to attack the Boer held heights. The cavalry was in close support in case it saw an opportunity to break through into the open country beyond. Jack, just nineteen years old, had arrived two days before and rode out with his brother into his first active service with the South African Light Horse. All that day and the next the infantry failed to make any dent in the strong Boer positions and they were withdrawn back across the river. Ladysmith would have to endure the siege a little longer.

On 12th February 1900, Dundonald's cavalry brigade, including the SALH, made a wide sweep out to the right to clear Boer patrols away from Hussar Hill, from whence Buller's staff officers carried out a reconnaissance of the Boer positions. With the mission accomplished, the Light Horse was riding back to camp. Winston, with that second sight that came with experience of patrolling on the North-West frontier and on the veldt, suddenly felt the situation to be dangerous and warned his men accordingly. Immediately they came under very heavy Mauser fire and the regiment dashed over a crest some two hundred yards off before dismounting and returning fire.

In the ensuing firefight Jack, who was in the line beside Winston, gave a sudden jump and wriggled back down the slope. He had been shot in the calf by a Mauser bullet that must have but narrowly missed his head.[3] Winston helped him back to an ambulance wagon and, after the skirmish was over, visited Jack in the field hospital where he was prepared for evacuation to Durban. By an extraordinary coincidence the first wounded officer received by Jennie on the *Maine* was her son, Jack.[4] Winston was able to visit them both there.

While Jack convalesced, Winston rejoined the SALH as Buller's force finally began to out-manoeuvre the Boers and force its way through to relieve Ladysmith. Buller held the Light Horse back and allowed British regular cavalry to enter the town first, but Winston was soon on the scene, gathering first-hand impressions and looking up old friends like Ian Hamilton. Winston had provided some light

25. Jack: one of the best riders in the regiment.

26. The King of Portugal visiting the Oxfordshire Hussars.
Jack, fourth from left, top row; Lady Gwendeline Churchill (Goonie), *third from left, second row;* Miss Hozier (Clemmie), *second from right, third row;* Winston, *third from right, front row.*

27. Arthur Bertie, 7th Earl of Abingdon, Goonie's father.

28. Gwendeline Mary, Countess of Abingdon, Goonie's mother.

29. Goonie as a child, 1889.

30. Wytham Abbey, the Bertie family home.

31. Jack and Goonie on their wedding day, 1908.

32. Family silver, featuring the gift of the Duke and Duchess of Connaught.

33. The Oxfordshire Hussars at the wedding of Jack and Goonie.

34. Winston and Clemmie on their engagement.

35. St. Margaret's Church, Westminster Abbey.

36. Winston arriving at the church, with best man Lord Hugh Cecil.

37. Clemmie arriving, with her brother, William (Bill) Hozier.

38. Jack and Goonie, 1908.

40. 'Beno' begging for forgiveness!

39. Johnny as a baby.

41. The two families in 1915: Winston, Diana, Clemmie and Sarah, Randolph, Jennie, Goonie and Peregrine, Johnny, Jack.

42. Jack at Dunkirk 1914, sketched by a fellow officer.

43. Jennie and Peregrine, 1915.

44. Jack at Gallipoli, 1915.

45. Jack, Winston and Eddie Marsh, Lille, October 1918.

relief for the officers of his regiment as reported by Lord Dundonald himself. On 26th February, Dundonald had walked over from his brigade headquarters to the bivouac of the SALH where he found Colonel Byng laughing. "I must tell you what Winston said this evening", Colonel Byng went on: "Winston said he wanted to get the DSO, as it would look so nice on the Robes of the Chancellor of the Exchequer." He added, "I told him he must first get into Parliament, if he could get any constituency to have him!"[5]

Byng could not have known that Winston was now so famous at home that the Southport Conservative Association had already cabled asking him to be their next parliamentary candidate. With a commendable loyalty he replied that he felt obliged to contest Oldham again at the next opportunity.

Buller's army remained relatively inactive for nearly two months after the relief of Ladysmith. Winston was able to obtain an extended leave of absence from his regiment. The *Morning Post* had applied for him to join Lord Roberts' main army as it prepared to march on the Boer capitals of Bloemfontein and Pretoria. Winston found himself kicking his heels at Cape Town without the necessary accreditation. He applied to two friends on Roberts' staff, Ian Hamilton and William Nicholson, to help him and they had to tell him that some of Winston's writings had greatly upset Lord Roberts himself. His friends were able to patiently win their chief over and the press accreditation was finally received. He attached himself to Ian Hamilton's fighting command as it protected the flank of the main army in its relentless northward advance. The despatches he wrote were published as *Ian Hamilton's March* and did much to add lustre to that popular general's name. Hamilton later asked Winston to carry his despatches back to Lord Roberts, and he was able to tell 'Bobs' that Johannesburg was taken. In the long talks about this, their previously friendly relationship was restored.

As Winston accompanied the main army to Pretoria and the battle of Diamond Hill, Jack had recovered from his wound and had rejoined the 1st South African Light Horse. In April, he wrote to his mother of the dreary service in and around Ladysmith:

> We are still here in this camp to which you came to tea, and
> the life is becoming very monotonous. Winston has gone off to

the other side to join Lord Roberts, and although he has left
his ponies and a good deal of his kit here, I doubt whether we
shall see him again. At present there is no attempt at a move on
this side, and it is getting very tiring. We have any amount of
drill all day long in the sun – but that is not very interesting –
and after that is over there is nothing to do. The regiment has
been here nearly a month and the camp is very smelly. There
are also some 30 or 40 horses rotting around the camp and a
few are in the water. But the health of the regiment is good and
I feel as fit as a fiddle.[6]

By the end of April, Jack was wondering why he had not heard a
word from his mother since he last saw her on 17th March. He wrote
of the daily patrols looking for Boer raiders in the area and he made
light of the dangerous work:

We are living quite a cowboy sort of life and ride about all day
long in our shirtsleeves. I spend about 12 hours a day in the
saddle and am as hard as nails and up to now I can boast of
not having been sick, although very many other officers are
down with fever etc… I have seen a few Boers lately. We climb
up kopjes and have a glimpse at them and then gallop away
before they can come after us. Sometimes they lay traps for us.
But we have grown very cautious.[7]

By June, with still no word from any of his family, Jack was feeling
really neglected.

I am beginning to feel like the prodigal son who is sent away to
these horrible colonies with instructions never to be seen or
heard of again. I have not heard one word of you or about you
since you sailed away from Durban nearly 3 months ago. I
picked up an old *Vanity Fair* the other day and found that you
were probably not coming out again. That and a little
paragraph in some Natal paper saying that the *Maine* had
sailed again for Cape Town is all I have heard or seen since
you left. I expect I shall find a lot of letters waiting for me
somewhere – but my squadron has been detached from the

regiment and we have been roaming about on our own for some time.[8]

His squadron had left Ladysmith but was detailed to guard Buller's lines of communication, which meant more tedious and occasionally dangerous daily patrols. He regretted not applying to rejoin the Yeomanry cavalry that was serving with Roberts' principal field army as it advanced on Pretoria. He had, however, vowed to himself that he would stick with the SALH until the end of its service. In common with most soldiers at the time he thought the end for the Boers was not far off and hoped to be home by August. As the nights grew colder and he often camped out with just a blanket he was critical of the cautious approach of General Buller. The nastier side of the war was intruding itself by now:

> We have been doing a little Rebel hunting round here. It is very sickening to find these devils smiling in their comfortable farms when all the loyal farmers have had their places sacked and often burnt. However we have packed a good many off to prison. Some of them are almost pure English and they meet you at the doors of their farms with beaming faces saying they have waited so long for our troops. And then when the evidence comes along you find they have been shooting at you for the last 6 months.[9]

Jack was finding his fellow officers "rather rough diamonds" and, though he had never felt so fit, concluded that he could "do with a bit of London".[10]

On 26th June he could at last acknowledge a letter from his mother, having learnt that she had been writing to Winston with instructions to send on the letters to Jack. Winston consistently failed to do any such thing. Jennie had, herself, been wondering why she got no reply from Jack to any of her 'epistles', as she called them. She had, for instance, announced her intention to marry again! On hearing that Alice Keppel was about to deliver a child widely believed to be fathered by the Prince of Wales, Jennie immediately arranged her marriage to George Cornwallis-West. She began importuning Jack to come home, to be at the wedding. She naturally expressed concern for his safety, with a horrid disease being a greater anxiety than a chance bullet in action. She was also rather desperate to get him back into the employ of Sir Ernest Cassel, lest he renege on their arrangements and take on someone else. Before long, Winston was writing to advise Jack to 'chuck' the regiment and get back home to work. They were already seeking financial advice from Jack and clearly wanted him home for that purpose.

Jennie was again seizing the headlines in society. She was still beautiful and George adored her. He had been obliged to resign his commission on marrying her. And, instead of a dowry, Jennie brought a raft of unpaid bills, including one for Lord Randolph's brougham coach, that had lain unpaid for a decade.

Jack, with a new sense of confidence born of active service, was not to be put upon quite so easily. His squadron had rejoined the regiment and they had been "very busy". In an "exciting week" they had played a leading part in a major move by Buller to turn the Boers out of formidably strong positions. "We were only allowed one days rest, and then off again round the country making the men surrender as much as possible. We found a few men, but in most cases the farms had white flags outside and an old 'vrow' or two in. They sold us eggs & bread at very high prices while the Boer owner was probably 'on commando' for they know we do not loot and that their farms are quite safe. If we threatened to burn all farms found without their owners, and if we made a few examples, I am sure that every farm we came across would have its Boer in it. And every Boer on his farm means one less 'on commando'."[11]

Jack had heard that Winston was leaving South Africa for home on 4th July and had a twinge of regret that he was not joining him. He reiterated that he would stick with the regiment until its term of service was over. In his next letter home Jack pointedly remarked that one letter from his mother and one cable from Winston (saying he was leaving) was the sum total of his mailbag to date. He skirmished with the enemy on a daily basis. He noted that nearly all the war correspondents were going home and deduced from this that the war must soon finish. He hoped so as "the novelty has worn off, and even a little fight does not seem to exercise the men much."[12]

His next letter to Winston, dated 10th July 1900, described some very significant fighting, but opened with a jibe against having only

City of London work to return to. "...although I am very sick of all this here, I should feel very unhappy if I were home before it is all over. The quills of the City can I think wait a little while and so can the arms of the ladies." The SALH "had a great day" playing a leading role in turning the Boers out of their Laing's Nek – Majuba Hill line. The regiment had seized a height that commanded Botha's Pass. For six hours they lay out in extended order, defending a three-mile front against repeated Boer attack, until relieved by infantry in the evening. A further ten days manoeuvring and fighting followed to put the Boers to flight and the British buried 142 dead Boers after it. He could write like the veteran he now was of the 'heroics' of a regiment new to the fight:

> Strathcona's Horse have just arrived – a very fine body of men
> full of fight. They came out with us the other day and the
> Colonel gave them the advanced guard. They promptly lost 3
> wounded and 2 prisoners and kept us out until 10 at night
> finding them. As soon as they were fired on, they charged right
> in close. They came home much elated and condoled with us,
> because we had been engaged all day and had not lost
> anybody![13]

A short letter of 5th August acknowledged a wire from his mother, who was still trying to get him to come home. He said he would like to do so but had no intentions of leaving the regiment while there was work to be done. Buller was just starting a major sweep towards the frontiers of Portuguese East Africa and Jack expected the SALH would "have the fun" if there was any. A week later he was writing from an army field hospital. They had been travelling light, with no tents or blankets during some very cold nights, in the operations against Botha's forces. During a break he had taken a nasty crack on the ankle playing polo and this had put him in hospital for a spell.

On being discharged from hospital, Jack travelled in an open railway truck for two days to rejoin his regiment. He was very dirty and dishevelled when he alighted at Pretoria to stretch his legs. There on the platform was Lord Roberts, assorted generals and the 'gilded staff', many of whom Jack knew personally. He was in such a sorry state that none of them recognised him until he went up to them and introduced himself. Lord Roberts was kindness itself, insisting that Jack get a good rest and suggesting that he waited in Pretoria to be able to bring forward important letters to Roberts at his forward headquarters at Middleburg. Colonel Valentia of the Oxfordshire Hussars gave Jack his room in Pretoria for him to use.

Jack wrote to Winston about his increasing annoyance at the general abuse directed towards Buller. He reminded him of some of the fierce fighting in the broad sweeping operations against the Boers. The Guards said that Buller gave them their toughest battles since the disaster at Magersfontein in the 'Black Week' of December 1899. Jack recounted the terrible fight at Burgerdale where a force of some 130 Johannesburg Police, called 'Zarps', and two guns held a stony kopje. They were heavily shelled by British artillery and attacked by the Rifle Brigade. They fought magnificently and inflicted 80 casualties on the attackers. Only seven 'Zarps' escaped from the hill. That evening Jack rode beside Lord Roberts over the gruesome field and he relayed the scene in some detail to his mother. After a few days on the staff, Jack returned to his regiment and was soon engaged in an action in which he displayed the greatest devotion to duty.

> Then we marched into this awful country NE of Lyndenburg. After 2 days uphill we reached 'Hell's Gate' from which the path falls about 1500 feet into a rugged country. The advanced infantry had just reached the top of the gate when they began shouting. We galloped up and there below us not 6 miles away we saw all the Boer wagons and guns trekking away up a steep hill. Then one wagon stuck. Next moment we were galloping down the hill at breakneck speed with 3 battalions of infantry cheering & shouting at us. I only found out what the road was like afterwards. In places it dropped 5 feet sheer. But we took it at a gallop. We arrived at a Nek, beyond which was a little gully, then another Nek. The gully was steep & the road zigzagged down and up the other side. And there on the other side were 300 desperate Boers, a pom pom & a 9lb field gun. We ran into a very heavy fire. But we soon got to work and presently the air fairly hummed with lead. The wagons were now quite close but moving away. The Colonel ordered an attempt to be made to cross the gully. One troop was to start

& if successful to be supported by a squadron etc. It fell to my
troop to lead. No one knew how the road ran or how to get
there. I was simply told to continue the pursuit. The range was
about 1200 [yards] and I started off full gallop. The road was
very rough. I got about ¼ of a mile & then finding that I only
had about 5 men left I jumped head over heels into a donga. I
crawled back to the regiment & was very glad to find that only
one man had been hit, the rest had taken cover earlier. The
Colonel said he was very sorry I had gone & that he had tried
to stop me etc. As luck would have it, it turned out allright.
But why 15 mounted infantry should be ordered to charge
Boers in position on a mountain road I don't know. The order
was cancelled almost as soon as given but I had started. It was
a very exciting ride but rather unhealthy. However the men
were very pleased. Why I don't know.[14]

Jack surely deserved a gallantry award of some sort for this display
of courage and leadership. Perhaps his colonel realised that he had
made a serious error of judgement in ordering the charge and did not
wish to draw attention to the matter.

Jack's last two letters to Jennie and Winston from South Africa,
dated 3rd October, display a maturity that had been building over
these months of active service. Campaigning was as tough as ever.
The rainy season had set in and they were saturated all the time. They
were riding hard, sharing their blankets with snakes, and living on
half rations. All their stores were used up. There was "no milk, no
butter, no whisky!" He expressed annoyance at being shown into a
camp within range of some hills that had obviously not been scouted
properly. No sooner were the fires lit for dinner than Boer artillery
shelled them very heavily. Ten men were killed or wounded, and the
rest went without food because of this piece of carelessness. He could
still admire the "pretty sight" of explosions at night, and they called
it a "Brock's Benefit" after the famous fireworks manufacturer. He
thought it particularly sad that men should die in this, surely the last
battle of the war. This sorry misconception was still rife throughout
the army.

This battle hardened twenty year old could now stand up very
firmly for his Natal army when it was routinely abused by 'the other

side' (meaning Lord Roberts' men). His vocabulary was no doubt 'improving' all the time:

> The ill-feeling here between our Natal Army and 'the other
> side' is growing more and more. It is such a pity. But it drove
> me mad in Pretoria hearing everybody abusing Buller. I went
> on a 40 mile trek the other day as escort to a convoy to
> Nelspruit. We were received by a staff officer who asked what
> he could do for the "jam army". Did we want more jam?
> Really we ate an awful lot. We told him we thought him very
> unkind to grudge us food considering we did all the fighting for
> him. We also mentioned his impudence in uncomplimentary
> terms and he went away his red collar and face blazing – I
> don't know who he was.[15]

He also stood up to his elder brother in a very firm manner. "I am very glad now that I did not chuck the regiment at Standerton. It would have been very uncomfortable coming home for no reason whatever while the fighting was still going on. I wonder that you advised me to do so. They are not saying nice things about those who have gone home just because they are sick of it."

Having 'stuck it out' Jack could take his leave of South Africa confident that he had done his duty and had enriched his life beyond imagining.

The drive to the north was over by October 1900, and Buller's army was broken up. As the SALH had existed for almost a year by then, those early volunteers who had signed on for a year were given the option to leave. At this time many believed the fall of the Boer capital cities signified the end of the war and Jack took the opportunity to return to the United Kingdom. Before he left, Julian Byng wrote this high commendation to Winston:

> Volkerust 23.X. [1900]
>
> My dear Winston
> I am sending Jack home now as to all appearances the war as a
> war is over though I am afraid there is a lot of dirty work still
> to be done but I cannot let Jack go without sending you a line

to say how well he has done. Of course I always knew he
would, but still I thought I would let you know how all his
good work has been appreciated by me.

Since Ladysmith the Regt. has always been at it – with
scarcely a week's rest anywhere, except a short time at
Standerton – and had some exceedingly hard work and heavy
losses. Jack has always done his share with the greatest
keenness – he is most gallant in action, and most trustworthy
and hard working in camp.

In fact I am very sorry to lose him.

I must sincerely congratulate you on your victory – and am
glad the Regimental wire reached you.

I don't know what is to become of us but it looks very bad
for getting home for some time. It seems to me a strong and
efficient police, backed up by garrisons of Regulars would
finish the whole thing, if it is ever to be finished – but Jack will
tell you the situation better than I can write it and will also
narrate all our doing since you left.

Ever yours

J. Byng.[16]

Chapter 15

Getting On
1900–1906

Jack returned a mature young man, having done his duty faithfully, to a familial landscape that had changed dramatically during his days of soldiering. His mother had re-married, presenting him with a step-father not much older than himself. His famous brother was newly elected as a Member of Parliament, whose urge to get on saw him described as 'a young man in a hurry'. Jack was obliged to return to work he openly despised in the City of London.

George had moved into 35A Great Cumberland Place with Jennie. Luckily for the happy couple, George's father did not disinherit him, and his allowance, though not very great, supplemented what little money he had of his own. Jennie still had her rental income from New York and the interest from Randolph's estate, but she was as extravagant as ever. George had been obliged to resign his commission and now had to find work. Jennie once again sought the assistance of Ernest Cassel, who knew of a vacancy with the engineering company, British Thomson-Houston, contractors for the Central London Railway. Initially, George became one of the unpaid members of the company's staff in Glasgow in order to learn the business. He later described his work: he had to wear overalls and act as a "sort of unpaid plumber's mate to the highly paid experts who were building this vast power unit".[1] He would stick to the work and eventually became Chairman of the company, and of several other companies, and did really well. He was working in Scotland five days a week, whilst Jennie was in London working on *The Anglo Saxon Review*, and they met only at weekends. Since re-marrying, she had lost the privilege of entrée that had been granted to her by Queen Victoria as Randolph's widow. A defiant Jennie dropped the title 'Lady Randolph Churchill' and called herself 'Mrs. George West'. This signature appeared for the first time on 10th August 1901 in the Blenheim Palace Guest Book.

The couple made a brave show of things and their weekends were filled with endless rounds of parties and visits to country houses. All was not faring well on the *Review,* which was losing money. Jennie tried to hold onto her friendship with the Prince of Wales, sending him a birthday present in November 1900. He replied, thanking her and congratulating Jack on his return from South Africa but nothing more.

Winston had landed back in England on 29th July 1900, and was soon drawn into the election campaign in Oldham. The returning hero was well received. On 1st October, Winston split the Liberal ticket and secured the second seat, only sixteen votes behind the winner. The Conservatives were back in government, with a majority of 134 seats. With an eye to his financial requirements, Winston immediately embarked on a well-organised lecture tour of the United Kingdom, which netted him a profit of £3,782 (about £190,000 today). Rather than take up his seat in Parliament, he left on 1st December 1900 for a lecture tour of America and Canada. This was in the hands of a Major Pond, "a vulgar Yankee impresario", and, apart from some success in Canada, was a disappointment. Still, a profit of £1,600 over two months, when added to his successful books and speaking engagements, meant he could boast to his mother of having made £10,000 in two years entirely by his own efforts. He wisely put most of that money in the safe hands of Cassel for investment.

On 22nd January 1901, Queen Victoria died, and the following day the Prince of Wales was proclaimed King Edward VII. On the same day, Winston had just completed his trip to America and set sail for home. He wrote to his mother wondering if 'the Keppel', as they called Alice, would be named 'First Lady of the Bedchamber'. The family had good cause to resent the powerful hold Alice now had over the King. Jennie began a bitter 'guerilla war' against her amongst her friends. Mary Curzon wrote to her husband in India of Jennie's spiteful behaviour. A letter of 11th September 1901, sent from Braemar Castle, Scotland, where she had met up with Jennie, conveyed the extent of the latter's anger and jealousy of Alice:

> Mrs Favourite Keppel is bringing forth another questionable
> offspring! Either Lord Stavordale's or H. Sturt's!! Lord

Stavordale is going to be married off to Birdie Stewart as Mrs
Keppel made a promise to Lady Ilchester to *allow* him to
marry at end of this summer! Jenny [*sic*] said people were
seriously disgusted at goings on of King – his pursuit of the
Keppel and daily visit there in his green brougham & his boon
companions Ernest Cassel etc. She said King was miserable in
the company of any but his few bridge friends as he feels
himself so hopelessly out of it with intelligence or intellect – on
the whole he had begun *badly*! I thought I scented personal
pique in much of her tirade, as since she married she has
dropped out of her old position ... .[2]

Alice was not pregnant; the King was a popular monarch; Jennie was
hardly in a position to criticize women who were 'visited' by Bertie.
In every respect Jennie was, indeed, displaying personal pique. Even
her passing, disparaging, reference to Lord Stavordale (a former
lover of Alice) may have been motivated by the fact that his future
wife, Lady Helen Vane-Tempest-Stewart ('Birdie'), had but recently
rejected the amorous attentions of Winston.

Winston's love life was going nowhere. He had loved Pamela
Plowden truly, but would make no real commitment to her. He
wrote to her, and of her, as if she 'belonged' to him, but her patience
ran out eventually. She once declared that he was "incapable of affection". She was attractive enough to arouse interest in several men
and acquired the reputation of a 'plate spinner', as Jennie spitefully
called her. Jack picked up some gossip, which he passed on to George
West, that Pamela was 'engaged' to two or three men at the time
Winston felt her to be his own. The inimitable Jean Hamilton, no
great friend of Winston at this stage, recalled several stories about his
troubled relationships. One of Winston's fibs sets the tone for Jean's
dislike of him:

At dinner last night Winston Churchill's name was mentioned
and I told the story of how, just after he had published "Ian
Hamilton's March" I asked him to dine, receiving a
typewritten answer beginning, "Dear Madam. As Mr.
Churchill is so much engaged by his political work I write to
say he is sorry, etc., etc.," and signed by a secretary. I was

furious at this impertinence, and had it framed and placed in my drawing-room. I had invited Pamela Plowden that same night, knowing Winston was very devoted to her and the next day I got a letter from her, telling me she had quite forgotten when she accepted that she had promised Winston to dine with him and hear his speech afterwards. She said she had written him trying to get out of it as she wanted to come to me but had got no answer. She did not give me her address and it gave me great pleasure to send my letter (telling her that of course she must dine with Winston) to him to address.[3]

Things did not go well for Winston and Pamela. Jean Hamilton recalled one severe spat. "I remembered the little scene she had told me about, with such bitter tears, when in a ballroom he had gone up to her, and brutally asked her 'if she had no pride, because he had heard she was going about saying that Winston had treated her badly'."[4] Pamela later married Victor, Earl of Lytton in April 1902.

On the rebound Winston seems to have attempted to court 'Birdie' Stewart, only to lose her to Lord Stavordale in January 1902. Once again, Jean, a great friend of 'Birdie', recorded a joke made at Winston's expense:

Lady Warwick [Daisy] said once at dinner to Winston and me that she would rather be in bed with a dead horse than with Count Metternich: we had been discussing who was the best looking man we knew and I suggested Count Metternich! After that Winston announced "I would not change my own face for those of any man!" I said something disparaging and he replied, "Ah, you say that after an exhaustive study of my profile." I replied, "Yes, I have had an exhaustive study of your profile, *often*; but I infinitely prefer the back of your head!" which made Birdie Stewart rock with laughter, and as Winston at that time meant to marry her he was wild. [5]

Jean Hamilton was reminded of an amusing episode with Winston, when they had stayed at Blenheim Palace the previous year. It gives an extraordinary portrayal of Winston's attitude to women and marriage, and helps explain his marked lack of success:

'Lady Hilda [Brodrick] was excited over Winston Churchill's
pursuit of Birdie ... and kept urging me to tell her and Lady
Londonderry of the way he had spoken to me about marriage,
at Blenheim. He told me one night at dinner there that he
intended love should have nothing to do with marriage – he
wanted a woman who would look well at the head of his table
and be a pleasant companion "*pour couchez avec*" [to sleep
with]; this last I did not repeat to Lady Hilda – it would have
made her hair stand on end – he then proceeded to ask me if I
thought Birdie pretty, etc., etc. Birdie anxiously asked me after
dinner if he had said anything about her! I did not tell her what
he *had* said but she confided in me that she should not like to
wake up and find the face of Winston on her pillow...' [6]

Sadly Winston was subsequently rebuffed by the wealthy Muriel
Wilson and the lovely American actress, Ethel Barrymore. His confidence in this field of activity took a severe beating.

Winston took his seat in the House of Commons on 14th February
1901, and made his maiden speech, during a debate on a settlement
in South Africa, four days later. It was a good speech, arguing for a
moderate approach to the Boers, to secure their early surrender and
future friendship. He had been in correspondence with his friend, Ian
Hamilton, and knew that many soldiers in the field shared this
approach. He had worked hard on its composition, and he learnt it
by heart to give an effective delivery. His next major intervention, in
May, was in a debate over Army estimates, in which he took up the
"tattered flag" his father had fought under many years before. He
took strong objection to an increase in Army expenditure of some
five million pounds a year, while accepting that the Royal Navy
needed all the money spent upon it.

While he annoyed many Conservatives with this stand, he caught
the attention of the Liberal opposition, just like his father had done.
Winston paid fulsome tributes to Lord Rosebery, a great friend of
Lord Randolph, and even hoped for a while that he might create a
new, centrist party. Like his father before him, Winston seemed to sit
uneasily in the Tory ranks. Winston's technique of committing
speeches to memory, made him an impressive performer in the
Commons. However, once in 1904, he was in full flow of speech

when he had a complete mental block. Unable to continue, he sat down with his face in his hands. Some MPs immediately remembered the failing performances of Lord Randolph towards the end of his career, and the first doubts as to whether Winston might go the same way surfaced.

Based on the great success of his books to date, and using Frank Harris as his agent, Winston was able to secure a very healthy advance of £8,000 from Macmillans to write a major study of his father's political career. This two-volume work was published in 1906, and sold some 11,000 copies in three years. While he gets all the credit for this magisterial work, which demonstrated what a great reforming parliamentarian Randolph was, there was another associated with it, who receives no credit at all. There is not one word of acknowledgement in the book to thank Jack for the huge amount of work he did in sorting and transcribing the hundreds of letters written by Lord Randolph. Peregrine conveyed some of this effort to the authors. On 15th August 1902, Winston wrote to Jennie, saying that Jack was "very busy" with all the letters, and how he had reduced them to good order. He said that if Jack wanted more work in that line, there were all the letters of the late Duchess of Marlborough to be read and sorted. Winston found her "crabbed" handwriting made his eyes smart.

Jack might have undertaken this work to give him something interesting to do to relieve the tedium of a City office. After all the inspection work he had done in Egypt, it must have been galling to see Winston invited out by Cassel to attend the opening ceremony of the Aswan Dam. On 9th October 1902, he wrote to Jack with this news, asking Jack to exercise his horses while he was away, and suggesting that he might speak to Cassel and get Jack a month off, to rest quietly at Blenheim Palace. This is, at least, some recognition of how hard Jack was working on the book. Jack was not very well at that time and was seeing a specialist. Winston thanked him for arranging "all the letters and scrapbooks". His conscience must have troubled him a little, for he wrote from Egypt in December to his mother saying he was worried about Jack, asking her to concentrate her attention on him as he was "rather untamed and forlorn". It would have cost nothing to recognize Jack's work in the Author's Preface and would have been most gratifying to his devoted younger brother.

The failure to make any such gesture is an act of selfishness towards Jack that reflects badly on Winston.

Jack, while living at Great Cumberland Place and working in the City, had resumed his duties with the Oxfordshire Hussars, and his recent combat experience was greatly appreciated within the regiment. In May 1901, he attended a course of instruction at Aldershot preparing him for promotion to captain and the command of a squadron. His commanding officer on the course, Lt. Col. Lawley, 7th Queen's Own Hussars, signed him off as "Intelligent and capable. Quite qualified to command a squadron", having evinced a competent knowledge of the subjects prescribed in the Yeomanry Cavalry Regulations. Jack would make a fine squadron commander. His horsemanship was superb and he won the regimental cup for riding.[7] He would see to it that his squadron was at peak efficiency and ready to mobilise for war in an instant. In the many photographs of Jack serving with the regiment, he looks every inch the soldier, tall, broad chested and fit. He is often seen amongst his fellow officers as a great prankster.

Writing to Jennie on 23rd March 1902, the King told her he had made arrangements for her ticket to attend the coronation. A truce had been called between them over Jennie's marriage to George. On 16th May, he accepted an invitation from Jennie to dinner when George was probably present. He wrote again on 22nd May, accepting an invitation to her "charming party" but it was now acknowledged that invitations to Bertie automatically included Alice. The only exceptions were the homes of about half a dozen who remained loyal to Queen Alexandra, and who professed religious views that forbade adultery. On 8th August, Edward and Alexandra were crowned King and Queen at Westminster Abbey. The King had invited several of his mistresses to the coronation, making available to them his personal box at the Abbey. The Earl of Crawford, who was the acting Deputy Marshall at the coronation, and who was something of a wit, dubbed it 'the King's loose box'. Seated in the King's box were: Patsy Cornwallis-West, Mrs Arthur Paget, Lillie Langtry, Sarah Bernhardt, Daisy, Countess of Warwick, Jennie Cornwallis-West, Daisy, Princess of Pless (George's elder sister, who was one of the Prince's favourite daughters), and Countess Torbay, wife of the Grand Duke Michael. The best position of all had been reserved for Alice Keppel, glittering in diamonds, and deemed the most beautiful woman there. Next to her sat the Prince's other favourite, his love daughter, Baroness Olga de Meyer, whose mother, Blanche, Duchess of Caracciolo, had recently died. Bertie stood sponsor for Olga, who was born on 8th August 1871, and she bore his middle name as Alberta. The Caracciolos lived mainly in France, and Blanche had been the Prince's French lover at the time Patsy Cornwallis-West had been his English lover.

Jennie had deliberately made a friend in Alice and they were often seen chatting together at social events. Bertie and Alice, and Jennie and George dined together quite often. On 16th March 1903, Lady Sarah Wilson gave a small, intimate, dinner at her home. Bertie arrived with Alice who looked positively dazzling, in a shimmering gown of oyster satin, designed by Worth of Paris. Other guests included Georgiana, Lady Howe, Jennie and George West, and General Sir Ian and Jean, Lady Hamilton. Jean left an amusing account of the evening.[8] From the same source we hear of the splendid Christmas 1903/New Year 1904 house party at Gopsall, the home of Lord and Lady Howe. Here Jennie once entertained the guests by standing on a chair and singing a saucy ditty. But Jean Hamilton reveals the bitterness simmering below the surface:

> Mrs George West and family departed to-day – an interesting, dominating, vulgar woman; [line drawn through vulgar] yesterday when she and I walked back together from skating, she told me that the other day she had said something about Fiscal Policy, and that Lady Howe and Co. had seemed so bored that she, Mrs West, had flown into a rage, and said, "Oh, I forgot, nothing must be mentioned in this house but golf and bridge," and flounced out of the room ... .
>
> Alice Keppel, she declared, seemed very anxious to be well informed, and to pass for a clever woman. ... it was shocking how initiated little Violet Keppel is, and that on Xmas morning Mrs West said to her, "What a lovely brooch – is it a Xmas present? Who gave it to you?" Violet looked carefully all round the room, then whispered "The King".[9]

Winston had been increasingly disturbed by the swing in the Conservative Party towards 'protectionism', a tariff reform measure that would favour the produce of the British Empire by putting higher tariffs on 'foreign' goods. Shaken by reading reports on the dire poverty suffered in many parts of the country, Winston could only see an attack on Free Trade making the situation worse, profiting capitalist oligarchs at the expense of the working people. This would soon lead him to make a move that many might have expected of his father but which never came to pass. Cynics might notice that the Conservatives were heading for electoral defeat and a change of party might be a shrewd move.

Whatever the motivation, Winston did find himself increasingly at odds with his own Party, both at the national and constituency level. His speeches were radical, often in defence of workers' rights and against capitalist interests. In November 1903, he had once exclaimed, "Thank God for the Liberal Party". By January 1904, he was threatened with the loss of the Tory Whip. Given that he was researching his father's stormy Parliamentary career at this time, it must have seemed like life imitating art. On entering the House of Commons on 31st May 1904, Winston paused and looked about, before crossing the floor to sit beside David Lloyd George. He had cast his lot with the Liberals.

In yet another parallel with his father, he now felt the full force of Tory rage, expressed both through their domination of the Press, and through the icy reaction of Tory society closing its doors to him. Of course, the Liberal grandees opened their doors to him, and he was marked out as a young man of great promise.

His reputation as a radical was soon established, with a fine and spirited opposition to an unpleasantly reactionary Tory 'Aliens Bill', aimed at giving the police powers to control a wave of largely Jewish immigrants. He kept up his opposition to what he considered excessive spending on the army. He was sent on a series of public speeches, in the great working-class areas of the country. He shared a platform with David Lloyd George in North Wales in October 1904, and told a Glasgow audience that he feared an Independent Capitalist Party more than he feared an Independent Labour Party. In December 1905, the Tories, sensing imminent defeat, resigned as the governing party and the Liberals were invited to form an administration until an election could be arranged. Winston was immediately recognized as a 'coming man' and was offered the post of Financial Secretary to the Treasury, a stepping-stone to the Cabinet. He knew that he was too new to politics to shine as a deputy to Herbert Asquith, but that as Under-Secretary to the Colonies, he would handle all the Department's work in the Commons, as the Secretary, Elgin, sat in the Lords. Before the year was out he had appointed an 'obscure clerk' in the West African Department to be his Private secretary. Edward (Eddie) Marsh had been praised to Winston by Leonie Leslie and Pamela Lytton, and thus began a lifelong friendship.

In the summer of 1904, Winston attended a ball given by Lord and Lady Crewe at their house in Curzon Street, W1. Winston was intrigued by a beauty there, and asked his mother who she was. Jennie arranged an introduction and discovered that this beautiful girl was Clementine, the daughter of her old friend, Lady Blanche Hozier. Clemmie recalled that Winston had stood and stared at her, but had not ask her to dance, and someone else whisked her off. He appeared to have lost all confidence with women. She was 19, he was 30, and he may have thought he was too old for her. Neither was much impressed with the other, and Winston was still far from over the loss of Pamela.

Clementine Hozier had a somewhat disturbed upbringing, as her mother and father parted acrimoniously, and there were wild stories about who may or may not have fathered all the four Hozier children. There seems little doubt that Hozier had fathered Clementine and her elder sister Katharine (Kitty), but there was a question mark over the twins born later, William (Bill) and Nellitina (Nellie). Part of her childhood was spent in Dieppe where her mother had fled to avoid her estranged husband. Hers was no privileged existence. To her beauty was added a natural charm and great intelligence. She was Head Girl at Berkhampstead School and excelled at French and German. She made a living giving French lessons. She was a Liberal in her politics and saw Winston in action in the Commons. She would grow to admire him as he stormed across the firmament in a whirl of reforming zeal.

Jennie and George, as usual, were wrestling with precarious finances. They decided to sell 35a Great Cumberland Place and buy a country home, Salisbury Hall, near St Alban's, Herts. Although not a stately home it had royal connotations of a saucy nature, as it was there, in 1669, that King Charles II had set up his mistress, Nell

Gwynne. Jennie's surviving house book shows that they took residence on 16th July 1904. Jennie spent months refurbishing her new house, having it redecorated to a high standard, and buying new furniture and more antiques. Jennie and Winston planned the gardens, deciding together which flowers they should plant following his experience of gardening in India. Jack advised on the bathroom renovation and planted a vegetable patch. George supervised the installation of electric lights. Jennie and George had been happily married for just over four years, and George, who loved shooting, now had his own estate for pheasant shoots, and Jennie had taken up golf instead of riding. Cordial relations existed between Jennie and the King, and Alice, and Bertie surely could not resist an invitation to an autumn shoot with his son, followed by a fine dinner laid on by Jennie. The advantage of a home in the country was that Jennie could entertain Edward and her other friends, well away from the prying eyes of London society. Her house book bears testament to the signatures of those who spent adulterous weekends there, as well as those making normal, social visits[10]. When Jennie selected Salisbury Hall as her new home, she clearly had a mind to create a microcosm of the King's 'Marlborough House set', though her over-spending would see to it that her plans were short-lived. Edward had grown so enormous that he could not climb the stairs to the bedrooms. At Salisbury Hall, she was able to get around the problem by having a down-stairs drawing-room converted into a bedroom specially for him, complete with a huge, four-poster bed. To provide washing and toilet facilities she had a down-stairs cloak-room turned into a bathroom. King Edward and Alice visited Salisbury Hall on several occasions.

George West had matured during the years of his marriage to Jennie. In addition to their enjoyment of hunting, shooting, and fishing, they took to the new thrill of motoring. The Wests were the first family in their circle to buy a motorcar. He had spent four years with the British Electric Traction Company, whilst earning a good income from his directorships, consultancy fees and investments. The year 1906 began well for him as he and a friend had by then established their own brokerage firm, Wheater, Cornwallis-West & Co, and the Company's earnings the previous year had reached £23,000. They had expanded, holding large interests in steel companies and copper mines, and George was travelling about on business more than ever. Unfortunately, the economic boom did not last, and George got into financial difficulties. In an additional blow, he was swindled by a lawyer who left him £8,000 in debt. His brother-in-law, the Duke of Westminster wrote to Winston in August 1906, concerning George's financial problems and offering to help. To spare George any embarrassment, the Duke sent a cheque for £3,000 to Winston with whom he secretly agreed that the money should be paid into George's bank account under another pretext.

The General Election of January 1906 was a landslide victory for the Liberals. Their 377 seats was an 84 majority over all other parties. The 83 Irish Nationalist and 53 Labour members were their allies; the Tories were left with 157 seats. Winston won his seat as part of a Liberal/Labour clean sweep in Manchester. He was confirmed in post and worked hard at the Colonial Office, where Lord Elgin did not always enjoy his flamboyant style. He was much concerned with the settlement of problems in South Africa; some of his speeches caused great resentment in various quarters, others were warmly received.

Jack was now working as a stockbroker with the firm Nelke, Phillips and Co. He applied himself to the work but could never be said to have enjoyed it. He was essentially cautious in his approach to financial affairs. A more flamboyant character may have taken greater risks for greater rewards, and might have crashed spectacularly (like his American grandfather). Jack had neither the temperament, nor the capital, to take such risks. He was made a partner in the firm in 1906. He was a constant source of steady advice to his brother. On 23rd August, he wrote a long letter to Winston relating to sharp movements on the Stock Exchange that had caught many dealers short, but which Jack was negotiating carefully. It would take a lot of hard work to make the half-year "look nice". He said that London was very hot but that he had to work in his office every day from 10am to 8pm, and that he was "tired out". It is in keeping with his character that he would sign off, "Mustn't grumble". It is equally in keeping that Winston would send a petulant reply complaining that some shares had been sold just before a big rise in their price. But he did ask Jack to come out for a weekend to join him on holiday at the 'Villa Cassel'. Jack was also of use to his mother in this respect, and she often left him to conduct her complicated financial affairs. Lumleys had still not finalized Randolph's estate, twelve years after his death. She wrote to Winston that Jack was "quite competent" to manage such matters. His joy was the Oxfordshire Hussars, and his photography. Through the former he was to meet the great love of his life.

In May 1907, Winston was appointed a Privy Councillor. The Liberal Government was already finding much of its reforming legislation being blocked by the House of Lords, where 355 diehard Tories easily dominated the 124 Liberal Unionist and 88 Liberal peers. A powerful campaign developed to confront this problem, and the speeches got very radical indeed. Winston was very much associated with this movement, and became an ally of the fiery David Lloyd George. Winston likened the House of Lords to "a footpad in the dark", and Lloyd George famously named it "Mr Balfour's poodle". A demand arose for a new, progressive tax that, if it had been implemented, would have done more to alleviate widespread poverty at the expense of the super-rich than any other legislation in this country's history. The call was for a tax on land value, where the increase of value in land because it was needed for a public purpose was to be declared a social, and not a private, value. The great land owners would not be allowed to enrich themselves simply because the people needed land for housing, transportation and the like. Small wonder that the House of Lords would engage in an open warfare with the Liberal Government that would shake the nation to its very foundations.

During the summer recess in 1907, Winston took himself off on a long vacation to British East Africa (until January 1908). In his absence Jack looked after his affairs at home. On Winston's return from South Africa, 'Sunny' Marlborough had generously provided him with rooms in Mount Street W1. Winston had subsequently taken out a long lease on the property. In September 1907, Jack was entrusted to see the property let out at a good rent (ten guineas a week). Jack also made sure the servants working there were kept on. Winston wrote en route, from Malta, to express his thanks for all Jack was doing. In October, Jack had to write that there was a panic on the New York stock market, where the Churchills were heavily invested. While the London markets were not too badly affected,

Jack said "it was not very pleasant" working in his office until 8pm every day "watching the crumbling prices". It got so bad that he warned Winston that their losses were very heavy, and loans might be required when he got back from his trip.

In 1907, Jennie and George were in deep financial trouble, and in a calculated attempt to make money, Jennie began writing her auto-biography *The Reminiscences of Lady Randolph Churchill*. Winston helped her by proof reading some of the chapters. The colourful volume was published in 1908, under the name of Mrs George Cornwallis-West. With an eye to the American market, Jennie painted a view of her life as if she had been the 'queen of society' from the day she married. We have already pointed out that this was not an accurate depiction of her early, married life, and actually detracts from her better qualities displayed at that time. In an attempt to further glamourise her life, Jennie recounted many stories of life at the court of the Second Empire as told by her elder sister, Clara Frewen, and passed them off as her own. She also borrowed some of Clara's letters that had been written to her by King Milan of Serbia, and quoted them as if they had been written to her. Jennie's naughtiness paid off and the book was a best seller in America. With the onset of their financial problems Jennie's temper, which was not good at the best of times, got worse, and there were quarrels over money as she continued to spend beyond her means. There is at the Churchill Archives in Cambridge a file of cheques returned by the various banks over the years that had been written out for items she purchased when there was no money in the bank to cover them. George was not robust and was taken ill with worry about his finances. The doctor sent him to St. Moritz to recover but it was too expensive for Jennie to accompany him so she had to stay at home. George's problems had been further compounded in that year, by losses on the stock exchange, due to the financial panic in New York. Jennie wrote to Winston, 21st November, "George hasn't been able to draw one penny from his business this year – so we have no nest egg to fall back on … . It preys dreadfully on poor George, who is getting quite ill over it all". Over the next few years the marital relationship would become more strained, another curious reprise of Lord Randolph's life.

CHAPTER 16

Two Brides for Two Brothers
1907–1908

The Churchill brothers had matured into two very good-looking young men. Winston at 5 feet eight inches tall, with pale complexion and high colour, was slightly smaller than his younger brother. Jack always looked tanned in the face from his outdoor pursuits, and was well developed physically, though his black hair was somewhat sparse, and he went prematurely bald due to some unnamed condition in the years following his return from the Boer War. Like their father, both brothers smoked cigars.

During his duties with the Oxfordshire Hussars, Jack was often in camp at Blenheim Palace. A neighbouring estate, Wytham Abbey, was owned by Montagu Arthur Bertie[1], the 7th Earl of Abingdon. The Berties, a family of ancient noble lineage, had known the Churchills for many years. Letters extant from 1890, show a ten-year-old Jack reporting that members of the Bertie family had been asking after his well-being. Jack found himself falling in love with the lovely Lady Gwendeline Bertie, a daughter of the Earl by his second marriage. Born on 20th November 1885, Gwendeline was nearly six years younger than Jack, and customarily with young ladies of the aristocracy, had been educated by a governess at home. When Gwendeline and her younger brother, Arthur, were children, he could not pronounce her name, and called her 'Goonie', which remained her nick-name for the rest of her life. Goonie was tall with a good figure, dark hair, clear, blue eyes, and pale complexion, and there was something of an air of innocence about her. Hers was a unique personality, to which all her friends attested. Goonie was "not considered beautiful in the conventional sense of the word", but she was described as lovely, and was "adored by all who knew her". It was her "atmosphere and charm", which lent her a unique kind of inward beauty[2]. She was a good conversationalist, and of a kind and understanding disposition, but witty, with a great sense of humour, and was very artistic, painting in oils. She was pleasant and happy, with a pleasing nature, and was full of fun, which made her extremely popular at parties. Everyone who came in contact with her loved her, and felt at ease in her company.

Jack and Goonie had been attracted to each other for some time, especially since Goonie's eighteenth birthday, in November 1904, by which time she had blossomed into a lovely young woman. They had been introduced by her same relative, Frank Bertie, who had introduced Randolph to Jennie in 1873. It is widely assumed that Winston also admired her. The Berties, however, would not have accepted Winston as their son-in-law. They "saw Jack as the brains in the family, Winston they viewed as a wild, maverick sort of character".[3] Jack a model son, was equally well liked, and was popular with the ladies for being quiet and well adjusted, kind, and considerate.

In the beginning, Jack had not felt confident enough to tell Goonie of his love for her, but had confided about it to Winston. When it became evident to Jack that Goonie, now aged 20, had feelings for him, he declared his love for her, and their romance began in earnest, in the early summer of 1907. As Jack had little in the way of money, and no title, they could not, for the time being, let her parents know about their romance. The Earl would not have considered Jack a desirable suitor for his daughter. The back of Wytham Abbey was surrounded by Wytham Woods, providing a forest and grass lands for horses and riders. Jack used to make the seven-mile ride on horseback, from Blenheim, where he was stationed, to Wytham Woods, where Goonie was waiting on horseback, and they met in secret trysts. Meetings between them were few, lest they should be found out, and for months they had to be content with keeping in touch by letter. Meanwhile, Jack tried to improve his financial prospects sufficiently that he could approach Goonie's father for permission to marry her.

Jack told Winston that he was in love with Goonie, and he responded graciously. If he harboured any romantic feelings for Goonie, he at once 'cleared the field' for Jack. Winston would later write to his mother that Jack had a very much better understanding of women than he did. Jack easily "got in touch" with them, and greatly depended on feminine influence "for the peace and harmony of his soul". Winston freely confessed to being "stupid and clumsy" in that respect.

Goonie had become friendly with Alfred, 4th Baron Lyttleton, and feeling the need to talk to someone, she had confided in him. Jean Hamilton got wind of it and wrote up a conversation she had with Lyttleton, 6th October 1907, "During our walk he was raving about the beauty of Gwendoline Barty [*sic*] who is engaged to marry Winston's brother, Jack". The engagement was strictly unofficial.

A love-lorn Jack would agonise about how to increase his financial prospects so that they could wed. Montagu Bertie was a severe man, though he was himself feckless with money, losing heavily at the races. The Earl had converted to Roman Catholicism with his first wife, and though Goonie was by his second wife, Gwendeline Mary, eldest daughter of the late Lieutenant General The Honourable Sir James C. Dormer, KCB, the children were all brought up in the Catholic faith. Goonie had been given a very strict upbringing, and reflecting upon her childhood, remarked how other aristocratic children were allowed to attend children's parties but her mother would never allow her or her sisters to go.

Jack had written to Winston on 14th November 1907, telling him that he had declared himself to Goonie:

> I am writing to tell you that a very wonderful thing has happened. Goonie loves me. I have loved her for a long time – but I have always attempted to put thoughts of that kind out of my mind – because I thought that I had nothing to give her – and also chiefly because I never for one moment imagined that she would ever care for me.
>
> *This is absolutely secret*. Only my mother and George know about it. Her parents know nothing. Nor must they – *until I can come with some proposition* .
>
> ... You understand all this?
>
> I wish you were here. You were in love really once – and you know what that meant. But you had other things to think of. Your career and your future filled more than half your life. I love the same way you did – but I have no other thoughts. All dreams of the future – my career and everything else, are

wrapped up in one person. Nothing else matters to me in the least. I suppose that sounds very silly – but the only people who think it so are those who have never been able to feel these things themselves.

Write to Goonie – but I impress on you, keep our *secret absolutely*. If her family suspected now – her life at Wytham would be unbearable ... .

I am going through a mixture of happiness and fear, that is not enviable.

For months the young couple could not risk seeing each other in public, lest they should be found out. Discussing Jack's love for Goonie in a letter to Winston, 21st November, Jennie had commented: "I sometimes thought you had designs in that quarter". It was now over five years since Pamela had married Victor Lytton, and Winston was still in love with her. Whatever coldness Jean Hamilton had observed at Canford had long since been resolved, and Winston and Pamela saw each other at intervals, and wrote long letters. On occasion, Winston stayed with the Lyttons. Regarding Jack's predicament, Winston replied to his mother, with his usual big heartedness, that they must do all they could to ensure his happiness, and saying he was thankful that he had not "married some beastly woman for money".

Goonie had plucked up the courage and told her mother of their love for each other, but she had not been sympathetic, and forbade her to see Jack. Goonie poured her heart out to Winston, in Africa, in a long letter of 16th December:

I am writing from my old classroom at Wytham. You are far away from us all, I had no idea you were so far – it is nice to think that your thoughts are not, and it is nice of you to write to me again. It was only yesterday afternoon that your Mother read out to me bits of your letter to her, while I was driving about with her in the streets of London ... .

Jack & I are so happy; but, Winston, is it not cruel that I am not allowed to see him, & even writing has been forbidden, though I do write all the same! Don't you think that it is positively cruel to impose this on us? You see, this dreadful

> financial crisis has upset the City & it has upset Jack – &
> though Mother has been told that we want to marry, Father
> has not been yet, because nothing definite can be settled about
> money, and Jack does not know exactly how much he has got
> & how much he will have & all that, and as my Father is –
> well, rather difficult to tackle we thought it would be better to
> wait & tell him when everything is absolutely straight &
> square, which it is sure to be very soon – and meanwhile my
> Mother does not allow me to see him; and we do love to!

Since she was not allowed to see Jack, Goonie went back and
forth on short holidays to Holland to fill her days of anxiety. A
further six months of this excruciating situation went by with Jack
reaching near desperation. The secret meetings and letter writing
continued, and all was confided to Winston in Africa. In New
York, there had been panic selling of shares on Wall Street. There
were serious problems with the copper market and the price had
slumped. The faithful Goonie vowed to Jack that she would wait
and wait, until he could come and claim her for his own. Jack had
been given partial information presumably from the solicitor concerning his and Winston's inheritance from their father, left in
Trust, and found that part of it was in trust for *their* children in
the future. In that letter of 14th November, Jack wrote to
Winston:

> I am also rather disturbed to hear that our American property
> and the English 'Will' property are settled on our children and
> we have only a life interest in these things. The only thing
> which we absolutely have for our own are the 'settlements'
> amounting in all to about £13,000.
>   I cannot think that this is quite right, and I must have a
> closer look into things.

This confusion over the terms of their father's will, kept from them
by their mother, would persist until early in 1914, when a rather
shocking truth revealed itself. In December, Jack was able to tell
Winston that he had spoken to his employers, and his financial
prospects now looked more favourable:

Nelke has been very affable and has promised to make some new arrangements about me. I am waiting to hear everyday. I am afraid he will jib at giving me £1000 a year.

Phillips [a partner in the company] has retired at last – and the whole firm is being reorganised. This is lucky for me and means probable promotion. ...

But it is still rather misery – Since I last wrote to you I have only seen Goonie for two minutes at a Railway Station!

Was there ever such a way of making love. ...

We write pages to each other all day – but I never see her.

1908 was to be a year of great happiness for both brothers. In his next, lengthy letter to Winston, 2nd January, Jack said he had had further talks with Nelke, and had told him he wanted a guarantee of £1,000 a year, but he would not agree, and would only allow him £500, a modest sum for a family of the Churchill/Bertie status. He was, however, also to have 1% of the profits of the firm, and in the worst times he would get a thousand pounds a year, and in a good year two, three, or even four thousand. He told Winston: "Many people marry on less". He believed that Goonie would "have something given to her", by way of a dowry, from her father, "if it is only £200 it is something. I am looking forward very much to your return in order to have your advice and your help". Jack had been able to bring some of Nathaniel Rothschild's business into Nelke Phillips, and he continued: "This has been a feather in my cap – and I have rubbed it in. ... Write to Goonie, Poor thing, she is very miserable that we have to wait so long – but at the same time she writes me that she is prepared to wait until I come for her".

Jack's financial situation was finally settled, and he approached Goonie's father, who gave his consent to the marriage. At last, Jack would place an engagement ring on Goonie's finger. It was a family heirloom, a sapphire & diamond ring, that Randolph had given to Jennie on the day they were married. It was one of two, and it had been their father's wish that each would be passed down to his son's intended brides. The engagement was announced and they could now be seen out together in public. Jennie's house book shows that Goonie and Jack visited Salisbury Hall on 3rd July. Underneath Goonie's signature is Jack's, and a drawing of a heart with an arrow through the centre. Whilst staying with Norah, Lady Lindsay, the renowned gardener, Jean Hamilton met the happy couple and Goonie's mother at Sutton Courtenay, on 12th July. They had come to view the house and the beautiful gardens, which were open to the public:

> Shoals of people arrived by motor to see Sutton, Lady Susan Townley and Lady Gwendeline Bertie with Jack Churchill being the most interesting. [4]

Jack agreed to be married in the Catholic Church. In accordance with the law of the land, Catholics had also to register a civil marriage. They were to be married first in the Registry Office on 7th August, but the marriage would not be consummated until the religious service took place in the Church of St. Aloysius, Oxford, the following day. Winston was to be the witness at the Registry Office, and best man at the church service, and came to stay with his cousin, Captain Freddie Guest and his wife, at a rented house they had taken, 'Burley Hall', near Oakham, which was convenient for the wedding. Also staying were other wedding guests: Winston's secretary, Edward (Eddie) Marsh, and Sir F.E. Smith, the Attorney General, and his wife, Margaret. After a jolly, and somewhat liquid, evening meal, they all went to bed. Wherever Winston went he seemed destined to be at the centre of a drama. A fire started in the early hours of the morning of 6th August. By the time any of the soundly sleeping party awakened, the house was engulfed in flames. The fire brigade arrived, and Winston, donning a fireman's helmet, took control, and proceeded to direct the operations of the firemen. Lady Smith later related how, in heroic style, Winston climbed a ladder onto the roof with a fire hose in his hand, and tried to put out the blaze all by himself.

The Registry Office marriage was just a quiet affair to legalise matters. The following day, 8th August, the 23-year-old Gwendeline Theresa Mary Bertie was escorted down the aisle on her father's arm. Her wedding gown was of ivory satin charmeuse, the under sleeves were of white embroidered Brussels net, delicately ornamented with silver. She wore a wreath of myrtle, and a veil of white tulle, and carried a huge bouquet of roses and lilies. Her betrothed, Captain John

Strange Spencer-Churchill, wore a morning suit in tails, as did Winston as best man, and both looked most elegant. Goonie was served by five bridesmaids: her sister, Lady Elizabeth (Betty) Bertie; the Misses Doris and Olivia Harcourt, cousins of the bride; and the Misses Iris and Daphne Grenfell, cousins of the bridegroom. They wore dresses of white muslin over silk, tied with soft, satin sashes of pale-blue; on their heads they wore white lace caps. The pageboy was dressed in Directoire costume, a style inspired by the French Revolution, of white nankeen trousers, and a blue satin coat. The Woodstock Squadron of the Queen's Own Oxfordshire Hussars, Jack's men, formed a guard of honour outside the church, making an arch of crossed swords.

The reception was hosted by the Earl and Countess, at Wytham Abbey. The seven course luncheon menu was published in all the newspapers. Jack and Goonie received dozens of wedding presents, amongst them two inscribed, hallmarked, silver wine goblets, from 'their Royal Highnesses the Duke and Duchess of Connaught'.[5]

The happy couple left by motorcar for 'Highgrove', Pinner, a house owned by Jennie's old flame, Hugh Warrender, which he had kindly lent them for the honeymoon. When Jack and Goonie got into the car, instead of starting up the engine, the men of the Oxford Yeomanry insisted on pulling it some distance along the road. Photographs show the newly weds happy and in high spirits, enjoying the fun. The presence of Winston, now a rising star in politics as President of the Board of Trade, ensured full press coverage. There were headlines like: MARRIAGE OF A CABINET MINISTER'S BROTHER, and photographs of Winston, walking arm-in-arm with the Countess of Abingdon, under the arch of crossed swords. They noted Jack having served in the Boer War, and having been wounded and mentioned in despatches, and that he held a captain's commission in the Oxfordshire Yeomanry. It was remarked that he had inherited his mother's fondness for music, and that he often accompanied her to the opera. As to his position in business, he was described in a throw away remark as a 'something in the City'. One disparaging press reporter wrote:

It must be exceedingly unpleasant on such an all-important occasion as one's marriage simply to figure before the world as

the brother of someone else. Captain Churchill has so far
contrived to elude fame, and the Earl of Abingdon probably is
not well known to the man in the street, therefore the only way
of attracting attention to the pretty picture made by Saturday's
bride and her husband ... was to label them as belonging to Mr
Winston Churchill, who had most conveniently for himself
found a place in front of the picture at a fire a day or two
before. [Jack] looks old for his years. I heard somebody say he
was forty-seven, which is ridiculous; he is only about thirty,
thought he certainly looks seven years older.

Life in a City office obviously did little for one's appearance. Jack,
actually twenty-eight, was always proud to be Winston's brother,
and nothing would have given him greater pleasure than for them to
be associated in the newspapers. In the other newspapers, there was
an abundance of photographs of Jack and Goonie, taken during the
marriage service in church, and afterwards walking out, under the
guard of honour, and of the bridesmaids and the pageboy, and with
the regiment.

The Churchill family motto is 'Faithful But Unfortunate', and was
an apt description of Winston's romances to date. The thought of his
political career and a life in the public eye, together with his lack of
fortune, was too daunting a prospect for most young ladies to whom
Winston proposed. Jennie wanted to see him married and settled, but
he was clumsy with girls, and even had to seek the advice of Aunt
Leonie for the love scenes in his novel *Savrola*. All this was to change
dramatically soon.

Winston and Clementine (Clemmie as she was known in her
family), had met again when, in March 1908, her great-aunt, Lady St
Helier, had given a dinner party at her London home. Winston
arrived, late as usual, to find the guests half way through dinner, and
seated himself in a vacant chair next to Clemmie. On this occasion,
he finally got up the courage to engage her in conversation. Now
aged 22, Clemmie had matured into a radiant, beautiful, redhead,
with a fine complexion, and sparkling, green-hazel eyes. She, a firm
Liberal, had witnessed Winston in action in the Commons and was
impressed by his speeches and admired him. He was taken by her
beauty, charm and intelligence, and they had something in common

in their interest in politics. She was a no-nonsense type of girl, with her feet firmly on the ground, and was, without a shadow of a doubt, the best girl in the world for Winston. He had at last met his soul mate, and this time it was going to be a story with a happy ending. Winston spent the rest of the evening in Clemmie's company. He asked her if she had read his recent biography of his father, and when she told him she had not, he offered to send her a copy, but true to Winston, he forgot.

In the spring of 1908, Henry Campbell-Bannerman, the Liberal Prime Minister, had been forced to resign through ill health. His successor was Herbert Henry Asquith, whose wife Margo was a friend of both Jennie and Winston. Asquith had made Winston President of the Board of Trade. On his appointment, he asked his mother to invite Clemmie to spend the weekend of 11–12th April at Salisbury Hall. Clemmie wrote to Jennie, Monday 13th April, thanking her for the weekend:

> Dear Mrs West,
>   I want to thank you very much for making me so happy during my visit to you.
>   At this moment your whole mind must be filled with joy & triumph for Mr Churchill, but you were so kind to me that you made me feel as if I had known you always. I feel no one can know him, even as little as I do, without being dominated by his charm and brilliancy. I wish I could be with you in this stirring fortnight. ...
>   Yours affectionately,
>   Clementine Hozier[6]

If Jennie had harboured any doubts about Winston's success as a lover, Clemmie's letter would have dispelled them, and Winston would have been reassured by her affection. Unfortunately for the couple, Clemmie had to leave immediately to accompany her mother to Germany to collect her younger sister, Nellie, from a clinic, where she had been successfully treated for tuberculosis. As a new Cabinet minister, Winston was obliged to stand again in a by-election to retain his parliamentary seat in North-West Manchester, so a long and arduous campaign lay ahead for him during the time his beloved was away. The separation between Winston and Clemmie lasted for six weeks as the Hoziers did not return until the end of May. Absence duly made the heart grow fonder, and love was blossoming on both sides. Winston had found the woman he wanted to make his future wife, and he wrote to her frequently. In his first letter he told her, on 16th April 1908, that he took "comfort and pleasure" from meeting "a girl with so much intellectual quality & such strong reserves of noble sentiment". Clearly his attitude to the qualities of a future wife had matured.

Winston suffered the humiliation of defeat in the Manchester election, and fun was poked at him in the newspapers. One report, mocking his initials, asked: "What's the use of a W.C. without a seat?" A lesser girl might have been put off by this setback, but Clemmie possessed a mature interest in politics and stood by him. Jennie did everything she could to further the relationship, and when Clemmie returned, she was invited to Salisbury Hall again. On 28th May her signature is recorded in Jennie's house book. Winston, meanwhile, had to undergo the entire, exhausting process over again, this time for a seat in the working-class constituency of Dundee in Scotland. His humour and wit in speech-making obviously went down well there, where he entertained the crowds, pouring scorn and ridicule on the Tories, telling them that the Conservative Party was:

> ... filled with old, doddering peers, cute financial magnates,
> clever wire-pullers, big brewers with bulbous noses. All the
> enemies of progress are there – weaklings, sleek, smug,
> comfortable, self-important individuals.[7]

The working-class crowds loved this grandson of the 7th Duke of Marlborough attacking his own class, in language that even they probably would not have dared use. Clemmie, who possessed a keen sense of humour, must have been in raptures, when she read the reports of his speeches in the newspapers. Winston had stepped into his late father's political shoes with a vengeance, and he won an overwhelming victory in the Dundee constituency. His life as a Cabinet Minister was packed with engagements. Clemmie could not be seen alone with him in public, as she did not have a personal maid to act as chaperone, and they only managed to see each other at intervals over the intervening weeks. However, Jack and Goonie and Winston and Clemmie did meet, at the Oxfordshire Hussars' manoeuvres, and were photographed together for posterity. Clemmie visited Salisbury Hall several times that summer. Unfortunately, she had to accompany her mother to Cowes week and missed the marriage of Jack and Goonie. In his letters Winston combined his wish to see Clemmie at Blenheim Palace and Salisbury Hall, with somewhat hilarious accounts of Jack's wedding and the fire. The Registry Office ceremony was "for all the world as if it was an elopement" and "the fire was great fun & we all enjoyed it thoroughly". He signed off, "Always yours, W".

Clemmie must, indeed, have had strong nerves to take on Winston, who was presently trying to finalise arrangements with his mother for her to visit Blenheim. It was all building up to a proposal of marriage in that historic setting, the place of his birth. He wrote to her again the following day, 8th August, with a joyous report of Jack's wedding, and the most ardent desire to see her at Blenheim soon.

Clemmie felt shy about going to the overpowering ancestral Marlborough home. Her family had little money, and she had so few clothes, she was down to her last starched dress, and had not another if it should be required. Her mother could not accompany her to Blenheim so Jennie went with her, acting as her chaperone, and they spent the night there. On the morning of 11th August, Clemmie presented herself at breakfast on time, but no Winston appeared. She nearly went home. Sunny had to send up a note to Winston to get him out of bed. Whilst Winston was getting dressed, Sunny took her for a drive round the grounds in the buggy. The story of Winston's proposal of marriage has become part of both British and American legend. In the afternoon, he took Clemmie for a walk in the garden, but the unpredictable British weather put a damper on his romantic plan to show her the lovely gardens and the roses. The heavens suddenly opened and a torrential rainstorm blew up, and they had to take refuge in the ornamental Greek temple, overlooking the lake. Winston dithered and dithered, and did not pop the question, and Clemmie saw an insect crawling across the stone floor towards a crack. She said to herself that if he did not propose before the beetle reached the crack, he never would. But Winston's courage returned, he declared his love for her, and asked her to marry him, and she accepted. For once in Winston's love life everything was going right for him. He was a Cabinet Minister in the Government, earning a salary that was sufficient to support a wife. The betrothal was supposed to be kept a secret for the moment, but Winston was so excited that he got completely carried away, and ran across the lawn and told the others the news. The following day Clemmie was leaving to return home, and Winston escorted her as far as Oxford, sending with her a letter to her mother. Though neither rich nor powerful, he felt that Clemmie's love would give him the strength to take on the "great and sacred responsibility" of giving her the happiness "worthy of her beauty and her virtues".

Clemmie wrote to her sister, Nellie, telling her of the engagement:

> My dear I have the most lovely ring – a fat ruby with 2 diamonds – I must tell you about it – When Lord Randolph married he gave her [Jennie] 3 lovely rings – one all diamond, one sapphire & diamond & one ruby & diamond – she wears the diamond one, & Goonie has the sapphire & diamond & I have the twin ruby one – Lord Randolph said they were for his sons to give their wives.[8]

Winston wrote to Pamela Lytton, asking that they remain "best friends", just as she had done when she married. Winston and Clemmie, and Pamela and Victor, would remain friends for the rest of the their lives. Clemmie's grandmother, the Countess of Airlie, wrote to both Jennie and Winston of her joy at the match. To Winston she said: "A good son is a good husband". It was undoubtedly one of the best compliments anyone had ever paid him. Winston had been a loving son and would be a kind and dedicated husband and a good father.

The official announcement of the engagement appeared in *The Times*, on Saturday, 15th August. King Edward VII telegraphed his good wishes from Marienbad. Clemmie wrote to her aunt, Lady Mabell Airlie, that every day was "heavenly", but it was a "scrimmage getting ready in time".

Clemmie visited Salisbury Hall again on 22nd August, and the marriage was planned to take place three weeks later. In the midst of trying to find a wedding dress, Clemmie wrote to Winston: "My darling ... I feel there is no room for anyone but you in my heart – you fill every corner". And in another: "... how I have lived 23 years without you. Everything that happened before about 5 months ago seems unreal". Winston replied: "There are no words ... to convey to you the feelings of love & joy by which my being is possessed. May God who has given me so much more than I ever knew how to ask keep you safe and sound".[9]

On the wedding day, 12th September 1908, the bride and groom passed through the City and were cheered by large crowds assembled in Parliament Square. The wedding took place at 2.00 pm, in St. Margaret's Church, Westminster, the church of the House of Commons. It overflowed with family, friends and political dignitaries. Clemmie was given away by her brother, Willliam (Bill,) who was a sub-lieutenant in the Royal Navy. She wore a shimmering white, ivory satin gown, with flowing veil of soft, white tulle, held in place by a coronet of white American orange blossoms. Clemmie's bouquet was of white tuberoses; she was a religious woman, and she carried a prayer book bound in white parchment, a gift from her godfather, Sir John Leslie. Her only jewels were diamond earrings, a gift from Winston. She was served by five bridesmaids: Nellie, her sister; her cousins Venetia Stanley and Madeleine Whyte; Winston's cousin, Clare Frewen; and Horatia Seymour, a friend of Clemmie's. They wore gowns of biscuit-coloured satin, and large, black picture hats, wreathed in roses and camellias, and carried bouquets of pink roses. Winston's old Headmaster from Harrow, now Bishop Welldon, Dean of Manchester, gave the address:

> There must be in the statesman's life many times when he
> depends upon the love, the insight, the penetrating sympathy,
> and devotion of his wife. The influence which the wives of our
> statesmen have exercised for good upon their husbands' lives is
> an unwritten chapter of English history, too sacred perhaps to
> be written in full.[10]

How very appropriate for the role Clemmie would play in Winston's life and career. Winston had been prevented, by Jennie, from having Jack as his best man, and that honour was extended to Lord Hugh Cecil. The only flaw in the otherwise immaculate turnout was

Winston's suit which, according to a report by the *Tailor and Cutter*, had something of a "flung together at the last minute" appearance about it, "neither fish, flesh, nor fowl ... one of the greatest failures as a wedding garment we have ever seen, giving the wearer a sort of glorified coachman appearance". George West did not attend due to business appointments. The vainglorious Jennie, knowing all eyes would be on her, made Jack escort her down the aisle. What power she wielded over him. Although she was immaculately and expensively dressed, and was glamorous for a woman of 54, photographs show she had a double chin, a big bottom, and looked plump and middle-aged. As Clemmie was 'unknown', the press endeavoured to build the story round Jennie. A report in *Current Literature*, in December, would have its readers believe that Jennie stole the show, providing a greatly inflated description of her. Such reports kept alive the myth in America and Europe of the great Lady Randolph Churchill, still enough to push up sales of newspapers and magazines, and bring in advertising revenue. One report gave a detailed description of what she wore, which had obviously been obtained from her in advance, and an insult to Clemmie was thrown in:

> ... golden beaver-coloured satin charmeuse, made in the exacting princess style that is so merciless to the hips of middle-aged women. The gown was finished with the widest of metal embroideries. The hat was of satin antique of the same colour, with large velvet and satin-petalled lilies in metallesque colouring with bronze and silver centres around the brim.
>
> As the widow of 'Randy' and the mother of 'Winny' swept up the aisle on the arm of her strapping son John there was a murmur of admiration among the crowded pews which the appearance of the bride herself quite failed to provoke.
>
> It seems too cruel to say, his mother seemed the junior of the bride by at least two years.

Jennie undoubtedly looked well, and was greatly admired, but she certainly did not outshine a beauty like Clemmie, who, with her 22 inch waist, looked beautiful in both her engagement and wedding photographs. Small wonder that she never really warmed to her mother-in-law. A more considerate mother-in-law would have dressed plainly, and taken a back seat, but that was not in Jennie's nature.

Clemmie's going away outfit was a grey costume, tied with a deep, black satin sash, and she wore a large black and tan picture hat, lined with velvet, and adorned with a long, sweeping ostrich feather. The young couple left to begin the first two nights of their honeymoon in the splendid surroundings of Blenheim Palace. Amongst the jolly crowd cheering them on their way, when they stepped out of the door of Portland Place, were the East End Pearly Kings and Queens. Winston as President of the Board of Trade had helped protect the rights of costermongers to street trading. When Winston and Clemmie arrived at Woodstock, there was another crowd waiting to cheer them, and the bells of the church of St Mary Magdalene rang out.

Winston wrote to his mother on 13th September, of his wedded bliss and the marvelous honeymoon in Italy. How many sons would write to their mother on the first day of their honeymoon? Jennie would soon be a grandmother twice over.

After so many failed 'romances' it does seem remarkable that Winston should have determined to marry Clemmie so quickly. We must inevitably wonder if the idea that Jack was 'stealing a march' on him in life had something to do with Winston's fast moves.

CHAPTER 17

Liberal Britain
1909–1914

Jack and Goonie had a modest honeymoon, staying for just a couple of days at the country house of a family friend, and their first home had to be as the guests of Jennie and George at Salisbury Hall. They signed the house book on 10th August 1908 for the first time as husband and wife. Goonie, as the daughter of an earl, retained her title as 'Lady Gwendeline Spencer Churchill'. She was, no doubt, grateful to Jennie for providing a home for them until they could set up on their own. Their finances would be constrained for a while, until Jack became more established as a partner at Nelke, Phillips and Co. Goonie was initially fond of Jennie, and was soon calling her *Belle Mère*, as she liked to be known by her boys. She had fond memories of the beautiful furniture, pictures and antiques at Salisbury Hall, and of the pervasive aroma of Jennie's favourite Chanel perfume. But she would have difficulty reconciling the somewhat easy virtue existing in Jennie's household with her own strict Catholic upbringing. The devout Goonie took her religion seriously. Within a few weeks of her wedding, Goonie was able to announce she was expecting her first baby.

Jack had also taken on a strict air concerning public morality, perhaps in reaction to his mother's well-known conduct, and certainly under the influence of the devout, and ordained, Dr Welldon. Just before they were married, Jack had unburdened himself to Goonie on the question of women riding astride horses:

> … on Monday I did kiss you darling, because you did not make a sight of yourself riding astride at Hartham. Was it for my sake? Thank you, Dearest, but it should also be for your own. You know these girls who do that sort of thing, only do it to show their legs – and the men urge them [to] do so, in order that they may see them! I think it is so undignified – and

if you could hear the remarks, made about people who do such things, your little cheeks would grow pink!

... if I felt that you Darling, whom I love so much and so deeply, were doing such things in front of others, I should be so unhappy and most frightfully angry. Don't think I am a prude – and you cannot be cross if I am jealous that way. I am Goonie most frightfully jealous about that sort of thing.

But Dearest you did not do it – and so give me your lips that I may kiss you my thanks.

You know it should be your own dignity that should prevent you – but I expect I am even more strict than that – and so perhaps you were right to think of me and of what I should wish. ...

Good night Darling give a great kiss – and Dearest I am so glad you did not jump on that pony. What would *my* knee, that I kissed, have thought, if anyone else had seen it!! [1]

What a curious mixture of priggishness and sexuality. Apparently Goonie had injured a knee in riding and her gallant husband-to-be had 'kissed it better'.

On the return of Winston and Clemmie from their honeymoon, he was immersed in the duties at the Board of Trade. His predecessor, Lloyd George, had put it in such good order that Winston found he had little more to do. In characteristic style, he looked for other parliamentary work to keep himself busy. He championed the Miners' Eight Hours Bill in the Commons, only to see it mutilated in the Lords. He strongly backed the provision for old age pensions in the 1908 budget, fulfilling promises he had made to himself that he would not see elderly folk like his beloved 'Woomany' suffer indignities in their old age through poverty. Like his father before him, he supported legislation aimed at curbing the power of the great brewing companies. He was a radical reformer in the interests of the working people. In 1909, he visited Germany to see how their Labour Exchanges alleviated the plight of long-term unemployment. A year later he would see them introduced in Britain.

British politics entered an extraordinary phase, in which the language used made it sound as if a bloody social revolution was in the offing. Despite the urgent need for a considerable increase in tax revenue, to fund the new welfare provisions and pay for a major re-equipment of the Royal Navy with 'Dreadnought' class battleships, the Cabinet emasculated Lloyd George's first 'People's Budget' to reduce its impact on the wealthier classes of society. Still the Lords flung it out and began a series of battles with the House of Commons that would end with the Parliament Act of 1911 greatly reducing the powers of the Lords, by then under the threat of the Liberals creating enough peers of their own to destroy the 'natural' Tory supremacy there.

Winston, with Lloyd George, was responsible for some of the most revolutionary speeches ever delivered in Britain. He once described the House of Lords as "five hundred randomly selected unemployed". He pointed out that 23 dukes owned 3.5 million acres of land, and 23 million people owned not one inch. Despite the huge crowds Winston attracted in the northern districts, the Liberals lost heavily in the February 1910 Election, which encouraged the Tory reaction. Now, with only a two seat majority over the Tories, the 71 Irish Nationalist and 41 Labour MPs were vital to Liberal survival.

In 1910, Winston was offered the Irish Office but turned it down in favour of the Home Office, one of the great offices of state. He was a proponent of less harsh prison conditions, and a reluctant supporter of the death penalty. He commuted 21 of the 43 capital sentences that crossed his desk for confirmation. While he is routinely criticised for his prominent role in the 1911 'Siege of Sydney Street', where he was filmed directing the police and troops in their confrontation with armed anarchists, his handling of large scale strikes in the South Wales coalfields has been grossly distorted. Far from ordering troops to fire on strikers, he is on record as warning consistently that the police must deal with local disorder and that the use of troops must be kept to an absolute minimum in support of the civil power.

At their marriage, Winston had taken Clemmie to live in his former bachelor house at 12 Bolton Street, London, but only while a larger house, 33 Eccleston Square, was prepared for them. From the outset, the four younger Churchills got on well together. Clemmie was particularly fond of kind, easy-going Jack. In early May 1909, Winston and Clemmie moved into their new home, with an 18 year lease, at £195 per annum.

Life at Salisbury Hall was proving a strain for Jack and Goonie. George West, still depressed over the swindle, thought he saw the ghost of Nell Gwynne. Poor Goonie, who was rather nervous and highly-strung, must have been frightened out of her wits. Within six months, by which time Goonie was already six months pregnant, the newly weds beat a hasty retreat. By February 1909, with his usual thrift and good order, Jack had managed to buy a modest house of their own, 10 Talbot Square, Hyde Park, in reasonably fashionable W2. Whatever Goonie made of it all, she never complained. Those who knew her spoke of her as kind and sincere, and not one to pass harsh judgements upon others. George West later said of her, "One had not got to know her long without realising what a truly loveable character she was. I can never remember her ever saying an unkind word about anyone, and there are precious few women one can say that about."[2]

Goonie gave birth to John George, (Johnny), on 31st May 1909, who was born at home in a top floor bedroom. Jack excused himself from duty with the Oxfordshire Hussars, and insisted on remaining with Goonie throughout the time she was giving birth. For its day it was very gallant and courageous of him, and typical of the extent of his consideration towards his wife. Winston wrote to Clemmie from Camp Goring, giving her some encouragement for their own expected child, which they affectionately referred to as P.K.(Puppy Kitten). He said that Jack was like a "little turkey-cock with satisfaction", exuding an "alone I did it sort of air". He detailed how Goonie gave birth within two or three hours, with minimal discomfort and no complications. Like any new father-to-be, Winston was anxious to reassure his wife that all would be well with her confinement.

On 11th July it was Clemmie's turn, and she gave birth at home to a daughter, Diana. Clemmie and Winston were overjoyed with their new baby, and when Winston wrote to Clemmie, he would include in his letter: "Kiss especially the beautiful P.K. for me". His own father had never concluded a letter to Jennie without a message to "kiss the baby". On Diana's christening day, Jennie sent her latest grandchild Winston's Victorian coral rattle.

Clemmie suffered from post-natal depression, though that medical term had not yet been coined. The pregnancy left her exhausted and low in spirits. She therefore took a holiday in Brighton, and was joined by her sister, Nellie. Diana was left at home, and the nurse and Winston minded the baby. In another reprise of his father's life, Winston wrote loving reports to Clemmie of how 'Puppy Kitten' was progressing. But he also told her to prepare for a demanding time in politics in the near future, as the battles with the Lords over the Budget were getting under way.

When Clemmie returned from Brighton, she still had not entirely recovered her strength, and took yet another holiday. While Goonie led a life of domestic bliss, painting pictures in tranquillity, and meeting her friends, the Asquiths, to play cards, Clemmie was surrounded by the hulry-burly of political affairs. Her personal interest in politics enabled her to share and cope with her husband's hectic life and she possessed a sharp mind for the subject. She was a supporter of votes for women, but was opposed to the law-breaking actions of the militant suffragettes. Goonie, too, was politically minded, and though she was never actively involved, she was an ardent supporter of Liberalism and remained a member of the Liberal Party all her life. Jennie was an enemy of women's suffrage, but seems to have modified her ideas under the influence of her daughters-in-law.

After the traditional family get together on Christmas Day 1909, and New Year at Blenheim Palace, Winston and Clemmie immediately set off together to Dundee, to campaign for the coming General Election. Winston won his seat handsomely. 1909 was a hectic and demanding year for Winston, and Clemmie was very patient over the number of days her husband was away.

Jean Hamilton revealed something of Winston's deep compassion for a troubled society in a record of a dinner conversation with him:

> ... about the middle of the feast he suddenly turned to me and said: "After all we make too much of death." "Yes, " I said, "I think we do – but why do you say so now?" "Because I have had to sign a death warrant for the first time to-day and it weighed on me." "Whose?" I said "For what?" "A man who took a little child up a side street and brutally cut her throat." I was relieved and said cheerfully: "That would not weigh on my mind." "Think" he said rather savagely "of a Society that

forces a man to do that." "I can't", I said. "If that man lived in our society his crime would be much worse – not brutal like that but some horrible, unnatural, decadent crime." He was not satisfied and we discussed whether the man was of unsound mind. I argued that criminal lunatics were just the people who ought to be put away, as if a man was in his senses he might repent but a criminal lunatic was a danger always to all. I was *very* interested in all he said – he was sensitive and in an excitable mood – alive.[3]

King Edward VII died suddenly on 6th May 1910, and political life was suspended during the week of his lying in state and his funeral. His successor, King George V, was not long enthroned before Winston sent him a long memorandum on prison reform, making arguments for reducing the number of inmates sent down for trivial offences that could have come straight from the debates in our own times.

Close association with Winston would intrude into the lives of Jack and Goonie, after the Sydney Street affair. Baby Johnny had a pet dog named 'Beno' which went missing at the beginning of 1911, and Goonie quite innocently placed an advertisement in the *Daily Mirror*, offering a £2 reward for his safe return. The newspaper ran the lost dog as a headline story, with double page spreads. The heading read:

MASTER CHURCHILL'S LOST TERRIER
Search for Pet Dog of Home Secretary's Nephew
WHERE IS BENO?

A photograph was printed of a dog exactly like Beno, to make it easier for anyone finding a stray to identify him. The newspaper later claimed that it was due to their publicity that the dog had been found, safe and well, and returned to its owner on 21st January. The *Mirror* published a picture of Beno, sitting with Johnny in his pram. But by this time the story had been turned to more sinister use, having degenerated into an attack on Winston over the siege of Sidney Street. A mock anonymous letter, purporting to be from the dog, was published:

To Lady Gwendoline [sic] Churchill, from "Beno,"
the White West Highland Terrier.

'MY DEAR LATE MISTRESS, -
I am not lost. I ran away. Do not blame my disappearance on
to some luckless tramp. I left you of my own free, deliberate
will.

Let me tell you why I left. It was not your fault; it was your
misfortune. You can't help being one of the Churchill family. I
can, and will.

Even a dog has feelings. I stood Winston a long, long time –
for your sake, dear mistress. But Sidney Street settled me. I
could no longer hold up my head. It was vain for me to deny
relationship. The black-and-tan dog next door cut me dead
after the battle of London, and the Charles II poodle at the
corner scarcely gave me a bark.

When I say that every respectable kennel in Mayfair is
closed to me, and that countless Whitechapel curs claim me as
a boon companion, you can guess my misery.

I say Bow-wow to you with tears,
Your old
BENO'

Besides a photograph of little Johnny printed below the letter, the
home address of Jack and Goonie was given, leaving the family and
their home vulnerable to attack by mobs. This was an age when radicals, including the suffragettes, thought nothing of attacking the
private houses of leading society figures. Goonie cut out all the press
articles and stuck them into a picture album, which exists to this day.
They received threatening letters in the post. As could been seen in
one of the press photographs, their house was without a garden or
pathway to the front, being approached immediately from the street.
There were steps down to the basement, which led to the servants'
quarters and the kitchen, making the house rather exposed and easily
accessible. Within months of these events, Jack sold the house, and
bought another, and the family moved to 41 Cromwell Road, South
Kensington, their long-term home. As to Beno, he lived to be fifteen
years old.

Jack's full-time, demanding, and tiring job as a stockbroker in the City carried a lot of responsibility. While constantly monitoring the rise and fall of stocks and shares, he gave financial advice to Jennie, George, and Winston. Jack provided a comfortable income, though they would never be rich. When he was not preoccupied with business affairs, he would relax in a brown leather armchair, and read *The Times* or a book by his friend A.E.W. Mason, author of *The Four Feathers*, who was a frequent visitor. Jack inherited a great love for classical music and the opera from his mother, which was shared with Goonie, and they went frequently together to the Covent Garden Opera House.

Goonie was not educated in the strictly academic sense, in the way that Clemmie had been, and joked about the gaps in her education. But she had a taste for literature and drama, and kept herself abreast of modern literary developments by reading reviews and books on the topical subjects of the day. She was a keen artist, and her artistic talent, and interest in literature, gained her many intellectual friends, like the artists William Orpen and Sir John and Hazel, Lady Lavery, and the playwright, J.M. Barrie. Goonie's friends adored her, she could light up a party with her wit and humour as soon as she entered the room, and Jean Hamilton and Pamela Lytton described her as a gorgeous creature. One of her friends commented that "there were many Gwendelines but only one Goonie", and another said she was "a unique character". 'Beb' Asquith said she had "great charm", a "subtle and delicate wit", and a "sense of the ironics and comedies of life". Others spoke of her great kindness and ability to understand everyone else's troubles, and she was a good listener. Pamela Lytton described the mature Goonie of later life, as "a living poem", and wrote that:

> ... her personality combined the greatest distinction and
> sweetness with a truly original, almost fastidious, mind. To be
> with her was to enjoy the best company and the sweetest
> companionship. She had a way of illuminating people by her
> sudden enchanting comments. She found you unusual books,
> she gave you unusual thoughts, she had unusual humour. She
> was lovely, with rare, almost medieval, looks – her gentle
> presence always counting in every setting.[4]

Sir John Singer Sargeant did an excellent charcoal drawing of Goonie as a young girl, capturing the dreaminess of her sweet blue eyes, and the trimness of her perfect figure, which picture is now cherished by her daughter-in-law, Mrs Peregrine Churchill. Her artist friends favoured her as a subject for their art, and as an interesting conversationalist and confidant. Her home was a regular haunt of writers, musicians and artists

The Cornwallis-West's marriage on the other hand, having been in difficulties since George's financial crisis in 1906, had never really recovered. To make matters worse, George seemed to have gradually tired of his bossy, mother figure of a wife, and had a roving eye for other women, and wanted the son and heir that Jennie could not provide. In 1909, Jennie had written and staged a play in which the famous actress, Stella, Mrs Patrick Campbell, had the leading role. 'Mrs Pat' met George, who was engaged in a minor role, and they fell head-over-heels in love. The West's financial difficulties, and George's flirtations, were taking their toll on Jennie. However, she seemed to have an endless aptitude for reinventing herself. Following their financial difficulties, and a breakdown of their marriage, the Wests got back together again. Jennie hit on a new plan, probably suggested by Sir Ernest Cassel, and entered the property market. She first bought the house of a friend, Madame Melba, who had been a neighbour in Great Cumberland Place. Having restored it to a high standard, she rented it out to tenants. Developing her skills further, she moved on to buying old, run-down, Victorian houses, refurbishing them, and selling at a substantial profit. Winston was so impressed he said she had earned a Minister's annual salary in two or three months.

Within a year, however, Jennie was in a bad way. Jean Hamilton described how she found her, whilst staying with a party at Taplow Court, the country home of the great society hostess, Ettie Desborough:

> Mrs. George West ... looks a terrible wreck of her former
> brilliant self – Lady Londonderry looked at her scornfully as
> we stood together before dinner for a moment and said "How
> can that allow itself to get like *that*?" ... Mrs. West was
> certainly very unsuitably dressed.[5]

A draft of a letter exists which Jennie wrote to her mother-in-law, whilst staying with Maggie Greville at Polsden Lacey, dated 12th August, just two months after the King's death:

> He [George] can have his freedom if he wants it – free to marry
> Mrs Patrick Campbell or anyone else he thinks would make
> him happy – I have done my best and have failed. In respect of
> money and extravagance with which he has reproached me
> there is absolutely nothing to choose between us.[6]

Clearly George had wanted a divorce but she had probably talked him out of it, and his family were opposed to the idea. The first whiff of scandal that the West's marriage was seriously in trouble had leaked into society, and found its way into Jean Hamilton's diary:

> Minnie Wyndham ... astonished me by telling me that George
> West is now madly in love with Mrs. Patrick Campbell, and is
> trying to get Mrs. West to divorce him in order to marry ...
> and Mrs. Pat is urging him on to this – what a mad world it is.
> George West has a fine taste in impossible old women, as I
> hear Mrs. Pat's temper is even worse than Mrs. George West's
> ... his longing is to have a child, and Mrs. Pat has assured him
> she can do this for him!!![7]

It was not until the spring of 1911 that Jennie wired Jack, to let him and Winston know of her predicament with George. Jack replied, 4th April, expressing in most sympathetic terms his sentiments at the breakdown of the marriage, and in an endeavour to cheer her, assured her he had paid some of her outstanding debts to the bank:

> Dear Mama
>   It was a shock to get your wire this afternoon. I sent it off to
> Winston who is much upset on your account – We tried to get
> hold of G., [George] but he will not be back until tomorrow. I
> will see him then, and have a clear understanding with him as
> to our opinion of affairs. What he can hope to gain by
> behaving like a blackguard I cannot understand.
>   Don't be too depressed – when all this is over – you will find

yourself more settled and happier than you have been for some
time, and you will come back again nearer to W. [Winston]
and me whose love is always just the same.

Don't be pessimistic … best love from both of us.

I sent £100 to Smith Bank – from both of us – £50 is from
Winston.

Jack.

George, an only son, was due to inherit the estate from his ailing
father, William. He wanted a son and heir, and was still besotted
with Mrs Campbell, the most famous actress of her generation.
Unknown to him, she was, like Jennie, also past childbearing age. In
an endeavour to economise, the Wests had given up Salisbury Hall,
and had moved back to London, but were living apart. George then
had regrets and asked to come back, and Jennie wrote to him from
her latest home, 2 Norfolk Street, Mayfair, 19th April: "Certainly
come back to your own home – & with God's help we shall start
afresh". The quarrel was patched up and they got back together
again. The marriage staggered on for another two years, and
Winston and Clemmie, and Jack and Goonie, had all written letters
to *Belle Mère*, pledging their love and support for her.

On 28th May 1911, Clemmie gave birth to Winston's only son,
Randolph, at their home in London. Military duty called Winston
away within days of the birth, and the daily letters between parted
husband and wife are full of a deep love and joy.

The brothers continued to enjoy their membership of the
Oxfordshire Hussars. Winston had joined the regiment in 1902 and,
with his regular cavalry background, was soon made a squadron
commander, and Jack served under him as a lieutenant for a while.
Jack was then made commander of the Woodstock Squadron. In
June 1911, they handled their troops at the summer camp at
Blenheim Palace with great dash, reporting that the Berkshire
Yeomanry couldn't keep up with them at all.

On hearing that Clemmie was somewhat weak after the birth and
felt unable to attend his coronation, King George V went to great
lengths to arrange a special carriage for her, that would deliver her
for the crowning ceremony itself, and then get her home quietly,
avoiding all the crowds and waiting about. It was an act of kindness

that reflected well upon the new king and his respect for his ministers.

In July, Clemmie went on holiday to the Bavarian Alps with her cousin, Venetia Stanley. Winston was so completely involved in the wave of strikes sweeping the country that he could not get away. Later, Jack and Goonie went out to join Clemmie and Venetia. Winston and Clemmie would get to holiday together in Scotland in September. In October 1911, Winston was appointed as First Lord of the Admiralty, a post he had been expecting after some heavy hints, and one that ideally suited his temperament and talents. Clemmie had grown accustomed to appearing with her husband in public, and participating in official duties. She launched the battleship *Centurion* at Davenport on 18th November. Their future home was to be the large and prestigious Admiralty House. But it would be expensive to maintain, and for a time Clemmie put off moving in. As Winston's workload increased, Clemmie, already a fine swimmer, put a good deal of her energy into sport, taking up fox hunting, and playing golf and tennis.

In February 1912, Winston, as the chief spokesman for a government steering a new Home Rule Bill through parliament, had some major speeches to deliver in Belfast. He took a newly pregnant Clemmie with him. They received a hostile and noisy reception from 'Loyalist' crowds, which contrasted ill with the friendly cheers of Nationalists. The couple had to be escorted away by secret routes and the strain of the frightening experience caused a miscarriage for Clemmie. Her health suffered for several months, and doctors were in constant attendance. She kept up her interest in women's suffrage. In March, an eminent physician, Sir Almroth Wright, had published a hostile letter in *The Times*, opposing votes for women, seeing them as being psychologically and physically incapable of making important decisions. Clemmie wrote a satirical reply that was published, asking if, perhaps, women ought not to be abolished altogether? She signed it, 'One of the Doomed'.

Winston was working with the First Sea Lord, Admiral Sir John ('Jacky') Fisher, at a time when the Royal Navy had increased its power enormously, through the introduction of the 'Dreadnought' class of battleship. Winston fully understood the importance of the Royal Navy in any future conflict, and was anxious that it should be able to deploy its full power, immediately, in the event of hostilities.

Like many others he watched the German build up of military and naval power and expected a war. With the enormous energy that probably only Winston could muster, he applied himself to inspections of the fleet, to policy measures, and to finances, all of which were necessary to ensure that the Navy was in a state of constant readiness to strike at a moment's notice to defend the country.

In May, Clemmie and Goonie accompanied Winston on board the Admiralty yacht, *Enchantress,* for a Mediterranean cruise. Jack could not take time off from his job in the City. The party also included Herbert Asquith the Prime Minister, his daughter, Violet, Nellie Hozier, Prince Louis of Battenberg, (the Second Sea Lord), and Winston's Private Secretaries, Eddie Marsh and James Masterton-Smith. During this important tour of inspection, Winston joined Lord Kitchener and General Sir Ian Hamilton at Malta, for important amphibious exercises. Three years later these three would be intimately involved in the great attack at Gallipoli, putting this training to practical use. On 28th May, a large dinner followed by a ball was held at the palace in honour of the visitors. Clemmie was still too unwell to attend, and Winston escorted Goonie. As hostess, Jean Hamilton sat next to Herbert Asquith, and "Ian sat next Lady Gooney [*sic*] Churchill and was happy – she looked a poem ... . Winston was grumpy on Lady R's [Rundle's] other side". Jean and Winston had little time for each other, and clearly he was eager to return to the ship, not wanting to leave Clemmie alone for too long:

> He [Winston] was civil for five minutes in the ballroom and said "this life suited him etc." but he was not going to enter into details with the likes of me. His manners did not last longer than five minutes, then he yawned in my face and said he must take Gooney [sic] back to the yacht. [8]

At another ball Jean recorded the observation of a rather strait-laced Mr Diggle who:

> abhorred all the *Enchantress* lot, especially all the women ... he said with bitter vigour that Lady Gooney [*sic*] looked positively *sinful* when she danced; that made me laugh, and I think there is some truth in it – she is seductive.

While they were away, Jack had been "yeomanizing" with the Oxfordshire Hussars, and had promised Winston he would look into the whole question of insurance companies offering special policies for submarine officers. This is just one more example of how Jack, using his particular financial expertise, assisted Winston in his work in an unsung way.

By the autumn, Goonie was again pregnant, and gave birth to her second son on 25th May 1913. She had wanted a girl, and had been thinking in terms of girl's names. The christening took place in Westminster Cathedral, with Winston as godfather, and there emerged a good story that Peregrine liked to tell. Goonie went to the front of the church to pray, and the priest came out to baptise the baby, and asked: "What name is this child to be given?" Someone said "Henry", then Winston (of course) suggested: "Winston". Goonie had not heard what was being said, and by the time she came to the baptismal font the priest had poured the water over the infant's head, and named him Henry Winston. Goonie had intended giving him the historic name of Peregrine that had been in the Bertie family since 1570. She did not approve of the change, and insisted on calling him Peregrine, by which name he would be known throughout his life. Little Johnnie, now aged four, could not pronounce it and called him 'Pebin', an affectionate nickname by which he was known to all the family.

In early April 1913, Winston and Clemmie moved at last, from Eccleston Square, into Admiralty House. The situation between Jennie and George had reached the point of no return. He was again besotted with Mrs Patrick Campbell, and if Jennie had not agreed to divorce him, she would have had to suffer the humiliation that he would divorce her. Throughout their lives, Winston and Clemmie, and Jack and Goonie, were devoted to each other, and to their children, and no infidelities ever occurred. The sexually deviant behaviour of the respective mothers of Winston and Jack, and Clemmie, would not be repeated. No doubt the younger Churchills were embarrassed by the entanglements and scandalous love affairs of their predecessors, and the gossip surrounding them. Clemmie and Goonie privately censored Jennie's extravagances, and her inability to live within her means, and questioned her sense of judgement in relation to her choice of men. Both the wives had received the steadying hand of religion in their upbringing, and both had good husbands.

Winston is notorious for the amount of time he spent on the *Enchantress*, his boundless energy demanding endless visits to naval installations. It was a very happy time in all of their lives. Jack accompanied him as often as he could, usually sporting a naval style uniform. In November 1913, Winston wrote to Clemmie from Portland, saying how Jack was "always happy in the circle of military things". Did he ever pause to reflect how Jack had been deprived of the military career he yearned for? While there was no malice in Winston, he was frequently quite thoughtless regarding Jack's situation.

Although their divorce had been granted in July 1913, George was legally obliged to wait another nine months before he could marry Mrs Campbell. Once again it was Jack who had to sort out the incredible tangle into which the finances of his mother and stepfather had descended. George seems to have washed his hands of the whole mess. Jack wrote to Jennie that George's business partner, Mr Wheater, "is almost at the end of his tether and is very bitter at George leaving him to face the music".[9] Writing on 31st December 1913 from Blenheim Palace, to his mother holidaying in Germany, Jack reported that little Johnny was trying to come to terms with the changes: "What used to be Granny West is now Granny Churchill – I don't know why but I know its true!" This chatty letter ended with a warning that at least £950 of bills needed to be paid before the decree absolute.[10]

On 9th January 1914, Jennie celebrated her 60th birthday, and Leonie gave a dinner for her. Afterwards a depressed Jennie went to her sister's bedroom and bemoaned the loss of her youth, when she used to sweep into a room, and knew that every man turned his head to look at her.

Family relationships would come under their greatest strain yet as Jack made the remarkable discovery that their mother had been deceiving the two brothers for many years over the exact nature of Lord Randolph's will. He had left his estate in a Trust Fund for the benefit of his wife while she lived, and for his two sons and their children after her death. But he inserted a clause that said:

"... after the decease or second marriage of my said wife whichever shall first happen to advance ... any part not exceeding in the whole one half of the presumptive share of any child or issue in the said trust fund towards his or her advancement in the world".[11]

Entirely unknown to them, Winston and Jack could have had a claim on their father's estate since Jennie's second marriage in 1900.[12]

In a long letter of 14th February 1914, Jack unburdened himself, giving full vent to the exasperation he felt:

Dear Mama

Winston and I, Woodhouse and Lumley, had a long consultation yesterday at the Admiralty on the new situation which has arisen, owing to this new discovery in the will.

We had always thought that Papa was very wrong in not making any provision for us during your life. We thought the will left us in the possible position of being for many years without a penny while you were in receipt of over £5,000 a year. This did in actual fact happen & you were unable to give us any allowance.

It now appears that there is a clause in the will providing that while in the event of your remarrying the trustees could demand on our behalf or on behalf of our children, should we be dead – a sum of about £1,200 a year – £600 a year each.

This discovery makes little difference to you – but it alters the security against your loan very much. Your Guarantees are not nearly in such a safe position ... . The position is this. Winston and I are now making our own living and as long as we do so of course nothing will be claimed – although I believe that at the present moment we could each demand about £600 a year.

But supposing I found myself in a state of penury with a wife and family – I might have to ask for the money – I am only – I hope – thinking of remote possibilities.

Again if I or Winston die before you – our wives will be left very badly off. There is nothing for them to bring up the children on except our insurances – in my case amounting to

£400 a year, and in that case there is no doubt that our
children's trustees would demand the money for their keep and
education ... .

The will was drawn up by the old Duke's solicitor – I forget
the name – he went to prison afterwards. How it escaped all
the other solicitors who have seen it, I cannot understand. Its
discovery would have facilitated my marriage settlement. As it
is the discovery does you no harm and makes a great difference
to us by giving something to our children should we die before
you ... .

Cox's overdraft will have to be paid off gradually out of
income.

You have nothing whatever to keep up and you have over
£2000 a year, and you certainly ought to be able to pay them
off quarterly. I do not see any chance of your raising another
penny.

It makes a considerable difference finding that Papa's will
was not made – as we were always led to suppose – carelessly
and without any consideration for us.

It is quite clear that he never thought that while you were
single you would be unable to pay us an allowance, and the
clause in the will covered the situation – which did actually
arise – of your remarriage ... .

You must save something out of your income to pay off
Cox. We have begged you so often to live within your income
– which is not a very severe demand. Your income is larger
than mine in most years and you have nothing whatever to
keep up. Unless you are able to do so and if you start running
up bills again – there is nothing that can save you from a crash
& bankruptcy ... . Lots of others whom you know are in much
worse positions than you ... .

Your loving
Jack SC[13]

For nearly twenty years Winston and Jack had thought their father
had made no useful provision for them in his will; for nearly fourteen
years their mother had denied them a half share of their full inheritance. If Jack, returning from the Boer War a combat veteran, had

received his £600 a year from 1901 he could easily have become a professional soldier. His inheritance would have supplemented his army pay, and he could have pursued his preferred career and lived very comfortably.

The financial problems escalated as the creditors moved in on the separated couple. They went after George first but he was vigorously denying his liability and blaming Jennie for reckless spending, even after they had started divorce proceedings. On 27th February,[14] Jack listed four writs in court for the recovery of sums from £56 to £220. One covered a jade jewel that Jennie had bought after they had agreed to separate. In all £900 was owed and George insisted he had not a penny. On 3rd March, Jack was able to report that he was juggling the various creditors, getting some cases postponed and doing everything he could to keep it all out of the papers. "You must decide all this yourself but as it stands they will sue G[eorge] – he will deny liability – if he loses the case I should think his bankruptcy will shortly follow. If he wins the shops will sue you. I am not at all sure that your name is not already in the case. You have denied liability – now G does the same – the only course open to the shops is to sue you both. You have the goods; and both you and G deny liability. It is no good saying he promised to pay. He has not got the money and his promises are of no value".[15]

These entanglements had drawn in many friends. £2,000 was owed by George to Cassel directly, but by defaulting on loan repayments the couple had obliged their 'Guarantees', the Dukes of Marlborough and Westminster, and Cassel, to carry on paying out £400 a year. "Naturally they are all furious". Jack reminded his mother – again, "Keep within your income, which is about £2,000 a year – much more than I have got".[16] Jack said Winston would write soon but was heavily involved "with aeroplanes and estimates".

The younger Churchills were understandably exasperated with Jennie's perpetual financial crises, her marital failure, her debts, and her uncontrollable spending, that was all impinging on their own lives in such dramatic fashion.

In the spring of 1914, Jennie wrote to Jack from Monte Carlo, where despite all the warnings from her family, she was back at the gambling casinos. She was in a depressed state and complaining somewhat pathetically about feeling unwanted, and may have been intimating that she was suicidal to gain sympathy:

> ... apart from Goonie & perhaps little Johnnie, who cares if I return or not? Not that I do not know that you and Winston love me, & are very good to me – but you lead busy lives, & have your own families to be absorbed in. What am I? Only an old 5th wheel – I am not complaining, only stating facts ... .

On 16th April, the decree absolute was granted, and on the same day, two hours later, George married Mrs Patrick Campbell. Jennie would soon meet another even younger man. She attended a Frewen family wedding in Rome, and at a ball was introduced to the 37-year-old, Montagu Porch, who fell in love with her at first sight. Porch was serving in the Colonial Service in Nigeria, and was very handsome, with a slim figure, and hair that was prematurely white. A month later, whilst he was on his way back to Nigeria, she would receive a letter from him, 16th May, which shows he was besotted with her:

> ... I remember you, dear kind friend, all the nice things you said of me. I would they were true or at least that you believed what you said.
>   Have you so soon forgotten that I want your photograph – will you send it to me please – one that can live in my lettercase ... & a kind word straight from you would buck me up enormously...Goodbye, dear Lady Randolph – I want your friendship & I mean to get & keep it.
>   Montie

Jack was not well in May 1914. Goonie had nursed him back to health, as Winston explained in a letter to Clemmie. He must have been a good deal better by July, as Winston was commandeering his services as an accountant for Clemmie. With the mounting political crisis, Winston had expressed concern at their monthly outgoings, though Clemmie was always careful with money. He advised Clemmie to send all the bills to him so that measures could be taken to control expenditure.

On 28th June the Arch-Duke Franz Ferdinand of Austria-Hungary, and his wife, were assassinated at Sarajevo in Bosnia. The threat of war was in the air. Winston at the Admiralty kept his family informed of the risks involved. Jack with his intimate knowledge of the financial sector in London and New York, sounded warnings to the family in July, regarding money:

> The world has gone mad – the whole financial system has completely broken down ... Be careful with what you have got – Gold will soon be unobtainable ...

Jennie wrote to Leonie in Ireland of political matters, and the financial squeeze, from her latest exquisitely decorated and furnished home, 72 Brook Street, London, on 1st August:

> W. [Winston] tells me Poincarré has written an impassioned letter to the King imploring his aid – The fleet (British) will be mobilised today probably – Germany is holding up English vessels – & has mobilised & massed troops on the French Frontier – Money is fearfully tight here & one cannot get a cheque cashed – & the Banks will give no gold. But W. says the financial situation will be easier as they are going to issue at once paper pound notes – Paris is in an awful state, risings in the streets – The whole world seems to have gone mad. I am depressed beyond words ...[17]

Since January 1914 Clemmie was expecting another baby, a new 'puppy kitten' to look forward to. The sisters-in-law were spending their summer holidays together, during July and August, in two rented cottages by the sea, at Overstrand, Cromer, Norfolk. Clemmie had taken Diana and Randolph to live at 'Pear Tree Cottage', and Goonie, with Johnny and Peregrine, occupied 'Beehive Cottage'. Winston and Jack were able to join them there and supervise the children in building great sand fortifications on the beach. On 3rd August, Germany declared war on France, and invaded Belgium. Britain, now forced into the position of having to maintain the balance of power in Europe, declared war on Germany the following day. Clemmie's third child was expected in eight weeks' time. Her mother was living in Dieppe, and had to be fetched back to England by Nellie, as it was not safe for her to remain in France. Blanche Hozier joined them at Overstrand, or as Clemmie put it to Winston, Nellie dumped her mother on her to look after, whilst she went off with a nursing corps to Belgium. What had begun at Overstrand as a happy, family holiday for the wives and children, in the sunshine and sea air, had rapidly turned into a nightmare. Immediately war was declared, Jack left his job at Nelke, Phillips, and joined his regiment, the Oxfordshire Yeomanry, to train for active war service. He had expressed a decided wish to go and fight at the front, and for Goonie the prospect was frightening beyond belief. Winston had huge responsibilities in wartime. Once again the family was off to the wars.

CHAPTER 18

A World at War:
From the Western Front to Gallipoli
1914–1915

Winston read the developing crisis in masterly fashion and quietly began to prepare the Royal Navy for war. That navy, even without its French, Russian and Japanese allies, was larger than the combined fleets of Germany, Austria-Hungary, Italy and Turkey. The Home Fleet was moved without fuss to its main base at Scapa Flow, from where it dominated the North Sea. The navy was formally mobilised on 2nd August.

It has to be said that Winston was exhilarated by the turn of events; the excitement of war suited him, and he shared a good deal of the elation that swept most of Europe in the summer of 1914. While Clemmie and the children stayed at Overstrand, he worked tremendously hard at the Admiralty. He easily dominated his political colleagues in the Cabinet, who were wholly lacking in military experience or expertise, and he was the equal of the political novice, Secretary of State for War, Lord Kitchener. Though technically only the civilian head of the Royal Navy, he completely ruled the First Sea Lord, Prince Louis of Battenburg, and interfered prodigiously in naval operational matters. At the Admiralty, Battenburg's nickname was 'Quite Concur'.

The Oxfordshire Hussars were mobilised for war on 4th August. Jack reported to his squadron at its camp near Blenheim Palace. As a squadron commander he would have had all the concerns in making sure all his men came in on time, that their horses were in good order and their kit was complete. Their brigade assembled and training to toughen up both men and horses began immediately. In common with the whole Territorial Force their first duty was the defence of the United Kingdom, but many were anxious that the fighting in France would be 'all over by Christmas' and they might miss the

chance to get into action. This is where a regiment with such powerful social connections as the Oxfordshire Hussars was well placed.
Having the brother of the First Lord of the Admiralty in its ranks was
an added bonus.

In his letter to Jack of 20th August, Winston was discussing the
possible deployment of the regiment. The first two squadrons might
be needed for divisional cavalry in the regular divisions – "a great
honour for the regiment". "I am trying to get the 3rd Squadron
(yours, I hope) for the infantry division I am forming from marines
and naval reservists". This was an early reference to the creation of
the Royal Naval Division (RND), which would go on to achieve
great fame at Gallipoli and on the Western Front. It came about
because, when the naval reservists were recalled to duty in August,
there were far more of them than there were ships in which they
could serve. It was one of Winston's excellent ideas to combine them
with the Royal Marines to form an extra division of infantry.

On 24th August, Winston wrote from the Admiralty, conveying
the serious news of the battle of Mons, where the British army stood
up well to the enemy but had to retreat. Already Winston was opin-
ing that if Britain did not win, he had no wish to live. "But win we
will". He was still lobbying on behalf of Jack and the regiment to get
them employed at the earliest opportunity. Such letters were always
signed, "your loving brother".

On 31st August, Winston had to write to Jack telling him that the
Yeomanry Cavalry were to be formed into a separate cavalry division
of four brigades, and would have to assemble and train at Churn for
some months. Winston wanted to talk the whole thing over with
Jack. He was anxious about his brother's clamour to put himself in
harm's way.

Winston came in for some personal criticism that autumn, after a
number of naval losses, but he retained the confidence of Prime
Minister Asquith, who admired his combative spirit. In his exuberant
desire to engage the enemy more closely, Winston took a keen interest in the military campaign, which he was partly able to do by
identifying with the exploits of Jack and the Oxfordshire Hussars.
Some of his colleagues avowed that one government department was
not enough for Winston, and they wondered if one war was enough.

Winston was desperate to get some results and an opportunity soon presented itself that, while his critics seize upon it as grist to their mill, in reality had a profound effect on the long-term development of the war in Europe. He had already deployed naval assets in the form of squadrons of the Royal Naval Air Service (RNAS) to Europe, based initially at Dunkirk, and sent further units to protect them. As the Germans suddenly threatened the early capture of Antwerp, which would have had the direst consequences for the BEF fighting in Belgium, Winston took the urgent step of sending everything he could by way of military force to support the city garrison. He also finally persuaded Lord Kitchener to release the Oxfordshire Hussars as divisional cavalry for the RND. Prime Minister Asquith, in one of his typically indiscreet letters to his mistress, Venetia Stanley, told her that Kitchener was "heartily glad to get rid of them", which gives us some idea of the persistence of the lobbying to get them into active service. Asquith rather gloomily predicted that "we shall see very few of them back again", and in a separate letter cast doubt on the "fighting or staying powers of the Oxfordshire Yeomanry".

The regiment left for France on 19th September; some of its latest recruits were still in civilian clothes. Jack, with no real knowledge of where they were off to, only that Winston had cabled promising a "really good show", fired off a message to his brother with a long list of demands for stores and equipment his men needed. His D Squadron was the first across, ahead of the rest of the regiment, and his first duty was to protect the planes of the RNAS.

One early sighting we get of Jack is from the diary of Baroness de la Grange, whose Chateau de La Motte au Bois, in the Forest of Nieppe near Hazebrouck, was used by a succession of British corps and divisions as their headquarters. On 20th September, she recorded: "The R.F.C. is at Morbecque, together with a company of the Oxfordshire Hussars, commanded by Major J. Churchill; these troops are acting as escort to the naval air squadron, commanded by Commander Samson"[1]. Their paths would cross many times before the war was ended. On 28th September Jack wrote to Jennie, asking her to look after Goonie: "I am afraid she feels my going very much – but I know she would have hated me to have stayed behind".

At the end of September, D Squadron re-joined the regiment at Hazebrouck, where Jack was surprised to be asked by the local priest if he was the son of the man who made that great speech entitled "Trust the People". Apparently the priest, who was also the local member of parliament, was an ardent admirer of Lord Randolph, and could quote his speeches at length. Early in October the regiment, still protecting Samson's planes and armoured cars, was skirmishing with German uhlans, and offering itself to the local French commander for active service. In their busy patrolling in this area, the Oxfordshire Hussars were the first unit of the Territorial Force to come under enemy fire in the war. The presence of British cavalry in this part of Belgium had been highly confusing for the German staff officers studying the British order of battle and its deployment – a useful side benefit from Winston's lobbying on behalf of the regiment.

As Winston was preparing for one of his by now routine visits to Dunkirk, his train was halted and returned to London. At a crisis meeting he learned of the Belgian decision to evacuate Antwerp, a move that would have released major German formations for action against the hard-pressed BEF. On 3rd October, with Kitchener's blessing he proceeded at once to Antwerp, promised the Belgians that his new Royal Naval Division would join them (the brigade of Royal Marines arrived the very next day) and, at his persuasive best, got the Belgians to promise to hold on for ten more days as new British formations would be arriving in Belgium by then, and the line from Lille to the sea could be secured.

Antwerp did not hold on for so long. For four days Winston was in his element, witnessing the front line fighting under enemy fire, and directing a stream of telegrams back to the Admiralty. He even asked Asquith if he could resign as First Lord and take an army commission as commander of the Antwerp garrison. Kitchener would have made him a lieutenant-general; it took Asquith to point out that promoting a former lieutenant of Hussars and Light Horse to lieutenant-general, a leap of seven ranks over a number of major-generals, brigadiers and colonels, was asking for trouble. In truth, Asquith needed Winston in both the Admiralty and the Cabinet.

That the city fell after seven days, and that the wretchedly inexperienced RND lost so heavily, is all held against Winston. Even the RND's own history describes the two Naval brigades as "a slender asset from the military point of view".[2] But it does go on to stress what a tremendous boost to morale their arrival was for the city garrison. Winston accepted much of the criticism and later wrote that he would have done things differently with hindsight. Even Clemmie, clearly annoyed that he had dashed off to war just as she was about to give birth to their daughter, Sarah, thought he had lost his sense of proportion.

But this courageous and imaginative stroke did have an extraordinary effect on the campaign. That extra five days of resistance early in October tied up German formations and allowed the Belgian army to fall back along the coast towards its British and French allies, keeping it in the fight and allowing the savage fighting around Ypres to run its course and halt the German offensive for the year 1914. Depriving Germany of victory in the short term condemned her to ultimate defeat in a long war of attrition she could never really hope to win.

After the RND was obliged to return to the United Kingdom, the Oxfordshire Hussars put in a few weeks training, during which time they received more modern rifles and had to fight off the threat of being sent home by a direct appeal to the commander-in-chief, Sir John French, to be allowed to stay. They became attached to General Head Quarters and provided a daily guard there. On 29th October, Jack dined with Sir John, where his lobbying to have them attached to a front line division drew the alarming response that they would be needed at GHQ for some considerable time.

The crisis of the First Battle of Ypres changed all that. The regiment was ordered to join De Lisle's 1st Cavalry Division, then locked in battle along the Messines Ridge. Jack was appointed as second in command of the regiment, handing command of D Squadron over to a Captain Molloy. Within twenty-four hours they were in place at Neuve Eglise behind the ridge, tired and very wet, and about to intervene at a critical time in the ferocious fighting of 30th October. Jack was ordered to take half the regiment (A Squadron and two troops of D) to reinforce the hard-pressed 1st Cavalry Brigade. As the rest of the regiment dug in, Jack dismounted his men and led them forward for a quarter of a mile until they located the brigade headquarters in the valley of the Steenbeek. With no detailed orders, or even a clear situation report, he was told to take his men up on to the ridge, select a well-covered position and support the cavalry fighting in the village of Messines. He deployed his men just below the crest of the ridge and then advanced the whole line up to the top, where they took post along the thick hedges bordering the Messines – Ploegsteert road. The rest of the regiment soon joined them, and they held their ground under a heavy fire, and with the frustration of having little in the way of enemy targets to fire back at. When the fire increased dramatically in the late afternoon, Jack got his men to fall back to the covered position just below the crest. He was able to keep casualties down to just seven men wounded (one of whom later died). During the 31st October, D Squadron was manning a barricade in Messines and was hotly engaged, beating off German charges at about one hundred yards range. The regiment was relieved by the 18th Hussars and went into support. That evening the Germans made their big push to storm the ridge and were defeated by the timely intervention of the 14th Battalion, London Regiment (London Scottish). The British were forced to abandon the Messines Ridge the next day and the Oxfordshire Hussars covered the withdrawal of the gallant remnants of the London Scottish towards Wulverghem. The regiment had been moving and fighting for sixty hours without any real break for sleep.

For two or three days more the regiment served in or close behind the front line, taking its part in the defeat of further German attacks and the final stabilisation of the line. When the 1st Cavalry Division in which they were serving was finally relieved the regiment made its way to safety in the rear and found that Major Churchill and one of his subalterns had made excellent arrangements for their accommodation and the distribution of hot food and mail from home. After a short rest they were returned to front line duty, including the manning of the trench lines that were solidifying all along the Western Front. Jack again showed his excellent organisational skills when put in charge of the regiment's horse lines. The headquarters of the BEF was desperate for good, reliable officers to serve in a number of important staff roles and so it came to pass that, on 19th November, Jack was ordered to report for duty as the Camp Commandant of a new training centre for Territorial Force units near St. Omer. The BEF knew it was in for a 'long haul' against the Germans and had begun to organise the training of its formations with some new sense of purpose.

Having heard from Jack about the fighting at Messines, Winston wrote to say how proud he was of the regiment in its first major battle and how helpless he felt to be "one who merely cheers from the bank the gallant efforts of the rowers". Sending his best regards to the regiment he penned one postscript: "It is my fault you are in it all". When Winston heard from Jack that Sir John French had personally asked for him to take up a staff appointment, he understood immediately that Jack would feel a great wrench at having to leave the regiment but he asserted that: "It is very clearly your duty to go where you can be most use. I expect you will do this work very well and as more and more Territorials arrive its importance will grow. Your brains and business training should be useful and will find a wider scope. You will know more of what is going on ... . In your position you will have lots of opportunities of helping the regiment and the Territorial interests in general. There will be plenty of chances of being shot at before the end is reached"[3]. Goonie, who had been "very good and brave" while Jack was serving with the regiment in action, was "enchanted at the news". Jack did, indeed relay his feelings about the new job to his mother: "Goonie will tell you that I have been ordered back here for some staff job – I do not quite like leaving my regiment ... . I am out of the firing line for the time being – I don't mind that one bit – but I do not like leaving the others in it".[4]

In a long conversation with Jack at St Omer, that Jack wrote up into a memo and sent on to Winston, Sir John French spoke of the terrible crisis of the First Battle of Ypres and how narrow had been the victory. He said that Winston had been a great help to him, and that his letters were always so encouraging. He wished he had been more informed about the Antwerp operation but Jack intervened to say that if Winston had not stiffened the resolve of the Belgians to resist there by the despatch of the RND, the Germans might have been able to release heavy reinforcements to seize and hold Hazebrouck and complete the ruin of the BEF. Sir John French could only agree.

While Jack was serving on the staff on the Western Front, he was able to pass on news of the latest developments in warfare to his desk-bound brother. Winston wrote to him a 'Secret' letter from the Admiralty on 26th February 1915, thanking him for a report on the first use on the Western front of the new heavy guns that were in such desperately short supply at this stage in the war. Winston sounded a little deflated as he talked of the "long vistas of pain and struggle" that lay ahead and how he toiled away but that the real inspiration to the government was the "true insight and courage" of the indefatigable Lloyd George. He was always hopeful of American intervention on the Allied side and thought that 'an incident' might turn them powerfully towards the Allies. This, in February 1915, was a rather bizarre prediction of the sinking of the *Lusitania* in May with its heavy loss of American lives. These letters were always very affectionate, this one beginning with "My Dear" and concluding with "Dear Jack do write to me. I am so glad to hear from you. With best love, Ever and always yours. W", fondly wishing to see him home on leave and passing on news of Goonie and the children.

Winston was also keeping Jack informed of the important new operations against the Turks at the Dardanelles. When an appeal came in early in January 1915 from Britain's Russian allies for some action, even a diversion, against Turkey to take the pressure off the Russian armies in the Caucasus, Winston responded immediately and generously with an offer to use the strength of the Royal Navy in that capacity. He asked Admiral Carden, commanding the forces blockading the entrance to the Dardanelles, to work out a plan for the bombardment and reduction of the forts guarding the straits and the Gallipoli peninsula. Some early success in silencing the outer forts was soon frustrated by the inability of British minesweepers to clear the way for the capital ships. In part they found themselves underpowered to cope with the flow of the current leaving the straits but, more significantly, they were always under heavy fire from mobile batteries of Turkish artillery operating from the Gallipoli peninsula itself. It was this problem that finally determined the need for troops to land on and clear the peninsula, to enable the fleet to batter its way through to Constantinople. In something of a rush, Sir Ian Hamilton was appointed to command a force comprising the 29th British Division, the Royal Naval Division, two divisions of newly-recruited Australians and New Zealanders (the Anzacs) then training in Egypt and a newly-created division of French infantry. It was a force largely unprepared and certainly inadequate in strength for the heavy responsibility it carried.

The winter of 1914–15 was a hard one and the BEF struggled to make itself comfortable as its strength increased by leaps and bounds. In a letter to his mother in February, Jack described how dirty and literally smelly the town was where he was based. He reckoned that the most modern drains dated from the time of the Duke of Marlborough! One of his worries had been relieved by the news that Jennie had taken in Goonie and the children to live with her. She would perform many such kindnesses during the war. Jack's good humour shines through in a typical soldier's story he told his mother. "I must try and pay a visit to Boulogne I think and see the *hors de combat* – I hear the place is full of lovely ladies – ready to bandage anyone anywhere. We call it the Remount Depot!"[5]

As the dreary winter progressed, and the rain and snow fell unrelentingly turning the country into a quagmire, Jack wrote to Jennie of how dull the GHQ had become. He clearly enjoyed stimulating company and found very little of it there. He thought it so full of "such awfully stupid people" that "one never hears two interesting words strung together!" There were frightful jealousies going on, especially once the Honours list was published. Jack wondered whether the Staff would ever be the BEF's strong point. He heard that all leave was cancelled from 1st March and regretted that he would not see his family for some time. Jennie's kindness was unstinting and she arranged a week's holiday for the children in Brighton. Jack commented on how excited everyone was by the naval attack on the Dardanelles, and how it should be "a tremendous thing, if successful". He could not imagine how he was shortly to become closely involved in the campaign.

As the BEF prepared for its first offensive action on the Western front in 1915, Jack was beginning to find the life of a staff officer at St Omer "a bit of a bore". On 12th March, he was feeling at a loose end as most of the General Staff went off to the front to observe the progress of the battle of Neuve Chappelle, when Winston suddenly rang at noon and asked if he would like a posting elsewhere. "Would I not!" he recorded in his diary, especially as it involved working with their old friend General Sir Ian Hamilton, who was putting together his staff for the Gallipoli campaign. An official letter requesting his services was brought out by 'Sunny' Marlborough, arriving at about 2.30 pm. Jack had to leap into a car and drive to

Hazebrouck to seek out Sir John French and ask his permission to go. He had to kick his heels for a while as the general watched the battle, but Sir John gave his immediate consent.

He was in London by 13th March, with just enough time to see Goonie and pick up some items of kit. Hamilton and his staff left that very day for the Mediterranean. Winston and Clemmie, Goonie, Jean Hamilton, and other family and friends all gathered at Charing Cross Station to see their train off. Sir Ian wrote to Winston the next day, as their train raced through France heading for Marseilles. He said what a lift it was for them to be seen off by so many well-wishers, and that Jack seemed cheery and fit. He thought he would be a great addition to "our little band of adventurers". Indeed Sir Ian had asked for Jack, not just out of friendship with the family, but because he was the only one of his staff officers with practical combat experience in the current war. Hamilton said he looked forward to dining with him regularly at the staff mess, where he would be able "to keep a close eye on him".

Taking a fast train to Marseilles, they boarded HMS *Phaeton* and set off for the eastern Mediterranean. Ian Hamilton and his staff were very crowded on board, and frustrated in their haste by the delay in getting the ship fully fuelled up at Toulon. Thereafter they raced eastwards at 23 knots. Jack was now basking in warm sunshine, when he had not ventured outdoors without a mackintosh for four months. The Admiralty demanded more haste and the ship hit 25 knots on 16th March, reaching the island of Tenedos next day, having covered 1,200 miles in 43 hours. Jack was deeply impressed by the assembled ships of the Allied fleet, British, French and Russian. Most striking was the new super dreadnought, *Queen Elizabeth,* on loan to the expedition to test her formidable 15" guns and complete her sea trials.

Sir Ian Hamilton met the new admiral, De Robeck (Carden had retired sick), and learnt of the major naval attack due to take place the very next day. On 18th March Jack accompanied Sir Ian and the French general, D'Amade, on a reconnaissance by destroyer along the west coast of the Gallipoli peninsula. What they saw was very sobering. The peninsula itself was rocky and offered very few landing places. The open area at Suvla Bay was too far from the real objective (the Narrows of the Dardanelles) and the neck of the peninsula at Bulair was very heavily fortified by the enemy and could only be attacked at great cost.

The party returned to the entrance of the Dardanelles and witnessed the climax of the great naval attack of 18th March. They watched in awe as the guns of the British and French battleships battered the Turkish forts. Having seen the devastation at the outer forts, they fondly imagined that the enemy positions must soon crack. Then they saw six battleships lost to enemy mines, three sunk, three severely damaged, before their eyes. The attack was broken off, a disappointing failure; they could not know then that the Turkish forts were perilously low on ammunition and could not have resisted for much longer. The Royal Navy would not be rushing the Dardanelles. Troops would be needed to storm the Gallipoli peninsula, and clear the way for the warships to close upon and destroy the forts at the Narrows.

Though Winston would assure his admirals that their losses would be replaced and that the naval attack should be resumed as soon as possible, De Robeck was content to leave the next phase of the operations to the army. It was obvious that the whole expeditionary force would have to be re-organised, not at Lemnos, but back at the major port facilities of Alexandria. Jack was on board the *Queen Elizabeth* when the vital meeting between the army and navy staffs took place and the decision to delay the assault taken. Ships began to leave Mudros harbour for Alexandria, where everything would have to be unloaded and re-arranged for some very serious fighting.

Jack's ship was diverted to Port Said, a dreary spot that he remembered with no fond memory from his time there in 1897 with Sir Ernest Cassel. He moved by train to Alexandria, spending an awful first night there in a vile hotel disturbed by drunken American sailors in the next room! From 28th March the staff settled down in a new venue and the hard work began. Jack had been appointed Camp Commandant at General Headquarters, an unglamorous post but vital to the smooth running of the headquarters and so to the well-being of the campaign. Jack had to scour the town laying in hard-to-find office furniture and supplies to enable the General Staff to get on with the vital planning work. Just as things were settling down into a routine, the *Arcadia* arrived on 1st April with the rest of the administrative staff. Suddenly Jack had to accommodate another

47 officers and 200 men. He had such a difficult time galvanising Egyptian government officials into activity that he "went into business" on his own account and negotiated privately with a "rich old Turk" for the exclusive use of a large empty hotel. Now the enormous amount of staff work could proceed apace and it is interesting to note that Jack thought the lately arrived staffs of the Quartermaster General and the Adjutant General settled in rather well. There were to be many accusations of ill feeling on this score when the failed campaign was being investigated later.

Jack frequently accompanied Sir Ian Hamilton and, on Good Friday (2nd April) they were going to lunch and noted a large number of Greek flags flying at half-mast. The general asked in a shop, "Who is dead?" "Jesus Christ", was the mystified reply! Jack was a great support to Sir Ian Hamilton and his diary entries clearly reflect the thinking of the force commander on many issues. When Hamilton's fellow generals began to express doubts about the forthcoming operations, Jack was quick to condemn their "gloomy forebodings" and wanted everyone to get on with their work and help the success of what was expected to be a difficult enough task. His excellent command of French was already proving useful in the numerous contacts necessary with the French component of the Mediterranean Expeditionary Force.

Just as he had got the Alexandria staff offices working smoothly, they were all back on ships heading for Lemnos again. The General Headquarters had to work from the battleship *Queen Elizabeth*. Once again the Camp Commandant had to make it all go smoothly. "There is a good deal of difficulty in trying to fit up the ship as an office. Everyone comes to me for everything".[6] Jack accompanied Sir Ian Hamilton on a reconnaissance of the Gallipoli coast on 12th April. From the *Queen Elizabeth* they could see Turkish defences being strengthened all the time and noted the few available beaches for an assault landing. They were confident that the landings could be affected but expected heavy casualties in the process.

As there was no official post of Camp Commandant, Jack was delighted when he was appointed a Deputy Assistant Adjutant General on the staff, at a useful salary of £550 per annum. He was constantly liaising with all manner of officers, of the assault formations, the Navy, the French, and so he leaves us a very valuable record of how the operation was planned and executed from a unique perspective. There had never before in history been an assault landing against a coastline defended by an alert enemy armed with such terrible weapons as machine-guns, quick-firing artillery and magazine rifles. There were only the most general instructions on how to carry out such an attack and everyone had to learn their task as they went along. Army and Navy were equally exasperated with each other's procedures and peculiarities and Jack's good nature was frequently called upon to smooth out difficulties.

On 20th April, Jack wrote to his mother, bemoaning the chaotic state of the postal service, and hinting that, before she heard from him again, she would hear of great happenings in the news. Presumably this letter passed the censor after the landings had taken place or it would never have been delivered. It is interesting because it gives the lie to a common myth that Sir Ian Hamilton and his staff made light of the problems they faced and underestimated their Turkish enemy. "This is a tremendous undertaking. No one has ever attempted to land on a large scale in the face of a prepared enemy before. Everyone is sanguine of success, but it will be very difficult and I expect there will be heavy casualties."[7] He told his "dear mama" how he lived and messed with Sir Ian who was very kind to him, and how he got on well with everyone. He would still find time to ask after the children, wondering if Peregrine could talk yet and whether he would know his father when he finally returned from the wars.

Finally the great day arrived. 25th April 1915. Jack spent the whole day on board the *Queen Elizabeth* with Sir Ian Hamilton and his General Staff. In fifty-seven timed entries in his diary, he recorded the confusing picture of the battle based on the messages received on the headquarters ship. They first watched the Australians go ashore above Gaba Tepe and then steamed south, past Y Beach, where things appeared to be going well. At Cape Helles they could see that the infantry was having a torrid time against a very determined defence. The *Queen Elizabeth* lent support with her huge 15″ guns and 6″ ordnance. Frustrated by their inability to do more, they watched as the troops landing at W Beach gradually improved their foothold, linking up with X beach and putting pressure on the Turkish defenders of V Beach. Only slowly did they realise that

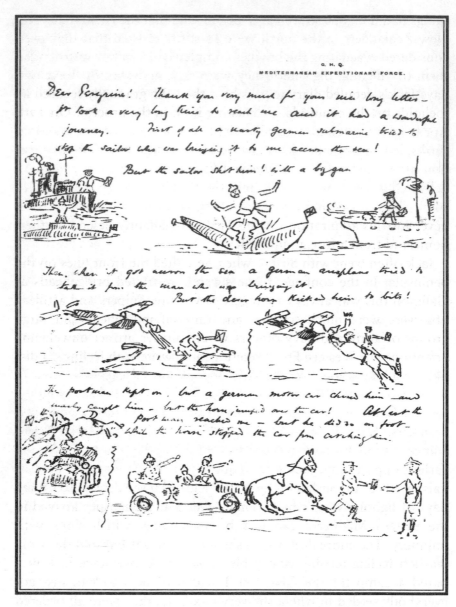

An example of Jack's illustrated letters to the infant Peregrine, from Gallipoli 1915.

things had not gone so well at Y Beach[8] and that the Australians and New Zealanders in the north were so stiffly resisted that they even considered evacuating the beaches completely. Hamilton encouraged them to "dig,dig, dig" until they were safe, and over the next two days Jack's detailed diary tells us how the MEF gradually secured its toeholds on the peninsula, exhausting itself in the process. On 27th April, Jack witnessed a terrible sight. A company of one hundred Turks, led by a gallant officer, sword in hand, attacked a British position along the coast. The *Queen Elizabeth* had them in sight and delivered a volley of 15″ shells into the attackers. When the dust and smoke blew away, not a living soul remained of the attackers. Jack never lost his admiration for the Turks so gallantly defending their homeland from a foreign invader.

Jack often went with Sir Ian when he visited the front lines on the peninsula. In the confines of the severely restricted bridgeheads at Gallipoli this was always a dangerous venture. Snipers and artillery observers were quick to spot any unusual movement and large groups of army and navy officers would always attract unwelcome attention. The Western Front veteran could write with feeling, "I disliked walking about trenches with people in red caps and men in white cap covers!"[9] From artillery observation posts he witnessed the Second Battle of Krithia, another defeat for the poorly equipped attackers. He saw his old RND friend, 'Oc' Asquith, the Prime Minister's son, brought in wounded and took Sir Ian to see him at the earliest opportunity. Jack was frequently at risk serving as a kind of liaison officer for Sir Ian on the battlefield. As if the defeat after three days of fighting wasn't bad enough, German submarines arrived in the eastern Mediterranean and began sinking British ships with impunity. The entire fleet had to shelter in Mudros Bay and the army was left feeling terribly vulnerable on shore. At one stage Jack prepared a camp for the GHQ on Tenedos island and had just got everybody settled in when, the very next day, they were all ordered back aboard the headquarters ship. To add to this exasperation, the first news began to trickle through of some political crisis at home affecting Winston.

Winston had been finding himself increasingly at odds with Admiral Fisher. Fisher was quite sure he could be as good a First Lord of the Admiralty as, say, Kitchener was a Secretary of Sate for

War. With these ambitions, he had the misfortune to be tied to the most energetic and interfering First Lord in history. Winston delighted in writing memoranda of the most intricate detail that were tantamount to orders for the Royal Navy. Winston had brushed aside Fisher's doubts about the viability of the Dardanelles expedition; Fisher had always favoured operations in the Baltic to threaten Germany and succour Russia more directly. Famously he thundered in one memo to Winston, "Damn the Dardanelles! They'll be our grave!" During a critical War Cabinet meeting in mid-May, Fisher used a discussion about the problems of the BEF in France and its desperate shortage of artillery ammunition to roundly attack the Dardanelles adventure. Winston later tackled him about it, saying Fisher had not been fair. He did not notice the odd looks Fisher gave him as he concurred. That night Winston fired off his usual detailed orders to the Board of Admiralty for reinforcing the fleet at Gallipoli and to one document added the ill-considered words, "First Sea Lord to see after action". He might have thought this was a routine matter that shouldn't have taken up the First Sea Lord's time but, for Fisher, perhaps understandably, it was a last straw and he fired off a letter of resignation and promptly absented himself.

Fisher's resignation, at a time when the war was not going well in general, created a political crisis in the House of Commons. The Conservatives were ready to withdraw their support for the Government and Asquith was obliged to accept the notion of a national government to include ministers from all the principal parties. One of the conditions for Tory acceptance was that the hated Winston must leave the Admiralty. He eventually settled for the Chancellorship of the Duchy of Lancaster, a post 'without portfolio' that allowed him to remain in the War Cabinet where he could remain a champion of the Dardanelles expedition.

All this came as a terrible blow to the embattled soldiers and sailors at Gallipoli. Jack recorded that Sir Ian was very upset at the loss of their staunchest ally in London; the naval commanders wrote very kindly to Jack saying how much they were going to miss Winston at the Admiralty and how they suspected that Fisher had been angling for the job himself. Jack duly passed these warm feelings on to his brother. He was glad that Winston's family was able to move in with Goonie and the children at 41 Cromwell Road.

Winston's ministerial salary, £4,360 per annum, after all government ministers had pooled their remuneration and taken equal shares, would mean that both families were economically safe and sound. This was a relief to Jack, always worrying about how Goonie was managing with him away at the front. He had written to his mother that, although Goonie had some £1200 a year, she was "not very practical" and might have found it difficult to cope but for the help of the wider family.

As the German submarines continued to take their toll of British ships it was finally decided that running the headquarters of the MEF from on board the *Arcadian* was no longer safe or practical. Jack was involved in selecting a permanent campsite on the island of Imbros. For several days he oversaw the erection of the tented camp, sleeping in the company of "animals with various numbers of legs". When the staff came ashore on 31st May there was an unseemly rush to snatch as many tables and chairs as could be had. An aggrieved Jack recorded, "Some people seem to think that they are at Aldershot and expect to find everything to hand". When Hamilton landed on 1st June the camp was running smoothly. Jack's new responsibilities kept him away from the front line now and he only reported the next battles, without witnessing them. The headquarters now totalled over sixty officers, sixty servants, a one hundred escort detachment, fifty signallers, fifty clerks and about forty police, cooks, printers, postals and "hangers on". All these depended on Jack for their daily needs. The weather had turned very hot, the plague of flies was "frightful", and the arrival or non-arrival of the post from home became a constant refrain. Ordinary camp life developed and only the lack of a decent drink and the sound of distant gunfire made it different from many other camps Jack had served in. He was kept very busy with all the details of an extensive camp and he found stores difficult to obtain "owing to the ships wandering about". He became very critical of the Naval Transport Officers and their lack of understanding for the needs of the army. On 24th June he was particularly vexed to see the *Immingham* interrupted in her unloading of an electric light plant for GHQ. She was ordered out to sea with three quarters of the plant still on board, only to be rammed by another steamer and sent to the bottom. "She might just have well have waited with us and emptied herself", wrote the weary staff officer.[10]

Jack carefully observed the fighting on the peninsula, which showed a number of tactical victories towards the end of June but at a terrible continuous drain on the divisions in the line. The 29th Division reckoned it lost 125% of its officers and 96% of its men in the month of June alone. A regular refrain in Jack's letters to his mother was the growing admiration of the MEF for their Turkish enemy. "The Turks are very brave at this particular kind of warfare. They seem to behave fairly well as regards wounded etc" "The Turks are still fighting very well and, although there are signs that they are not quite so good as they were two months ago, they will certainly hold on to the end. If we can effect a big smashing blow on them – it may make a difference – but they are very fine trench fighters and are showing themselves determined to fight for their country. The prisoners say they do not like fighting England, but that as we have attacked their country – they have no choice".[11]

Then came news that massive reinforcements were on their way for a final push to victory. As more troops poured into the eastern Mediterranean Jack also found himself coping with a GHQ that now numbered 650 personnel. While busy with his normal staff work he had the unenviable opportunity to watch the new offensive out of the Anzac area go horribly wrong. The new troops put ashore at Suvla Bay were keen enough but were very badly led and, before long, were thrown into confusion and passivity. The mainly veteran forces attacking out of Anzac were defeated by the terrain, their own exhaustion and another brilliant battlefield performance by the Turkish commander, Mustapha Kemal. Jack went ashore on 8th August with Lieutenant Colonel Aspinall of the General Staff and saw at first hand the appalling incompetence of the Suvla generals. He couldn't help wondering that if they could have put Hunter-Weston and the 29th Division ashore against such weak opposition they would have accomplished their mission in short order. His record paints a depressing picture, as nothing Sir Ian Hamilton tried had any effect on the overall situation. As each new division went ashore it seemed to break in his hands.

Then came the bombshell of Sir Ian Hamilton's dismissal as commander, to be replaced by Sir Charles Monro. In letters home Jack would deplore the fact that the continuous efforts of his companions were held to no account by people who knew little or nothing of the extraordinary difficulties under which they laboured.[12] He blamed the Foreign Office for its many diplomatic failures in the region, and had a special loathing for the journalist Ellis Ashmead-Bartlett for the way his reports were used by the campaign's enemies in London to bring it down. He wondered what might have been if the men lost in the "idiotic slaughter" in France had been made available to Sir Ian for use in this campaign that offered such great strategic prizes if it had only been supported with vigour from the very start.

In the short term Jack was cut adrift; "I am a dog without a home", and he expected Monro to bring out his own staff and send Jack back to his regiment in France. Birdwood became the temporary Commander-in-Chief and all the staff were kept very busy coping with the many changes. The weather turned increasingly bad and added to all their difficulties. With wry amusement Jack noted that Monro's staff officers, fresh from their chateau in France, were shocked at the Spartan encampment of GHQ MEF and wanted all sorts of things doing for them that were quite impossible.

Birdwood took kindly to Jack, retained him as Camp Commandant and asked him to prepare encampments on Imbros for anything up to 16,000 men. Jack was busy on this, and nursing an injured ankle, when Kitchener made his one and only visit to the Dardanelles. He was sufficiently shocked at the conditions the troops had endured there for so long that he became less of an opponent of the school of thought that saw evacuation as the only real choice.

Towards the end of November severe winter weather wrecked camps, small boats and piers and caused many deaths from exposure. Jack's personal worries grew, especially on the financial front. The news that Winston had finally left the government and was to return to the army had implications for the well being of his family in London:

> I am afraid it will be a great struggle at C[romwell] Road. I am paying about £250 a year interest on the money borrowed to pay for the house & the rates & taxes make the house cost about £350 a year. I get £375 from Nelke & £500 from my present job which is precarious and Goonie has £400 making £1325 in all. Deduct the house and Goonie should have about £950 a year at the moment. I believe things are better in the City – & I hope I may be able to produce a little more".[13]

Jennie wrote on this letter that the money worries should be kept private!

When Jack heard that the plan was to evacuate Anzac and Suvla but hold on at Helles he quickly predicted that the Turks, by massing all their artillery in the south, would make the latter place utterly untenable. The first part of the evacuation was carried out brilliantly, without the loss of a single man. Jack's new camps on Imbros were soon filled to overflowing and he was mightily involved in getting the troops processed through and sent on to Egypt. He was not surprised when the order to evacuate Helles came through at the end of December. By Sunday 9th January 1916, the last Allied soldier had left the Gallipoli peninsula, most heading straight for Egypt. Jack moved to Mudros with Birdwood, who had offered him a posting on the Staff of the Australian and New Zealand forces. Jack thought the success of the evacuations had handed the Government a lifeline for which they should be grateful. All he could think about now was getting home on leave to see his wife and children. He often wondered if little Peregrine was talking yet, he was only just walking when he last saw him. But the problem was that, in order to secure a position with Birdwood's Anzacs, he had to remain in Egypt so as not to be passed over by a man in theatre. He was greatly heartened to receive two honours – a 'Mention' in Sir Ian Hamilton's Final Despatch, and from the French, the medal of the Legion of Honour. This was a personal recommendation from the French commander in gratitude for all the liaison work Jack had done with the French forces. He regaled his mother with descriptions of the medal ceremony at Mudros, being kissed by the general and foreseeing how fine he would look on the boulevards with the rosette of a *chevalier* on his tunic.

Back in Cairo, Jack could at last wash and shave regularly, wear clean clothes and learn again to dine in safety with civilian acquaintances. His money worries were heightened by the news that Nelke was obliged to reduce the retainer salary he was paying him to £250, and if he were sent back to his regiment in France he would lose another £200 a year. While living on active service he "had not spent a fiver since March last!" and all his pay went to Goonie. There had been a suggestion that Goonie might try and come out to Cairo to see Jack but he was glad it didn't happen. Too many ladies were making something of an exhibition of themselves in their zeal to 'do something', especially for the wounded men in the hospitals. Jack thought they more often than not got in the way of the efficient working of these important institutions. One can hear him sympathising with the wounded when he related to his mother that Lady Maxwell had taken to singing 'Abide With Me' to them!

It had been expected that, when he went to the BEF on the Western Front, Winston would get at least a brigade. That he was colonel of the 6th Royal Scots Fusiliers and likely to spend some time in the front lines was an added worry for Jack. He fervently hoped that Winston would not be about when the next big attack began. Knowing that both families were crowded into 41 Cromwell Road was another concern. He wondered aloud if Clemmie could bear it without any of her "high strikes" [hysterics] at this difficult time.

It was something of a relief to be finally appointed to the staff of 1st ANZAC Corps and to know that he would accompany them to France for service on the Western front – with secure employment and a much higher chance of getting home on leave to see his loved ones.

CHAPTER 19

Seeing it Through
1916–1918

The Churchill womenfolk, in common with women around the world in wartime, got on with their lives as best they could. Jennie, buoyed up by the love of Montagu Porch, and still doing well financially from her property enterprise, joined the opera singer, Maud Warrender. Ever the accomplished pianist, Jennie accompanied her on a series of morale-boosting concerts. Before long she was engaged in hospital work. She still kept a fine house, and when her man servants went off to the war, she recruited 'footwomen', that she dressed in a long black skirt and a footman's livery of waistcoat and a red and gold jacket. Goonie was shocked at the luxurious dining that still went on at Jennie's establishment, but was grateful for the invitations none the less.

Goonie's highly-strung nerves made her very fearful as the war started. She unburdened herself to Jennie about her dread of Jack being injured or killed, and wondered how she would cope now that his income was so drastically reduced. While she was proud that Jack was serving his country well, she confessed that "we have not a 'bob' left in the world and I do not know what the future holds in store for us". She jokingly wondered if she and Clemmie, staying on the coast under threat of German bombardment from the sea, might qualify for a medal. Returning to 41 Cromwell Road, she had to start drastic cuts in her expenditure, and she let three of her six servants go, retaining the cook, the nanny and one other. Johnny had learned to ride a bike and often rode off, and Peregrine was equally prone to walking off if left unattended. The nanny described the boys as "a pair of pickles".

In September 1914, Goonie wrote to Jack of her work for All Saints' Hospital, preparing a small ward for seriously wounded soldiers. "I am going to organise and arrange, and feel quite competent, cool, collected and confident that it will be done beautifully, and I think I shall be made a Lady of Jerusalem". She would later help at Blenheim Palace, where part of the building was given over to a military hospital.

Clemmie at least had Winston at home, though fearfully busy, while she brought up three children, including a very young baby. She had the anxiety that her sister, Nellie, had been captured by the Germans when her nursing unit was overrun. Mercifully, the unit was repatriated before too long. In June 1915, Clemmie took up important war work by joining the Munitions Workers' Auxiliary Committee formed by the YMCA. Lloyd George headed the new Ministry of Munitions and women flocked to the arms factories to take up posts vacated by men going into the armed services. To maximise production, canteens were provided to feed the workforce. Clemmie became responsible for opening, staffing, and running nine canteens in the north and north-eastern metropolitan area of London, each one providing meals for up to 500 workers. Her job was to tour the areas and enlist ninety unpaid volunteer helpers and to liase with, and obtain the co-operation of, factory managers.

When Winston lost the Admiralty in the coalition re-shuffle, they lost their London home. With Ecclestone Square leased out, they had to move temporarily into the Wimborne's house at 21 Arlington Street. To economise, Goonie and her children also moved in. With two households, five children and their nannies, under one roof, it was cacophonous. Winston promptly moved out to live with his mother. But a scheme whereby all government ministers pooled and shared their salaries gave them a useful boost to their income. By October 1915, they all moved together into Goonie and Jack's house at 41 Cromwell Road. Jennie would eventually join them there, and was able to contribute to the upkeep of the chaotic and noisy *ménage*.

Winston greatly missed having a decisive role in the higher direction of the war. In late 1915, he took up the great love of his later life, painting, as a means of coping with his bouts of depression. It seems that Goonie helped in starting this interest. But, once again in his remembrances of this important development in his life, he never gives due credit to his parents. In this case we already know that Jennie had introduced her own love of painting to both her sons when they were children. The taking up of the brushes in 1915 was part of a long family tradition, and not quite the revelation Winston recalls.

Frustrated by his inability to influence policy as Chancellor of the Duchy of Lancaster, Winston resigned from the Cabinet on 30th October 1915. He wanted to go back into the army. He vainly sought command of British forces in East Africa, and got the hint that Sir John French might get him a brigade command in France. In November 1915, he decided to rejoin the Oxfordshire Hussars in France. His anxious mother wrote to him:

> Please be sensible, ... I think you ought to take the trenches in small doses, after 10 years of more or less sedentary life – but I'm sure you won't "play the fool" – Remember you are destined for greater things ... I am a great believer in your star ...

He went out to the front, attached to the 2nd Grenadier Guards, and saw service in the Neuve Chappelle area. But in December 1915, Sir Douglas Haig replaced Sir John French as Commander-in-Chief, and he told Winston that, with no vacancies for a brigade command at present, he would have to make do with a battalion. Thus Winston found himself, as of 5th January 1916, a lieutenant colonel commanding the 6th Royal Scots Fusiliers. This battle-hardened battalion, part of the excellent 9th (Scottish) Division, were not certain what to make of their 'political' colonel but, by dint of hard work and attention to military detail, Winston won their trust. They went into the line at Ploegsteert Wood, known to the Tommies as 'Plugstreet'. It was a 'quiet' sector, and the winter months saw no great actions. Winston worked his men hard improving their defences, but was never a ferocious disciplinarian. He was once criticised from higher command for 'undue leniency'. He never shirked danger, and did his share of front line duty and patrolling. But by March 1916, he was anxious to return to the House of Commons, where he thought he could make a more meaningful contribution to winning the war. On hearing that his under-strength battalion was due to merge with another, he took the opportunity to resign his commission in May 1916.

Jack had sailed with the Anzac Corps from Egypt to France in

March, landing at Marseilles and moving by train to the front. After some training, they went into the line in the 'quiet' Armentieres sector. This was just a few miles south of where Winston was serving and Jack had the opportunity of dining with him on occasion. Jack was, as usual, responsible for the smooth running of Corps Headquarters, and his quiet role in the performance of this fine military formation would, inevitably, remain unsung. His duty included the selection of the site for the corps offices and, on 8th April, he presented himself at the door of his old patroness, Baroness de la Grange. She recalled that he apportioned all the rooms to the officers, putting labels on the doors of each room. He was renowned for his high humour and practical jokes, and he tried to play one on the Corps' Chief Engineer, the French-Canadian Joly de Lotbiniere. He wrote a caption, 'Bouffe de Lotbiniere 1660', and attached it to a picture of a Roman Catholic cardinal, and got everyone to ask the general about this 'interesting ancestor'. It seems de Lotbiniere spotted the joke, that he could be descended from a supposedly celibate priest, immediately. He made a great show of quizzing the Baroness about how a priest could have direct descendants, and who might have written the caption. The Baroness, whose legs had been unmercifully kicked under the table to ensure she maintained the joke, had to say it was her mother. The canny general had, in fact, recognised Jack's beautiful calligraphy, and replied, "Well, that's true, it looks like the writing of an old-fashioned *grande dame*". He who laughs last, laughs longest.

Jack's letters to his mother from April say what a waste it was to keep Winston in a dug-out in France when he could be doing more important work at home. While Winston found himself unpopular at Westminster, with no effort being made to bring him back into useful governmental employment, the Anzac Corps moved south to the battlefields of the Somme. Once again, Jack had to oversee the upheaval of moving the great concern that was a corps headquarters, and see them all settled in a new camp. The Australians were plunged into the savage fighting around Pozieres. He wrote to Jennie on 16th August:

> The offensive continues slowly and there seems to be no idea of stopping yet. Worn out troops are relieved & sent off to

recover and be reinforced – then back they come and again 'go in'. All the time the artillery never stops day or night. The supply of munitions is quite wonderful & there does not appear to be any falling off yet, in spite of the enormous amount used in the last 6 weeks.

The Anzacs have done very well – as fighting men they are hard to beat. The awful shell fire was a surprise to them – but they have gone on making frequent attacks, nearly all of which have been successful. The German resistance is wonderful, but they are without doubt hard pressed. They depend entirely on machinery now & if it were not for their guns & machine guns we should be chasing them. The letters found on prisoners give very gloomy accounts of life in Germany – all are longing for peace, but the majority are still convinced that they are winning and will, in the end, win a complete victory. The most pessimistic think that no one will win the war – and I am not sure they are not right![1]

In the midst of all the fighting, Jack, to the great good fortune of the Churchill family, kept a close eye on their finances, and changes in the regulations. So this letter concluded, "I wrote some time ago to Winston & told him that he should look after the American securities which are at Parr's Bank. I hope they have been exchanged. If not, they should be as soon as possible, otherwise the extra tax on the dividends will have to be paid." As a staff officer he was, of course, able to get more leave and was delighted to meet Goonie in Paris that summer and spend more time with her than he had in the previous two years. In September he told Jennie:

I have not had time to write before as we have again been moving. The Somme battle is going on as hard as ever – but we have had to come away. The losses have been heavy & the men who have escaped are tired. It is impossible to keep men very long in the firing line under such conditions. Troops have to be relieved frequently. The 'Anzacs' were 'in' for 6 weeks and during that time they captured more ground than any other corps and they took about 900 prisoners – so they are quite pleased with themselves.[2]

This letter concluded, "Goonie seems to be going a round of visits & if I get home I shall try to join her wherever she is for the week. Best love Your Jacky". He was referring to Goonie's propensity for living the life of a nomad, constantly on the move, staying with her many friends around the country. This was mainly to save money by living at the expense of other people who could well afford it, but may also have been a means of distraction to reduce her anxiety for Jack's safety. It was certainly to escape from the terrible crush at 41 Cromwell Road, where effectively three households were living cheek by jowl. An added bonus was the separation of Johnny and Randolph who, when allowed to go about together, were as mischievous as it is possible for two small boys to be.

This constant changing address made it hard for Goonie's friends to keep in touch with her. There is a moving series of letters from one such, Harold Brassey, commanding 8th South Lancashires in France. In June 1916, just before the opening of the Battle of the Somme, he wrote gently chiding Goonie for having written "a very serious and gloomy little letter … . Really I must take you to task for writing letters calculated to create despondency among the troops on the eve of an important battle. You say you find life very strange and difficult. Oh, dear, what can the matter be?" When he got no reply he thought he had given her offence and sent a stream of letters begging her to answer. "Why won't you write to me?" In a tragic end to this sad little story, Harold Brassey was killed by a German sniper's bullet on 16th July, never knowing whether Goonie had received his desperate pleas. Her letters were all being re-directed to Blenheim Palace as a sort of *poste restante*.

The Jerome sisters were enduring the harsh realities of war, each in their own way. Leonie Leslie was utterly distraught when her most loved son, Norman, was killed in battle serving with the Rifle Brigade. Shane had tried to serve as a stretcher-bearer at Gallipoli but had been invalided home with a nervous breakdown. Clara Frewen had to comfort her daughter, Clare Sheridan, when her husband, Wilfred, was killed in action. Clare would raise two children alone, and become a distinguished sculptress, and notorious admirer of the Bolsheviks. Jennie, while grieving for her sisters and their loss, had her house at Brook Street burgled. She lost large amounts of valuable jewellery, and many of the exquisite gifts made to her by Bertie, both as Prince of Wales and King, and from Queen Alexandra. The burglar also took trinkets from George West and a gold locket containing portraits of Winston and Jack. She might have been sustained by receiving, while being courted from afar by Montagu Porch in Nigeria, a proposal of marriage from her old flame, Hugh Warrender, then serving on the Western Front. She was enamoured of Porch and turned Hugh down. Jennie was kept busy with voluntary war work, and helping out with her grandchildren.

In November a letter from Jack to Jennie showed what a strain the constant fighting was on officers and men. He wrote of the "indescribable mud" of that winter, and of men getting stuck fast and needing to be hauled out, and of some drowning in shell holes. Jack said he was "in a paradise compared to the poor people in the so called trenches & dug outs".[3] There was bad news from the Eastern Front. It seems that, while in this slightly depressed state, Jack made a bad impression on the Bishop of Perth during his visit to the Australian troops. Sir Douglas Haig recorded in his diary on 8th November that he saw General Birdwood and "I told him that the Australian Bishop of Perth had been greatly upset with the pessimistic views of his (Birdwood's) Camp Commandant (a Major Churchill, a brother of Winston Churchill). Birdwood said he was an exception, all were in the best of spirits and full of confidence."[4] This was surely an unfortunate episode, as those who knew Jack both at Gallipoli and on the Western Front found him to be a hard-working, good-natured and amusing companion. The grim fighting on the Somme and the hard winter must have told on him, and he was always a critic of the attritional battles on the Western Front. No doubt he conveyed these views to Winston, who would, in his later writings, become one of the leading critics of that strategy.

When the corps headquarters was in a fixed location for a long period, Jack's duties became fairly routine. He was then used as a sort of public relations officer, receiving visitors, and escorting General Birdwood on some of his trips. In February 1917, he showed 'Birdie' the sights of Paris during a few days leave. Though most places seemed shut, Jack's fluent French, and ribbon of the Legion of Honour, got them into all the things they wanted to see, including the Palace of Versailles. In April, he was tasked with showing visiting Australian journalists the battlefields where the Corps had seen severe fighting around Bullecourt. The Australian newspapers carried a report that included this description of Jack, that was more in character than that of the Bishop of Perth: "Sir William Birdwood had caused Major Churchill, younger brother of Mr Winston Churchill, who is a very winsome and brotherly kind of man, and wholly without 'side', to conduct us along some of the more historic portions of the front". During an aerial dogfight, anti-aircraft shell splinters fell around them. "Major Churchill immediately caused us to take refuge in dug-outs until this battle in the air was over".[5]

Domestic arrangements continued to cause concern. When his employer, Mr Nelke, died, Jack was worried that his place at the firm would not be kept open. He now envisaged the war ending and finding himself without any job or regular income. From his letters to his mother we see that Jennie, better off than she had been for a long time, was being very kind to his family. She had moved back into her own house, and Johnny was so happy staying there that he refused to move back to Cromwell Road. Jennie also paid for summer holidays for Goonie and the children, renting apartments for them.

Clemmie and Winston had moved back to 33 Eccleston Square, and in the spring of 1917, Winston bought a country home, Lullenden Farm at East Grinstead, Sussex, for £6,000 by selling £5,000 of his Pennsylvania Railroad stock, and £1,000 of Exchequer War Bonds. It was a beautiful, half-timbered Elizabethan house, built of grey stone, with a Great Hall and a solar room. It was the ideal location for Winston's new hobby, painting. There were extensive gardens, which Clemmie enjoyed landscaping, and it was well away from the London bombings. Attached to the house were a 100-acre working farm, and a barn, which they converted into a nursery, where the children lived with their nanny. The older Churchill children, Johnny, Diana and Randolph, were sent to a boarding school at St. Margaret's Bay, Kent for a time.

With David Lloyd George as Prime Minister since December 1916, Winston might have expected a return to government duties sooner rather than later. He did not allow for the bitter resentment felt for him by the powerful Tory hold on the Coalition. It was not until July 1917 that his old radical ally felt secure enough to appoint Winston to a ministry. He took over Lloyd George's old role as Minister of Munitions. The restoration of a ministerial salary was good news for

Clemmie and the family. This was very important work for the successful prosecution of the war, and Winston was as vigorous and
demanding as ever in seeing the work was done well. In a diary that
is usually filled with invective against politicians, Sir Douglas Haig
recorded the visits of Winston to the armies in France most cordially,
complimenting him on "excellent work", and on his enthusiasm to
concentrate all resources on winning the war on the Western Front
"by August 1918".

Jack's letters home give an interesting commentary on the conduct
of the war as seen by the men engaged in it. America joining the war
in April 1917 was a lift, though by July he notes sardonically that in
Paris "England is quite forgotten & everything is American now. I
met several American officers. They have got a great deal to learn and
I am afraid they will do this learning in a very hard school." In
September he reported on the victories in battle that form the middle
part of the Third Ypres campaign, so often forgotten because of the
costly battles of Passchendaele that followed. "The Bosche's great
defensive schemes have been defeated". He was able to show
Winston some of the scenes. "I saw W[inston] & Eddie [Marsh] over
here for a moment on their way to Paris. Eddie appeared delighted at
being shot at!" But by November the tone darkened again, with the
onset of atrocious winter weather and more bad news from the East
as Russia was taken out of the war by revolution.

The spring of 1918 opened with a series of huge German offen-
sives, as the enemy tried to force a decision in battle before the
Americans arrived in sufficient numbers to tip the balance against
Germany. The Anzacs were not engaged in March, but by late April
had made decisive interventions to stem the German advance. Jack
summed up the situation with an expert eye: "The Germans must be
disappointed with the result of their two great attacks. They achieved
a great deal and captured much ground and great booty. But they did
not do anything decisive, and the line remains intact."

With everyone moved out of 41 Cromwell Road, and the children
at school, Goonie was able to arrange the letting out of the house on
a three year lease. Much of the furniture was stored at the Duke of
Westminster's stables, and the excess was sold at a good price. All
this was joyful news to Jack and his constant worries over money,
though he did observe that "it is very unpleasant having no home –

and nowhere to live". Goonie continued her nomadic existence, changing addresses often. It was probably during this time of worry and anxiety that she became a heavy smoker.

Montagu Porch got home on leave and he and Jennie went to Castle Leslie in Ireland for a holiday. It was there, in May 1918, that he proposed to her and she accepted. Once again, Winston and Jack were presented with a stepfather almost the same age as themselves. On 25th May, Jack's reply to the announcement, sounding more like that of a parent to an errant child, says it all:

> What a surprise! Your letter has just been forwarded to me. Whenever I go to a war you do these things!
>
> I feel sure that you have thought it all out carefully and that you are certain that you are acting wisely. I know that the last few years must have been lonely for you. With both of us married it was inevitable that you should be alone. I do not remember hearing you talk of him and I have never met him. If he makes you happy we shall soon be friends. I wish I could get over for the day – but it is impossible as I am just taking a new post and I shall probably be moving on the 1st June.
>
> Now, my dear, you know that no one can make any change in our love for one another, and it will be something to know that you are no longer alone. And so I send you my best love and wishes, and pray that all will be well.

The Australian Corps, for some time under the command of an Australian general, Sir John Monash, had decided to 'Australianise' its staff, and remove all British officers. Jack ended his long association with them and joined General Head Quarters, BEF, as an Assistant Military Secretary. General Birdwood paid tribute to the hard work Jack had put in for the Anzacs by seeing that he was awarded a Distinguished Service Order. With typical humility, Jack wished that there were a suitable decoration other than the DSO, which he felt properly belonged to the fighting troops. But, in that "age of medal ribbons", as he described it, he would wear it with pride. He got a home leave that summer, seeing Goonie and the children in Oxfordshire, not knowing that it would be his last leave until the war ended.

Jennie and Montagu Porch were married at Harrow Road Registry
Office on 1st June 1918. She was sixty-four and he was forty-two. He
had a little money, and large family estates. Winston and Jack Leslie
were the witnesses, but Clara Frewen, Goonie and Clementine also
signed the register, and Lady Sarah Wilson attended. This time there
would be no dramatic change of name. Jennie would remain Lady
Randolph Churchill. Montagu had to continue working in Africa
and, because of wartime restrictions, Jennie was refused a passport to
join him, not even for a visit, and had to remain at home. Within
three weeks of the marriage, Jennie was as lonely as ever, having confided in Jean Hamilton, who wrote in her diary, 20th June: "Jennie
Churchill ... very sad at the departure of her young Porch". Her husband had bought the lease on a new and more prestigious house, 8
Westbourne Street, Hyde Park, and Jennie put all her energies into
redecorating and furnishing it. She still spent freely and debts were
never far away. Both her daughters-in-law were somewhat exasperated by her extravagance, and by the endless stories about her in the
popular press, usually centred around her penchant for younger men.

Clemmie was still continuing with her canteen work. Jean
Hamilton recorded on 14th June 1918, how Clemmie and Frances,
Lady Horner, had to leave a dinner party at Lord Haldane's house at
11 pm. to work a night shift at the Hackney Canteen. Clemmie was
at that time four months pregnant with her fourth child, but she had
not allowed her pregnancy to deter her from her duties. There were
many worries beginning to accumulate for Clemmie. The Ministry of
Defence had decreed that farm land must be cultivated as part of the
war effort, and straightened financial circumstances meant that
Winston could not afford to pay for the machinery to cultivate
Lullenden. Though they loved the place they were eventually forced
to put it up for sale. Also at around that time the cost of the lease on
33 Eccleston Square was being increased, and the Churchills could
not afford to renew it. At a dinner party at the Hamiltons' London
home, 1 Hyde Park Gardens, on 18th June, Clemmie unburdened
herself to Jean. She did not know how she could afford the cost of the
birthing and Jean offered her the use of her home. Then, during a discussion about whether the childless Jean should adopt two children
she was fostering, the compassionate Clemmie offered to give her
unborn child to Jean or, if Clemmie had twins, she was to have one

of them.[6] It was a momentary crisis and when the child, a little girl, Marigold was born, kindly Aunt Cornelia Wimborne had loaned the Churchills her house for Clemmie's confinement.

After four years of war events began rapidly to move in favour of the Western allies. Germany's allies fell away and, on 8th August 1918, one hundred days of offensive operations began on the Western Front that saw the German field armies in full retreat and suing for peace by November. Jack was able to guide Winston over the Amiens battlefield just two days after the victory. Fresh corpses littered the area. Jack then found himself working for his old chief, Birdwood, on the staff of Fifth Army. His letters home describe the victories, and the news of the interior collapse of the German army. He thanked Jennie for her kind offer to pay Johnny's school fees, but one of her cheques bounced! In October Jack was able to greet Winston as they witnessed the triumphal march of Allied troops through newly liberated Lille. The official photograph of the scene shows Winston and Jack in close proximity to another staff officer, Bernard Law Montgomery. It is common for 'Monty' to be retained in the photo and for Jack to be 'cropped out'.

On 11th November 1918, the German plenipotentiaries signed an armistice that brought the fighting to an end. The transition to peace would not be as smooth as one might have wished.

CHAPTER 20

Post War Britain
1919–1929

An end of hostilities did not mean everything returning to normal quickly. An armistice was not peace, and theoretically hostilities could recommence at any time. Jack would be kept busy on the staff of Fifth Army for many more months, at first keeping the army in the field and, later, supervising the demobilisation of the citizen soldiers as they were finally allowed home to civilian life.

He wrote to Jennie on 6th March 1919:

> Dear Mama
>
> I have been hoping to receive orders to come home. My job has practically finished and although I have been fairly busy up to about a week ago – I have now very little to do and am very anxious to get away. I have written to Winston and hope that orders will come through soon. It is very dull & tiresome here and I am wanted in the City, where things are beginning to look better.
>
> Goonie is coming up here from Paris I believe to see Norman's grave[1] – I shall meet her and take her round – but it is a bad moment – for everything is in a state of mud and squalor. However she is lucky if she has obtained leave to come. Birdwood has gone, and the Army is breaking up generally … . I think Goonie has taken on Bedford Square for 6 months – and we will live there until the autumn – but it is going to be a great struggle.
>
> W. seems to be getting on very well – but nobody here knows what is to become of themselves – and of course it is impossible to make definite appointments etc. until peace is declared.
>
> I hope to see you next week & to return for good. Yrs Jacky[2]

It seems that, on one of his final leaves home, he had made useful
connections in the City that would guarantee him a job. Cromwell
Road was, of course, out on a long lease to Lady Tree to raise much
needed funds, so they had to find temporary accommodation for
Jack, Goonie and the boys, at Bedford Square in the London home of
Lady Ottoline Morrell. She rather ruthlessly put them out at the end
of the short lease and they had to find another temporary abode in
Ebury Street, in a house once occupied by Mozart on his visit to
Britain. Later in 1919, they finally settled back into their own home.

Jennie moved into her new home at 8 Westbourne Street in May of
that year, after making a good sale of Brook Street. Montagu Porch
left the colonial service and was finally able to join her, and she was
very happy living with a man who clearly adored her. His comforting
presence got her over the news of the death of Charles Kinsky in
Austria in December 1919.

Winston must have wondered what his fate would be in a peace-
time coalition in which the Liberals were so weak and the
Conservatives, who still regarded him as a turncoat, so very strong.
How fortunate that his friend, David Lloyd George, now bestrode
the world stage as one of the victors of the most terrible war in
Britain's history. He was sufficiently in command of his government
to confidently offer Winston either his old job at the Admiralty, or
the important role of Secretary of State for War, with the added
responsibility of the Air Ministry.

First there was a general election to be fought. Winston campaigned in Dundee on a radical programme, advocating
nationalisation of the railways, and a savage attack on wartime prof-
iteers. He would have capped war profits at £10,000 and seized
everything above that to reduce the National Debt. He even toyed
with the idea of continuing the state control of industry, since it had
worked so well during the war. He won his seat handsomely, and so
did the Lloyd George Coalition in the country, but it was massively
dominated by the Conservatives. Lloyd George promptly appointed
Winston to the Cabinet, in charge of the double ministries of War
and Air.

He and Clemmie were back in their home at Lullenden, with a
rented house in London at 1 Dean Trench Street, with their children,
Diana, Randolph, Sarah and their new baby, Marigold, who was not

'given away' to Jean Hamilton. Winston was, as usual, deeply committed to his ministerial duties, and just as often delving into the business of other ministers. The ever-sensible Clementine advised him to drop the Air Ministry and concentrate on one at a time. Winston was too keen on all things related to air power to consider that. He had taken flying lessons before the war and, on 18th July, was piloting a plane over Croydon airfield when it crashed spectacularly. Though badly shaken, he still delivered a speech at a dinner that night. Winston, it seemed, was indestructible. Clemmie accompanied Winston on a visit to the British Army on the Rhine in August, and wrote to him soon after, "I love to feel that I am a comfort in your rather tumultuous life". Winston did not help his reputation greatly by the violence of his reaction to the Bolshevik Revolution. With a war-weary nation looking forward to enjoying peace, he kept large numbers of British troops in north and south Russia, fighting to maintain an anti-Bolshevik coalition, to no avail. His language was colourful to say the least, referring to Russia's leaders as "troops of ferocious baboons" and to their creed as a "pestilence", a "plague-bearing bacillus" and the like. This belligerence soured his relations with Lloyd George, and encouraged sections of British society to see him as a warmonger.

Winston and Clemmie could not keep up the expense of Lullenden, and sold it to their friends, General Sir Ian and Lady Hamilton. Clemmie felt its loss keenly and asked the Hamiltons for a 'first refusal' if they ever decided to sell. There would be other rented houses before they finally bought 2 Sussex Square and were able to settle into a real family home.

When Jack returned from the war he was without a job. He had been very kind to one of the Rothschilds at Harrow School "and this was remembered". Leo de Rothschild was putting money into the stock-broking firm Vickers da Costa, and asked for Jack to be a party to the negotiations. Jack soon after secured a partnership with the firm as a stockbroker.[3] Goonie had domestic problems of her own to deal with. It was rumoured in society that her mother was a 'bolter'; that having finally had enough of her over-bearing, gambling husband, Lord Abingdon, the Countess had run away with another man named Johnson, but "had to return, a broken woman" according to the inveterate diarist, Jean Hamilton. Lady Abingdon looked young and attractive compared with her aged husband. Goonie vigorously denied that any such thing had happened. Still Jean Hamilton thought she looked distraught when they met at a summer house party at Frances Horner's Mells Manor:

> ... what a shock of joy that I saw Gooney [sic] suddenly appear like a pale and dreamy ghost. I dreamed of her all last night – I felt so sorry for her, and I made her come and lie down on a long chair and was hoping to have a real heart to heart talk with her when Sir John [Horner] appeared and all chance of it was gone.[4]

Goonie's troubles did not last. Desperate to have a girl, having borne two sons, by October she was pregnant with her third child.

Jennie and Montie were busily spending the proceeds of their house sale. They travelled through France visiting Jennie's friends there, and there were new and exciting people at the parties – Stravinksy, Picasso, Ravel, Proust, James Joyce. Some of them later visited Jennie and Montie in London. Jennie still invited old friends like Queen Alexandra to her soirees. When the Queen came, Porch had to "telephone for a constable to be outside" to control the sightseers. Jennie, effervescent as ever, particularly enjoyed entertaining younger people. Let us hope she did not notice that she was being 'cut' by at least one of her daughters-in-law. Jean Hamilton wrote in her diary:

> I have been lying here thinking of the many lonely women I know – women who have been lovely spoilt, petted – Jennie Churchill! ... still full of doughty deeds and restless longing to be happy; she was a brilliant woman and adores Winston, but Clemmie, when she 'phones to them to come and dine with her, just casually says "Oh, it's too far, we won't go, we must not begin this kind of thing." I heard her say this the other day when we lunched with them. They now live at Westminster ... but they have two motors and it can't take more than ten minutes.[5]

Winston, once the great radical, was moving steadily to the right in his politics. He approved the creation of the Auxiliary Police in

Ireland, the infamous 'Black and Tans', a formation of ex-soldiers so called for the colour of their uniforms. In an increasingly ugly guerrilla war for Irish independence, these men would commit some notorious atrocities by way of retaliation for Irish attacks. In May 1920, Winston clashed with British trades unionists who had refused to load the ship, the *Jolly George*, with weapons and ammunition bound for Poland to fight the Bolsheviks. Increasingly, he would make the mistake that was to cost him so dear in 1945, of branding every holder of any opinion of a left wing or progressive character as an agent of Soviet communism.

In June 1920, Goonie got her dearest wish, a daughter was born, to be christened Anne Clarissa Nicolette (always known as Clarissa). Goonie would lavish a great deal of love on this precious child, her last. Her anxiety at the time of the birth was heightened by the continuing scourge of what was known then as the 'Spanish Influenza'. We now suspect this to have been an early visitation of an avian 'flu; it killed more people in Europe and America than died in the First World War. In 1919, Isabelle, the Scottish nurse to baby Marigold, had died of it, and there had been great concern for the infant. Several members of the Churchill families caught milder forms of the illness and survived.

Johnny and Peregrine had followed in the footsteps of their father and uncle and built up a huge collection of toy soldiers, with a fine transport section. Their model electric railway covered the entire ground floor of their home, and they collected model ships. Their moving model of the battle of Jutland was so accurate that it impressed Admirals Beatty and Keyes when they were invited to see it. It would later be taken to Chartwell to show 'Uncle Winston'. While Johnny would become an artist, Peregrine was already showing an interest in engineering matters.

Goonie continued to attract artistic friends. William Orpen, who had written her a series of illustrated letters from France while he was an official war artist, called to see the new baby. Hilaire Belloc was a valued friend. He went boating with Jack, and Johnny remembered them singing bawdy songs together. The family would visit Belloc at his home in Horsham.

1921 was to be a terrible year for both families. On 5th January, Clemmie's grandmother, Countess Henrietta Blanche Airlie, died. At ninety years old she could be said to have lived out her natural span. But later that month a relation on the Londonderry side of the Marlborough family, Lord Henry Vane-Tempest, was killed in a railway accident in Wales. By a curious clause in his grandmother's will, Winston inherited some property as a result of this unforeseen event. Having left the County Antrim estate, Garron Tower, to Lord Henry, the will stated that, on his demise, it would pass to Winston. While it was not quite worth the £4,000 per annum that Winston first thought, it still contributed some £2,000 a year after tax to a permanently cash-strapped family.

More dreadful news followed. Clemmie's younger brother, William (Bill), had been a heavy drinker and a debt-laden gambler. Winston tried to straighten him out, encouraging him to give up gambling and begin to pay off his debts. Suddenly, on 14th April, Bill shot himself dead in his Paris hotel room.

Jennie was left alone again when Montagu Porch returned to Nigeria to explore some business opportunities to aid their ever-precarious finances. In June, Jennie went to one of the marvellous house parties at Mells Manor, the home of the Horner family. She had some new Italian shoes, and normally a maid would scour the soles to make the new leather less slippery. It seems this was not done and Jennie took a very nasty fall down stairs and broke her ankle. A local doctor set it and she was brought back to London, where she was attended by her sister, Leonie, and a nurse. Jean Hamilton was to go to the theatre with them, and arrived at Jennie's house to much worse news, for gangrene had set in and the foot would have to be amputated.

Jean went on to tea with her nieces, Margot Warre and Betty Godley, the daughter's of Ian's brother, the artist Vereker Hamilton. Before her marriage Margot had been a ballet dancer, and now gave dancing lessons. A class was in progress, and one of her pupils was Sarah, the 6½-year-old daughter of Clemmie and Winston. Jean forgot herself, and blurted out the news in front of the little girl:

I forgot the presence of lovely little Sarah Churchill and told
Betty and Margot about poor Lady Randolph's foot, then I
saw the child's eyes full of horror on my face.[6]

Jennie's leg had turned black, and Winston, upon seeing it, had brought in a surgeon who thought the leg should be amputated from above the knee. She had been very brave, telling the surgeon to "be sure and cut high enough". After the operation, Jennie seemed out of danger, though hardly relishing a life on crutches. Then she suffered a sudden haemorrhage, on the morning of 29th June, and died, aged 67. She was laid to rest at Bladon beside Randolph. Jack looked after poor Montagu Porch, who had rushed back from Nigeria too late to attend his wife's funeral. He declined to inherit any of Jennie's property, and it was Jack who was left to sort out her estate. She left debts of approximately £70,000, mostly to Rothschild's Bank. Winston and Jack only retained items of sentimental value which included some of her jewellery and furniture. Her creditors were demanding large sums, and Jack had been paying them out of his own pocket to keep them at bay. Settling her financial affairs was no easy matter. Solicitors for Sir Arthur du Cros wrote quickly to remind Jennie's executors that she had borrowed £3,000 from him in March 1916 at 6% per annum, none of which had been paid. Most of the debt was covered by a spectacular auction sale of her house contents, and the sale of the house itself. It would be 1927 before Jack was able to draw a line under this task.

Winston reflected in a letter to Anne, Lady Islington, that Jennie had died before she had to cope with "old age, decrepitude, loneliness" and that she had been spared a "long ordeal". In death "very beautiful and splendid she looked". Both received numerous letters of condolence; Jack heard from some of his old wartime friends, sending the warmest greetings and fond memories.

That summer, Goonie had first rented the house, 'Menabilly', in Cornwall, which was leased by the Horners but is more famous as the home of the novelist, Daphne du Maurier. They had an idyllic summer there, with many friends visiting them. Jack could only get down for three weeks, but everyone remarked how much better he looked when he left than he did when he arrived. Katherine Asquith, wife of Raymond, and her twelve-year old daughter, Helen, were guests. Jack thoughtfully sent a telegram to congratulate Helen on winning a scholarship. This brought a self-deprecatory letter from Goonie to Jack:

Poor Johnnie [sic] and poor Peregrine, they have no chance
with a stupid and indolent mother like me – and will Clarissa
ever get a scholarship? I wonder – This morning I spent in
trying to teach Peregrine to read a large printed and simple
story of Helen of Troy – it took me ages, painful and
laborious, but I am thankful that we are going to have our
faithful nice Miss Jupe [a tutor] at Mells – I was right in getting
her wasn't I? ... I thought that both John and Peregrine ought
to do a *few* lessons during the holiday, because otherwise they
forgot everything – and P. really has gone back here terribly –
and I can't bring him forward and he is 8 now – and he really
ought to be able to read and write, ... and also during the
holidays, if Johnnie and he have nothing to do, they quarrel so
after a bit ... .

Write and tell me what you are doing and if you are
comfortable? – I am so looking forward to Mells – and I do
hope you will be able to get away and be there for a long time,
for the whole time in fact.

Clemmie remarked how much she would like a country home, if
only to be able to see more of the 'Jagoons', the delightful collective
noun her family gave to the family of Jack and Goonie. This would
spark the search that ended with the finding of Chartwell. In early
August there was more sorrow. Thomas Walden, Randolph's old,
and faithful valet, who had become Winston's servant, had died.
Winston wrote, in sorrow, to Clemmie, 10th August, from the
Colonial Office, that he had taken flowers from both of them, and
that all the servants had attended. There were 40 at the funeral. But
the hardest blow of all was about to strike. Marigold, aged 2 years
and 9 months, their adored 'Duckadilly', died suddenly, on 23rd
August. She had previously had coughs and colds, but it was not
known that she was very ill, until it was too late. She died of septi-
caemia, whilst Clemmie sat singing her favourite nursery song to
her. Winston and Clemmie were utterly devastated by their loss,
and were plunged into deepest mourning for a beloved child.
Winston took his children to see the grave, and a story is told by the
guides at Kensal Green Cemetery, where Marigold is buried, that
the wartime Prime Minister would arrive in a limousine and stop

and get out and sit on a bench there for a time meditating in silence.[7]

That dreadful year also saw the death of an old and valued family friend, Sir Ernest Cassel, in September. It was another loss, in a way, when the Queen's Own Oxfordshire Hussars was converted from yeomanry cavalry to a unit of the Royal Artillery. The Churchill brothers did not follow the move.

While Winston was busy with the affairs of the Colonial Office, Clemmie had searched out a new London home for them, 2 Sussex Square. That summer they were able to holiday with Goonie, who had again taken a house in Devon for some months. Clemmie wrote to Winston, asking him to look after Jack. It seems that, with all the servants gone to Devon with the family, Jack was being cared for by one housekeeper, a policeman's wife, "who nourishes him exclusively on salted haddock"!

Some joy was restored in September 1922, with the birth to Clemmie and Winston of their daughter, Mary. Things may have been looking up for them, for he had bought for £5,000 a fine house in Kent, 'Chartwell', set in lovely grounds but needing a good deal of work done before it was truly habitable for a family. But in October, Winston suffered from appendicitis, which took him out of political life at a crucial moment. At loggerheads with his Conservative partners, David Lloyd George had resigned as Prime Minister and forced a General Election. Winston wasn't able to visit his Dundee constituency until 11th November 1922, just four days before the polls. He bombarded them with letters and manifestos, but again erred on the side of extremism. He attacked the Labour candidate, the irreproachable E. D. Morel, trying to paint him as a bloodthirsty communist. Despite Clemmie's personal intervention and best efforts in Winston's absence, it all backfired terribly. Winston was thrashed into fourth place. On his forty-eighth birthday he was out of office and out of parliament altogether. The Conservatives were back, with no place in their ranks for the turncoat.

He and Clemmie went on a long winter holiday in the South of France. He tried to put a brave face on things, but the 'black dog' of depression sat heavily upon him. He found solace in his painting, and began to sketch out plans for his monumental history of the period

1914–1919, "The World Crisis". By May 1923, they were back in Britain. Chartwell was eating up the money very quickly, and, though he felt some moral qualms about accepting, Winston took £5,000 from the great oil companies, Royal Dutch Shell and Burmah Oil, to discuss with Prime Minister Baldwin a possible merger with the Anglo-Persian Oil Company, in which the government owned a majority share. His meeting with Baldwin was most cordial, and he realised that, at the highest levels, he was not so unwelcome to the Conservatives.

As each volume of "The World Crisis" appeared (between the years 1923 and 1931), their finances improved steadily. This encyclopaedic work on the origins, conduct and aftermath of the Great War was an opportunity for Winston to explain many of his decisions, and to vindicate his stand on such major issues as the Dardanelles campaign. It is criticised as being very partial in its presentation of the history of the war, to put all Winston's decisions in the best possible light. Even the friendly reviews found it "remarkably egotistical"; Balfour described it as "Autobiography, disguised as a history of the universe". But it had been supported in the writing, and drew praise from, naval authorities and all those who opposed the attritional fighting on the Western Front. What we can add to the story, from papers that have come to us from Peregrine, is that, once again, Jack was assisting with the preparation of the book, for which he would get no acknowledgment whatsoever. He read accounts and biographies, especially of the Gallipoli campaign, which he then summarised and sent to Winston, to guide him in his writing.

In November 1923, Baldwin called one of the more unnecessary General Elections, over some protectionist issue, leading to a hung Parliament. The Conservatives had 258 seats, the Labour Party 191 and the Liberals 157. When the Labour and Liberal parties defeated the Conservatives in their first vote, Ramsay Macdonald was invited to form a minority Labour government. We see the extraordinary event of Winston standing in that 1923 election as an 'Asquith Liberal', fighting the seat of Leicester West against the formidable Labour radical, F. W. Pethwick-Lawrence. Winston's speeches were well to the right of most Liberals and it was no surprise to see him defeated yet again.

A Labour government was anathema to Winston. He feared the very worst, though it turned out to be a very timid and short-lived administration. At the earliest opportunity, in February 1924, he fought a bye-election in Westminster. There was the curious stance of him being backed by most of the national leadership of the Conservative Party, but reviled and rejected by the local party. He stood as an Independent Anti-Socialist, even though there was an official Conservative candidate. He ran a fine campaign, helped by the young Brendan Bracken, and only missed victory by 43 votes. The Conservatives won, and Winston helped beat the Labour candidate, Fenner Brockway, into fourth place. His path back into the Conservative fold was now wide open.

In April 1924, Winston was able to spend his first night at Chartwell. Sadly, Clemmie was away in Dieppe with her mother. But it was the start of a long and happy association, where so much great writing, painting and sheer physical labour would reward Winston's diligent efforts to secure the place.

Jack would send both his sons to Harrow. (Winston had chosen Eton for Randolph). Both Johnny and Peregrine were good at athletics, especially acrobatics and diving. Less is said of their academic record. Jack, whose own handwriting was described as "educated and scholastic looking", did criticise Johnny's letters for the poor writing. Jack gave lots of practical advice, like getting to know the 'Custodians' well. These men, a sort of school police, could help one out of a jam if they liked you. Johnny's artistic temperament developed and, in 1925, aged 14, he sold his first work, a poster for the Great Western Railway. Jack treated his sons with care and consideration. He introduced them in their mid-teens to the pleasure of good wine, especially port. Jack and Lionel de Rothschild pooled their resources to buy really fine wine and shared the cellar. Jack's taste was much more developed than Winston's in this respect. Goonie, too, had a very discerning palate when it came to claret.

Before he went to Harrow, Peregrine was at Summer Fields Prep. School, near Oxford. He must have complained about his loneliness there. In a charming letter, reminiscent of the sort of anxiety shown in Lord Randolph writing to his boys at school, Jack asked what was the matter:

2nd February 1925

Dear Pebin

I was very sorry to see your letter this morning – What is the matter? You are doing quite well now and have reached quite a high form. As I told you your report last term was quite good. Is anybody being unkind to you? You must write to me and tell me exactly what is the matter, and you know I will try to help you. Of course it is hard having to go back to school and nearly all boys dislike it. I used to dislike going back very much and Johnny does not like it any more than you do – but all sorts of things have to be done which one does not like doing.

You know you cannot expect to stay home all the time doing nothing but play. What is it that worries you so much? Is it the lessons or the games or the other boys? Are there no boys with whom you can make friends? You keep so much to yourself that I do not think you can make friends easily. But you must realise that you cannot expect others to be nice and friendly to you, unless you take a little trouble to be friendly to them. And if you have no friends you will of course be very lonely and feel homesick.

But write to me and try to tell me what the trouble is. There are thousands of other boys at school and many of them at schools which are not nearly so nice as Summerfields.

Perhaps you would like to go to Harrow as early as possible. You might be happier then with Johnny to look after you.

In the meantime – cheer up – and don't be unhappy. Tell me what is in that noodle of yours. In a very short time you will have to come home to have your ear seen to.

Best love
Your loving Father
John S. Churchill

All seems to have gone well, for the Headmaster, E.H. Alington, wrote a warm letter to Jack in August 1926 on the occasion of Peregrine leaving the school. In a remarkable reprise of the life of Lord Randolph's children, it is exactly the sort of letter Jack's teachers wrote about him, just as Johnny was a 'harum scarum' fellow like Winston:

Dear Major Churchill

I must just put in a line to say how sorry we are that Peregrine's time with us has come to an end. Everybody likes him, and we would have been glad to have him a bit longer.

He has been here a longish time, and I don't believe he has ever had a bad report, which is something to be able to say, and he has been a manly straightforward fellow with it.

It was a pity he missed all that time before the entrance exams, but if they have put him too low, he will rise all the quicker, provided that he sticks to it – it was bad luck too to be cut out of all the games in the summer, and specially gymnasium, where he would have had a good chance of carrying off the medal.

Perhaps he will come to the fore at Harrow in gymnastics.

I have spoken to him quite plainly on the temptations that come to boys as they grow and develop, not that I want to claim your prerogative, but because I consider it all comes "in the day's work" – He struck me as a pure minded and wholesome boy, and not likely to be attracted by any unmanly form of evil, as he has a good stock of self respect and common sense.

I hope he will be happy at Harrow, and always be a credit to you.

Yours sincerely
E.H. Alington

Johnny gives us a portrait of domestic probity at 41 Cromwell Road.[8] Jack would come home from a long day in his City office. Johnny thought his parents got on very well but spoke very little. After dinner they might play a little mah-jong; more often Jack retired to his study to read the newspapers or books by one of their many author friends. Goonie held court every morning – 'elevenses' with digestive biscuits and port, and a constant stream of writers and artists calling to see her. Jack would go round the house closing shutters; Goonie would follow opening them! Goonie's great foible was the poking of fires, often poking them to death. Her friends took to hiding the pokers when she came to call upon them, lest she leave them with desolate hearths.

The social graces were imparted, with lots of practical advice. Jack insisted that the boys always present themselves "clean, shaved and powdered", for the ladies at close quarters notice every detail. Goonie advised them to pause before entering a gathering and run a wet finger over their eyebrows and eyelashes. It made one look fresh and alert. Both Jack, very much guided by his mother, and Goonie were great music lovers. They were often seen at the opera, and imparted this love, especially of Wagner, to their sons. When they returned from a social event, Goonie would sit up late into the night discussing with Johnny all the finer points of the evening's proceedings.

After a huge success in Liverpool addressing the Conservative Associations there, Winston was adopted as the Conservative candidate for Epping in September 1924, and he was duly elected on 30th October with a majority of nearly 10,000 over his Liberal opponents. His critics suggest that, once again, he had managed to change parties just as his new friends swept to victory. What is truly astonishing is that Stanley Baldwin, to the amazement of large sections of his party, promptly handed Winston one of the great offices of state, making him Chancellor of the Exchequer. Baldwin reputedly liked giving people "enough rope to hang themselves". Winston would be so busy mastering the complexities of the Excheqeur that he would be less trouble than as a 'loose cannon' on the backbenches. After all those years in storage, he could finally wear his father's robes. Winston seized the offer as if he had never been away and, with his usual burst of energy, began imposing new limits on all the spending departments. The Royal Navy was an early victim, as he vetoed plans to deploy more submarines in the Far East.

Winston and Clemmie were able to sell 2 Sussex Square because they moved into the house at No 11 Downing Street that went with his job. At the first budget he presented in 1925, Winston benefited greatly from the caution of the previous Labour Chancellor, Philip Snowden, from whom he inherited a surplus of some £37 million pounds. Winston was able to cut Surtax (though he did increase rates of Death Duty), and increase many rates of pensions and insurances for widows and orphans. He was very severe on the armed services, cutting naval estimates and eschewing any continental alliance with France.

The big debate at the time was whether the pound should be valued against gold at its pre-war rates. This 'return to the Gold Standard' would make British exports expensive and imports cheap and Winston, never really at home with economic theory, somewhat reluctantly went along with the collective Cabinet decision.

Chartwell required a great deal of repair and refurbishment, as well as the programme of bold and imaginative alterations to the grounds instituted by Winston. It seems a mortgage had to be raised on the property to finance all this. Once again, Jack was to the fore in the family's monetary affairs. In April 1926 the solicitors Nicholl, Manisty and Co were writing to him as a Trustee, to see if he was happy for a loan of £10,000 to be raised on a property valued at £18,000. "As this is a family transaction, the question of a forced sale is hardly likely to arise ... but, of course, this does not affect your responsibility as a Trustee to see that a proper security is obtained".[9]

One of the first industries to suffer from the return to the Gold Standard was Britain's coalfields. With their export markets destroyed, by the strong pound and the cheap German coal being dumped around Europe to pay off war reparations, the mine owners simply cut the pay of their workers. Not unreasonably the miners withdrew their labour and a bitter eighteen-month dispute set in. In May 1926 the Trades Union Congress tried to force a decision by calling a General Strike in support of the miners' claim. Winston saw this as a call to arms. Paternal reforms for the workers was one thing; seeing the organised working class making demands of the government was quite another. This was the socialist menace he had campaigned against since 1917 writ large. With the Fleet Street newspapers shut down by sympathy strikes, Winston got approval for the creation of a semi-official newspaper, the *British Gazette*, to keep the public informed about the course of the strike and what the Government was doing to combat it. Run by volunteers, with paper commandeered from Fleet Street, and with editorials thundering forth in typical Winston style, the circulation peaked at two million copies a day.

The call went out for volunteers to break the strike by carrying out vital work in transport and the distribution of goods. Jack was one of the first to answer the call, and he worked every day in and around Paddington Station as a Special Constable and general strikebreaker.

He would be presented with a fine silver salver by the Great Western Railway Company for his services to them during the strike. There was no revolutionary intent in the TUC, and the strike was called off after just nine days. It is entirely in character that Winston then became one of the chief contributors to an effort to find a peaceful settlement between the doughty miners and their equally stubborn employers. 'Beer and sandwiches' were employed long before the Wilson government earned a reputation for using such diplomacy. The mine owners were recalcitrant and the miners were literally starved into submission.

Winston produced useful budgets each year, something he never seemed to manage for his own household, and found plenty of time for long holidays. In 1927, he was touring in the Mediterranean with Jack, and met Mussolini once or twice in Italy, saying some nice things about him that would come back to haunt him later. He once took himself off to Chartwell from August to October, getting a good deal of writing done. The artist Walter Sickert became a friend and assisted in developing Winston's painting technique. Jack, always keen on new technology, would bring his portable radio down to Chartwell and many a pleasant dinner was rounded off with the lights turned low, listening to some music. Winston grew increasingly agitated about the campaign launched by Gandhi for the independence of India. He savagely denounced this mildest of men as a dangerous troublemaker and feared that the Conservative Party was too lenient towards him.

The General Election of 1929 put the Tories out of office, and gave Ramsay Macdonald's Labour Party their first real chance to govern. It was their misfortune to be in office when the great recession hit the world's economies. Winston held his seat but returned to the backbenches, for far longer than he imagined.

CHAPTER 21

From the Wilderness to Downing Street
1929–1940

Having never taken more than three weeks holiday at a time in his life, Jack expressed a new sense of solid well being by accompanying Winston on a three-month trip to North America. Randolph and Johnny, both down from university for the summer, would accompany their fathers for part of the holiday. Goonie expressed no desire to be so long away from England and, to everyone's regret, Clemmie was not well enough for the journey. They sailed on 3rd August 1929, on the *Empress of Australia* and travelled in great comfort. Winston wrote continually to his wife, "the citadel of his life and soul", and regaled her with tales of long sessions of Bezique with Jack, on whom he "inflicted most cruel defeats". He found time to write two major essays for publication, and began an intensive course of reading in preparation for his proposed study of John Churchill, the first Duke of Marlborough.

Once in Canada, the Canadian Pacific Railway Company provided them with excellent accommodation for their tour across from Quebec to Vancouver. Besides luxurious double cabins each for Winston and Jack, and sleepers for the boys, the company even provided a travelling secretary to take Winston's endless stream of dictation. The trip paid for itself with a series of lectures made along the way. Jack, still a great horseman, had an interesting encounter with a grizzly bear while out riding alone. Meeting on a narrow path, they stared each other out for some moments. To his great relief, the bear fled from the incident first. After twenty-six days in Canada, twenty days were spent in California. They were often the guests of very wealthy Americans, and took great delight in visiting the locations and stars of the film industry that had settled in and around Los Angeles.

Clemmie had recovered from minor operations and illnesses. She was sustained by her loving daughters, and by Goonie who, with 'Pebin' (Peregrine) and Clarissa, was a frequent visitor to Chartwell. She wrote to Winston that the sixteen-year old Peregrine and the (nearly) fifteen-year old Sarah "seem more wrapped up in each other than ever". In another curious reprise of family history, Johnny had grown up a 'bit of a handful', always in scrapes with the equally rumbustious Randolph, and now rebelling against sobriety in favour of bohemianism, while Peregrine had become a serious, quiet young man, always with his nose in a book if he wasn't pondering some problem of a practical engineering nature.

Another generous captain of industry, the head of the Bethlehem Steel Company, provided the train that took the touring party back to the east coast of America. From there Randolph and Johnny, due back at university, were sent home on the *Berengaria*, under the charge of Lord Birkenhead (formerly Sir FE Smith). Winston and Jack extended their holiday with a visit to Gettysburg and other Civil War sites. Winston regaled Clemmie with a confident statement of how his writing was earning such good advances and payments, and that some solid investments were producing handsome and steady returns. By the end of October the great 'Wall Street Crash' had devastated the American economy and sent shock waves around the world. Winston estimated that his investments shrank by £10,000 in the twinkling of an eye, and, no doubt remembering his own upbringing, he felt a great anguish about his family's finances and prospects. In a throwaway remark in his memoirs, Johnny would say, "Certainly our families avoided the tragedy which overwhelmed so many others".[1] Once again a lot of very hard work by Jack is passed over lightly. What a blessing at this time to have a well-established stockbroker in the family.

There was retrenchment at Chartwell. Only the study was kept in use and the family repaired to a cottage that had been intended for a butler. Winston embarked on such a sustained programme of writing for money that they kept their heads well above water, and could even take out long leases on quite comfortable London homes. The year 1930 saw the publication of the very successful *My Early Life*. This humorous, charming and engaging 'memoir' has influenced most subsequent books about Winston, but should be read, as we have argued, with caution. It was followed in 1931 by *The Eastern Front* (a supplementary volume to *The World Crisis*, after criticism that he had badly neglected that aspect of the war), by an abridged edition of *The World Crisis*, a collection of essays (*Thoughts and Adventures*), and then the four volume *Marlborough* (between 1933 and 1938).

Jack was back in his office, wrestling with the turbulent stock markets in the wake of the financial disaster in New York. He could do little to recover their position in America, where things were bad and getting worse. But Vickers da Costa were paying close attention to world market trends, and Jack was able to make short term purchases and quick sales to keep a small flow of profits coming back to the family. He managed the families affairs, ordering their debts into a sequence for payment (putting everything off for as long as possible), setting losses made on the Chartwell farm against tax liabilities, and steering their investments along safer lines, towards basic commodities that would always be in demand and companies with a brighter future: copper in Rhodesia, oil in Alberta, and into Marks and Spencer, Gaumont British Films and Sherwood Starr Gold Mining.

While the new Labour government was beset by worldwide recession, the Opposition Front Bench met infrequently. This suited Winston who was hard at work with his writing. But he soon found himself once again at odds with the Party leadership. Baldwin was steering them towards some partial recognition of India's demand for self-government. In another extreme stance, Winston was utterly opposed to this. He spoke of the benign Mahatma Gandhi as if he were the devil incarnate. He was egged on by Tory press barons and found himself entrenched in a very right wing segment of the Conservative Party. Winston formally resigned from the Shadow Cabinet in protest, and when a coalition National Government was formed in 1931, he was not offered any ministerial position by the dominant Conservative Party. He was well and truly 'in the wilderness'.

To Jack and Goonie's dismay, Johnny was becoming increasingly wayward at university. He gave up his regular line of study and enrolled in the Ruskin School of Art. He was encouraged in these endeavours by his radical cousin, the sculptor, Clare Sheridan, and

46. Winston, Clemmie and Randolph.

47, 48, 49. Johnny and Peregrine growing up together.

50. Montagu Porch.

51. Jennie's funeral, 1921. Winston, Jack, Johnny, Oswald Frewen (Clara's son), Clara Frewen, Leonie Leslie, Goonie, Clemmie, and Sir John (Jack) Leslie.

52. Clarissa as an infant.

54. Clarissa as a teenager, 1935.

53. Clarissa out riding with her father.

55. Clarissa as a young woman.

56. The family at lunch: Jack, Peregrine, Clarissa, a guest, Goonie.

57. The family on holiday: Jack, Peregrine, Goonie, Clarissa, and Johnny.

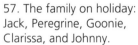

58. Jack and Goonie playing bezique in their garden.

59. Jack in his library. His great solace.

60. Winston and Jack on a tour of inspection, July 1941.

61. Peregrine, Royal Naval Volunteer Reserve.

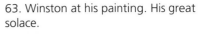
63. Winston at his painting. His great solace.

62. Goonie's grave. Her birth date should read 1885.

65. Bladon Churchyard: the Celtic cross marks Lord Randolph; next to him lies Jennie; next to her are Jack and Peregrine. Winston and Clemmie lie in front of Jennie.

64. Winston's state funeral, 1965.

66. Peregrine and Yvonne, 1958

67. Peregrine and Yvonne, on his 80th birthday, 1993.

by the friends of the family, the great artists Sir John Lavery and Sir Edwin Lutyens. The riotous parties were many; one summer was spent pursuing a 'lost love' across Italy and Germany before she dropped him dead. When he threw up his studies and resigned from Oxford, Jack promptly enlisted his son into the firm, Vickers da Costa, at fifty pounds per annum and a half-commission for new business won. Another of Jack's friends, Sir Reginald McKenna, the head of Midlands bank, put a £200,000 contract Johnny's way, earning a very nice £250 commission for the apprentice. Johnny in a suit and bowler hat was to be a brief phenomenon. He had developed a talent for mural painting and another family friend, Lord Birkenhead, secured a £100 commission for him to do a mural for 'Chips' Channon. Johnny left Vickers da Costa on 1st January 1932, after a very amicable interview with Mr Vickers, and devoted himself to perfecting his chosen profession, with some courses taken at the Royal College of Art (who candidly admitted there was not much they could teach him) and the Central School of Arts and Crafts. In 1933, Uncle Winston would give him his most famous and enduring commission, to paint the 'Marlborough Pavilion' in the garden loggia at Chartwell.

Jack had frowned on Johnny's antics to date. He had called his artistic leanings 'playing the ass'; his chasing of women 'playing the ass in the bulrushes', and viewed an artist's career as 'playing the ass in the gutter'. But he did give Johnny a £10 a month allowance to help him get started, and Goonie, always more lenient with her children than her parents had been with her, was happy for him, though she did not appreciate the eccentric attire he affected – of beret, cloak and riding breeches. Johnny always admired his father's dress sense, so moderate and unostentatious, yet always the height of good taste and elegance. It seems that Jack gave him no advice on clothes, and even kept the name of his tailor a close secret, no doubt lest Johnny would order suits at his father's expense.

At the end of 1931, Winston and Clemmie were able to travel together to America, where Winston embarked on what was expected to be a successful lecture tour, scheduled to bring in some £10,000. But, soon after the first talk, he was attempting to find a private address in New York to which he had been invited when he was knocked down by a car on Fifth Avenue. It was a nasty accident, with eight days in hospital and all of Christmas and the New Year confined to bed at the Waldorf Astoria hotel. Three weeks convalescence in the West Indies helped a lot, but he was depressed at this turn in his fortunes. He was very sad at what he considered three great blows in the last two years – the loss of money in 'the Crash', the loss of office in the Conservative Party, and now the road accident – and he wondered if he would ever recover completely from this trio of woes. He gamely tried to complete the lecture tour, but was only able to manage about half of it. Clemmie had returned to England ahead of him and was delighted to cable him that 140 friends, organised by the faithful Brendan Bracken, had raised a subscription to present him with a very handsome new Daimler car.[2]

Winston was writing on an industrial scale by now. He was working on the study of Marlborough, on a whole series of essays and began negotiations with Cassel for the major work that would become his epic *History of the English-Speaking Peoples*. An advance of £20,000 (perhaps £600,00 today) was most acceptable, especially for a work not due to be delivered until the latter half of the decade.[3] Although Winston dictated his words to efficient secretaries, he always employed first-rate researchers, usually rising stars in the world of history[4], to assemble the raw material on which he worked.

It is as well he was kept so busy. His continued extremist stand on Indian freedom alienated him from many Conservatives who might otherwise have shared many of his ideals, like Anthony Eden, Harold Macmillan and Duff Cooper. This became a significant problem with the rise of fascism in Germany. It has been observed before that, if Winston had passed away at some time before 1939, he would have been remembered as a rather fine writer and journalist, a good and improving painter, and a failure as a politician, in the sense that he might have achieved so much more had he been less of a maverick. How like his father in that respect.

In 1932, Winston had travelled extensively in Germany, a country he admired, visiting the battlefields of the Duke of Marlborough. In Munich, he saw at close quarters the burgeoning influence of the Nazi Party on the brink of assuming complete control of the nation state. A severe bout of paratyphoid fever laid him low, and he was confined to a sanatorium in Salzburg for two weeks. Jack wrote letters to cheer him up, saying "There was a rumour that you had been poisoned by drinking water! I contradicted this libel at once!" While he, in common with most people at the time, did not outwardly disapprove of the new regime in Germany, Winston does seem to have instinctively grasped the danger it would pose for Europe.

In May 1932, Winston's son, Randolph, left Oxford University before his finals to take up a career in journalism. Thanks to his father he secured a job on Lord Rothermere's *Sunday Graphic* and was soon reporting on the elections in Germany. Winston had very high hopes for Randolph, and there were to be many disappointments ahead. Having determined that his own parents were too distant, Winston had vowed to be a good father to his own children. We are left wondering which approach to parenting was the more successful. He may have lavished care and attention upon them, but they may have found "living under the shadow of a great oak" to be more of a strain than anyone realised at the time. Diana would have two broken marriages and would die in 1963 from an overdose of sleeping pills. Randolph is variously described as 'thorny', 'patrician', 'over-bearing', 'comprehensively disliked' and even 'a fascist beast'. He, too, had two unhappy marriages, and is remembered as a heavy drinker, gambler and womaniser. Sarah, full of charm and vitality, was won over by the amateur dramatics engaged in at Chartwell and Blenheim to a life on the stage and in films. Of her three marriages, the first ended in divorce, and the second in separation and the suicide of her ex-husband. After the terrible loss of Marigold, what a blessing the lovely and balanced Mary would prove to be.

With Johnny embarked on an artistic career, Jack and Goonie were glad to see Peregrine safely into Cambridge University to study engineering, for which he had always displayed a natural affinity. Goonie had so longed for a daughter that she lavished an ocean of love and affection on Clarissa. This was so pronounced that it drew comment from others, including cousins and their nannies, who felt it to be almost unhealthy. The child could be demanding. In one letter to Peregrine, Goonie remarked, "I have just cuffed C.[larissa] over the head – she is too spoilt". A little unfair, that, since Goonie spoiled her more than anyone else living. More than once Jack had to tell 'Pebin' that he could not come down to see him at school "as C.

insists on riding". Reminiscing about her father, Clarissa later recalled him as a distant figure, getting in from work and repairing to his study to read the papers. Yet there exist many photographs, and a series of home movies, taken by Jack of their family holidays abroad, and of Jack and Clarissa together, usually riding, a love of his that he had imparted to her. Clarissa was a very clever child and would be remembered as a fine intellect.

January 1933 saw Hitler appointed Chancellor of Germany. The Nazis moved quickly to seize the apparatus of the state, making their removal impossible. In February the Oxford Union passed the motion, "That this House refuses in any circumstances to fight for King and Country". A week later, addressing the Anti-Socialist and Anti-Communist Union, Winston denounced this "abject, squalid, shameless avowal" and warned of the "splendid clear-eyed youth" of Germany demanding the re-armament of their country. His powerful talents, as writer and speaker, swung into action as a warning to Britain and Europe of the danger they faced. He was not helped by people reminding him of his stance, before and after the Great War, against military spending and of the cuts he had made in defence budgets at every opportunity. But he had seen, with a clarity denied to others, the logical outcome of the Nazi accession to power and he would not desist. There were great moves afoot in Europe to negotiate further disarmament as a guarantee of peace, and France was put under great pressure to set an example and reduce her powerful armed forces. When Winston suggested that these measures made war more likely he was shouted down in the House of Commons. His old reputation as a 'war lover', however unjustified, was at odds with the mood of the country. How curious that it was Anthony Eden who, using phrases like "a fantastic absurdity", had to refute Winston's arguments in the House.

After barely a year of marriage, Diana's union with John Bailey, son of Winston's wealthy South African friend, Sir Abe Bailey, broke down. Clemmie had not favoured the match and, according to Mary, her relationship with Diana sadly grew cold. The divorce was finalised in 1935. Another stormy relationship burst upon the joint family scene. In May 1934, Johnny, working as an artist in Italy, married his latest love, Angela Culme-Seymour. They both professed to be atheists and Angela declared, after their 'pagan' wedding, that

she would never 'belong' to anyone. Jack and Goonie received notifi-
cation of this wedding by letter, after the event. Goonie commented
in a letter to Peregrine, "Johnny seems to have written to the whole
of London about his marriage ... and Papa sent her [Angela] today
1000 lira with a jocular letter – isn't he sweet?"[5] The couple, surviving many tantrums, returned to England, for a rather strained
meeting with Jack and Goonie at Cromwell Road. Johnny painted a
major mural at the home, in Churt, of David Lloyd George. Soon
after, on 26th March 1935, his daughter, Sally (christened Cornelia
Sarah) was born. That summer, Johnny and Angela (minus the baby,
left with Angela's mother) were invited to join the family on a holiday cruise to Sweden. Almost every year, Jack took his family on a
cruise to Scandinavia and the Baltic. He was now well established at
Vickers da Costa, and could offer his family a very comfortable existence – a new motorcar, one of the first electric pianos, a permanent
country home, Holworth, on the Dorset coast. In 1936, they sold 41
Cromwell Road and moved to a smaller, but more prestigious house,
No. 42 Chester Terrace, overlooking Regent's Park.

In the late summer of 1934, Winston and Clemmie had taken a
delightful holiday as guests of their friend, Lord Moyne (Walter
Guinness), cruising on his motor yacht *Rosaura* in the
Mediterranean. He then told them that he had a commission to capture some Komodo dragons from the Indonesian islands for the
London Zoo. He invited them both on a long voyage. Winston was
incredibly busy, working on the ever-expanding life of Marlborough.
He could see Clemmie would love to make the voyage and graciously
gave his consent. She left in December 1934, and was away until the
end of April 1935, having sailed 30,000 miles. It was a remarkable
experience for her, and the letters between husband and wife are
deeply moving in their declarations of love. It is not significant that
Clemmie is widely held to have 'fallen romantically in love' with one
handsome and charming younger man, Terence Philips, on the
cruise. Winston's nastier critics might suggest their marriage was in
trouble, but Clemmie recalled those times with "detached amusement", in the words of her biographer-daughter, Mary, who gamely
never shirks such issues in her family history.[6] There was more than
a hint that Philips had a preference for other men.

In 1935, Randolph, against the advice of his father, stood for

Parliament on an anti-Indian independence ticket, and had merely split the Tory vote and let in a Labour candidate. Diana, soon after her divorce, had met and married Duncan Sandys, a former Foreign Office diplomat and new Conservative MP. Clemmie liked him and was pleased that Diana had found happiness. Sarah began her stage career that year. Clemmie, who did not greatly approve of this development, was nevertheless impressed by her performances. She was less enamoured of Sarah's passionate attachment to Vic Oliver, the much-married American music hall star. In September 1936, Sarah 'bolted' to America, without parental consent, and married in New York on Christmas Eve.

Late in 1935, to avoid an English winter, Johnny had taken his family to live and work in Spain. They settled in a village near Torremolinos, where Angela promptly fell in love with a French count and left her family home on Sally's first birthday. He was so ashamed of this development that, when invited back to London to paint the hall and staircase of his parents' new house, he could not tell them of his dilemma. Sally had been left in the care of Angela's mother, but, in July 1936, Johnny had to rush back to Spain, where a savage civil war had broken out, to rescue her. He used his family name to get the British Consul at Gibraltar to arrange for a Royal Navy destroyer to call in at Malaga and take off all foreign nationals anxious to escape the fighting. When he landed up in London, expecting his parents to assume the care of little Sally, he was in for a shock. Jack and Goonie did not wear their religious beliefs lightly. They had disapproved of the irreligious marriage in the first place and refused to take the child into their household on a permanent basis. They did, of course, look after the innocent child until Johnny could get set up in London, and arrange for Sally to be taken into the Marchioness of Tweeddale's residential crèche. Johnny was not told at the time that both his mother and his father were quite ill. Jack was looking after Goonie, already in the early stages of cancer, while he had been told by his own doctors that an aneurism might give him only two years to live.

In Parliament and the press Winston continued to warn of the danger of disarming in the face of German re-armament. He admitted that he was having little impact on the majority opinion in the country. While he maintained that his writing, and his idyllic life at

Chartwell sustained him, there were many 'black dog' moments of depression, and a noted increase in the enormous pleasure he took in alcoholic beverages. It was only partly in jest that the sarcastic Lord Rothermere bet Winston that he could not renounce alcohol for the whole of 1936. Winston settled for promising to eschew brandy or undiluted spirits for a year. When German troops re-occupied the Rhineland that year, it was one more example of the Western powers appeasing the anti-communist powers – Japan in Manchuria, Italy in Abyssinia, Germany in Central Europe. By now the pretence of a unified 'National' government was over and the Conservatives had assumed the reigns of office, with Stanley Baldwin as Prime Minister. If Winston hoped for a moment that he might be invited back into government, he was soon disappointed.

Randolph crashed to another bye-election defeat in January 1936, having stood against Ramsay Macdonald's son, Malcolm, in Ross and Cromarty. The death of King George V that month brought to the throne the popular Prince of Wales, as King Edward VIII. It also saw Winston go off on another of his quixotic tangents that made him such a distrusted figure to the British Establishment. It became obvious that Edward intended to marry Mrs Wallis Simpson once her current (second) divorce was made absolute. The prospect of a twice-divorced, clearly adulterous American as Queen of England united the ruling elite, and a large section of 'middle England', in opposition to the idea. The cold and heartless official stance was anathema to the warm-hearted and chivalrous Winston. He argued, repeatedly but in vain, for the government to stop pressing the King for a statement of his intentions. By 10th December 1936, Edward had been forced to sign a Deed of Abdication. Winston had so completely misread the mood of the House of Commons on this issue that even his friends thought he had undone two years of important work on the German question with five minutes of tomfoolery over the affairs of another man's heart.

Winston predicted that 1937 would be a "mournful year". His innate anti-communism coloured his attitude to the Spanish Civil War. He was content to see General Franco's rebellion against an elected government succeed, despite the active support given to it by Germany and Italy. He received a constant stream of letters, reports and visits from all those who viewed the increasing military might of

Germany with alarm. It is clear that brave individuals in the armed services and the Civil Service risked their careers to pass on classified information to Winston, spelling out the dangerous shift in the balance of forces, especially in the air, in favour of Germany and against the Western allies. The Establishment continued to feel that Winston was endangering the international situation by his public stance on these issues.

In May 1937, Baldwin retired and Neville Chamberlain, Chancellor of the Exchequer since 1931, became Prime Minister. If his accession saw the first steps towards an increase in military readiness on the part of Britain, it also coincided with a more determined effort to engage with Hitler and secure peace by international treaty. In October, Chamberlain might, on receipt of yet another published volume of essays, express his ardent admiration for Winstons's writing, but there was to be no place for him in government in these dangerous times. But permission was given to several senior officers, including Vice-Admiral Sir Reginald Henderson and the C.I.G.S., Field Marshal Sir Cyril Deverell, to correspond with Winston in answering his questions on defence issues. He had again drawn close to Anthony Eden, Duff Cooper and a growing band of parliamentarians who were alarmed by the international situation. When Anthony Eden resigned as Foreign Secretary in February 1938, over the issue of appeasement of Italy, Winston spoke vehemently in his defence. He declared it had been "a good week for Dictators", but the band of seers around him remained a tiny minority as the nation prayed earnestly for peace.

Both Mary and Clarissa recall that, for many years, the whole talk at Chartwell was of the threat of war. Winston and Clemmie took great comfort from their family gatherings. The 'Jagoons' were frequent and popular visitors. Mary described her Uncle Jack as "a peaceful addition to any party". The children used to make him repeat his party trick of clicking out the tune of 'God Save the King' on his teeth with his fingernails! When Sir John Leslie was asked of his remembrance of Jack, he could only recall him as a quiet, good-natured man. By the late Thirties he was much concerned with Goonie's health, and stoically bore his own problems in that regard without any fuss. Johnny was quite a successful artist now, with regular commissions for mural decoration. With Sally's upkeep, and a studio-cum-shop in London to maintain, he was usually cash-strapped. Jack did make him several substantial gifts of money, and Winston, when he heard of his difficulties, wrote him a generous cheque. Peregrine was gainfully employed on major engineering projects. Clarissa, in an effort to escape the cloying love of her mother, and displaying great academic ability, went off to the Sorbonne in Paris to study. In January 1939, Goonie wrote a frantic letter to Winston asking if the situation was so dangerous that Clarissa should be got home. She described Jack as being, in equal parts, deeply depressed and very cross. Winston assured her that the immediate danger was not that severe and that there would be time enough to get Clarissa home.

It was not long before their Uncle Winston advised both Johnny and Peregrine to get themselves into the army. Johnny at first applied to the Royal Engineers and Signals Board, hoping to use his artistic talent to specialise in camouflage work. There was no vacancy at that time, so the brothers both joined the family regiment, the Queens Own Oxfordshire Hussars, now a Territorial Army anti-tank artillery unit. They remembered that one of the first lectures they attended explained, with commendable honesty, that their two-pounder anti-tank guns would be perfectly useless against the known strength of the new German panzers. This was related to Winston, who said it merely confirmed his fears about Britain's unreadiness for war. Before the war started, Johnny was invited to join the camouflage service of the Royal Engineers.

Hitler threw caution to the wind in 1938, and absorbed the whole of Austria into Greater Germany, before making territorial demands upon Czechoslovakia for the 'return' of the mainly German Sudetenland to their 'mother country'. It was a sign of the true feelings of the country at large, that Chamberlain could fly to Munich, make shameful concessions to Nazi aggression, and return to a hero's welcome waving his promise of 'peace in our time'. If German ambitions could be diverted to Eastern Europe, what need had Britain and France to concern themselves? Winston's group of patriots were roundly denounced as troublemakers, and the machinery of the Conservative Party was deployed to make their political lives difficult. Clemmie supported Winston completely in his stand, and there are many stories of guests at Chartwell incurring her wrath if they expressed pro-appeasement views. It can have come as little comfort to watch as Hitler promptly invaded and occupied the whole of Czecho-slovakia, and turned his attention to Danzig. Belatedly Britain and France began military preparations to face the crisis; somewhat bizarrely they issued a guarantee to Poland that her territorial integrity would be protected against German aggression.

Thus it came to pass that, when Germany attacked Poland on 1st September 1939, Britain issued an ultimatum demanding German withdrawal. That ultimatum was ignored and Britain declared war on Germany on 3rd September. Chamberlain had to create a War Cabinet and immediately invited Winston back as First Lord of the Admiralty. A signal flew around all the bases and ships of the Royal Navy: "Winston is Back!" He was at his desk that very evening, and a blizzard of letters to him followed, thanking God that he had kept such a true course for the best part of a decade, and was back in office where his undoubted talents were so badly needed.

One early appeal for help came from Goonie, terrified that Clarissa, then travelling in Romania, might be in danger. Once again, he assured her that she could get home safely from that relatively quiet part of Europe. Indeed, after the rapid defeat of Poland, the whole of Europe went into a quiet phase known as the 'Phoney' War. The BEF established itself in Northern France; Johnny was with them as a Staff Captain at 1st Corps Headquarters, specialising in camouflage work. Peregrine was employed at the Air Ministry as a civilian expert on similar work. Winston saw the Royal Navy win a great success by forcing the pocket battleship, *Graf Spee*, to scuttle itself after being trapped in Montevideo harbour following the Battle of the River Plate. Once again the frustration of inactivity saw him firing off new schemes for action, including some very dangerous ideas about sending the fleet into the Baltic. He was initially interested in the plan to send British and French troops to assist the Finns in their separate war with the Soviet Union, but later argued that it would not impact at all on Germany's war effort. These discussions did draw Allied attention towards Scandinavia, and the vital iron ore mines in Sweden that found their outlet through Norwegian ports like Narvik. Winston became a major advocate of pre-emptive action in Norway to seize these assets for the Allies and deny them to Germany. Early in April 1940, Chamberlain appointed Churchill to preside over the War Cabinet's Military Co-ordination Committee, which sounds rather more authoritative than it actually was. Preparations were well under way for an intervention in Norway when the news came that Germans were massing in their northern ports with a similar plan in mind.

Both sides set out on 7th April 1940; the Germans, having a much shorter journey, arrived first and in strength. Denmark was overrun; Norway invaded. The Royal Navy had some remarkable successes against the German fleet, but Allied land forces were contained and driven back by the German Army and Luftwaffe. Before April was out the Allies were planning for the very difficult evacuation of their beleaguered troops from some parts of Norway, as other troops were still going ashore into extremely perilous situations. A mounting tide of criticism of the whole handling of the campaign inevitably made Winston something of a target. How extraordinary that, in the ensuring parliamentary debate, he should emerge the victor.

CHAPTER 22

Their Finest Hour
1940–1945

Though he was as culpable as anyone for the fiasco in Norway, Winston emerged strongly from the debate in the House of Commons on 7th and 8th May 1940. There was such a tide of opinion running against Neville Chamberlain that a vote of censure reduced the government majority from 213 to 81. Chamberlain left the Chamber to cries of "Go! Go! Go!" On 9th May, he tried to cobble together a new coalition but the Labour Party refused to serve under him. A suggestion that an aristocrat, Lord Halifax, become Prime Minister was met with a stony silence. The next day the Germans launched a huge offensive against Holland, Belgium and France. Chamberlain tendered his resignation to the King and, when asked to nominate a successor, advised that Winston be called upon. His reputation, built over several years, as the siren voice warning about Nazi aggression made him the natural choice.

Plunged into crisis and near-disaster from the day he achieved the highest office, this was the moment Winston was born for. The stubborn streak in his character; his love of British history and institutions; his certainty in the correctness of his own opinion – all this came together at the hour of his country's greatest need. His unflinching leadership over the next couple of years are why he was, is now and always will be regarded with the greatest admiration by freedom-loving people in Britain and throughout the world. His utter refusal to contemplate a negotiated peace with the most evil regime in history was what carried an ill-prepared and battered nation through many trials until more powerful allies stepped up to take the strain of the war.

He would face many more humiliating military defeats, and the pressure of responsibility would see many more 'black dogs' gnawing at him. Throughout his travails a close and loving family would sustain him and they made a vital contribution to Britain's success in war in this, their own way.

Jack, himself diagnosed with a heart tumour, and devoting all his spare time to nursing Goonie, gamely went out every day to work in his office in the City. He would later provide useful services to help Winston function to his best ability. Johnny was caught up in the retreat to Dunkirk, commanding a provost company at very short notice. From the beaches his commanding officer despatched him to London, to convey to his uncle the desperate need for small ships to get the men off the beach and out to the ships waiting to get them back to England. He went on to serve for three years at Anti-Aircraft Command, Stanmore. Peregrine worked on camouflage projects and, commissioned into the Royal Naval Volunteer Reserve, as an interpreter of photographic reconnaissance. Clarissa went to work decoding ciphers in the Communications Department of the Foreign Office. Greatly admired for her keen intellect, she continued to be somewhat aloof from her own family.

Randolph, who had married the beautiful Pamela Digby in 1939, was returned unopposed as the Conservative MP for Preston from 1940 to 1945. He went out to the Middle East with No. 8 Commando in January 1941, and was frustrated to be kept in Cairo, doing various liaison jobs, by commanders too afraid of his father to put him in harm's way. Diana served in the Women's Royal Naval Service but had to leave in February 1941 to look after her two small children and her husband, Duncan Sandys, who had been seriously injured in a car accident. Sarah continued her acting career until she parted from her husband, Vic Oliver, in 1941. She then joined the Women's Auxiliary Air Force and worked on photographic interpretation. Stationed at Medmenham, she was able to get to Chequers often to see her parents. By September the whole family was in uniform, as Mary joined the Auxiliary Territorial Service and immediately applied for active service with a mixed anti-aircraft battery.

The matriarch, Clementine, was the guiding genius of the family. She was as perceptive as ever, realising that a well-meant attempt to get little Sally (Johnny's daughter) evacuated to America would look like the Churchill's were abandoning ship. She moved swiftly to get the passage cancelled and the child re-located in England. She frankly warned Winston that his "sarcastic and over-bearing manner" was alienating the friends he must work with.[1] She was sure this was just the strain of his work, but the value of such timely advice was beyond calculation. Of course, she embarked on a punishing schedule of work and visits in her own right. In particular she investigated the conditions in which Londoners spent the night during the Blitz, and made many important and practical suggestions for improvements.

The German bombing was intruding upon the family in many ways. Goonie, so ill now that she had to reside permanently in the country, was staying at Hamstead Marshall, the home of her friend, Rosie Ridley, when she received an alarming letter from Peregrine:

> Dear Mama
>
> It has been rather noisy here lately. Up to yesterday afternoon Chester Terrace was still there but there have been a large number of bombs everywhere. The Travellers has been bombed and the Carlton Club is no more and one or two other landmarks have vanished ... .
>
> I was very nearly killed by a direct hit on a restaurant on Monday night. I was dining between Berkley Square and Bond Street on the ground floor when two bombs landed and demolished the entire building. I was buried for a while but found I still could move and eventually dug myself out. I found I wasn't in the slightest bit hurt which was amazing. With assistance from the rescue squad, who seemed to appear from nowhere, we got out an Air Force boy who was cut about the head but otherwise alright. We two were the only people not hurt. There were eight others all rather mashed. Why I am not dead is incredible as there is literally not a brick standing.
>
> I think I was knocked on the head cos I still feel a bit dizzy and as soon as I have settled a few things I am going to take a rest for two or three days. Shall I be able to see you?
>
> Love, Peregrine[2]

It is no wonder that Goonie had been saying she was "trembling and worrying" for her family still in London. It was not long before Chester Terrace did receive bomb damage serious enough to make Jack move out and live at 10 Downing Street. This was in an even more heavily bombed part of town, and he spent a good deal of time in the extensive bombproof shelters below ground, "in quarters resembling third-class accommodation on a Channel steamer", according to 'Jock' Colville. The ailing Goonie was greatly heartened by a visit from kind Clemmie, and she had written to 'Darling Pebin':

> I meant to give Papa this letter to take to you this morning – but he went early, Poor Old Bird, and I was asleep.
>
> What I want to say is, if I can help you about your holiday, let me.
>
> I had an idea that perhaps you would like to spend it at Crab Wood with me?? [Crab Wood was a 'cottage' owned by Goonie's dear friend, the Duke of Westminster.] It's empty, all the servants are there, and food – so if you would like to go there, it is all ready for you and me. ... Aunt Clemmie came here from Aylesbury (that is Chequers) yesterday, clack clack clack clack clack; she was in roaring spirits, and says perhaps invasion imminent – urah! urah!! But it was very sweet of her to come and see me –
>
> All my love, Mum[3]

Between working in the City, where he said things were rather flat, and travelling down to see Goonie every weekend, Jack helped Winston by using his organisational and financial skills to set up and run a canteen for Winston's immediate staff at the Downing Street/Foreign Office complex. Their productivity in the service of this most demanding of masters was enhanced by being able to have their meals at any time at their place of work. Lord Moran, Winston's doctor, remembered Jack dining with the secretaries every night, always "the life of the party". Moran knew that Jack was seriously ill and marvelled that "he went on his way as if he had no care in the world". It is also known that Jack's office skills, shorthand, typing, and administration, were called upon for some of Winston's most secret correspondence.[4]

Winston's restless spirit saw him constantly moving about the country, visiting installations, inspecting units and meeting officials. Jack was an inseparable companion for much of the time. He was always there when asked, but would 'make himself scarce' when secret matters were discussed. Jock Colville commented at one stage that Winston's "naturally affectionate nature disposes him towards nepotism". On one trip Jack was loudly applauded by the crowds, and it was belatedly realised they had, not unreasonably, mistaken him for the Soviet Ambassador, Ivan Maisky. The presence of his brother helped Winston through some difficult times, and, when the chance to relax at Chequers came, he needed as many of his family and friends about him as could be arranged. Winston refreshed himself for the fight in this setting, and with these people.

Leading by example, Winston saw the nation through the invasion scare after the retreat from Dunkirk, when the defiance of his great speeches was as powerful a weapon as the scarce resources available to Britain's armed forces. The sustained bombing of British cities that autumn was stoically borne, while the might of the Royal Navy and the extraordinary dedication of the Royal Air Force and anti-aircraft services during the Battle of Britain kept Britain's shores inviolate. Not content with resisting the fascist enemy, Winston declared that he sought nothing less than complete victory and the extirpation of the enemy creed from the world. All the while he devoted himself to drawing that great 'arsenal of democracy', the United States of America, into the war on Britain's side. It was no easy task. Despite many leading Americans recognising the threat posed by a victorious Nazi Germany, there were as many and more agreeing with the majority of the American people that this was a 'European civil war' best avoided by the USA.

Winston must have hoped that his half-American heritage would appeal to the decision makers in America. His direct appeals to President Franklin D. Roosevelt, by cable and personal meetings, drew much sympathy but no commitment to enter the war. America, to the great benefit of its depressed economy, sold arms and equipment to Britain until the entire gold reserves of the country had found their way to Fort Knox, and only then did Roosevelt send Harry Hopkins over with the offer of 'Lend Lease', a sort of deferred payment scheme that suggested Britain was only 'borrowing' the sinews of war to keep its armed forces in the fight. Winston cleverly reminded the Americans that Britain was so heavily indebted to them that they could no longer afford for Britain to go down to military defeat, and thus he bound them ever closer to Britain's fortunes. He walked a fine line between persuading America that Britain was far from beaten and only needed American tools to 'finish the job' and asking whether America would really like to see the British defeated and her mighty fleet at the disposal of a triumphant Germany.

In his enthusiasm to actively prosecute the war Winston could be both inspired and mistaken. From the moment British forces were expelled from the European mainland, he ordered the creation of commando raiding forces and the Special Operations Executive to carry the war back to the enemy, as well as pushing ahead with a bombing offensive. He courageously sent all Britain's reserves of armoured fighting vehicles to Egypt, where they won a spectacular victory over far larger Italian forces in the Western Desert. He would then dissipate that success by throwing forces he could ill afford to lose into Greece, where they were soundly defeated by the invading Germans.

All this was a prelude to the first of the two great acts that would ultimately lead to Germany's downfall. On 22nd June 1941, Germany and her allies attacked the Soviet Union, unleashing the greatest and most violent campaign in military history. Winston, the inveterate enemy of Soviet communism, began immediately to offer assistance to his new ally, Joseph Stalin. He reminded one and all that if the Germans invaded Hell, he could be relied upon to make at least a favourable reference to the Devil in the House of Commons! The Soviets suffered such a string of massive defeats in 1941-2 that many doubted if they could last much longer, but their spirited counter-attack at the gates of Moscow in December 1941, showed that they were not giving up easily.

On the extended family, so completely taken up with the war, a great sadness now descended. Goonie, who had continued to be a heavy smoker, with Jack by her side, had bravely fought lung cancer for some three years. Jack visited her in the country every weekend. She knew she was getting weaker, and she raged against her fate. She resented the idea of dying at the age of only fifty-six. Early in July 1941, a severe chill developed into pneumonia and she died on 7th July. The letters and tributes to her were, quite simply, astonishing. A tidal wave of love and affection, private and public, was released to the great comfort of her family. A few examples must suffice.

One poignant little card from her mother, who survived her by a

year, read, "Now comes peace, my darling"; Lord David Cecil wrote
the lyrical obituary that appeared in *The Times*:

> Lady Gwendeline Churchill's extraordinary charm was implicit
> in her appearance, her subtle twilight beauty, the fastidious
> grace of her dress. But it disclosed its power fully only in
> intimate conversation. Even then it was hard to analyse, so
> unexpectedly diverse were the elements of which it was
> compounded. Pensive, dreamy, with an intense refinement of
> feeling and a delicate sensibility to the beautiful, she exhaled
> romance. But unexpectedly mingled with romance was a touch
> of the eighteenth century, elegance, clear-eyed shrewdness, and
> amused scepticism, expressing itself in an enchanting
> mischievous irony, which flickered over every phrase of her
> talk. Distinction was above all the keynote of her personality,
> an exquisite fineness of quality, beside which most people
> showed up as lamentably crude and common-place. She was
> like the single flower of a high civilization, bred through
> generations to bloom once only for the wonder and delight of
> mankind.[5]

Winston's old flame, Pamela Lytton, who had known Goonie since
she was eleven years old, wrote to *The Times* describing her as 'a
living poem'. "Those who knew and loved her will always find her 'in
the shining of the stars, in the flowering of the fields'."[6] Violet
Bonham-Carter thought her "unlike any other human being I have
ever known – more rare and perfect". It was the kind Katharine
Asquith who directly addressed the role Jack had played during the
long illness: "I know the terrible strain you have been under for three
years – and how you dreaded the pain and suffering for her – and
how wonderfully you took it. Your love must have been a great pro-
tection for her".

The devout Roman Catholic, Lady Gwendeline Churchill, was
buried on 10th July 1941, at Begbrook Convent, some three miles
from Blenheim Palace.

On 7th December the Imperial Japanese Navy, without a declaration of war, attacked the United States base at Pearl Harbour in the
Hawaiian Islands. Astonishingly, in the second great act of folly

referred to, either in a fit of Hitlerian madness or a bowing to inevitability, Germany declared war on the United States of America. Winston could hardly contain his glee. He felt that the war had been won from that moment forward. There would be much hard fighting for more than three years, but in slightly more than one year the battles of Midway in the Pacific, El Alamein in North Africa, and Stalingrad on the Eastern Front had decisively wrested the initiative away from the Axis powers.

It was, of course, some while before the real might of the United States, industrial and military, could be fully mobilised. For most of 1942 the Allies endured further reverses that seemed all the more bitter after the jubilation released by America's accession to the war. A Russian offensive failed and her armies were driven back to the Volga and the Caucasus Mountains. The Japanese burst out over South-east Asia and the Pacific. The surrender of Singapore to the Japanese was arguably the worst disaster in British military history. The surrender in North Africa of Tobruk so quickly, after its heroic defence the previous year, was shameful. An experimental amphibious raid on Dieppe was bloodily defeated. The Royal and Merchant Navies suffered grievous losses in the Pacific and Atlantic Oceans and the Mediterranean Sea. With his deep knowledge and understanding of military history, Winston saw these setbacks as the episodes they were. He faced down a vote of no confidence in the House of Commons in July, and later that year he persuaded Sir Stafford Cripps, a challenger to his position as Prime Minister, to defer his resignation from the Cabinet until after the Anglo-American invasion of Vichy French North Africa (Operation Torch) had taken place. Success in North Africa, soon followed by the Soviet counter-attack at Stalingrad that surrounded the German Sixth Army, secured Winston's position as Britain's war leader.

Once again Britain was a junior partner in a great war coalition, and, while the Soviets were actively fighting the vast majority of the German armed forces, the Americans were pouring troops and equipment into Britain, anxious to open a second front in France at the earliest opportunity. Winston had a larger strategic vision that he found increasingly difficult to 'sell' to the Americans. As the Soviets gradually assumed the initiative on the Eastern Front, he determined to develop an Allied offensive in the Mediterranean that would bring

British and American troops into central and eastern Europe long before any invasion of France could be mounted from the west. It was to forestall the Soviets in the long term that Winston inveigled the Americans into joining attacks on Sicily and then Italy. The German defence of Italy neutralised that strategy, and the Americans were able to impose their will and press ahead with plans for the cross-Channel invasion. From November 1943, when Roosevelt and Stalin combined at the Teheran Conference to insist on a second front opening in France the following summer, Winston finally lost control of the overall strategy of the war. It also guaranteed that the Soviets would be in central Europe in force and laid the foundations for the Cold War that ensued. Perhaps Winston was right all along, but with Soviet allies dying in such numbers in such savage fighting, it was impossible to spell out his visionary understanding at that time.

Winston, who celebrated his seventieth birthday in 1944, kept up a punishing schedule of work. He spent a lot of time overseas, at summit meetings or meeting with his service chiefs. Jack was always there to greet him on his return, often escorting Clemmie. Mary recalls that Clemmie drew strength and comfort from the constant and calming presence of Jack through these difficult years. The strain began to tell on Winston and his health began to suffer. Clemmie, too, was ordered by her doctors to convalesce by the sea in April 1943. Ten days rest at Weymouth, with the amiable Jack for a companion, saw her return to the fray in the best of spirits.

Randolph was seeing his share of active service in the Middle East and, with Evelyn Waugh, was sent into Yugoslavia to liaise with Tito's guerrilla partisan army. After the Normandy landings, Mary's anti-aircraft unit went over to join the armies fighting their way through North-west Europe. Johnny also went out to join the headquarters of 21st Army Group as the Inter-Service Liaison Officer dealing with Air Photographic Headquarters in England. He went in close behind the leading British troops, with the special task of rushing captured enemy airfields and seizing their photographic records.

Clemmie did important war work as President of the YWCA's Wartime Appeal. She did not enjoy public speaking but her delivery improved as she took her duties seriously and spoke up with spirit, appealing for money to help women war workers and service women adjust to the demands of war. She was a diplomatic host to the ener-getic and outspoken Eleanor Roosevelt, during her three-week visit to the United Kingdom. But her most triumphant work was for the Red Cross Aid to Russia campaign. This non-political appeal to send medical aid to embattled Russia was an ideal way for all political classes to express their support for a real fighting ally. The Russians were demanding recipients; polite pleasantries did not figure in their vocabulary. But Clemmie drove the appeal along forcefully, raising two and a quarter million pounds by December 1942. She deliber-ately let the fund get overdrawn as it shipped aid off as fast as it could be collected. A fine New Year appeal saw the overdraft cleared in a trice, and the fund boomed along – over four millions by October 1943, and six millions by December 1944. It actually ran on until June 1947, by which time over seven and half million pounds had been raised. The Soviet authorities were moved to honour her on behalf of all the volunteer workers associated with the Red Cross, of which more later.

After the Allied breakout from the Normandy bridgehead in August 1944, the German armies were chased back to frontiers of the Fatherland. Their success against the airborne landings at Arnhem in September, and the last desperate counter-attack in the Ardennes in December, could not prevent their ultimate defeat. In particular they could not prevent the armed forces of the Soviet Union pouring across the 1941 frontiers and driving into Romania, Bulgaria, Hungary, Czechoslovakia Austria, Poland and Germany itself. Late in January 1945, Winston flew out to Yalta, on the Black Sea, for an important summit conference with Stalin and Roosevelt. There was little he could do to restrain the triumphalist Stalin; he got little help from the dying Roosevelt.

In March 1945, as Winston watched the Allied assault across the Rhine, Clemmie flew out, via Cairo, to the Soviet Union as the hon-oured guest of the Red Cross. She and her companions, Grace Hamblin and Miss Mabel Johnson (secretary to the Aid to Russia Fund), were lodged in the State Guest House. A full programme of visits to hospitals, children's homes, factories, the ballet, and to offi-cial lunches and dinners, and one interview with Joseph Stalin himself, was laid on. The Soviet Red Cross awarded Clemmie the Distinguished Red Cross Service Badge, "amidst stormy applause".

The party travelled to Leningrad by train to see the heroic city that had withstood a Nazi siege for some nine hundred days. After more morale-boosting visits, the City Council awarded Clemmie the Order of the Red Banner of Labour, and Miss Johnson the Medal of Labour. On to Stalingrad, to see a city more completely devastated that anything Clemmie could ever recall. After a 'rest' on the Black Sea coast, punctuated by more visits to recovering wounded soldiers and to the theatre, they went on to Rostov-on-Don, where the Fund was rebuilding two shattered hospitals. They were in Odessa, via the Crimea, for May Day, and returned to Moscow on 5th May. She was there when the news of Germany's surrender finally came through. The next day, Clemmie broadcast over Moscow Radio a message from her husband looking forward to friendship and understanding between the British and Russian peoples. Clemmie was home by 12th May. Winston, unable to break the habits of a lifetime, was late in arriving to meet her.

Jack's poor health had given them all an anxious moment. In the last week of April he had suffered a heart attack while staying at the Royal Dorset Yacht Club, Weymouth. After a week he was judged fit to be moved to London. The doctor accompanying him, Adam Gray, recalls that as the stretcher-bearers were loading him into the ambulance, Jack decided he needed a pinch of snuff and insisted on getting it. Winston was in daily touch with the doctors for the fullest details of Jack's condition, and he visited him at University College Hospital several times. Jack spent his final recuperation at Chequers, although that facility was soon to be removed from the family. Society obviously thought the worst as the diarist, James Lees-Milne, spoke at a dinner party of Jack "now dying in hospital". He thought that Winston was so devoted to his brother because he was "the repository of his confidences". Another guest, Emerald Cunard, remarked, "You are a very perspicacious man, Jim".[7]

In 1945, there had been no General Election in Britain for ten years. With victory in war guaranteed, the political parties began to turn their attention to the demands of peace after such a protracted and expensive struggle. Partisan attitudes began to replace coalition co-operation. Winston greatly offended the organised working-class, as represented by the Trades Union Congress, by refusing to consider an amendment to the Trades Disputes Act of 1927, still resented as an act of vengeance after the General Strike. The Labour Party became more assertive and the party conference at Blackpool in May declared that it was not prepared to wait for victory over Japan before insisting on an election. The Coalition ended on 23rd May, and Winston technically headed a caretaker Conservative government until the election.

Winston worked on his electioneering speeches over the first weekend in June at Chequers. He made one of the most astonishing blunders of his long and interesting life. His old Labour colleagues immediately became 'Socialists', abhorrent to a free Parliament. Despite the predictably sensible advice of his wife, he inserted the gross slander that such a party could only govern with some sort of 'Gestapo' to nip free opinion in the bud. His broadcast unleashed a storm of protest and did irreparable harm to the Conservative campaign. Well might an admirer like Vita Sackville-West ask, "What has gone wrong with him?" He may have realised, too late, that he blundered but he still campaigned as vigorously as one would have expected.

The election was on 5th July, but the result would not be declared for three weeks, to allow all the service votes to come in from around the world. On 15th July, Winston flew out to the Potsdam Conference, where the Allied powers were to discuss the war against Japan and the many, intractable issues about the settlement of post-war Europe. He returned to London on 25th July for the declaration of the results. He expected a victory; the Labour leader, Clement Attlee, apparently expected to lose by a narrow margin. Winston was returned unopposed in his new constituency of Woodford. The unelected Randolph proved to be unelectable and lost his seat. The Conservative Party crashed to one of its greatest ever defeats. Labour, with 393 seats to the Tories 213, had an outright majority of 146 over all other parties. The British people might love 'Winny' and admire his defiant stand at the moment of the nation's greatest ever peril, but they could not forgive his party for the hardship of the Thirties and the drift to war that had blighted so many lives.

CHAPTER 23

The End of it All
1945–1965

Clemmie, concerned at the enormous strain the war years had been on his constitution, remarked to Winston that electoral defeat might well be a blessing in disguise. He famously replied that it seemed quite effectively disguised. Admitting that the size of the Labour majority made him feel slightly ashamed, it was not immediately obvious to Winston that not having to cope with the enormous problems of de-mobilisation and reconstruction in a long drawn out 'age of austerity' would actually work entirely to the advantage of the Conservative Party and its embattled leader. Meanwhile a new house had to be found in London, a new role as Leader of the Opposition was embarked upon, and a well-earned holiday was arranged. Villas in the possession of wartime colleagues, Generals Alexander and Eisenhower, were made available in Italy and the South of France, and some fine paintings were completed, which must have helped to calm frayed nerves. He submitted two paintings anonymously to the Royal Academy in 1947. Both were accepted for the summer exhibition. His family report that he was more than usually tetchy for a while, and some spectacular rows took place, most notably with Randolph at a Claridge's dinner. He took comfort in his favourite champagne by Pol Roger.

Jack moved in with his son Johnny, and his second wife, Mary (Cookson), in their home at Camden Hill. He was in such pain a lot of the time that Mary had to inject him with morphine at regular intervals. When he improved in health he insisted on returning to his office in the City, travelling each day by tube train. Johnny and Mary found him a nice apartment of his own, where he could have all his own books and possessions around him. It was next door to an old friend, Katie Trefusis (now Mrs Arthur Crichton). He took great pride in being, finally (after previous failures), elected to the Turf Club, Piccadilly, and he took pleasure in entertaining his family there. Peregrine, who was as yet unmarried, spent much time with his father in his last years and was very kind to him. It was during these years that Jack imparted much of the family history to his younger son.

In October 1945, Winston had received an invitation from a small college in the Midwest USA to give their next annual lecture. He was encouraged to accept by a promise from President Harry S. Truman to introduce him to the audience in his home state. So it came to pass, during a holiday in America, that Winston delivered one of the great speeches of his life at Westminster College, Fulton, Missouri, on 5th March 1946. It was the product of his deep understanding of history and his worries about the effect on Europe of a resurgent Soviet Union. It is made famous by the dramatic description of Europe divided by 'an iron curtain', though he had used the phrase many times before and it was not original to him. But it certainly made a captivating newspaper headline. He warned against a new appeasement, and stated that the Soviets understood strength and despised weakness. He did recognise that the Soviets had legitimate state interests, but warned that they could only be contained by a united English-speaking world, that shared a 'special relationship'. It was a warning to the West not to drop its guard in the face of new perils. Condemned by some as the first shot in the Cold War, and fiercely denounced by Stalin as "a call to war", the speech gradually assumed a mantle of wisdom as the way to avoid future war, from a position of strength, rather than to drift into catastrophe from one of weakness and irresolution.

The defeated premier returned home as a world statesman re-born. He launched immediately into the preparation of his war memoirs, presented as a magisterial general history of the war. (A planned five volumes would eventually become six.) He had already been stung by some personal criticism coming from several American memoirs of war service. Winston had always said that personal reputation was vindicated by history, and that he would make certain that he was the historian. He negotiated a remarkable series of contracts with British and American publishers, guaranteeing the most enormous income. He then set about recruiting a powerful team of researchers and writers, including the 'coming' historian, William Deakin, and the consummate staff officer, General Sir Henry Pownall (who was paid £1,000 a year for his contribution). He doggedly wrestled with the Whitehall bureaucrats to be allowed unprecedented access to all the state papers relating to the war. Many items now in the 'Churchill papers' were released bearing a cover note requesting their early return to the Cabinet Office.

It was a remarkable achievement for a septuagenarian, absorbing the work of several assistants, editing their texts and dictating his own linking narrative. The succeeding volumes were always published first in the USA, the most lucrative market, and subsequently in Britain. The first volume, "The Gathering Storm" came out in 1948; "Their Finest Hour" in 1949; "The Grand Alliance" in 1950; "The Hinge of Fate" in 1950/1951; "Closing the Ring" in 1951/1952; "Triumph and Tragedy" in 1953/1954. In all 1.6 million words of text and nearly three hundred thousand words of appendices were produced in the inimitable, highly readable and massively popular style of Winston Churchill. He earned easily ten times what he was ever paid as Prime Minister. Indeed all his books took on a new lease of life and booming sales made him, really for the first time, a permanently wealthy man.

Like "The World Crisis" and its treatment of the First World War, this work is not an entirely objective study of history. The whole project is based on the careful selection of primary documents that show Winston's decision-making process in the best possible light. It also repeats the fault of the earlier work in a complete lack of balance concerning the events on the Eastern Front.[1]

In the midst of this tremendously hard work, Winston suffered a great personal blow. In the hard winter of 1946/1947 Jack's health collapsed for the last time. Sir Charles Wilson (Lord Moran), Winston's personal physician, recorded in his diary how Jack's illness had developed into an aneurism, which "throbbed under his breastbone like a great engine", threatening to burst and kill him at any moment. We have already seen that Moran marvelled at how Jack got on with life "as if he had no care in the world".[2] In late February 1947, Jack's doctor, Lord Horder, told the family that the end was near. Winston received telephone updates almost hourly. He gave a stream of advice to the nurses in attendance, encouraging Jack to 'fight to the finish'. On 22nd February, Winston was at Jack's bedside with Johnny, waiting for the end. Lord Moran remembered

Winston telephoning him with news of the illness. "Winston was sad about Jack. He has a tender heart". Johnny left the two brothers together for the final moments. With much shedding of tears, Winston sat with Jack as he slipped away on 23rd February, aged 67. Winston had always loved his brother Jack, and felt his loss keenly. He busied himself greatly with the funeral arrangements, revealing a prodigious knowledge of suitable prayers, hymns, psalms and incidental music. He discussed with Johnny the order of service and then, in a curiously Winston moment, pulled out a copy of his book, *The River War*, and began reading from it for some thirty minutes, seemingly to console them both at such an emotional time. Even Jack's dying was turned, by acts of well-meant sentimentality, into a 'Winston event'. Apparently he expressed a wish that he could still write as well as he did when a young man.

In a final irony, Winston was not able to see Jack buried. In the bad weather of that terrible winter, Winston's doctors would not allow him to attend the funeral at Bladon. Jack was laid to rest beside his mother. Winston was able to attend the memorial service held later in London. Of Jack's children, only Clarissa is alive at the time of writing. Johnny continued his career as an artist, specialising in murals, and married twice more. He died in 1992, leaving only Sally (Sarah Cornelia, Lady Ashburton) to continue Jack's line. Peregrine became a successful civil engineer, developing a line of pre-fabricated housing of enormous benefit to the Third World. He was keen to write about his father's role in the family when he died suddenly, without issue, in 2002. His widow, Yvonne, survives him. Clarissa (Countess of Avon), married Sir Anthony Eden in 1952, but has no children.

Despite a minor stroke in 1949, Winston was able to lead his party into an election the following year that almost wiped out the huge Labour majority of 1945. In October 1951, he was back as the properly elected Prime Minister of a Conservative Government. It was his sixteenth general election. He was feeling all of his seventy-seven years. But there would be a last flourish of that great heart. In 1953, Eden had to take a long leave from the Commons because of ill health. Winston took over the duties of Foreign Secretary and the extra work seemed to rejuvenate him. Thus it was that he was 'in post' when Joseph Stalin died in May. Winston was inspired to issue a warm, friendly invitation to the new Soviet leadership to a summit conference, and even referred to the possibility of a 'Locarno style' pan-European security system that would, presumably, replace the power blocs of the Cold War. The speech seems to have been instinctive. It came as a shock to his own party and to the Americans. The Korean War was just ending; the race for the hydrogen bomb was in full spate. The world was not ready for such bold initiatives. The moment passed; the baton fell. A few weeks later another stroke forced him to take a month's leave, resting at Chartwell. He did not abandon his hopes for a reduction in tensions between the Soviet Union and the West, but circumstances were not conducive to success. War in Indo-China and icy meetings between American and Soviet leaders militated against his ideas.

A great cult of admiration developed around Winston, with a constant stream of adulatory books about his life and times leaving the printing presses. He, who was of course half-American, was especially popular in the United States, and Dwight Eisenhower encouraged the cult by the several congratulatory forewords he provided to biographies of 'the great man'. He was rapidly assuming the status of the greatest living Englishman, and one of the greatest figures in British (and world) history. The British Government, at the behest of the new queen, had already awarded him a state funeral by 1953. The planning began based on the last great civilian state funeral, that of William Gladstone. It soon became a far grander affair and, under Winston's own guidance, looked more like the memorial to the mighty Duke of Wellington. Winston even asked for the great candlesticks that had stood at the corners of the Iron Duke's coffin during his lying-in-state to be resurrected for him. They were.

He had repeatedly refused a peerage, perhaps because it would have interfered with his son Randolph's parliamentary aspirations. But he was installed as a Knight of the Garter in 1953, and later that year made the coronation of the new queen, Elizabeth II, a personal triumph by his gallant speeches. His eightieth birthday in 1954 was a national event of the highest importance – 30,000 cards (one simply addressed to 'The Greatest Man Alive, London') and 900 presents were delivered. A collection by 30,000 subscribers raised £259,000 for a Churchill Trust that would go towards the creation of Churchill College, Cambridge (in 1958). Clement Attlee presented an illuminated address from both Houses of Parliament to him, together with a specially commissioned portrait by Graham Sutherland. This uncompromising picture of an elderly gentleman, that Winston famously described as a remarkable example of 'modern art', was not at all how he wished to be remembered and Clemmie was perfectly happy to throw it on the fire. Civic freedoms, prizes and awards poured in. He beat off the claim of Ernest Hemingway to achieve the Nobel Prize for Literature in 1953, something that only three Britons (Rudyard Kipling, John Galsworthy and George Bernard Shaw) had achieved before. There is a faint, and commendable, suggestion that he would have preferred to win the Peace Prize.

Clemmie had not been well in the summer of 1952, and had gone, with the Duchess of Marlborough, to take a rest cure at a health spa in Italy. It is worth noting that, just as in the days of Lord Randolph and Jennie, it was entirely natural for husband and wife to holiday separately, with friends, and usually as a relief for some ailment or other. While sharing a holiday at Capri with Sarah and her husband, she received a letter from Clarissa announcing her engagement to Anthony Eden. Winston and Clemmie, standing *in loco parentis*, saw her married that August from No 10 Downing Street. 1953 was a strenuous year for a man up in years, with the Garter investiture and the Coronation. At a large Downing Street dinner on 23rd June, Winston had a serious stroke, and his condition, kept secret, deteriorated over the next few days. He was taken to Chartwell to rest and the prognosis was not good. By the time speculation about his condition reached the British press via news stories from America, Winston had made a remarkable recovery. Clemmie was anxious that he should retire from office sooner rather than later. But he battled on, first to wait until the 'Party leader in waiting', Anthony Eden was recovered from his series of operations, and then to 'hold the fort' while the Queen and Prince Philip went on their long Commonwealth tour. He tired easily, and could get depressed, but still he managed to attend Cabinet meetings and the Party conference in October. A signal honour was paid to Clemmie when she was asked to accept the Nobel Prize for Literature on Winston's behalf. (Normally, if a recipient is unwell, his or her country's ambassador to Sweden accepts the prize).

The family had its tribulations. Diana suffered a nervous breakdown that made relations with her mother more than usually fraught. Randolph, a successful journalist, seemed intent on offending as many people as was humanly possible, and Clarissa broke with him completely over a spiteful attack he made on her new husband. Sarah had separated from her second husband. Clemmie was suffering acutely from neuritis, giving great pain to her right arm and shoulder. While nursing her husband and herself, Clemmie had then to help her sister, Nellie, through the last stages of cancer until her death, aged sixty-six, in February 1955.

The celebrations for his eightieth birthday, the Graham Sutherland portrait excepted, were a tremendous, rejuvenating boost to Winston, though Mary Soames recorded in her diary that her 'Mama' collapsed with fatigue. Senior members of the Conservative Party were now openly asking Winston to set a date for handing the premiership over to Eden. Winston would have liked to see another summit meeting to discuss the implications of the advent of the hydrogen bomb, but the Russians could not be brought to the negotiating table. Finally the date for retirement was set for 5th April 1955. Queen Elizabeth paid the unusual tribute of joining a celebratory dinner at No 10 Downing Street on 4th April. It was, of course, a sign of the enormous respect and personal regard she felt towards her Prime Minister, and it quickly became 'established' that this was a unique honour paid by a reigning monarch to her 'first citizen'. This is one more myth that has accreted around Winston, as King George VI had done the same for Stanley Baldwin when he retired in 1937. A party for all the staff at Downing Street was held the next day. Chartwell and life as a private citizen beckoned. At last he could get on and finish *The History of the English-Speaking Peoples*.

The long and gradual decline of life set in from 1958, when a bout of pneumonia left Winston much weakened. A fall in 1960 led to the breaking of a small bone in the neck, but a worse tumble in 1962, while staying at the Hotel de Paris, saw the breaking of a hip bone that had longer term consequences. His London home, 28 Hyde Park Gate, was fitted with lifts to enable him to get about, but he was not able to travel down to his beloved Chartwell for a year. Deafness, for which he resolutely refused to wear a hearing aid, and increasing bouts of lethargy, led to long periods of brooding silence.

Family life could bring joy and tragedy. Great comfort was taken from the arrival of grandchildren (two Churchills, three Sandys' and five Soames'), and the first great-grandchild (to Diana's daughter, Edwina). The Soames family lived at Chartwell Farm and were a constant source of pleasure. Their removal to Hamswell Manor, near Tunbridge Wells, was still within easy motoring. Sarah's third marriage, to Henry Audley, promised much happiness but was tragically ended after just fifteen months as Henry succumbed to a massive heart attack. The heaviest blow of all was the death of Diana in October 1963, by an overdose of sleeping tablets.[3] She had taken to doing excellent work with the Samaritans, and she had seemed in good heart to those of her family who saw her just before the end. It was mere happenstance that there was nobody about when she took the fatal dose. It fell to Mary to convey the news to her mother and father.

Winston remained the Conservative Member of Parliament for Woodford through the general elections of 1955 and 1959, with substantial, if slightly declining majorities. Clemmie kept an eye on constituency affairs for him, and his efficient secretariat dealt with the normal matters of an MP. His last attendance at the House of Commons was in January 1961. The question of how long he could remain as an MP was being increasingly discussed, not least by Clemmie who thought it really was time he stood back from public life. As a General Election approached in 1964, Winston took the decision not to seek re-election.

The Conservative Government of Sir Alec Douglas-Home planned to put before the House of Commons a vote of thanks for Winston's long and distinguished services to Parliament, which would then be conveyed to him at his London home. When Clemmie saw the utterly banal 'appreciation' offered she was deeply displeased. She looked out the stirring address made by the Speaker of the House when the Duke of Wellington left Parliament and compared it to the "mangy address" to her husband. Winston made a final visit to the House on 28th July, and the next day a much more fitting tribute was passed, paying proper respect to his inspirational wartime leadership.

He had been made an honorary citizen of the United States of America in the spring of 1963; his ninetieth birthday in November 1964 saw more national celebrations. But the end was not far off. Another stroke on 11th January 1965 left him semi-conscious but clinging to life. A priest was called to pray over the unconscious Winston. He lasted until early on 24th January 1965, when, with two or three long sighs, he died exactly seventy years to the day and almost to the moment after his father, Lord Randolph.

From 26th to 30th January he was Lying-in-State at Westminster Hall. The funeral coffin was borne to and from the gun carriage by men of the Grenadier Guards; the carriage was towed in procession by naval ratings. After the service at St. Paul's Cathedral, attended by some three thousand people, the casket was carried by motor launch from Tower Pier to the Festival Pier at Waterloo. It was then that the cranes along the river were famously dipped in silent salute. Men of his old regiment, the 4th Hussars, escorted the coffin into Oxfordshire, where Winston was laid to rest at Bladon Church in the bosom of his family. His place in history was secured forever.

Postscript

Winston Churchill's grave is visited by many thousands of tourists each year. It lies in close proximity to that of his father, Lord Randolph, (marked, appropriately with a Celtic cross as a symbol of the Ireland he loved), and of his mother, Jennie. We are frequently asked where Jack is buried. His grave is beside his father and mother, in the row immediately in front of Winston and Clemmie. In death as in life, Jack is in the shadows.[4]

It is something of a truism now that, had Winston retired from public life in the Nineteen Thirties (when he was in his sixties), he would be remembered as a failed politician, notorious for his opportunist changes in party loyalty. He would have established a reputation as a fine writer of history (though not necessarily as a historian) and a gifted painter. The year 1940 changed all that. By his iron will, the product of his family history and character, he became his country's saviour and, by extension, an important element in the fight against one of the greatest threats to freedom in the history of the world. His reputation as one of the great statesmen of the Western democracies is strong and well earned.

It only remains to remind our readers that Winston's early career was advanced at the expense of his younger brother, Jack. The extravagance of their mother in her struggle to maintain her place in high society, itself directed towards Winston's future, was utterly destructive of the family finances. In the chaos of loans and debt, Jack's career prospects were sacrificed in favour of his elder brother. His consistently good school record, and the help of an admiring headmaster at Harrow, would have guaranteed success at university. He might have studied law and would have had some choices of career. He yearned for the army life and, had his father lived, it would have been his. His record in the Oxfordshire Hussars, and on active service in South Africa and on the Western Front and at Gallipoli, show that he was suited to it. All this was denied to him because, in the absence of his father, his spendthrift mother would make no provision for his further education. His mother and his brother combined to coax him into life in the City, where he was supposed to become a stockbroker and 'make millions' for the family. To say that the work was uncongenial to him is to say the least of it. Yet he selflessly remained a constant support to his mother and brother, endlessly arranging their affairs for them, and assisting Winston in some of his great literary endeavours. None of this was acknowledged, then or since. Jack stuck to his path, seeing it as his duty to support them to the best of his ability. He built a successful family life of his own, with a charming wife and three talented children. He was content to be the brother of a famous man, and he was a quiet source of strength during the years of war when Winston needed the love and support of his family to sustain the struggle. We know that he worked on through the great pain of a long illness that he kept to himself. He died as he had lived, without complaint.

Notes

Introduction

1 David Higham *The Dark Lady: Winston Churchills' Mother and her World* Virgin 2006
2 *Finest Hour*, the journal of the International Churchill Society.
3 Ted Morgan *Churchill: Young Man in a Hurry 1874–1915* Simon & Schuster 1982
4 Shane Leslie *End of a Chapter* p.116. He continues: "Few sons have done more for their fathers", referring to Winston's biography of Lord Randolph.
5 Winston S. Churchill *His Father's Son: The Life of Randolph Churchill* Phoenix 1997 p.396
6 Jack Churchill to Jennie, November 1892. from the private papers of Mrs Peregrine Churchill.
7 4th November 1892. Printed in Churchill, R. S. Companion Volume I: Part I, p. 345–6

Chapter 1

1 The family comprised:
George 1844–1892; Frederick 1846–1850; Randolph 1849–1895; Charles 1856–1858; Augustus 1858–1859; Cornelia (Lady Wimborne) 1847–1927; Rosamund (Lady de Ramsey) 1851–1920; Fanny (Lady Tweedmouth) 1853–1904; Anne (Duchess Roxburghe) 1854–1920; Georgiana (Countess Howe) 1860–1906; Sarah (Lady Wilson) 1865–1929.
2 Churchill Archives: CHAR 28/112/8.
3 Churchill, Peregrine and Mitchell, Julian *Jennie* Collins 1974 pp. 23–25.

4 ibid. p. 32

5 ibid. p. 35

6 ibid. p. 61

7 Higham, Charles *The Dark Lady* Virgin Books 2006.

8 From authors conversations with Peregrine Churchill 2001.

9 Churchill and Mitchell *Jennie* p. 75.

10 ibid. p.82

11 Churchill Archives: CHAR 28/5/36.

12 Churchill and Mitchell *Jennie* p.99–101.

Chapter 2

1 Mrs Cornwallis West *The Reminiscences of Lady Randolph Churchill*.

2 R.F. Foster *Randolph Churchill* p.55. We can assume it was the younger sister, Leonie, engaged in such frolics.

3 René Kraus *Young Lady Randolph* pp 82–3.

4 Roy Jenkins *Churchill* Macmillan 2001 pp 7–8. John Lee was at the launch party for this book when Jenkins made his 'confession' about the lack of original research.

5 Peregrine Churchill to *Sunday Telegraph* 29th April 1990.

6 This Jerome family heirloom had gone first with them to Paris. Jennie brought it to London, and took it to Dublin. Jack and Goonie Churchill used it to rock their children. It was inherited by Peregrine who remained childless, and who bequeathed it to Blenheim Palace, where it is now on public display.

7 The Conservatives went from 351 seats to 237, the Liberals from 250 to 353 (an absolute majority) and the Irish Home Rule Party from 51 to 62. William Gladstone became Prime Minister.

Chapter 3

1 Quoted in Anita Leslie *Jennie* p.70.

2 Ibid. p. 77–78.

3 Mrs E.M. Ward *Reminiscences* (Ed. Elliott O'Donnell).

4   Despite our best efforts, we have been unable to trace any of Jennie's paintings. Peregrine did tell us that one good 'anonymous' portrait of Randolph on public display, in Winston's studio at Chartwell, was actually by Jennie. She sold several paintings and we think some must survive in Ireland. There is no record of her painting portraits of either of her sons.

5   W. S. Churchill *Lord Randolph Churchill* Vol I pp. 210–211. Winston refers to his father staying "at a little cottage near Wimbledon", a wholly inappropriate description. The modern writer is David Higham *Dark Lady* p.78.

Chapter 4

1   Quoted in Churchill, R.S. *Winston S. Churchill: Vol 1* p. 48–49
2   Sir Francis Laking, a top physician brought in by Mrs Jerome.
3   Peregrine Churchill and Julian Mitchell *Jennie* p.111.
4   Ibid. p. 114.
5   Virginia Woolf *Life of Roger Fry.*
6   Mrs Cornwallis-West *Reminiscences of Lady Randolph Churchill* p.149.
7   Maurice Baring *The Puppet Show of Memory* 1922.
8   Churchill and Mitchell op. cit. p. 128.
9   ibid. p. 130

Chapter 5

1   Sadly it was later stolen in a burglary. She had a miniature made of it, which passed down through Jack and Peregrine, and has been loaned, with the other medals, by Mrs Peregrine Churchill, to the American Museum at Bath.
2   Randolph won comfortably with 2,576 votes to his opponent's 769.
3   Conservatives: 316; Liberal Unionists: 78, against Liberals: 191 and Irish Nationalists 85.
4   Peregrine Churchill & Julian Mitchell *Jennie* pp. 142–3
5   Quoted in Winston Churchill *Lord Randolph Churchill* Vol II, pp. 171–2.

Chapter 6

1   Churchill and Mitchell. p. 162.
2   Mrs Peregrine Churchill gifted this tiepin, together with other valuable items of Jack's, to the National Army Museum.
3   Letter in the private papers of Mrs Peregrine Churchill.
4   Ralph Martin *Lady Randolph Churchill* Vol 1 p. 226.
5   Quoted from a booklet by Dr Tyerman in correspondence with Mrs Rita Boswell Gibbs, Archivist, Harrow Public School, December 2004.
6   The Manchester Cup was inherited by Jack, who donated it to the Royal Dorset Yacht Club, of which he was a member.
7   We suspect the baneful influence of 'Tante Leonie', of which more later.

Chapter 7

1   All Jack's letters are from the private papers of the late Peregrine Churchill, and have been deposited at the Churchill Archives, Churchill College, Cambridge, by Mrs Peregrine Churchill.
2   This is a reference to an accident that Jack had suffered at Deepdene, when a visiting friend had fired some sort of missile that injured his eye. Jack had to wear glasses for a while after, but it never interfered with his military service in later life.
3   Churchill Archives: 28/10/20.
4   Randolph has bee accused by some authors of profiteering from his political positions, especially where his friends, the Rothschilds bankers, are concerned. This letter suggests otherwise, as does his permanent shortage of funds.
5   Letter from Winston to Jack 11th July 1891.

Chapter 8

1   See Chapter 17;
2   MARB 1/15. RSC to Duchess 14th January 1892. Churchill College, Camridge.
3   From the personal papers of Mrs Peregrine Churchill.

4   Elizabeth Kehoe *Fortune's Daughters*
5   Daisy, Countess Warwick *Discretions*

Chapter 10

1   Dr Mather has deduced that this is symptomatic of Raynaud's Disease, a serious malady affecting heavy smokers.
2   For the record the son of Oscar Wilde told Peregrine that Harris repeated exactly the same story about his father. It seems Harris merely change the names to fit the latest of his victims of malicious gossip.
3   See Chapter 1.
4   Classic description of a bipolar disorder.
5   Source: The private papers of Mrs Peregrine Churchill.
6   R. F. Foster *Lord Randolph Churchill – A Political Life* p. 218.
7   Many of Randolph's problems would have been exacerbated by heavy consumption of alcohol. This was an age of heavy drinking but when writers produce huge wine bills as evidence of this, they fail to appreciate that a busy political/aristocratic household would require a large and well-stocked cellar.
8   Peregrine Churchill in conversation with the authors, 2001.
9   Manuscripts written by Peregrine Churchill, August and October 1991.
10 Churchill Archives. 29/98/41–42.
11 Authors interview with Lady Soames, who was quoting conversations between Winston and Anthony Montague Browne, Winston's Secretary.
12 From a letter of 9th August 1975, in the private papers of Mrs Peregrine Churchill. This letter claims that Sunny Marlborough said his father also died of syphilis, infected by the same French woman as Randolph! 'Blandford' in fact died of a heart attack.

Chapter 11

1   Of the three Trustees, one had died already, and Lord Curzon made no interference in the family affairs. Jennie was left in charge.

2   The Prince would have been referring to the day Randolph ordered him out of his house, on discovering him alone there with Jennie.
3   Shane Leslie *Long Shadows*.
4   The Duchess Lily married for the 3rd time, Lord William de la Poer Beresford VC (1847–1900).
5   Diary entry 15th August 1915: Jean, Lady Hamilton.
6   George Cornwallis-West *Edwardian Hey-days*.
7   Tim Coates *Patsy*.

Chapter 12

1   Quoted in Churchill, R.S. *Winston S. Churchill: Vol 1* p. 255
2   Printed in *Companion Volume 1: Part 2* to the above p.720–721

Chapter 13

1   See Chapter 12, where Jennie says "800 a year goes to you 2 boys"; we shall see that she was giving Winston an allowance of £500 a year.
2   Winston is here referring to what he expected to inherit after Jennie's death. This seems to be all the boys knew of the terms of their father's will, that they would share whatever was in the Trust Fund.
3   Printed in *Companion Vol 1 Part 2* p. 901 to Churchill, R. S. *Winston S. Churchill: Vol 1*
4   Ibid. p. 922
5   Ibid. p. 859
6   From an original manuscript letter in the private collection of Mrs Peregrine Churchill.
7   Consuelo Vanderbilt Balsan *The Glitter and the Gold*.

Chapter 14

1   See Winston Churchill *From London to Ladysmith* and *My Early Life*, and Celia Sandys *Wanted Dead or Alive*.

2   Amery, Leo *Times History of the War in South Africa* Vol. II, p. 94.

3   This bullet was mounted on a small chain and kept as a souvenir. It has been donated to the National Army Museum, London, with other Jack Churchill items by Mrs Peregrine Churchill, Jack's daughter-in-law. It has recently been on display at the Cabinet War Rooms.

4   A number of works say that Jack was the very first wounded man received on the ship, but other enlisted men had been treated on board before he, the first officer, arrived.

5   Griffiths, K. *Thank God we Kept the Flag Flying* p.344.

6   Jack Churchill to Lady Randolph. 3rd April 1900, CHAR 28/32/1.

7   Jack Churchill to Lady Randolph. 28th April 1900, CHAR 28/32/2.

8   Jack Churchill to Lady Randolph. 2nd June 1900, CHAR 28/32/3.

9   ibid.

10 Winston Churchill to Jack, 31st July 1900.

11 Jack Churchill to Lady Randolph. 26th June 1900, CHAR 28/32/4.

12 Jack Churchill to Lady Randolph. 2nd July 1900, CHAR 28/32/6.

13 Jack Churchill to Winston. 10th July 1900, CHAR 28/32/7.

14 Jack Churchill to Winston. 12th September 1900, CHAR 28/32/10–13.

15 Jack Churchill to Winston. 3rd October 1900, CHAR 28/32/14–15.

16 Original letter in the private papers of Mrs Peregrine Churchill.

Chapter 15

1   George Cornwallis West *Edwardian Hey-Days*.

2   John Bradley (Ed) *Lady Curzon's India: Letters of a Vicereine* 1985.

3 Jean, Lady Hamilton. Diary entry 27th April 1902, recalling an earlier incident.

4 Diary entry 3rd December 1903, recalling an earlier incident.

5 Diary entry 14th June 1903, recalling an earlier incident.

6 Diary entry 30th November 1901.

7 This cup is now at the National Army Museum, London, a gift from Mrs Peregrine Churchill.

8 Celia Lee *Jean, Lady Hamilton (1861–1941): A Soldier's Wife* pp. 41–42.

9 Jean, Lady Hamilton. Diary entry, Sunday 3rd January 1904, Gopsall.

10 The philanderer Colonel Harry Scobell would spend a weekend at Salisbury Hall with Lady Margerie Orr-Ewing, with whom he was having an affair. Scobell was the hypocrite who played a major part in having his brother-in-law, Colonel Charles A'Court, thrown out of the army for having an affair with Mary, Lady Garstin, the wife of Sir William Garstin. In 1906, Scobell and Lady Margerie were photographed in the garden at Salisbury Hall, (she swathed almost head to toe in a fox fur coat), whilst Jack Churchill showed them his vegetable patch!

Chapter 16

1 Pronounced 'Barty'.

2 From notes taken at an interview with her daughter, Clarissa, Countess of Avon.

3 ditto

4 Jean Hamilton Diary, Sunday 12th July 1908.

5 Now displayed in the National Army Museum, London SW3, a gift from Mrs Peregrine Churchill.

6 Quoted in Soames, Mary *Clementine Churchill* 2nd Ed. P. 41

7 Quoted in Churchill, R. S. *Winston S. Churchill: Vol II* p. 263

8 Soames, Mary op. cit. p. 49

9 Quoted in *Companion Vol II Part* 2 p. 803 to Churchill, R. S. op. cit.

10 Churchill, R. S. op. cit. p.274

Chapter 17

1   Jack Churchill to Lady Gwendeline Bertie, 15th April 1908.
2   George Cornwallis-West to Jack Churchill, letter of condolence, 9th July 1941.
3   Diary entry 21st February 1910.
4   Pamela, Countess of Lytton – tribute to Goonie in the *Times* 18th July 1941.
5   Jean, Lady Hamilton. Diary entry 9th July 1910.
6   In the private papers of Mrs Peregrine Churchill. It is not clear whether this draft was ever sent.
7   Jean, Lady Hamilton. Diary entry 17th August 1910.
8   Jean, Lady Hamilton. Diary entry 28th May 1912.
9   Jack Churchill to Jennie West 21st July 1913. CHAR 28/33/1.
10 CHAR 28/33/3.
11 Source: Lord Randolph's will dated 1883 from the private papers of Mrs Peregrine Churchill.
12 To the tune of £600 each – a total of £16,800 (£840,000 today).
13 CHAR 28/33/5. This vitally important letter has never been quoted at length before.
14 CHAR 28/33/7
15 CHAR 28/33/8
16 CHAR 28/33/12 7th March 1914.
17 Churchill and Mitchell Jennie p. 248.

Chapter 18

1   de la Grange, Baroness Ernest *Open House in Flanders* John Murray 1929 p.22.
2   Jerrold, Douglas *The Royal Naval Division* 2nd edition Hutchinson 1927 p.24.
3   Printed in *Companion Vol 3 Part1* p. 270 to Gilbert, M. *Winston S. Churchill: Vol3*
4   CHAR 28/33/15 20th November 1914.
5   CHAR28/121/1 1st February 1915.
6   Churchill, Major John S. Gallipoli Diary, Saturday 10th April 1915.

7   CHAR28/121/7 20th April 1915.
8   Later in the campaign, when this narrow landing place was secured, Jack captured its essence in a poem he sent to the newssheet published by Headquarters MEF:

> Y Beach, the Scottish Borderer cried,
> While panting up the steep hillside
> To call this a beach is stiff
> It's nothing but a bloody cliff.
> Why Beach?

9   Churchill, Major John S. op. cit. Thursday 28th April 1915.
10 ibid. Thursday 24th June 1915.
11 CHAR28/121/9 & 11 20th June and 29th July 1915.
12 Churchill, Major John S. op. cit. Saturday 6th October 1915.
13 CHAR28/121/18–19 22nd October 1915.

Chapter 19

1   Churchill College Cambridge, CHAR28 File 121/37.
2   CHAR28 File 121/39
3   CHAR28 File 121/42
4   The National Archives WO256/14.
5   CHAR28 File 121/53
6   See Celia Lee *Jean, Lady Hamilton 1861–1941 A Soldier's Wife* pp. 198–9.

Chapter 20

1   Norman Leslie, Leonie's son, killed in action in 1914.
2   CHAR28/121/82.
3   Authors interview with Clarissa, Countess of Avon.
4   Jean, Lady Hamilton. Diary entry 11th August 1919.
5   ibid 19th May 1919, 1 Hyde Park Gardens.
6   Ibid 10th June 1921.
7   Related to the authors by Claire Aston, guide at Kensal Green cemetery.
8   John Spencer Churchill *Crowded Canvas* Odhams Press 1961.

9 Nicholl, Manisty & Co to Major John S S Churchill, DSO, 20th April 1926.
   In the private papers of Mrs Peregrine Churchill.

Chapter 21

1 John Spencer Churchill *Crowded Canvas* Odhams 1961.
2 Subscribers included the press barons, Beaverbrook and Harmsworth, the Prince of Wales and Duke of Westminster, Sir Ian Hamilton, Charlie Chaplin, Harold Macmillan and Duff Cooper.
3 Because of the war and its subsequent six-volume history it would not actually appear until 1957.
4 Maurice Ashley and Keith Feiling worked on *Marlborough*.
5 Lady Gwendeline Churchill to Peregrine, 26th May 1934, private papers of Mrs Peregrine Churchill.
6 See Mary Soames *Clementine Churchill* (Second edition) Doubleday 2002 pp. 298–9.

Chapter 22

1 Clementine Churchill to Winston, 27th June 1949. See Mary Soames *Clementine Churchill* Doubleday 2002 p. 325.
2 Peregrine Churchill to his mother. Sent from Flat 7, 46 Upper Grosvenor Street, 23rd October 1940. Private papers of Mrs Peregrine Churchill.
3 Lady Gwendeline Churchill, Hamstead Marshall, Newbury, Bucks, Wed. 25th September 1940, to Peregrine. Private papers of Mrs Peregrine Churchill.
4 Amongst Peregrine's papers were a number of sheets of notepaper inherited from his father simply bearing Winston's signature at the bottom, suggesting that Jack was authorised to send out letters 'signed' by the Prime Minister on his behalf.
5 The Times. 11th July 1941.
6 These tributes are all from the private papers of Mrs Peregrine Churchill.

7   Diary entry – 9th May 1945. James Lees-Milne (Ed. M. Bloch)
     "Prophesying Peace:Diaries 1944–1945, p. 189.

Chapter 23

1   A masterly exploration of the whole work is in David Reynold's
     *In Command of History: Fighting and Writing the Second
     World War* Penguin: Allen Lane 2004.
2   Lord Moran *Winston Churchill: The Struggle for Survival
     1940–1965* Heron Books 1966 p.318.
3   It is debated whether this was suicide, or a tragic, accidental,
     overdose.
4   Peregrine Churchill has joined his father there and, at the time
     of writing, plans are being laid for the grave to be re-furbished
     with a more durable stone.

Sources and Bibliography

Primary Sources

Jennie and Jack Churchill's letters, Chartwell Papers, Churchill Archives, Churchill College, Cambridge

Lady Hamilton's Diaries, Liddell Hart Centre for Military Archives, King's College, London, by kind permission of Mr Ian Hamilton.

Peregrine Churchill's private papers, by kind permission of Mrs Peregrine Churchill.

Published Sources

Airlie, Mabel, Countess of, *With the Guards We Shall Go* Hodder and Stoughton 1933

Asquith, Lady Cynthia, *Diaries 1915–18*, Knopf 1969

Churchill, John Spencer, *Crowded Canvas*, Odhams Press 1961

_____, Peregrine and Mitchell, Julian, *Jennie: Lady Randolph Churchill: A Portrait with Letters*, Collins 1974

_____, Randolph S., *Winston S. Churchill I: Youth 1874–1900* Heinemann 1966

_____, Randolph S., *Companion Volumes, two parts* Heinemann 1967

_____, Randolph S., *Winston S. Churchill II: Young Statesman 1901–1914* Heinemann 1967

_____, Randolph S., *Companion Volumes, three parts* Heinemann 1969

_____, Winston S. *My Early Life* Thornton Butterworth 1930

Coates, Tim, *Patsy: The Story of Mary Cornwallis-West*, Bloomsbury 2003

Colville, John, *The Fringes of Power: Downing Street Diaries 1939–1955*, revised edition Weidenfeld & Nicolson 2004

———, John, *Winston Churchill and his Inner Circle*, Wyndham 1981

Cornwallis-West, George, *Edwardian Hey-Days*, Putnam 1930

———, Mrs George, *Reminiscences of Lady Randolph Churchill*, The Century Co. 1908

Foster, Roy, *Lord Randolph Churchill: A Political Life*, Oxford 1981

Gilbert, Martin *Winston S. Churchill III: 1914–1916* Heinemann 1971

———, Martin *Companion Volumes, two parts* Heinemann 1972

———, Martin *Winston S. Churchill IV: 1917–1922* Heinemann 1975

———, Martin *Winston S. Churchill V: 1922–1939* Heinemann 1976

———, Martin *Winston S. Churchill VI: Finest Hour 1939–1941* Heinemann 1983

———, Martin *Winston S. Churchill VII: Road to Victory 1941–1945* Heinemann 1986

Haffner, Sebastian, *Churchill*, Haus Publishing 2003

Harris, Frank, *My Life and Loves* Privately printed, Paris 1922

Higham, David, *Dark Lady: Winston Churchill's Mother and her World*, Virgin 2006

Hill, Malcolm, *Churchill: His Radical Decade*, Othila Press 1999

Holmes, Richard, *In the Footsteps of Churchill*, BBC 2005

Jenkins, Roy, *Churchill*, Macmillan 2001

Kehoe, Elizabeth, *Fortune's Daughters: The Extravagant Lives of the Jerome Sisters*, Atlantic 2004

Keegan, John, *Churchill*, Phoenix 2003

Kraus, René, *Young Lady Randolph*, Jarrolds n.d.

Lang, Theo, *My Darling Daisy*, Michael Joseph 1966

Lee, Celia, *Jean, Lady Hamilton: A Soldier's Wife 1861–1941*, Celia Lee 2001

Lee, John, *A Soldier's Life: General Sir Ian Hamilton 1853–1947*, Macmillan 2000

Leslie, Anita, *Edwardians in Love*, Arrow 1974

———, Anita, *The Fabulous Leonard Jerome*, Hutchinson 1954

_____, Anita, *Jennie: The Mother of Winston Churchill*, Hutchinson 1969

_____, Shane, *Long Shadows*, John Murray 1966

_____, Shane, *Men Were Different*, Books for Libraries Press 1967 (1937)

Lukacs, John, *Churchill: Visionary, Statesman, Historian*, Yale UP 2002

Martin, Ralph G., *Lady Randolph Churchill: Volume One 1854–1895*, Sphere 1974

_____, Ralph G., *Lady Randolph Churchill: Volume Two 1895–1921*, Sphere 1974

Mather, Dr John H. MD *Lord Randolph Churchill: Maladies et Mort* Finest Hour No. 93 Winter 1996–7

Moran, Lord, *Churchill: The Struggle for Survival 1940–1965*, Heron Books 1966

Morgan, Ted, *Churchill: Young Man in a Hurry 1874–1915*, Simon & Schuster 1982

Ramsden, John, *Man of the Century: Winston Churchill and his Legend Since 1945*, Harper Collins 2002

Reynolds, David, *In Command of History: Churchill Fighting and Writing the Second World War*, Penguin:Allen Lane 2004

Rhodes James, Robert, *Lord Randolph Churchill*, Weidenfeld & Nicolson 1965

_____, *Rosebery*, Phoenix 1995

Rosebery, Lord, *Lord Randolph Churchill*, Humphreys 1906

Russell, Douglas S., *Winston Churchill: Soldier*, Brasseys 2005

Sandys, Celia, *Wanted Dead or Alive*, Harper Collins 1999

Soames, Mary, *Clementine Churchill*, second edition, Doubleday 2002

_____, Mary, *Speaking for Themselves: The Personal Letters of Winston and Clementine Churchill*, Doubleday 1998

Woods, Frederick, *Young Winston's Wars*, Leo Cooper 1975

Annotated Index of Names

Abbreviations used: LRC or R – Lord Randolph Churchill; W – Winston Churchill; J – Jack Churchill; HoC – House of Commons; HoL – House of Lords; PoW – Prince of Wales; SoS – Secretary of State; DoM – Duke of Marlborough.

married 1952, Sir Anthony Eden: xx; relationship with mother and father 317–18; talk at Chartwell was of war 322; studying at Sorbonne, Goonie's cocerns 323, 324; decoding ciphers in the Communications Dept., Foreign Office 327; engaged to Anthony Eden; married from 10 Downing St. 343; mentioned 342, 344.

Churchill, The Honourable Clementine, (Clemmie), (*née*) Hozier; later Baroness Spencer Churchill of Chartwell GBE; born 1st April 1885, at 75 Grosvenor St, London; second daughter of Sir Henry Montagu Hozier and Lady Blanche (*née*) Ogilvy, daughter of Lord and Lady Airlie; married 12th September 1908, Winston Leonard, elder son of Lord Randolph Spencer Churchill and Jennie, (*née*) Jerome: Jennie first introduces to Winston summer 1904 211; education and family background 221; CH16 description of 234; a Liberal supporter 234–5; writes to Jennie 13th Apr. 08; goes to Germany with mother 235; WSC writes to frequently 236; visits Salisbury Hall 28th May 236; at Oxfordshire Hussars' manoeuvres; receives invitation to Blenheim Palace; engagement 237–8; writes to Nellie of family heirloom ring 238; wedding plans; St Margaret's Westminster; receives love letter from W 238–9; bride and wedding 239–40; going away outfit 241;CH17 moves into 12 Bolton Street 243; May 1909 moves into larger house 33 Eccleston Sq. 244; gives birth to Diana 11th July 245; suffers from depression 245–6; takes two holidays 246; supports women's suffrage 246; gives birth to Randolph May 1911 252; King George V sends carriage for to attend his Coronation 252–3; on holiday to Bavarian Alps; launches battleship *Centurion*; recreational activities; accompanies W to Belfast; suffers miscarriage; publishes letter on women's suffrage; goes with W on Mediterranean cruise 254–5; moves into Admiralty house April 1913; Eccleston Sq. rented out 255; on holiday with family 1914, 261; CH18 gives birth to Sarah 1914 267; CH19 takes up canteen work 285; moves in temporarily with Wimbornes 21 Arlington St 285; with children at Lullenden 291; offers to give away 4th unborn child Marigold 294–5; CH20 death of Marigold 1919 300, 303–4; death of mother 300–01; death of brother Bill 301; would like country home 303; finds Chartwell 303; new home 2 Sussex Sq 298, 304; holiday in Devon 304; birth of Mary Sept. 1922 304; CH21 W takes to travel in America 1931 315; cruising with Lord Moyne

to house 293; CH20 living at Bedford Sq. 296; going to Paris to see Jack 296–7; living in Mozart's house 297; mother said to have run away 298–9; pregnant and wishing for a girl 299; gives birth to Clarissa June 1920, 300; rents *Menabilly* for summer holidays 1921, 302; letter to Jack about the children 303; CH21 on family matters 313; CH22 ill with lung cancer; residing in countryside with Rosie Ridley 328; visited by Clemmie 329; Jack visits at weekends 329; 1941 death of; tributes to in *Times*; buried Begbrook Convent cemetery 331–2.

Churchill, Jennie, (Lady Randolph), second daughter of Leonard Jerome and Clarissa (Clara) (*née*) Hall: xix–xxi, CH1 meets and falls in love with Lord Randolph Churchill Cowes week 1873, 1–2; accepts LRC's proposal of marriage; 1870 comes with her family to live in London 5; education and piano training 5–6; returns to Paris; meets DoM 11; wedding day 15th April 1874 Paris 11–12; life at Blenheim Palace; pregnancy 12; first home No. 1 Curzon Street 12; W born at Blenheim prematurely 13–14; returns to Curzon Street Jan. 1895 14; appoints Mrs Elizabeth Everest nanny to W 14; money troubles begin 14–15; writes loves letters to R from Paris; R's medicine packed in her luggage in error 17–18; CH2 takes up residence in 'little' White Lodge, Phoenix Park, Dublin; falls from horse 19–20; assists Duchess with famine relief work 21; keeps R in touch by letter 21; not the life she had imagined 23; supports R politically and ambitious for him 23–4; strain of R dividing his time between home and London 24; discusses son with Empress Elizabeth 25–6; pregnant with second child summer 1879 27; *Reminiscences* 27; returns to England 29; new home St James's Place 29; CH3 writes to mother of shortage of money 1880 33; first mention of difficulty with W 33; hopes for R's success in cabinet 33–4; involved in politics 34; 1881 moves to live temporarily at Blenheim; writes to mother of unhappiness 34–5; dislike of in-laws; political functions a drain on finances 35; writes a diary 35–6; painting; taught W & J 36,38; family returns to St James's Place 1882 36; mid-Feb. R very ill 36; takes care of him at home 37; first meets Kinsky 1881 37; takes R to hotel 37; returns home April to St James's Place 38; sails with R to New York 38; family re-union; money from father 39; returned home 27th May 39; rents "Beech Lodge" for summer 39; CH4 new home 2 Connaught Place 43; typhoid fever 43–6; skeletons in cellar of St James's Place 44; exchange of letters between Jennie, her family and R 44–6; Money worries 45; PoW showers with gifts 48; spent part of summer 1883 at Blenheim with W&J and cousin Sunny 49; PoW introduces to Marlborough House Set 49; begins sexual relationship with Kinsky 50; founder member of Primrose League 51; Leonie's wedding 54; CH5 campaigns for R in bye-election; victory speech 59; expects to be first American lady in Downing St; active in charity for Women in India; Queen awards Order of Crown of India 61; sits by W's sick bed 63–4; fears R has another woman; confides in Dowager Duchess 65–6; Duchess raises their financial problems 66; advises against fast set and jealousy 67–8; CH6 year 1886 begins badly; financial and marital problems; press speculation about divorce 70; dismay over R's resignation; writes to R 71–2; with R at Cowes week 73; letter writing amongst family 74; visits W at Brighton School 75; with R to Russia 75–6; in Germany with Kinsky 76; W writes from Ventnor 80; riding with R and enjoying horse racing 80–1; visits W who is 'on reports' 83; R returns home early and finds PoW in house alone with 83; CH7 letter to W who did not acknowledge father's £5 88; R takes Banstead Manor; family holiday 89–90; holidaying for the winter at Banstead with W&J 92; W wants a gun 92; father ill in England 92; visited Harrow; in frequent touch with Welldon about W's progress 94; W finds breakfasting with Kinsky 96; summer 1891 with Kinsky at Banstead 96; writes to R in SA of holiday at Banstead 96–7; worrying about money; school fees a drain on finances 99; Banstead given up; moves in with Dowager Duchess at 50 Grosvenor Sq.; complains to R 101; R suffers from mood swings; deterioration in domestic lives 103; affair with Wolverton 104; in Scotland for her health; in great deal of pain; Roose calls in Dr Keith, gynaecological specialist 109; staying at Canford Manor 111; CH9 spends time in Paris 126; plans world trip with R 132; 2 Connaught Place sold 133; family dinner before parting 133; CH10 arrive New York 27th June '94; attends banquets, new Manhattan cocktail 134; writes to Leonie that R is not well; Keith optimistic; going from Vancouver to San Francisco; hounded by press 135–6; touring Japan; shopping; photographs taken with R and sends to W&J 140; arrives in China;

Paris 288; CH20 sends Johnny and Peregrine to Harrow Public School 306; domestic life 308; gives sons fatherly advice 309; attending to W's mortgage on Chartwell Apr. 1926 310; and strike breaking 1926 310–11; accompanies W to North America on a three-month trip 312; CH21 takes family on cruise of Scandinavia and Baltic each summer 319; CH22 home at Chester Tce. bombed 328; influence on W 334; CH23 moves in with Johnny; has new apartment 338; winter 1946–7 health collapses; Lord Moran's opinion of 340; death of; and memorial service 341; postscript to 346–7.

Education: Sept. 1887 Elstree Prep School 74; Elstree School reports; marks in gymnastics 82; Jennie sends newspapers 82; top of his form with 300 marks 87; returns to school autumn 1891; confidently predicts he can pass Harrow entrance exam a year early 104–5; father writes to Welldon about J's entry into Harrow; Welldon replies 105; enters Harrow Sept. 1892, youngest boy in school; shares room with W 107–8; father rewards with a fine gold watch 108; placed in class of 32 boys 108; school reports from Harrow School; passes Harrow entrance exam at first attempt; undertakes arithmetic exam and passes 108; soon rises to 20th place; coming top in essay 108; sets new record at Harrow for no punishment 110; popularity at Harrow 113; Jennie visits Harrow hears praises of J from Welldon 116; R writes of 'capital report' 116; finds W noisy and disruptive in their room 109; receives new clock and camera for his good work 116; French improves; returns to Harrow Sept. 93; father reprimands for not writing often enough; Welldon anxious to see R about J's career 124; father attends speech day 131.

Career: influence of W upon 170; Welldon's influence upon; possibility of degree at Oxford; intentions misunderstood by mother172; discussion of 173–5; 177–8; W pours cold water on 173–4; goes to France to learn French for a year 174; mother's letters to 180; on W's spending 175–6; aged 17 still treated as a child; Jennie wants him to go into the City and train as a stockbroker 177–8; returning from France 178–9; wants career settled 178–9; Jennie & W spend so much no money to finance J's career 180–1; cajoled into going into the City as a clerk for

GHQ personnel 280; Hamilton dismissed 280; without a job 281; Birdwood retains as Camp Commandant; prepares camps on Imbros; evacuation of Gallipoli peninsula 282; mentioned in Hamilton's Final Despatch; awarded French Legion of Honour; appointed to 1st ANZAC Corps bound for Western Front 283; sails from Egypt to France; moves by train to the front 286–7; responsible for smooth running of Corps HQ 287; writes to mother of savage fighting 16th Aug. 287–8; and battle of Somme 288–9; dreadful conditions; escorting Birdwood; and journalists 290–1; on the US joining in the war; on the Germans and spring 1918 offensive 292; 100 days offensive on Western Front; end of war Nov. 1918 295; Oct. 1918 brothers photographed together at triumph liberated Lille 295; war over – but not for Jack; writes to mother 6th March 1919 hoping to receive order to come home 296.

Returns to the City: Stockbroker with Vickers da Costa; later partner 298; 1921 leaves Oxfordshire Hussars 304; stock market crisis 314; well established at Vickers; family kept in comfort; sells 41 Comwell Rd.; buys 42 Chester Terrace, Regent's Park 319; moves into Downing St to help W 328; divides times between W and his job in the City 329; has new apartment 338.

Finances: finds Harrow School expensive; keeps account book 109; has to pay W's unpaid bills 112; money being spent on Jennie & W 175; careful account of spending in France 180; W asks to share burden of mother's loan 185; advises mother against casinos 195; ever cautious with money 223; Lumley has still not finalised father's affairs 224; salary insufficient on which to marry Goonie; effects of financial crisis in the City 227–31 increase in salary of £500 p.a. 231; discovers true terms of father's will and Trust Fund for first time 256–9; sounds financial warnings on threat of war 261; staff position salaried at £550 p.a.; writes to mother that Goonie has £1,200 to live on 279; writes home of financial problems of his family 281; money worries as Nelke reduces his retainer 282; finances during war 288; worried about place in firm when Nelke dies 291; rent from home; Goonie sells off furniture 292; helped minimise losses to family during Wall St crash 313;

Health: usual illnesses; measles, whooping cough, chickenpox,

2; background and school days; introduction to politics at an early age; interest in chess 4; student at Merton College, Oxford; youth after graduation; writes to his father about Jennie and marriage proposal 6; father's hostile reaction 7; wins over Mrs Jerome 9; goes into politics to secure father's consent 9; consent to marriage 10; father's marriage settlement 11; writes to Mrs Jerome of birth of W 14; buys lease on house 48 Charles Street 15; family and social life and love letters 15–16; anxious about W's health 16; row with PoW over Blandford's affair with Lady Aylesford 16–17; ostracised by society 16; threatens PoW with publication of intimate letters 16–17; looks after W whilst Jennie is in Paris; exchange of letters with Jennie 17; CH2 Sec. to his father in Dublin 19; torn between wife and political commitment 20; writes to mother of his marriage 25; finding a boarding school for W 41; CH4 holidaying in Algeria 43; March 1883, full reconciliation with PoW who dines at LRC's home 47–8; J and R restored to highest rank in society 48; death of father 49; in Germany 49; plans railway extension with Blandford 50; responds to Jennie's letters about W's stabbing 55–6; CH5 on railways construction in India 59 60; fishing trip with Roberts 60; rushes to W in Brighton 63–4; wife campaigning for R in election 64; writes from Europe; sending presents 67–8; CH6 writes to *Sun* reporter denying divorce 70; writes to Welldon about entry for W 73–4; returns home March 1887; buys *L'Abbesse de Jouarre* 74–5; trip to Russia 75–6; Germany 76; *L'Abbesse* wins PoW Handicap; Portland Plate; November 1889, the Oaks at Epsom; 1890, the Manchester Cup 80–1; sends W money for a bicycle 83; CH7 elected to Jockey Club 90; takes W&J on visit to the Astors; takes W&J and friends on expedition up the river 90; writes to mother, offered the Chairmanship of a gem mine 92; leaves for South Africa 93; *Daily Graphic* commissions series of letters 93; deep level mining finds gold 99; writes to Jennie Nov. 1891 of disillusionment with politics 99; returns from SA Jan. 1892 102; writes to Natty Rothschild saying Jennie is living with Wolverton 103; sends money and hampers to sons at Harrow 108; death of Blandford 110; CH8 sees Bismarck in Germany 116–7; CH9 writes letter to mother praising W 124; arranging J's army career 125–6; writes to W of meeting with Lord Roberts 127; CH10

may have been "Chronic inflammation of the brain" brought on by exhaustion 150; discussion of other possible illnesses 151; two-year study of medical reports by Dr John H. Mather 151–3; and Leonie Leslie 153–4.

Political career: enters politics 9; MP for Woodstock 10; election campaign and victory 10; travelling between Dublin and London 19; maiden speech 1874 20; meets Lord Justice Fitzgibbon 20–21; Sec. of mother's Famine Relief Fund 21; wife accompanies to all 32 counties of Ireland 22; on Irish Nationalist movement in HoC 22; expert on Irish matters: education funding 22; condemns England's record in Ireland 22; on Russo-Turkish War 1877–78 23; General Election 1880; holds his seat 29–30; political star is born 1880–2 31; joins 4th Party 31–2; on Employer's Liability Bill 32; opposes Irish Coercion Bill 34; murder of Cavendish and Burke in Ireland 39; returns to HoC 3rd July 1882, leads fight against Liberals; opposes war in Egypt; 40; Fourth Party developing Tory Democracy; NUCA 40; renewed friendship with PoW 48; Bradlaugh case 48–9; Primrose League 1883 50–1; redrawing of political boundaries 52; General Election; stands for South Birmingham seat 52; SoS for India 55–6, 57–8; opposes Coercive Crimes Act 57; stands in bye-election 1885; on Burma; on Irish reforms 60; General Election Nov. 1885; fails to win Centl. Birmingham; wins Paddington South 61–2; position on Ireland 62–3; public meeting in Belfast 63; goes fishing in Norway; election result; Tories triumph; Leader of the HoC and Chancellor of the Exchequer 64; talked of as next PM 65; Treasury shake up 68; resigns abruptly 68; letter to *The Times* 69; returns to HoC after foreign travels; addresses public meetings 72; Hon. Doctorate of Law at Cambridge 81; HoC July 1889 supports more money for the children of the PoW 83; attacks brewers 83; plans for local govt. in Ireland 84; backs down over South Birmingham seat 84; Piggot forgeries implicating Charles Stewart Parnell in Phoenix Park murders 85–6; writes to Paddington constituency 92–3; resumes seat in HoC Feb. 1992; recognises growing power of organised labour; 105–6; in favour of the mineworkers in 8 Hour Bill; Gen. Election called for July 1892; returned unopposed but Tories suffer election defeat 106; writes

state entry into Dublin 19; experiences in Dublin 21–2; subject of letters between parents; first signature 24; start of ill health 25; portrait painted 1878 25; suffers fall from donkey 25; start of education 26–7, 36; jealous of new baby J 29; CH3 7th birthday present 35; noisy and boisterous 35; taught to paint by his mother 36; at Blenheim with Everest during father's illness 38; early letter to papa 38; CH4 starts at St George's School 41–3; letters home 42; presented to PoW 48; toy soldiers 51; parents take away from St George's 53–4; dreadful legends about 53; wants revenge on Kynnersley 53–4; writes R for copies of autograph 56; CH5 father's school visits 60–1; upset father did not visit 61–2; CH6 at pantomime in Brighton 71; Buffalo Bill show 72–3; visits royal yacht; meets PoW and Prince George 72; bad behaviour at home; on holiday in Ventnor with Everest and J 73, 80; PoW presents with tie pin; 73; 1887 last term at Brighton School 74; 14th Birthday father inspects toy soldiers; W says he wants to join the army 81; CH7 thanks father for postal order 86; Kinsky sets up target range and teaches W&J to shoot 90; writes to father on Derby Day 95; and friendship with Kinsky 96; summer of adventure with J, Kinsky and Dudley at Banstead 1891. 97; June, receives long letter from father of his adventures in SA 97; replies 97–8; father brings antelope's head as present 102; fires gun and upsets father; long discussion ensues 107; receives letter from father of mother's illness 109; letter from Lady Wilton 111; accompanied by Eton master, goes on holiday to Europe; takes J boating and he nearly drowns 116–117; CH9 enters Sandhurst Sept. 1893; enjoys work; wants to go to London; R refuses 122–3; getting on well with father; out together socially 124; father writes to about meeting with Lord Roberts 127; causes upset by arriving late for lunch with father and Lord Roberts; in talks with Col. Brabazon to join the 4th Hussars 128; father writes objecting to too many visits to London; provides advice on importance of hard work 128–9; upsets father by loosing valuable gold watch 130–1; mother sympathises with 131; father writing friendly letters to again 131; CH12 falls in love with Pamela Plowden in India 171; CH14 *River War* pub. 197; CH15 heartbroken over loss of Pamela; tries to court Birdie Stewart 215–6; and Jean Hamilton on love 215–6; attends opening of Aswan Dam Oct. 1902 217; first

now 28 Hyde Pk Gate 344; becomes a grandfather 345; HoC vote of thanks to; Honorary citizen of the US 345; death of 24th January 1965; lying in state and funeral of; buried Bladon cemetery; Postscript 346.

Education: starts at St George's Prep. School 3rd Nov. 1882, 41–3; invoice for high fees 45; school reports St George's: 45–6, 50,51,52; tyrannical regime 46–7; very happy at school 51; father sends *Treasure Island* as birthday present 51; early sign of unhappiness 52; settles into Brighton School; begins stamp collection; 54; school reports Brighton School: rapid improvement in work 54–5, 57; stabbed 55; glowing reports of progress 72; 1887 top marks in several subjects 74; 1885 mother engages governess 61; father selecting public school for; took up boxing and swimming 74; Harrow entrance exam. 77–8; enters Harrow 17th April 1888 77–8; expenses 78; placed in special small house with Mr Davidson; joins rifle corps 78, 83; school reports Harrow School: Davidson writes to Jennie of W's bad performance 78–9; improves; wins prize for 1,200 lines of Macaulay from memory 80; denied remove; excels at Shakespeare 80; R writes to Welldon re W's career preference; R visits Harrow 81; gets his remove 1889 82; R writes to Welldon to take W into a big house; Welldon replies 83; Welldon places W 'on reports' 83; preparing for entry into army class at Harrow 83; obtains remove first term 1890, 86; writes letter to father complaining about Army Class; and mother's reply 88–9; J compares his bad conduct with his younger brother's good conduct 89; bad reports reaching his mother 90; she writes to R about 91; came 4th in preliminary exam. 92; swished by Welldon for breaking windows in factory 94–5; private tutor hired for part of summer holidays 1891; Jennie in serious discussions with Welldon; he insists that W spend the Xmas holidays with private tutor 98–9; Jennie writes to R in SA about W's learning German 98–9; refuses to study French over Xmas but mother insists 100–1; takes up sword fencing; wins a cup; father writes congratulating him on his success and encl. £2; spends all the money and R replies crossly 104; 1895 remove but not a double 104; predicts he will pass Sandhurst entrance exam. 106; failed Sandhurst entrance exam 390th out

Hussars 1902; made squadron commander 252; pub. biog. of father 1906 217.

First World War: rejoins Oxfordshire Hussars; goes to front attached to the 2nd Grenadier Guards; sees service in trenches; anxious mother writes to; lieutenant-colonel commanding 6th Royal Scots Fusiliers; resigns May 286; shown over Amiens battle field by J 295; 1921 leaves Oxfordshire Hussars 304.

Political career: political interest aroused 113–4; leads protest in London 1894 141–2; mother's ambitions for 170; introduced to Bourke Cockran; wants to capture father's seat as MP for S. Paddington 178; two political meetings 187; narrowly defeated at Oldham 197; CH15 elected MP for Oldham 212–13; lecture tour of US and Canada 213; death of Queen Victoria, writes to mother of Alice Keppel; returns home from US 213–4; takes seat in HoC 14th Feb. 1901; maiden speech; on army estimates; commits speeches to memory like father; breaks down in HoC 216–7; on tariff reform; crosses the House to Liberals; public speeches; Liberals form Govt.; Under-Sec. to Colonies 220–01; Liberal landslide victory 1906, 223; Privy Councillor; ally of Lloyd George; demand for tax on land value 224; CH16 President of the Board of Trade 235; fails to win seat North-West Manchester 235–6; wins seat in Dundee 236–7; Cabinet Minister 236–7; CH17 Miners 8 Hr. Bill; old age pensions; visits German labour exchanges 243; first People's Budget 244; reducing the powers of HoL; Liberals lose heavily in Feb.1910 Gen. Election; Home Secretary; on capital punishment; Siege of Sydney Street; South Wales strikes 244; campaigning with Clemmie in Dundee Jan. 1909; wins seat 246; concern over crime and death penalty 246–7; dealing with strikes 253; Oct.1911 First Lord of the Admiralty; goes to Belfast to speak on Home Rule Bill 253; Dreadnought; inspections of the fleet 253–4; Mediterranean cruise on *Enchantress*; description of 254–5; with Gen. Sir Ian and Lady Hamilton at Malta; 254–5; threat of outbreak of First World War 262–2; Germany declares war on France 3rd August 261; First World War CH18 prepares the fleet for war 263; battle of Mons; naval losses 264; discussion of naval strategies 265; witnesses front line fighting in Antwerp 266; asks Asquith if he can resign and take a com-

327;and inspections 329; and invasion scare; and appeals to Roosevelt for US to join in the war 330–31; and conduct of war; attack on Soviet Union; offers assistance 331; Japanese attack Pearl Harbour; Germany declares war on US; US enters the war; Soviet counter-attack at Stalingrad 332–3; Nov. 1943 Roosevelt, Stalin and second front in France 334; Yalta Conference Jan.1945, 335; 1945 first General Election in 10 years; refuses to consider amendment to the Trades disputes Act of 1927 336–7; heads Caretaker Govt.; Potsdam Conference; retains seat at Woodford; Tories lose election; Labour Govt. elected 337; CH23 1949 leads party into election 341; Prime Minister again Oct. 1951 341; takes over duties of Foreign Secretary 341; cult figure 342; on death of Stalin 341–2; retires as PM 5th April 1955; Queen joins at Downing St dinner; 344; remains MP for Woodford; last attendance at HoC 1961; does not seek re-election in 1964 Gen. Election 345.

Health: ill health begins in Ireland 25; home ill from school during holidays 1882, 44; home from school ill, accompanies parents to Germany 1883,49; home from school ill 52–3; bouts of asthma 53; attended by Dr Robson Roose 53; seriously ill with pneumonia; and recovery 63–4; Harrow School selected for health reasons 74; R writes to Welldon about W's health 78; ill over Xmas 1888; with Everest to Ventnor to recover 82; returned to school Jan.1889; and cigarettes 91; Kinsky gives alcohol to 96; Jan.1893 falls from bridge in Bournemouth; father rushes home; brings best surgeons money can buy; serious injuries; doctors order long rest from study 111; convalescing in Brighton 112; suffered 'black dog' of depression 304; car accident in US; convalesced for 3 weeks 316; laid low with paratyphoid fever 1932; in sanatorium in Salzburg 316–7; many 'black dog moments'; and alcohol 320–1; ordered by doctors to convalesce 334; too unwell to attend J's funeral 341; first minor stroke 1949 341; second stroke 342; third stroke kept secret 343; pneumonia 1958, 344; bad fall in 1960; second fall in 1962; home fitted with lift; deafness; lethargy 344; fourth stroke 345–6.

Finances: father grants £10 a month allowance 122; falls out with Frank Harris over money 153; £300 army pay plus £500 from